Panagiotis Dimitrakis holds a doctorate in War Studies from King's College London, and is an expert on intelligence and military history. He is the author of *The Secret War in Afghanistan: The Soviet Union, China and Anglo-American Intelligence in the Afghan War* (I.B.Tauris, 2013), *Failed Alliances of the Cold War: Britain's Strategy and Ambitions in Asia and the Middle East* (I.B.Tauris, 2012) and *Military Intelligence in Cyprus: From the Great War to Middle East Crises* (I.B.Tauris, 2010).

'This exciting new book by Panagiotis Dimitrakis is an imaginative and thrilling spy story based on a thorough study of the sources. It will inform and entertain and deserves the attention of scholars and general readers alike.'

**Professor Joe Maiolo, Department of War Studies,
King's College London**

SECRETS AND LIES IN VIETNAM

Spies, Intelligence and Covert Operations in the Vietnam Wars

PANAGIOTIS DIMITRAKIS

BLOOMSBURY ACADEMIC
LONDON • NEW YORK • OXFORD • NEW DELHI • SYDNEY

To Eleni

BLOOMSBURY ACADEMIC
Bloomsbury Publishing Plc
50 Bedford Square, London, WC1B 3DP, UK
1385 Broadway, New York, NY 10018, USA

BLOOMSBURY, BLOOMSBURY ACADEMIC and the Diana logo
are trademarks of Bloomsbury Publishing Plc

First published in Great Britain 2016 by I.B.Tauris & Co. Ltd
Paperback edition first published 2020 by Bloomsbury Academic

ISBN: HB: 978-1-7845-3399-1
PB: 978-1-3501-5316-5
ePDF: 978-0-8577-2758-9
eBook: 978-0-8577-2962-0

Series: International Library of Twentieth Century History, volume 83

Typeset in Garamond Three by OKS Prepress Services, Chennai, India

To find out more about our authors and books visit
www.bloomsbury.com and sign up for our newsletters.

CONTENTS

ABBREVIATIONS

ARVN	Army of the Republic of Vietnam
ASA	Army Security Agency
CCP	Chinese Communist Party
CIA	Central Intelligence Agency
CIO	Central Intelligence Organization
CORDS	Civil Operations and Revolutionary Development Support
COSVN	Central Office for South Vietnam
DAO	Defense Attaché Office
DGER	Direction Générale des Études et Recherches
DIA	Defense Intelligence Agency
DRV	Democratic Republic of Vietnam
EMIFT	État-Major Interarmées et Forces Terrestres
FCO	Foreign and Commonwealth Office
FRUS	Foreign Relations of the United States series
FTNV/ZOT	Forces Terrestres du Nord Vietnam and Zone Opérationnelle du Tonkin
GCHQ	Government Communications Headquarters
GCMA	Groupement de Commandos Mixtes Aéroportés
GCR	Groupe des Contrôles Radioélectriques
GRU	Main Intelligence Directorate, Russia
ICCS	International Commission for Control and Supervision
KGB	Committee for State Security of the Soviet Union
KMT	Kuomintang

MAAG	Military Assistance Advisory Group
MACV	Military Assistance Command Vietnam
MACSOG	Military Assistance Command Vietnam – Special Operations Group (later renamed Studies and Observations Group)
MI6/SIS	Secret Intelligence Service (UK)
MIA	Missing in Action
NARA	National Archives and Records Administration (US)
NSA	National Security Agency
OSS	Office of Strategic Services
PASF	People's Armed Security Force
PAVN	People's Army of Vietnam
PLA	People's Liberation Army (China)
POW	Prisoner of War
PRU	Provincial Reconaissance Unit
SDECE	Service de Documentation Extérieure et de Contre-Espionnage
SEAL	Sea, Air, Land (US Navy Military Special Forces)
SEPES	Political and Social Studies Service
SIGINT	Signals Intelligence
SMM	Saigon Military Mission
SOE	Special Operations Executive
SRO	Service de Reinseignement Opérationnel
SSPL	Sacred Sword of the Patriots League
STR	Service Technique de Recherches
TNA	The National Archives (UK)
Viet Cong or NLF	National Liberation Front of South Vietnam
Vietminh	League for the Independence of Vietnam
VNQDD	(Viet Nam Quoc Dan Dang) Vietnamese Nationalist Party
UCLA	University of California, Los Angeles
UN	United Nations
USAF	United States Air Force
USIS	United States Information Service
USMC	United States Marines Corps
USOM	United States Operations Mission

ACKNOWLEDGEMENTS

Professor Christopher Goscha of the University of Quebec, one of the authorities on the Vietnam Wars, helped me considerably with sources, and I thank him for this. Special thanks to Rosalie Spire for her prompt aid and advice with reference to the UK National Archives. I would also like to thank for their help Olympia and John Wood, William Rees, and Tomasz Hoskins and Sara Magness at I.B.Tauris. I owe a great debt to my parents Giannis and Mimi, brother Timos and wife Eleni for their support and interest in my work.

INTRODUCTION

THE KILLING MAZE

To paraphrase Thomas Hobbes, the noted English political philosopher, the rule in espionage is the duplicity of all against all. One should never, ever forget that the life of the secret agent is solitary, poor, nasty, brutish, short and betrayed. The spy operates in a maze of the chaotic, fragmented information gathered, and the spymaster endeavours to make an actionable meaning out of the information supplied to him or her. Spymasters often tell the top decision makers that they don't know the intentions of the enemy. This demonstrates the never-ending difficulty of intelligence gathering: often, the truth cannot be discovered in time. Policy makers rush to make up their minds without taking into account the limitations of the available intelligence. Sometimes they become interested in espionage, turning, themselves, into overconfident amateur spymasters.

***

Agent Nguyen Cong Vien (aka Lam Duc Thu, Nguyen Chi Vien or Hoang Chan Dong) and an agent codenamed Edouard were among the ethnic Vietnamese who worked for the Sûreté, the French security service with regional branches throughout French Indochina. Vien's task was to gather intelligence in post-Great War Paris, where optimism for a better, more peaceful and judicious world had spread with the establishment of the League of Nations. These agents, and their masters, watched and reported on Nguyen Ai Quoc ('Nguyen the Patriot'), an enigmatic young Vietnamese who had arrived in Paris in 1919 and, together with other Vietnamese, lobbied politicians and the press to argue the cause for an independent Indochina. In September of that year, Edouard informed the Sûreté that Nguyen Ai Quoc's real name was in fact Nguyen Van Thanh. But the security service remained uncertain of his true identity. In 1920, he was arrested and interrogated; the French tried to force him to reveal his real name, but they failed. Immediately after his release, the young Vietnamese complained to the Human Rights League that he had been the victim of police maltreatment.[1]

In 1923, Quoc left for Moscow under the name Cheng Van and worked for the Krestintern, the Red Peasant International. A few years later he reached China. The agent Vien (who had now infiltrated the circle of communist Vietnamese in Canton) continued reporting of his activities. In 1926, he informed the Sûreté that Quoc, with other Vietnamese in Canton, was 'preparing for revolution [in Indochina] methodically'.[2]

Eventually Quoc was exposed as a communist by Loi Teck, a spy working for British intelligence who has previously worked for the Sûreté. In 1931, Quoc was arrested in Hong Kong. The French governor of Indochina asked for the communist leader to be handed over. Nonetheless, the crown judge allowed him to leave the colony.[3] In December 1940, Quoc and his comrades reached the Sino-Vietnamese border, staying with Vietnamese refugees in Jingxi, on the Chinese side of the border. A Vietnamese uprising against the French in Indochina had failed. The Indochinese Communist Party competed with nationalist parties. The young Vietnamese who had appeared in Paris in 1919 now carried three identity papers: a membership card for the Young Chinese Newsmen's Association; a card identifying him as a special correspondent of the International News Agency; and a staff travel permit for the Chinese Nationalist headquarters of the Fourth War Area. All papers were issued to Ho Chi Minh, 'Ho the Enlightened'.[4]

***

In Vietnam's wars between 1945 and 1975, millions of Vietnamese were killed, and millions more were driven to misery and despair. The wars also led to the defeat of the United States, the global superpower, which counted over 50,000 dead soldiers; and to the demise of an influential colonial power of the past, France. Scholars and readers will always find fascinating the way that the Vietnamese became victorious. Even today, new declassified files are added to the pile, new archives open and new books are published. There is no doubt that the literature on the wars in Indochina, and Vietnam in particular, is expanding.

This book is about the spymasters and field agents who were recruited and handled secret sources. While providing the politico-military context of the war, we avoid any interpretation or argument that benefits from hindsight. One should never forget that, when hunting for secrets and trying to avoid arrest, spies do not think with the benefit of hindsight. If the reader of a book on espionage sometimes feels lost and confused about the field reporting, he or she approaches more closely what is like to be a spy – by making a bid to find out what is going on, by seeking the truth frantically and even by employing unreliable informers. By quoting from field reports, we attempt to present the atmosphere of fear and uncertainty at the initial stage where the spy's report has yet to be turned into 'finished intelligence'. Operatives, and low-rank diplomats who interact with them in information-sharing, *live* the war and experience the enemy's methods of espionage daily; they have no opportunity to sit back and distance themselves from a reality that consumes them – but which also makes them, in time, better able to cope with high pressure situations that are dangerous to their lives.

We will not analyse strategy, military operations, counterinsurgency or international diplomacy. This study does not provide a socio-economic analysis of Vietnam or the history of the politics of the Indochinese Communist Party or the Vietminh. Due to space constraints, the book focuses solely on Vietnam and not on Laos, Cambodia or Thailand – other countries affected by the war.

The stories of spymasters from British, French and US intelligence services (notably MI6, SDECE and the CIA), as well as the activities of North Vietnamese secret services, are presented chronologically and thematically in each chapter. Readers will witness events through the eyes of the spy: the first Franco-Vietnamese intelligence confrontation; intelligence officers' fear of a general war resulting from a Chinese military intervention in Vietnam; the confusing piecing together of evidence, gathered from various secret sources, to draft an accurate estimate of the opponent's plans; the assassinations of officials and communist cadre; the battle of Dien Bien Phu; the infiltration of DRV moles and the double-cross system of Hanoi; the coup against President Diem; the 1964 Bay of Tonkin incident and the 1968 Tet Offensive surprise; the fall of Saigon in April 1975. In the Aftermath, we provide a brief narrative about US intelligence warning the White House of the Sino-Vietnamese War of 1979.

***

In 1945, negotiations of the British and the Americans with the Chinese nationalist regime under Chiang Kai-shek led to an agreement for North Indochina: the 16th parallel was to be included in the theatre of operations of the Chinese. South Indochina was assigned to the British forces. On 24 July at the Potsdam conference, the arrangement was concluded. Nonetheless, the participants had not anticipated the end of the war with Japan by August. Thus, the political implications of a British and Chinese deployment of forces in Indochina were not thought out. President Harry Truman would not continue Roosevelt's (evidently vague) scheme of a trusteeship for Indochina. Under General Charles de Gaulle, the French sought to return as soon as possible, but for the time being their forces were inadequate to exert any control over Indochina. An expeditionary force, the Corps Expéditionnaire Francais de Extrême Orient (CEFEO), under General Jacques Leclerc, would reach the country by late autumn.[5]

After the Japanese surrender on 15 August, British and Chinese forces occupied Indochina. Key tasks were to keep peace and order, to liberate Allied prisoners of war and to disarm the Japanese forces. Churchill and the Foreign Office top rank wanted to support the French; the danger of a liberation movement like the League for the Independence of Vietnam (Vietminh) shaking the postwar colonial rule in South East Asia had to be averted. Nonetheless, saving the French colonial rule meant that Britain was about to face severe criticism among the neighbouring nations, as well as from Stalin and Mao, for working against the principle of self-determination of peoples and boosting imperialism yet again. The Vietminh cadre, who had approached the Americans throughout the war in vain, felt betrayed because Washington remained unresponsive. The British troops entered a killing maze where no one was willing to accept their authority – be it French colonialists, the Vietnamese nationalists (some of whom had sided with the Japanese) or the Vietminh under Ho Chi Minh. It was a war of all against all.

Captain Archimedes Patti, the OSS commanding officer of a mission of 12, reached Hanoi on 22 August 1945 to arrange for the release of Allied prisoners of war and to gather intelligence on the general conditions. Until then he had served in intelligence roles in North Africa, Sicily and Salerno. Patti arrived with Major Jean Sainteny, the French head intelligence officer in China.

On 19 August, tens of thousands of Vietnamese demonstrators swept through Hanoi, together with 800 armed Vietminh militia. The Japanese occupation forces did not react: in fact, they allowed the Vietnamese to take over some unguarded buildings. In turn, the Vietminh avoided confronting them.[6] For some time during the Japanese occupation, a mole had infiltrated the Hanoi postal service that handled the colonial telephone, radio and telegraph networks. The spy was Nguyen Thi Bich Thuan, who contributed directly to the Vietminh's seizing of the central office in Hanoi on 19 August. The Vietminh cadre immediately started to send messages to their comrades in South Vietnam, such as party directives and orders for their militias to raise the population against the return of the French. In their turn, on 31 August Vietnamese anti-communist nationalists started broadcasting from the Bach Mai.[7] (Until the Vietminh's withdrawal from Hanoi, the spies at the postal service overheard the conversations of their opponents, the local leaders of the Vietnamese Nationalist Party and the Greater Vietnam (or Dai Viet) Party. The mail was also opened.[8])

On 23 August 1945, Captain Patti met with General Tsuchibashi Jujitsu, the top ranking Japanese officer in Hanoi, emphasising the responsibilities of the Japanese to maintain peace and order until the arrival of Allied troops. Major Sainteny and his staff officers were detained incommunicado in the governor's villa. Patti recommended to the OSS that no French personnel be dispatched to the city for fear of Vietminh causing trouble.[9] He wrongly assumed that the Japanese would try to employ the Vietnamese as fifth columnists against the coming Allied occupation. Patti remarked on the political status of his OSS mission: 'Our OSS team had immediately become the center of Allied authority to which everyone with a cause or a desire for prestige brought himself to be heard. The French came to complain, make demands and play conspiratorial games. The Vietnamese came to be seen with the Allies and acquire status in the eyes of their adversaries, creating an image of "insiders" with the American mission.'[10]

On 24 August, Tran Van Giau, of the Central Committee of the Vietminh, urged the overtaking of Saigon. Vietminh militias seized the government building not guarded by Japanese guards. The

Vietnamese did not confront the Japanese who remained in the Bank of Indochina building, their posts and barracks or the governor-general's palace. A large pro-Vietminh demonstration of almost half a million took place.[11]

Two days later, Ho Chi Minh arrived in Hanoi for the first time in his life. During the following days, the appearance of Patti in uniform next to Ho Chi Minh and Giap gave the strong impression that Washington backed the Vietminh against the rule of the French. Patti had repeated discussions with the Vietnamese. Trying to get Patti's backing, Ho revealed to him that the Emperor Bao Dai was about to abdicate and that the draft of the Vietnamese declaration of independence would be along the lines of the American one. Patti was duly impressed.[12] For the time being the Vietminh sidelined Viet Nam Quoc Dan Dang (VNQDD) and the Dai Viet.[13]

Patti met another OSS officer, Lucien Conein, who would become a protagonist in covert operations in Vietnam in 1950 and 1960. Born in Paris in 1919 to an American World War I soldier and his French bride, he grew up in Kansas. Upon the start of World War II, he presented himself to the French consulate in Chicago, and, as a French subject, asked to join the army. After the fall of France, he returned to the United States and enlisted. He was recruited by the OSS in part due to his fluency in French and was assigned secret operations in his occupied motherland. Late in 1944, he undertook yet another mission: landing in Nazi-occupied southern France to hand over arms to the French Resistance. Later he was transferred to the Pacific theatre of operations. The OSS organised a mission for the sabotage of Japanese installations in North Vietnam. When the war ended, he and his team reached Hanoi. Avowedly pro-French, he suspected the Vietminh and discounted the potential of their military capabilities. He also distrusted Patti: 'I didn't like Patti. He was an arrogant Guinea [a disparaging term for those of Italian ancestry]. You'd never get the truth out of him.'[14]

Conein, who for a large part of his career in secret operations would confront the Vietminh and the National Liberation Front of South Vietnam (NLF, Viet Cong), had meetings with Ho Chi Minh and Giap in 1945. About Giap, he later said: 'You didn't really talk to Giap. He talked to you. . . . He had piercing eyes, and you knew he was sincere; he believed in what he was saying. . . . He was really fantastic and personable. I liked him.'[15]

In the meantime, the French had launched a top-secret operation on 28 August 1945: Mission Lamda, made up of six DGER (Direction Générale des Études et Recherches) officers who parachuted near Hue. Their mission was to contact Emperor Bao Dai and ask him to delay any of his initiatives until the agents had put him in communication with Paris. Eventually, four officers were killed and two taken prisoner by a Japanese detachment.[16]

The responsibility for South Indochina had fallen under Lord Mountbatten's South East Asia Command (SEAC), which had to tackle the issue of limited resources since the Attlee government was implementing massive demobilization (under operation Python). The SEAC was overburdened: it had to oversee the disarmament and repatriation of 500,000 Japanese troops scattered across South East Asia, and it had to liberate 123,000 Allied prisoners of war in a region of 1.5 million square miles. The first priorities for occupation were Hong Kong, Malaya, and Burma. Indochina followed because the Japanese headquarters for South East Asia were in Saigon. The British operation to occupy Indochina was codenamed Operation Masterdom.

The directive issued to Major General Sir Douglas David Gracey stated that he must maintain 'law and order and ensure internal security' and liberate 'Allied territory insofar as your resources permit'. He did not have enough forces to occupy South Indochina; his main force was the 20th Indian Infantry Division (which comprised about 20,000 troops). He communicated with the supreme Japanese commander in Saigon, Field Marshal Baron Terauchi Hisaichi, informing him of the disarmament obligations under the terms of the surrender signed in Tokyo.[17]

Back in London, the Foreign Office sought French support for its post-war colonial policy, fearing that the fall of Indochina to communism would spark a domino effect in the British South East Asian colonies. The escalating – and unjustified, given the contemporary intelligence reports – fear of the domino effect goes back to as early as 1944: '[T]he potential threat to Australia, New Zealand, India, Burma, Malaya, and the East Indies Archipelago resulting from Indochina being in the hands of a weak or unfriendly power has been sufficiently demonstrated by the action of Japan in this war.'[18]

The Japanese troops responsible for war crimes against civilians and Commonwealth forces turned into a willing post-war ally. On 27 August, the British met with Japanese top-rank officers in Rangoon; the latter concurred that they would follow Tokyo's orders and would maintain internal security in occupied areas until the arrival of the Allied forces.[19] Already the Vietminh, before the arrival of Allied troops and the OSS mission in Saigon, had had five secret meetings with the Japanese officers, who agreed that the captured French weapons be handed over to them.

A number of Japanese deserted. In Lang Son, Colonel Nakawaga and 4,000 men joined the Vietnamese.[20] Captain Patti wrote that 'three or four thousand Japanese dropped from sight into the clandestine pro-Asian movement'.[21]

The OSS had good timely intelligence; they knew that some weaponry was handed over to the Vietminh and other Vietnamese parties. A report, dated 18 August 1945, stated that 'well informed French and Annamese sources state that the Central Committee [of the Vietminh] has been negotiating with local Japanese military authorities for purchase of arms and ammunition with intent of using them should either the French or the Chinese attempt to reoccupy their areas'.[22]

Major General Gracey (nicknamed 'the Bruiser'), an old-school Indian army officer, was about to enter the maze of Indochina unprepared. He had received inadequate intelligence briefings for his hasty deployment. Field Marshal William Slim had issued a directive that claimed that the only threat to law and order could come from Japanese troops resisting surrender. In South Indochina a 'sustained uprising' was deemed unlikely; in North Indochina nationalists had some forces and had established a provisional government in Hanoi. At that time, Ho Chi Minh and the Vietminh were more considered nationalists than communists. Brigadier March Maunsell, the deputy of Gracey in the control commission, later claimed that the thought 'never entered our heads that there could be a problem caused by any source other than the Japanese'.[23]

In an emotive speech on 2 September 1945 in Hanoi, Ho Chi Minh proclaimed the Democratic Republic of Vietnam (DRV). From 1950, the army of the new republic would be named the People's Army of Vietnam (PAVN). Captain Patti, impressed by the formations of the Vietminh fighters, wrote to OSS headquarters: 'From what I have seen these people mean business. The French will have to deal with them. For that matter, we will all have to deal with them.' The OSS officer attended the ceremonies in Hanoi. Two American P38 Lightnings flew over the parading crowd. People wrongly believed that the Americans were saluting the birth of the new state; in fact, the Lightnings were just on a reconnaissance flight.

The same day, a surprising wave of violence swept through Saigon. The Vietminh demonstrations celebrating independence turned against other nationalist groups (among others, the Cao Dai and the Hoa Hao religious sects) as well as the underground network called the Binh Xuyen and the French. On receiving the news, Gracey assumed that the provisional government of the Vietminh in Saigon could not control the city. The OSS mission in Saigon put strong pressure on the Vietnamese to release 200 French women and children from prison; the men were released the next day.[24]

During those days, the Vietminh seized the abandoned archives of the Sûreté in Hanoi, Hue, Saigon and other cities. It was a unique opportunity to identify the spies who were among them in the 1930s and 1940s, as well as to supplement their education in espionage with the French manuals. Nonetheless, Ho Chi Minh's security officials, such as Nguyen Van Ngoc, realised that the low and mid-level Vietnamese security officers employed by the French were valuable assets for protecting their new state. He wrote in his memoirs: 'I once again realised that they [the French trained security personnel] were an invaluable resource which the revolution had to know how to use.'[25]

The first British officers and troops arrived in Saigon on 6 September.[26] In Indochina over 70,000 Japanese troops were waiting to be disarmed. On 13 September 1945, Gracey reached Saigon by aeroplane, escorted by a Gurkha contingent. The Japanese commander and his guard accepted the terms of surrender, but Gracey opted for the Japanese to keep their arms. He did not even bother to greet the Vietminh delegation who waited for him at the airport. He wrote: 'They came to see me and said "welcome" and all that sort of thing. . . . It was an unpleasant situation, and I promptly kicked them out. They were obviously communists.'[27]

On 14 September, the transport of Gracey's main units commenced; the 32nd infantry brigade of the Indian Division arrived on 7 October, followed by the 100th infantry brigade on 17 October.[28] On 14 September,

General Lu Han, the commander of the Chinese First Army Group, arrived in Hanoi. The DRV officials established a working relationship with Lu Han, whose soldiers, on arrival, supported themselves by looting. Ho Chi Minh met with the general. Eventually, the Vietnamese leader declared the need for the Vietnamese to donate all their gold to the provisional government to purchase arms. The donation week (euphemistically called 'Gold Week') commenced on 16 September. Lu Han, who was interested in the gold, obligingly agreed to sell US-made weaponry to the Vietminh. The Vietminh fighters acquired 3,000 rifles, 50 automatic assault rifles, 600 machine guns and 100 mortars. They also bought French and Japanese weapons, reaching 31,000 rifles, 700 automatic weapons, 36 artillery pieces and 18 Japanese tanks.[29] In November, Ho Chi Minh opted to dissolve the Indochinese Communist Party as a tactical move to prevent the nationalist Chinese becoming apprehensive of his plans.[30]

Stalin viewed Ho Chi Minh with suspicion. He was aware of the summer-1945 collaboration between the OSS and the Vietminh – as well as the presence of the OSS in Hanoi and Saigon, and Ho's appeals for support from Washington. At that time Stalin did not believe that anyone – not even Mao – could win the civil war with Chiang Kai-shek.[31]

In any case, the Vietminh were angry at Britain's stance because it paved the way for the return of the French. On 17 September, only four days after the arrival of Gracey, the nationalist Pham Van Bach (who was not a member of the Vietminh), frustrated with his talks on independence with Jean Cédile, the French commissioner for Cochinchina (the southern region of Vietnam with Saigon as its principal city), called for a general strike in Saigon. The Vietminh followed. Gracey, assuming a communist plot, closed down the local press. On 21 September, he declared martial law; two days later the British backed the French coup to oust the DRV provisional government.[32] On the night of 21 September, Cédile insisted that if resolve were shown, the local population would back the French bid to control the city and the surrounding areas.[33] Cédile informed Gracey that DRV forces were about to attack Saigon and asked for the 1,400 released French prisoners of war to be armed. But once armed, they stormed the city centre, turning against all Vietnamese indiscriminately.[34]

On 21 September, Gracey issued a controversial proclamation that he had to maintain law and order, commanding British, Indian, Japanese and French troops, as well as the local police south of the 16th parallel. By contrast, the 28 August instructions for Gracey required that the 'Saigon area' be administered by his forces, as well as the disarmament of the Japanese and the release of the Allied prisoners of war.[35]

The DRV provisional government of Saigon informed the Americans of a demonstration to take place on 23 September. They knew that it was illegal since the British major general had declared martial law. OSS Captain Peter Dewey, the head of the OSS mission in Saigon, who had a reputation for being pro-Vietminh, witnessed the indiscriminate assaults of the released armed French against the Vietnamese. Dewey was a Yale graduate in French language and history. In 1942–3, as an Air Corps lieutenant, he had taken part in intelligence missions and was awarded the French Croix de Guerre. In August 1944, he led an intelligence operation in southern France. He was a shrewd, resourceful and courageous intelligence officer who hated colonialism. Private First Class George Wickes, educated in French and Vietnamese, held an unofficial commission of second lieutenant while serving with Dewey in Saigon. He wrote to his commanding officer: 'Dewey talked to me most of all, and I was impressed by his account of what was going on ... what impressed me most was his interpretation of the complicated political manoeuvrings of the different individuals and factions represented in Saigon, which he frequently explained to me.'[36]

Fearing chaos, Gracey did not think for long; he would use the Japanese military because he lacked adequate troops to keep the order south of the 16th parallel. Nonetheless, the British found the headquarters of Terauchi 'disjointed, ill-coordinated and badly administered', and feared that some Japanese officers wanted to take advantage of the precarious security situation.[37] On 23 September, the French launched a coup, taking over government buildings in Saigon and killing Vietminh cadre. Dewey protested, but Gracey declared him persona non grata and demanded that he leave the city by 26 September.[38]

The same day, for the first time the US Army Security Agency (ASA) intercepted war-related communications between the French and the DRV. Station MS-1 at Arlington Hall intercepted a message from a French colonial radio station in Hanoi to the French embassy in Moscow. (Ostensibly, the French colonial authorities informed the embassy of the verbatim message of Ho Chi Minh, enclosing it.) The message was unencrypted and in English. Ho Chi Min addressed Stalin: 'We beg to inform Your Excellency that the Provisional Government of the Viet Nam Republic has been established under President HO CHI MINH. Ex-Emperor Bao Dai abdicated on 25 August, handing over the rule to a new government supported by the whole nation. Meanwhile, owing to the collapse of the river dam system, half of Tonkin is flooded, causing tremendous losses. The people have begun to starve. We appeal to Your Excellency for any positive help. Respectfully.' Three days later Ho Chi Minh sent a message to Prime Minister Clement Attlee (which was also intercepted by the ASA), asking for Britain to intervene in Indochina, to deter the French forces from moving against the Vietnamese. Both leaders ignored the patient Ho Chi Minh.[39] (Meanwhile, the Ministry of Colonial Affairs in Paris continued employing old, broken codes in its communication with the colonial authorities. In the postal service in Hanoi, the Vietminh was reading messages until late September 1945.)[40]

Gracey ordered that the former prisoners of war be disarmed, and that they return to their barracks; however this did not materialise because the next day the Vietminh retaliated: on 25 September they attacked the jails freeing their comrades as well as taking the airfield. In the suburb of Cité Herault, 300 French and Eurasian civilians were taken hostage; about half of them were massacred.[41] The nearby Japanese guards did nothing to stop the killings.[42] Gracey reprimanded Terauchi, who commanded about 4,000 Japanese troops in Saigon.[43]

The next day at noon, Dewey was murdered by sniper fire while he was driving just 500 metres from the OSS headquarters in Saigon. According to one account, he had spoken in French to Vietminh guerrillas ('Je suis Americain'), but they assumed that he was French. Two Gurkha platoons later dispersed the fighters, but the body of the officer was never found. Ho Chi Minh expressed his sorrow in a meeting with US General Gallagher, who was serving as an adviser to the staff of General Lu Han in Hanoi. According to the general, Ho stated that the murder 'might have been staged for the benefit of French propaganda by French agents, but [he] admitted it might have been the action of unruly elements of the Annamese'.

Ho Chi Minh wrote a letter to Truman emphasising his intention to find the culprits, but arguing that 'it is impossible to investigate into the matter now. Saigon being still in the hands of the Franco-British troops.'[44] Dewey's body was never recovered; it was buried secretly. One of the very few who knew where he rested was Cao Dang Chiem, who headed a team of Vietminh militia that day, guarding a nearby bridge. Chiem rose to become head of the Office of Strategic Intelligence of the DRV.[45]

It was an irony of history that the first American to die from Vietminh fire was an intelligence officer who despised the post-war colonial aspirations of the French and the British. Dewey was posthumously awarded the Cluster to the Legion of Merit medal for 'continuing his complex operations, without interruption to the steady flow of highly valued intelligence to Headquarters'. On 28 September, General Tsuchibashi, the supreme Japanese commander in Hanoi, officially surrendered to the Allies. General Lu Han did not recognise the authority of the French or Vietnamese in Saigon. Ostensibly, the intention of the Chinese was to put pressure on the French with the presence of their army in North Indochina so as to negotiate with Paris the end of the French presence in China. Eventually, Chiang Kai-shek agreed for the return of French rule and the withdrawal of Han's troops from Hanoi, in exchange for the abolition of French extraterritorial privileges in China.[46]

The same day, a French officer was murdered in northern Thailand – an episode the French top ranking officers (among them General Raoul Salan) would always remember, making them suspicious of the Americans even into the 1950s. Major Peter Kemp and Lieutenant Klotz of the Allied Land Forces Para-Military Organisation were moving mortars and heavy war material to the French secret agents of the Direction General des Etudes et Recherches (DGER) in Laos. On their way they met a Vietminh/OSS group. The Vietnamese demanded that Klotz be handed over to them. Kemp tried to protect Klotz, who was shot. The OSS men did not make any effort to protect the French officer who died; they declared their neutrality.[47] By November, the Vietminh presence in Laos had reached 2,000 fighters, according to the head of the DGER, who reported that two of his agents were killed and their heads displayed in Vientiane.[48]

By now, Field Marshal Slim had realised that Gracey was trying to accommodate contradictory orders: to disarm the Japanese; to restore peace and order; and to not support the return of the French colonial rule.[49] On 9 October, Britain signed an agreement with France: south of the 16th parallel the administration was in French hands.[50] Mountbatten was angry with Gracey for declaring martial law, but he did not change the operational directive of Operation Masterdom. The British feared a repeat of their experience in Athens. In December 1944, the British had turned against the main Greek guerrilla army, the National Liberation Front/National Liberation Army (EAM/ELAS), in support of the Greek government. The guerrillas tried to launch a rebellion in protest to the government's attempt to dissolve their army. Eventually, the British had to call an armoured brigade to confront the revolt in the Greek capital.[51] Mountbatten wanted to avoid a similar experience and insisted that the French must employ their troops in fighting the Vietminh.[52] He dispatched Brigadier E.J.C. Myers to Saigon. Myers was the former head of the British military mission with the Greek resistance. Myers divided the French into two categories: the Vichy ones who were 'rotten to the core' and the arrogant Gaullists who infuriated the Vietnamese.[53]

Now Gracey opted for direct communication with the Vietminh. On 1 October, the major general assured the Vietminh that his troops were neutral. Mountbatten had ordered Gracey to speed up any Franco-Vietnamese contacts. Nonetheless, the same day the chiefs of staff in London authorised Gracey to assist the French even outside the key areas prescribed in previous instructions. The frustrated and angry major general demanded that the Vietminh stop attacking the French, leave their roadblocks, control their militias and return the body of Dewey. They replied that they expected the British to free them from both the French and Japanese yokes. The pledge that the British act as 'arbitrators' and that they 'protect their nationals against French aggression' sounded impossible to Gracey. Eventually, it was agreed that a ceasefire would commence on 2 October. The Vietminh would consult with a French delegation on 3 October. The truce was extended to 6 October when another meeting was scheduled. According to the British, the Vietnamese 'claims' for independence were 'extreme'. The poorly armed Vietminh forces in Saigon did not abort their attacks against the Allied troops. On 10 October, a British-Indian patrol was ambushed. Gracey understood that Ho Chi Minh was escalating; he duly retaliated, waiting for the French expeditionary force to return to Indochina and take over.[54]

British-Indian, French and Japanese troops drove the Vietminh out of Saigon and the nearby villages on 11–14 October. On 13 October, a Vietminh attack on the airfield was repelled. Nonetheless, some Japanese continued to help the Vietnamese. Brigadier Hirst witnessed Japanese officers aiding the rebels around Thanh My. The same day, French troops captured two Japanese air force officers helping the insurgents and shot them on the spot.[55]

CHAPTER 1

OUR MAN IN HANOI

As the war between the DRV and the French escalated, Major General Gracey needed someone in Hanoi to inform him of Ho Chi Minh's intentions. MI6 headquarters dispatched their 'man', Lieutenant Colonel Arthur Geoffrey Trevor-Wilson. A former banker who was fluent in French, Trevor-Wilson was called up in 1939 as a driver in the Territorial Army; soon he was commissioned and dispatched as a liaison officer in France. On his return to England after Dunkirk, he joined the SOE and received training from, among others, Kim Philby, who soon left for SIS. A few months later, Trevor-Wilson applied to SIS and joined Section V.[1] Later, he recalled: 'My boss was Kim Philby. I found that he worked harder than anybody else. In spite of his stutter, he was a great leader, and in those days in SIS, leaders were at a loss. I found nothing wrong with him.'[2] The banker-turned-spy flew to Algiers and contacted the US diplomats who had remained at their posts after the entry of the United States in the war. Incidentally, in his hotel in Tangiers he met the Oxford-educated von Auer of the German Armistice Commission. 'Fortunately I had a Swiss passport on this occasion and I had to modify my voice so as to become French-Swiss man', Trevor-Wilson recalled. He soon returned to London where he was assigned to counter-intelligence duties as a commanding officer of four teams to be attached to US forces heading to Algiers. He was introduced to the top-secret source: the Bletchley Park decipherers.

The Italian Armistice Commission was about to depart on a plane stationed at an airfield south of Algiers. The French authorities delayed the Italians' departure. Trevor-Wilson arrived on time to inspect the cargo. The 'drums' (required by the Government Code and Cypher School) he discovered 'led to final re-arrangement of the terms to our army in Algiers, which caused them to go ahead towards Tunis and General Montgomery's fight with Rommel. The latter's troops were far below what our leaders thought.'[3] Trevor-Wilson broke a code for German military messages in the final phase of the North African campaign.[4]

The next assignment for Trevor-Wilson was Paris. Together with Lord Rothschild, Kenneth Younger and 40 troops that were part of the US Task Force, he was deployed to Gare Montparnasse to await the arrival of General Leclerc's armoured division.[5] He returned to London to receive more training in intelligence gathering methods and processing reports from Bletchley Park: 'It then happened that my employers decided to send me to General Douglas Gracey in Saigon', Trevor-Wilson wrote.[6]

While staying in Burma for a couple of days, he met with General Salan, the future commander of French forces in Indochina, who informed him of his forces' deployments and strategy.[7] Salan had been a risk-taking military intelligence officer in Indochina since the 1920s; he had also served in the Ministry of the Colonies in 1937. In 1938–40, posing as a correspondent of Le Temps, he had lured Spanish Republicans from refugee camps in France to Ethiopia to spy on the Italian forces and organise a revolt. The aim was to divert Mussolini's attention from the French occupied Djibouti. (Salan would seek to topple de Gaulle in 1961–2, leading the Organisation Armée Secrète (OAS) – a terrorist organisation.)[8]

On reaching Saigon, Trevor-Wilson was ordered to go to Phnom Penh to report on the attitude of the population in advance of the arrival of General Leclerc's force. He concluded that no trouble would arise, and that the Vietnamese were friendly towards the French.[9]

After several months in Saigon, Trevor-Wilson was sent to Hanoi as the head of the British military mission to General Lu Han. He had to facilitate the demarcation of the 16th parallel, dividing the British and the Chinese occupation zones. 'It was of course difficult to obtain Chinese agreement on any single matter', he remarked later. After repeated talks with Chinese officers who barely spoke English, Trevor-Wilson achieved an agreement on the borders between the Chinese and the British sectors.[10]

In parallel, the MI6 officer met with Ho Chi Minh on a weekly basis. He understood that the DRV had total control of the north. Despite his investigation, he had not found evidence linking the Vietminh to Moscow. Trevor-Wilson persuaded Ho Chi Minh to release a pro-French Cambodian member of the royal family about to be executed as a Japanese collaborator. In his discussions with Ho Chi Minh, Trevor-Wilson claimed that there was a secret 'Trade Union of Kings', with King George VI as 'secretary-general', who would be very angry if the Cambodian was executed.[11]

Together with Lieutenant Commander Simpson-Jones of the Royal Navy, Trevor-Wilson also searched for French troops imprisoned by the Vietminh. '[T]his took Lt. Commander Simpson-Jones and me several weeks, using a large number of very experienced Chinese people to visit the gaols.' After gathering all the intelligence, he paid a visit to Ho Chi Minh, eventually convincing him to sign a release document he could present to prison guards. He visited a prison on an island between Hanoi and Haiphong, presenting the document signed by the Vietnamese leader. Initially, the commanding officer doubted the authenticity of Ho Chi Minh's signature; but eventually he was persuaded and he freed 14 French officers and men.[12]

In addition, Trevor-Wilson arranged for the arrest of Major-General A.C. Chatterjee of the provisional government of India. 'I had to do [it] all alone', he later wrote. He persuaded Ho Chi Minh that the general who was staying in Hanoi, planning to go to Manchuria or Russia, had to return to India: 'I told him that I had received a message from India (which was, of course, wrong) saying that the Indian Government would welcome the return of these people who would do better in India than in Hanoi.'[13]

The MI6 officer visited the house where Chatterjee was staying. 'Ho Chi Minh told me that he would place a cordon of his policemen around the 123 rue Laloe if I went there. He gave me a whistle for me to blow if I had any disturbance, and then his policemen would come to my aid. In the airfield, I had a Dakota [transport] with several Royal Air Force men aboard.' He met the major general unarmed; the Indian was carrying a holstered pistol. After a long discussion, the Indian and his accompanying officials agreed to fly with Trevor-Wilson to Saigon the next morning, and then to Singapore, where eventually they were put under arrest.[14]

By November 1945, the French had deployed 10,000 troops in South Indochina. Two months later, the principal cities of Cochinchina, South Annam and Cambodia were reoccupied. The Vietminh took off for the mountains and rural areas to continue their fight.[15] Gaullist Admiral George Thierry d'Argenlieu took over as high commissioner for South Indochina. One of d'Argenlieu's aides sarcastically called him 'the most brilliant mind of the twelfth century'.[16] The French troops took control of the majority of the areas, and the 20th Indian Division was preparing for withdrawal. Gracey called the Japanese cooperation 'amazing'.[17]

Gracey described French operations in the Mekong Delta as having 'much unnecessary brutality. . . . The French troops are leaving a pretty good trail of destruction behind them, which will result in such resentment that it will become progressively more difficult for them to implement their new policy, and, I am convinced, will result in guerrilla warfare, increased sabotage and arson as soon as we leave the country.'[18]

Jean Sainteny, now commissioner for Tonkin and Northern Annam, and Ho Chi Minh had commenced discussions by mid-October in Hanoi. France insisted on the strategy of divide and rule: Cochinchina, Annam and Tonkin had to be considered separate state entities. Also, they wanted French troops to remain in Annam to safeguard its French population (of around 20,000). Their military would exert pressure on the Chinese to withdraw from Vietnam. Some French officials came to the straightforward conclusion that the Vietnamese simply hated the Chinese because of a long memory of Chinese invasions. The election, which took place on 6 January 1946, gave Ho Chi Minh a clear victory. Gradually, French forces started moving north. Ho Chi Minh argued – in vain – for independence to be included as a term in the final agreement.

French domestic politics influenced Ho Chi Minh's interpretation of the events. On 20 January 1946 President Charles de Gaulle, who had insisted that France maintain control of Indochina, resigned. General Leclerc was pressing north with his expeditionary force. He was no moderate; however he believed that he had inadequate troops to fight for total victory. Thus he had no option but to consider an agreement with Ho Chi Minh. The expeditionary force was not fighting many serious battles with the Vietminh, nor with their nationalist rivals (among them Hoa Hao and Cao Dai religious sects with followings in the countryside, and Trotskyites in the cities). They all disappeared to fight another day.

Leclerc agreed to independence for the DRV. Sainteny's new instructions, drafted by d'Argenlieu, spoke of self-government within the Indochinese Federation, which would be part of the French Union. Also, French military presence in Tonkin would be required. Three plebiscites would be organised for the people to decide if they wanted to join the Democratic Republic of Vietnam or the French Union.[19]

The British withdrawal commenced in mid-December; most of the 20th Division had left by 7 February 1946. On 28 February the French agreed with Chinese General Lu Han that the Chinese would withdraw from North Indochina in return for the revocation of French extraterritorial privileges in China; other key terms were the abolition of tax on Chinese exports coming through Tonkin and the protection of Chinese subjects in Hanoi.[20] In the meantime, General Leclerc was preparing an audacious plan to take over Hanoi. 'Operation Centre' called for a landing in Haiphong and an air-landing in Hanoi. On 1 March, 35 warships and landing craft sailed from Saigon to Haiphong.[21]

But Lu Han suddenly changed his mind. As the French ships arrived in Haiphong, Chinese artillery opened fire. The French responded. Trevor-Wilson and Lieutenant Commander Simpson-Jones intervened decisively, with the latter sailing with a small boat to the French ships. Eventually a ceasefire was agreed.[22] The engagement – which killed 20 French sailors, wounded 40 and led to an unknown number of Chinese casualties – lasted until 11 a.m. Vietnamese sources claimed that Vietminh spies who witnessed the bombardment were unable to reach a functioning phone line to inform the DRV general staff and General Giap of the developing situation.[23]

The Chinese compelled the French and the Vietminh to sign a 'preliminary convention'. The Ho-Sainteny agreement was a compromise: the French recognised the *etat libre* ('free state') of the Democratic Republic of Vietnam; the Vietnamese acceded to the dispatch of the 15,000 French troops to replace the departing Chinese occupation force in Tonkin. The military presence would last five years and the French accepted that they would respect the results of a referendum for the unification of the three provinces, which would be held in due course.[24]

In July 1946, Trevor-Wilson flew to Hanoi where he opened the first British consulate general. He met again with Ho Chi Minh ('he neither drank nor ate too much, nor had women friends but he smoked large numbers of cigarettes'); Pham Van Dong, the DRV minister of finance;

and Giap.[25] At that time, Ho Chi Minh was also preoccupied with another matter. A top Vietminh financial officer stole 10m piasters and escaped to Hong Kong. The crisis was kept secret. (Later, in the 1960s and 1970s, the son of the financial officer, Tran Van Minh or 'Albert', worked for the CIA as an interpreter/interrogator.)[26]

***

A wave of assassinations hit Saigon. On 29 March, 'known Vietminh extremists' murdered Dr Phat, a member of the Council of Cochinchina, who was against the province's union with the Democratic Republic of Vietnam.[27] Thach, a member of the same council, was assassinated on 3 May. He had voted in favour of the province joining Ho Chi Minh's state, but was killed 'evidently because friendly with French'. The French 'have retaliated with wholesale arrests and burning houses, villages where terrorists may have shelter', reported Charles Reed, the US consul in Saigon.[28]

A Vietnamese delegation with Ho Chi Minh, accompanied by General Salan and Lieutenant Colonel Emile Tutenges, left Gia Lam with two C47 Dakotas early on the morning of 31 May. Trevor-Wilson accompanied him to Paris, probably at the insistence of the Vietnamese leader.[29]

However, High Commissioner D'Argenlieu insisted that Cochinchina was a separate state, and surprised Ho and Sainteny. On 1 June, when Ho had reached Cairo, the French official declared the autonomous Republic of Cochinchina in the name of France. Thus, Ho had to work around this fait accompli in his talks with the French government. When interviewed by journalists, Ho Chi Minh played down his communism, claiming that his country was not yet ready: 'perhaps in 50 years' he remarked, adding that the DRV constitution was similar to the American one. The negotiations dragged on. The French government did not want to lose Indochina. Once again, D'Argenlieu aroused the anger of the Vietminh, shaking their confidence in French good will. He announced that a conference on Indochina was scheduled for 1 August in Dalat, where the establishment of the 'Indochinese Federation' would be discussed. The federation would encompass: Cochinchina, Laos, Cambodia, Southern Annam and the Central Highlands.

Pham Von Dong, one of the chief negotiators for Ho Chi Minh, concluded in September that no meaningful outcome was in sight and left for Hanoi. Ho Chi Minh showed patience and continued. He pleaded with Washington to get interested in Vietnam, also referring to the US administration of the Philippines – but to no avail.[30]

In early September 1946, acting Secretary of State William L. Clayton wrote to Charles Reed: '[I]ntelligence reports of uncertain reliability state USSR (a) anxious see Ho Chi Minh succeed unite three Kys under Viet Nam for possible eventual weapon against National Govt China and (b) has instructed French communists maneuver reliable French Officers to Indochina for training cadres future Viet Nam army.'[31] It was improbable information, indeed – but it influenced the evolving US thinking on Vietnam.

Sainteny and Overseas Minister, Marius Moutet, remained close interlocutors of Ho Chi Minh, who warned them that a less moderate cadre in the Central Committee of the Vietminh would oust him if no agreement was reached. Eventually on 14 September, he concluded a desperate agreement with the French: a ceasefire to commence on 30 October; no mention of independence. The so-called 'Modus Vivendi' was a 'pathetic agreement' for the DRV, Sainteny remarked.[32] Ho Chi Minh was booed by Vietnamese students as a traitor when he reached the port of Marseilles to return home aboard the warship *Dumont d'Urville*.[33] During the long voyage, a SDECE secret agent managed to enter his cabin and photograph some of his notes. Unfortunately for his superiors in Paris, the microfilm could not be developed.[34]

Reed had a meeting with Clarac, a French official and the chief of the Sûreté in Saigon. Both claimed that the Vietminh activities were increasing: 'Intercepted letters indicate Chinese communists are entrenched in Chinese centers Saigon and Haiphong and that Annamites chiefly in Tonkin and Annam, but also to certain extent in Cochinchina, are receiving much Communist propaganda.' The French officials said: 'Communists are already in French Indochina (no Russians), and close watch over [the] development must be maintained as agencies outside French Indochina are undoubtedly supplying propaganda.'[35]

*****

Ho Chi Minh was trying to reach an agreement with the French while General Giap built two large military bases in northern Tonkin and prepared for war. In May 1946, the Chinese troops started to withdraw from Tonkin and Hanoi. Vietminh clashes with the French occurred in the form of sabotages and ambushes. On 4 August, a nine-hour ambush took place, with heavy casualties on both sides.[36] High Commissioner D'Argenlieu was still confident that his forces were gaining the strategic advantage. However, he was surprised – and embarrassed – by the suicide of the pro-French president of the Republic of Cochinchina on 10 November 1946.[37]

General Leclerc was replaced by General Jean Étienne Valluy, who wanted to take the battle further to the enemy by taking over Hanoi and Haiphong in order to put strong pressure on Giap. The harbour was considered the 'lungs of Tonkin' because smuggled war material from China passed through the port to the Vietminh, who controlled part of the city. Valluy asked the French for more money for spies, and to pay off local village chiefs. He insisted: 'To get worthwhile intelligence, one has to pay for it, because the life of a clandestine agent is not exactly a leisurely activity in this country. One needs money, lots of money.'[38]

The general and D'Argenlieu sought decisive action without prior authorisation from the French. The high commissioner left for Paris for consultations, but on 13 November, the day of his departure, the confrontation escalated. The Vietminh noted the provocative stance of the French in Haiphong; Giap was already deploying his troops, warning them that confrontation was about to take place. Everybody was looking for a pretext for hostilities.

On 20 November 1946, a French patrol boat seized a vessel loaded with gasoline for the Vietnamese who in turn intercepted the French boat and arrested the crew. The French made an attempt to free the crew and an exchange of fire commenced. Almost simultaneously in another part of the city, a group of Vietnamese artists attacked French civilians, injuring them. Violent incidents occurred throughout the city, resulting in 240 Vietnamese and 7 French dead. A bid for a ceasefire failed. On 22 November, Colonel Pierre-Louis Debès, the French commander in the city, was ordered to deploy his forces in order to take an advantageous position. The Vietminh gathered its light-armed forces, who had few artillery pieces.

At 10.05 a.m., without authorisation from his superiors, Colonel Debès commenced the artillery, air and naval bombardment of the Chinese and Vietnamese quarters of Haiphong. The strike lasted for over two days; thousands of Vietnamese were killed.[39] The Vietminh had blocked the roads around the city. Ho Chi Minh made a vain effort to approach the Americans. In return for assistance with the French, he offered Abbot Low Moffat, a high-ranking State Department official dispatched to Saigon, Cam Ranh Bay as a naval base. The US administration concluded that the Vietminh were communists and that it would be better to support France. In their eyes, the DRV was ruled by a small group of communists who were 'possibly in indirect touch with Moscow and direct touch with Yenan [i.e. Mao's headquarters]'.[40] A State Department circular from 17 December emphasised that the French rule and deployment of forces should continue, 'not only as [an] antidote to Soviet influence, but to protect Vietnam and Southeast Asia from future Chinese imperialism'.[41]

In effect, the domino theory had been evolving since 1944. By 1948, the Foreign Office assumed that the fall of Indochina would enable communism to spread in South East Asia: 'If the Vietminh were to gain notable successes, this would have widespread repercussions in neighbouring territories. Indochina was the springboard for the Japanese attack against South East Asia, so it seems not impossible that it will become a springboard for the advance of Communism westwards across Asia.'[42] Some British ambassadors' comments, like those of Thompson in Bangkok, verged on hyperbole, claiming that 'the frontiers of Malaya are on the Mekong'.[43]

In mid-December 1946, the divided Hanoi became the locus of confrontation. General Valluy demanded that the Vietminh clear their barricades on the streets. The situation was more than tense. By the morning of 19 December, the French had issued three ultimatums for their opponents to abide by. French intelligence predicted that the guerrillas would attack on 19 December at 7 p.m. Giap made the last preparations.[44] Ho Chi Minh was convinced that the time for diplomacy was over. The warning issued by the Central Committee to the Vietminh secretaries, commanders, cadre and provincial organisations and units was clear: expect a French attack within 24 hours.[45]

The French eased their guard, assuming that the Vietnamese would not confront them. A Vietminh delegation met with the French, but no agreement was reached.[46] Charles Petit, a counterintelligence inspector of the Sûreté, infiltrated a group of the nationalist Tu Ve party, warning of an attack within two hours by the Vietminh. The French command received the intelligence without delay. General Morlière brushed off any hesitations and cancelled all leaves. Nonetheless, no attack took place at 7 p.m.[47]

At 8.03 p.m., the electricity in the city was cut off by the Vietminh supporters in the power plant. Shooting from both sides commenced immediately. The Vietminh opened fire, with some artillery pieces against the French installations and barracks killing soldiers returning from a special movie screening. Giap had deployed his irregular forces; many of the regular ones moved in safe mountain areas to the north. Three divisions remained outside the city in the suburbs and the Ho Tay (West Lake). French Foreign Legion and other units assaulted the city quarters, suffering casualties in close-quarter battles with their opponents; they experienced first-hand the ingenuity of the Vietnamese in organising defences with small arms fire and crude mines.[48]

Trevor-Wilson was at his office in the consulate general:

Late in the evening, we burned all our secret papers. My secretary from London got off to Hong Kong, and I was left with a Vietnamese secretary and two clerks from London. The Vietnamese managed to control one-half of Hanoi. The extent of villainy of the Vietnamese police and army authorities was incredible. I was taken to see, at the French police headquarters a number of French men and women who had been murdered in a vicious way. Many other people were chained together and marched off to a school nearby, and later on moved to a large number of kilometres. With their males in French police or army, they applied to me to get them out. In due course, all came out, some of them on stretchers.[49]

On 20 December, fighting took place in Bac Ninh and Nam Dinh (north) Hue and Da Nang on the central coast, and in Saigon. Ultimately, the Vietminh could not cope with the French military might, and withdrew. Nonetheless, almost two months after their apparent defeat, guerrilla teams stayed in Hanoi and harassed their opponents. The French established their presence in Hanoi, Haiphong, Hue and Hon Gai and, by March 1947, in the Red River Delta. Ho Chi Minh and Giap deployed their regional headquarters and bases in the areas of Thai Nguyen, Bac Kan and Tuyen Quang.

The French made a vain bid for negotiation. On 14 May 1947, French official Paul Leon Joseph Mus reached – by foot – Ho Chi Minh's headquarters in Thai Nguyen. Already in April the Vietnamese leader had proposed peace talks for a ceasefire. The terms set by the French were simply impossible to meet: the Vietminh were to lay down their arms; allow the French to deploy in their territory; and hand over legionnaires who had deserted the Foreign Legion. All in return for a ceasefire. Ho stated: 'In the French Union there is no place for cowards. ... If I accepted these conditions, I would be one.' Mus had nothing to reply.[50]

In its contact with the United States, which was still unwilling to support it openly, France insisted that the Vietminh was planning a massacre of French civilians with its 19 December attack on Hanoi. Marius Moutet, the Overseas Minister, showed Jefferson Caffery, the US ambassador in Paris, photos of people killed by the Vietminh. He claimed that just 'two hours before the time fixed for the general attack, the French authorities were warned by agents that the attack was impending, and, therefore, a general massacre was avoided'. The French official did not believe that Ho Chi Minh and his associates had planned the massacre, but he 'went along' with the extremists; the Vietnamese leader did not have control over the Vietminh, having been 'out-maneuvered and out-played', Moutet insisted. Nonetheless, the American ambassador was cautious: 'Most of what Moutet told me and much of the contents of the papers I saw have appeared in one way or another in public print.'[51]

**

By 1947, MI6 had set up stations in Hanoi, Hong Kong, Tientsin, Shanghai, Nanjing and Urumchi (north-west China). Now it sought to expand to Bangkok, Kabul and Seoul. Dick Ellis, the MI6 regional controller, sounded disappointed about the quality of intelligence received. Indeed, MI6 had few secret sources in China, and had to rely on a fragile collaboration with the KMT regime's Bureau of Information and Statistics (BIS).[52]

The MI6 station in Hanoi had information of Russian interests in the DRV capital. On January 1946, it was reported that the Russian mission was large enough to have rented 14 rooms in the hotel Metropol and a villa. The British kept contact with Ho Chi Minh to ensure a steady stream of intelligence about his intentions. Lieutenant Commander Simpson-Jones saw the DRV president as much as three times a week, in order to be informed about his continuing talks and negotiations with the French. The general impression in London was that Ho was a moderate who should not be 'eliminated' as the Royal Navy officer insisted. However, Giap, the defence minister, was deemed to lean towards the extremism of the Vietminh.

As the conflict escalated, many French people – men, women and children – were taken hostage by the Vietminh. In Hoa Binh, there were 171 captives (among them were 53 women; and one-third were children under 10). Two hundred civilians (among them British Indians) and 30 military personnel were there when the city fell; between 300 and 400 civilians had been missing since the end of 1946. A French doctor tried to convince the guerrillas to let him go to Hoa Binh: they repeatedly refused.[53] Trevor-Wilson mediated, but the Vietminh remained intransigent.[54] Eventually on 23 June, Trevor-Wilson succeeded in getting seven priests from the Redemptorist mission freed.[55] Approximately 800 other French remained in captivity. On 10 January 1949, French, Red Cross and Vietminh representatives conferred on the living conditions of the captives. The Vietminh, which refused to release its hostages, claimed that it could not improve their facilities because of a lack of communications and transport. Besides, its hostages were scattered in villages and were not held in a single camp. The British military liaison officer remarked 'the general impression gained at this meeting was that the hostages were being treated as well as can be expected, given the shortages, lack of communications and low standard of living to be found throughout Vietminh controlled zones'.[56]

Of the release of more hostages in September 1950, Trevor-Wilson wrote:

All were wretchedly clad, having neither underwear nor foot-gear, and looked exceedingly yellow as if suffering from liver diseases. Nevertheless, they stated that although there was at times very little food, and until the arrival of French Red Cross parcels in April 1949 no medicines, they were not deliberately maltreated. However, no fewer than forty-two have died in captivity – a high proportion. It is to be hoped that this action on the part of the Viet Minh will be followed by the release of the remaining hostages.[57]

***

The Ho-Sainteny agreement was undermined by d'Argenlieu, who, in Saigon on 2 June 1946, proclaimed the Republic of Cochinchina. France also promoted the role of Emperor Bao Dai, who was antagonist of

Ho Chi Minh, as a nationalist leader.[58] Charles Reed, now head of the State Department's Division of Southeastern Asian Affairs, called him a 'French-inspired and French-dominated political zero.'[59]

Meanwhile, Paul Coste Floret, the French Minister of War, said boastfully: 'There is no military problem anymore in Indo-China ... the success of French forces is complete.'[60] The State Department had sided with the French: 'We cannot conceive setbacks to [the] long range French interests [of] France, which would not also be setbacks [of] our own.' Intelligence which claimed that Ho Chi Minh, acting in a conciliatory manner, had side-lined extremists, led the Foreign Office to the conclusion that he was 'midway between Mao of the Long March and Gandhi at the spinning wheel'. Meanwhile, Dean Acheson, the US undersecretary of state, warned his diplomats that Ho Chi Minh was an 'international agent of communism'. Acheson did not believe that the popular Vietnamese leader could be included in a future government: he insisted that 'the question [of] whether Ho [is] as much nationalist as Commie is irrelevant. All Stalinists in colonial areas are nationalists.'[61]

The US consulate in Hanoi was trying to get intelligence about Ho Chi Minh and communism. Their secret sources were unsure. In November 1946, it was difficult to confirm the presence in Vietnam of Chinese communist advisers. Vice-Consul O'Sullivan wrote: 'Numbers are not known but estimates run to the hundreds. Traffic apparently is directed by sea from Shanghai to Hong Kong, thence to Haiphong. However, any reports concerning the presence of Chinese Communists in Haiphong itself should be regarded with suspicion. Pirates from South China have combined with Chinese Army deserters to blackmail Chinese congregating there. While calling themselves Communists, they are actually outlaws.'[62]

The French government insisted that Ho Chi Minh was a Stalinist. US Ambassador Caffery wrote to the secretary of state: 'A high Foreign Ministry official said they are particularly worried because they have "positive proof that Ho Chi Minh is in direct contact with Moscow and is receiving advice and instructions from the Soviets".'[63] But Vice Consul O'Sullivan had no further information on Ho Chi Minh's contact with the Russians. The French claimed 'that if Ho was not receiving instructions from Moscow it was only because of technical difficulties in transmission'. O'Sullivan warned, though, that 'French concern over

Communism may well be devised to direct Dept's attention from French policy in Indochina.'[64]

O'Sullivan had no solid intelligence at his disposal. He wrote of 'theories' with reference to the suspected Moscow–DRV link. The Vietminh attack of 19 December could have been on 'orders from Moscow ... possibly simply to upset Southeast Asia' or possibly to give the French Communist Party (which was deemed to rise to power) a good chance to reach an agreement with the Vietminh and show themselves as 'protectors of French interests'.[65] In any case, the French officials continued to speak of 'positive proof that Ho Chi Minh is in direct contact with Moscow and is receiving advice and instructions from the Soviets'.[66]

In 1947, a Special Projects Staff report from the State Department, which also had access to communications intercepts, concluded that there was 'no evidence of any control of the Vietnamese Communist movement by Moscow'. The following year, a similar report found 'no direct evidence, and that if there was any, a Moscow-directed conspiracy was "an anomaly"'.[67]

In their turn, the Chinese nationalists who employed BIS, an immense intelligence gathering machinery, were not sure of any Ho Chi Minh/Soviet liaison. On 31 December 1946, Chinese First Secretary, Tswen-ling Tsui, met with State Department officials in Washington. He said that he did not believe that any communications existed between the USSR and Vietnam; while he believed that Ho Chi Minh 'might receive moral support' from Moscow.[68]

By mid-October 1948, Hanoi was full of rumours that Ho Chi Minh had resigned in favour of the 70-year-old nationalist, ex-mandarin Bui Bang Doan, who had joined the Vietminh in 1946. It looked like Doan was a personality who could accept the return to power of Emperor Bao Dai. Trevor-Wilson, who was now consul in Hanoi, warned Britain that these were the same rumours that were aired back in August 1947, and that they were, as Consul-General Frank Gibbs in Saigon put it, 'probably French feelers or Communist smoke'.[69] By the end of 1948, secret intelligence at the disposal of Gibbs revealed the existence of a secret political organisation that aimed to unite all the nationalists, among them Ngo Dinh Diem (the future president of South Vietnam) and his Catholic following, the Vietnamese nationalist party VNQDD, as well as radical socialists. General Xuan and Emperor Bao Dai may have been involved in the establishment of the organisation that was both anti-French and anti-communist. Gibbs maintained that his report was based on 'fairly reliable information'.[70]

There was a clear French intent to share information with the British as early as 1947. Returning from a visit to Hanoi early in June 1947, the military liaison officer Major J.E.D. Street remarked that 'a very big impression has been made on the average Frenchmen in FIC [French Indochina] by the Franco-British Alliance. British stock is higher in FIC than it has ever been, and this is reflected in the very helpful way in which the French authorities are giving us information of all kinds (including details of secret military dispositions, etc.).'[71] He wrote that the scale of arms smuggling between Thailand and Cambodia had decreased in comparison to the past. The China–Saigon smuggling route had heavy traffic; cargo ships from Hong Kong sailed to Saigon, stopping outside the three mile limit, unloading the arms onto junks. The arms were 'the most modern American' ones, sold by Chinese merchants who had access to the surplus from the Chinese nationalist regime which had been armed by the US before the embargo.[72]

The French military offered their British counterparts secret intelligence on the Chinese in Vietnam. An official of the British consulate general in Saigon noted: 'I must ask you [Brain from the Office of HM Special Commissioner in South East Asia] to take my word for its [the report's] first-class authenticity, and since it concerns [French] intentions [towards the Chinese] which are not yet being carried out, I must stress its secrecy, and the necessity of there being no leakage of any part of it to any Chinese whatsoever.'[73]

By early 1948, the security of the French-held cities did not improve, despite the advance of the French forces in the surrounding rural areas. Frank Gibbs, the British consul general in Saigon, described the 'extraordinary situation [of siege] which prevails' every night with rifle and mortar fire. Lord Killearn, who paid a visit to Saigon, wrote to Bevin: 'If you suppress a nationalist severely enough you will find him tending towards communism because it is the communists who have consistently supported nationalist movements in dependent territories. And it is also true that once a nationalist movement is outlawed or driven underground it is usually the communists who gain control owing to their great experience and efficiency in clandestine organisations.'[74]

In June 1948, the Foreign Office had intelligence from MI6 to the effect that largescale arms smuggling was organised to support Saigon's needs, the South Vietnamese regime and the pro-French organisations and sects; arms of the Chinese nationalist army were being smuggled to Hong Kong and then transported in Vietnamese junks to Saigon.[75]

The French press speculated about a secret agreement between Mao and Ho Chi Minh.[76] British intelligence had information of Chinese aid to the Vietminh.[77] Also, the US consul general in Saigon had intelligence which claimed that Ho Chi Minh was receiving aid from the Chinese.[78]

In Paris, the US Embassy had secured a secret French plan for the possible evacuation of Tonkin and Northern Annam and the concentration of forces in Cambodia, Southern Annam and Cochinchina; this contingency would be activated only in the event of a communist victory in the civil war in China and the deployment of Mao's forces along the border with Vietnam.[79] A year later, in October 1949, after winning over the KMT regime, Mao declared the establishment of the People's Republic of China. The same month Vietminh guerrilla operations had expanded to Cambodia and Laos. Vietminh troops, 3,000 strong, were stationed in Kampot and Kompong Speu. Nonetheless, in a Thai newspaper Ho Chi Minh blamed 'French imperialist propaganda' for connecting him with Mao and Stalin.[80]

During the same period (autumn 1949), British and French intelligence exchanged information on communist leaders in South East Asia. The sharing of intelligence did not include the fight against arms smuggling, but both sides hoped that it would soon.[81] French files confirmed the Anglo-French intelligence cooperation in 1949.[82] Nonetheless, the French bitterly complained about not receiving intelligence on Siam (Thailand). To this, the British replied that Thailand was an ally of Britain and that divulging information on this country (and the Vietminh deployments there) would amount to an unfriendly act towards it.[83]

In any case, British and French military commanders were sharing military and public security intelligence on Indochina.[84] It was reported that approximately 18,000 Chinese irregular troops operated in northern Tonkin.[85] The Chinese were deemed more like 'pirates' who had infiltrated the Tonkin areas in December 1948 and January 1949. The cooperation between the Vietminh and the Chinese bands was 'evident from the coordinated timing of the communist offensive'. The French outposts and Route Coloniale 4 were threatened by the Chinese and the Vietminh. It was reported that, in a location north-east of Lao Kay, 600 Chinese and a DRV battalion operated together.[86]

The French government informed the British embassy in Paris that the Chinese General Chu Xia Pi had the Chinese bands 'in some degree' under his command. It was also reported that approximately 15,000 Chinese irregulars were deployed between Lao Kay and Ha Giang and 3,000 at Lang Son. In any case, the Foreign Office was warned by the French government that 'there is evidence of the existence of an organised military staff and of orders having being received from higher up. The French do not know whether these orders come from but do not exclude the possibility that they come from Mao Tse-tung himself'.[87]

The French and colonial forces managed to repel the joint Chinese-Vietminh assault in North Tonkin, which lasted from March to early April 1949. A French staff officer informed Major W.P. Lunn-Rockliffe, the British liaison officer in Saigon, that the Chinese bands were more 'pirates' than communists. He said that 'the French military commander at Lao Kay was able to buy, with a few old arms, a [Chinese] band just inside the Chinese border and had them beat up another Chinese band returning from a foray in Indochina'.[88] Many Vietminh documents were found after their retreat; the tactical commanders of the Vietminh were urged to 'keep the pressure up on the colonialists. Our Chinese comrades will soon bring assistance.'[89]

Foreign Secretary Ernest Bevin and Robert Schumann, his French counterpart, talked about ways of expanding intelligence-sharing through the British high commissioner in Singapore.[90] The Colonial Office worried that if the French withdrew from northern Indochina there would eventually be a 'direct strategic threat to Malaya'. Intelligence came from the intercepted broadcasts in Vietnamese. Ho Chi Minh thanked Stalin for arms aid.[91]

In Saigon, the consulate general and MI6 were trying to find evidence of Chinese–Vietminh cooperation. On 15 March 1949, it was reported that there was no information available but that 'there is probably no direct contact'. Gibbs wrote of Sino-Vietnamese 'local' contact across the Yunnan frontier, and 'some' arms smuggling, but there was 'no evidence' of 'high-level contact'.[92]

The intelligence that the Foreign Office received was inconclusive; a report from August 1949 emphasised that 'there is no direct evidence of co-ordination by Russia of communist activities throughout Southeast Asia though it is strongly suspected'.[93] On 6 April 1949, the consulate-general in Saigon informed the commissioner general in Singapore: 'We passed on the information to the French without revealing the source, and they said that it more or less confirmed reports they had already received. We understand that all troops in Saigon had already been told to be prepared for an emergency after 10th April, and guards will be doubled, etc. Meanwhile, acts of terrorism in Saigon are definitely on the increase.'[94] Over time, the Vietminh focused its attacks on the Tonkin area, while attacks on Saigon were limited. By early May it was reported the French had performed satisfactorily in minor operations not only in the Saigon area but also in Thu Dau Mot, Ben Luc and Long Xuyen.[95]

In October 1949, the Foreign Office blocked an RAF photo reconnaissance flight over Indochina, reasoning that it could be interpreted by the Vietminh as a 'prelude to active intervention' if taken into account together with two Royal Navy warship port calls and top ranking officers' visits to Saigon.[96] Nonetheless, by early December the Foreign Office agreed on air reconnaissance of Indochina. The French delayed in granting authorisation: eventually the order for aerial survey was given by the British Chiefs of Staff on 27 January 1950. While three British officers were attached to French units in Indochina in liaison duties; three French officers were attached to British units in Malaya.[97]

One of the officers, Captain P.N.R. Stewart-Richardson of the Coldstream Guards, was wounded in the thigh on 23 January 1950 when his mobile column fell into a Vietminh guerrilla ambush. He was taken to Saigon military hospital for an operation. The British tried to conceal the episode from the press. The authorities in Singapore, where the captain was based, were asked not to publicise anything. Nonetheless, a report appeared in the *Strait Times*. The French demonstrated their alliance with Britain against the DRV. General Carpentier (the commander in chief of French forces in Indochina) visited the captain in the hospital, and awarded him the Croix de Guerre.[98] Counselor-General Frank Gibbs remarked that the award 'seems to be a fait accompli, and it will not of course be possible to ask the French to take it back if this were considered desirable'.[99]

The French pressed for more military intelligence sharing. General Carpentier took a personal interest in an arrangement with the British, including the supply of his forces with British equipment. Nonetheless,

Prime Minister Attlee and his cabinet did not want to intervene in Indochina; the Foreign Office informed the Chiefs of Staff not to discuss anything with the French at any level that would imply British military involvement. Britain warned the United States that no British forces would be dispatched, even if the Chinese invaded Vietnam.[100] Meanwhile, the British ambassador in Moscow feared that 'the Soviet and Chinese leaders have decided that French Indo-china is the weakest link in the chain of Western defence in Southeast Asia and that the maximum pressure should be exerted there'.[101]

Meanwhile, in November 1949 a report on Indochina by the high commissioner of India was leaked to the press – much to the embarrassment of the Foreign Office. The high commissioner denied that his staff could have been implicated in the leak. But British intelligence disputed this, and informed the consulate general in Saigon: 'It has nevertheless subsequently confirmed from secret sources that the leakage did, in fact, occur there; the Indian High Commissioner showed the report to Frederick Kuh of the *Chicago Sun*, who must have passed it on to his colleagues of the Associated Press in order to cover himself. We are trying to check up whether the *Chicago Sun* carried the story under Kuh's name. So far, we only know of the Associated Press report.'[102]

In March 1950, the Ministry of Defence reported that the People's Army of Vietnam (PAVN) regular forces reached 86,000 in 188 battalions supported by 90,000 irregulars. The French had deployed 135,800 regulars, 50,000 Vietnamese 'colonial' regulars, Cambodia and Laos combined 6,000 regular troops and 41,000 Indo-Chinese troops. British military intelligence assumed that time was on the side of the PAVN, who were conducting a war of attrition, along with guerrilla attacks, until they were better prepared.[103]

The British were aware that rumours were spread against them. H.A. Graves wrote to Eden – who was now Foreign Secretary – on 18 January 1952: '[R]umors of negotiation with Mao Tse-tung have not been allowed to appear in the local press but they have even touched myself and it is widely said that my recent private visit to Hong Kong was in connexion with His Majesty's Government alleged appeal to Mao Tse-tung to take his hands off Indo-China. In the same way there was a tendency to dismiss as a smoke screen your own statement that his Majesty's Government would not tolerate Chinese intervention in Indochina or elsewhere in South-East Asia.'[104]

In Saigon, the Vietnamese Prime Minister, Tran, feared that Russia was directly arming the PAVN. He claimed that a large number of Skoda heavy machine guns — ostensibly from Czechoslovakia — was transported to the communists. In addition, it seemed that the number of Chinese instructors and advisers in the PAVN camp had increased.[105] As for Trevor-Wilson, he continued to report on the escalation of the war and the growing fear of a Chinese intervention (which we will explore in Chapter 4).

CHAPTER 2

FRENCH INTELLIGENCE AT WAR

French military intelligence had no time to reorganise to cope with the new war in Indochina. The intelligence apparatus in Indochina tried to reinvent itself. Beyond the Second Bureau of the French General Staff, which handled military intelligence, the intelligence machinery in Indochina comprised:

1. The Direction Générale de la Documentation (DGD) from 1950 onwards. (Previously it was named Bureau Federal de Documentation.) This was a coordination office, serving the high commissioner.
2. The Secrétariat Permanent de la Défense Nationale (SPDN) assigned to the collection of diplomatic/political intelligence from defence attachés in neighbouring countries, as well as from Japan and Hong Kong. The secretariat transferred intelligence to the DGD.
3. The Service de Documentation Extérieure et de Contre-Espionnage (SDECE).
4. The Sûreté Nationale (security service; a police organisation).
5. The Groupe des Contrôles Radioélectriques (GCR).

In Paris, the SDECE was under the premier's office; in Indochina it was put under the high commissioner. Its four branches covered domestic and foreign intelligence targets: the SDECE's Service de Renseignement (SR) gathered intelligence from outside Indochina (namely Thailand, China, Taiwan and other countries). Like the US and British intelligence services, SDECE spies could not penetrate the 'yellow wall' of Mao's China. (The SDECE had already lost its presence in China after the defeat of Chiang Kai-shek and the closing down of the consulates by Mao.)[1]

Maurice Belleux, an Air Force Colonel and Saint-Cyr graduate, led the SDECE in Indochina from December 1947 to April 1956. His intelligence background included his contribution in the merger of the DGER with the SDECE. General Roger Blaizot (the commander of the French forces in Indochina between 1948 and 1949) did not like Belleux, calling him suspicious and untrustworthy. 'I do not regret the quarrels I had with him', he said. The general feared that Belleux's girlfriend, a White Russian, was a spy in the service of the Russians. Throughout the occupation of France, Belleux was dispatched on air intelligence missions; until May 1944 he was one of the leading members of the 'Hunter' network on behalf of the Bureau Central de Renseignements et d'Action (BCRA). He later served in the section des études (research section) of the DGER. He was a former special operator who believed strongly in the value of commando raids guided by up-to-date intelligence. Thus, Belleux advocated the establishment of the Service Action of SDECE and the Groupement de Commandos Mixtes Aéroportés (GCMA) – something that would materialise only in 1951.[2]

In Indochina, the SDECE had a counterintelligence branch working with the Sûreté, as well as the military security service, the Brigades de Contre-espionage Opérationnelles. Signals intelligence were gathered by the Service Technique des Recherches (STR), another branch of the SDECE.[3]

To what extent mountain tribes could effectively confront the Vietminh was debated among high-ranking officers. The anti-Vietminh Montagnard tribes – or the three other 'maquis' groups overviewed by the GCMA: a Meo tribe in Laos, a T'ai group under Deo Van Long in north-west Tonkin and a Meo tribe in north-central Tonkin, east of the Red River – could not be considered forces that menaced DRV-controlled territories. A 1952 French report on the activities of the GCMA claimed that '98 percent [of the tribe fighters] are illiterate; they are incapable of giving precise intelligence.' Another report, from 1 October 1953, criticised the use of tribes as saboteurs. They were nothing more than village militias.[4] In any case, the French deemed the average Vietnamese 'an intelligent and a good observer with a tendency to embroil'. The Cambodians and the Laotians were characterised as 'sluggish, impressed by their superstitions'. The Mois tribes could not provide information because 'they could not even count'; they were distrustful and unwilling to hand over people they were associated with. On many occasions, the tribes had reported the movement of the same Vietminh group near their village, thus giving French intelligence inaccurate information on the enemy's deployment.[5]

The Groupe des Contrôles Radioélectriques (GCR), an agency established in 1945, was assigned to communications intelligence; it was controlled by both the SDECE and the Ministry of Defence in Paris. In Indochina, the GCR was put under the STR of SDECE, although it was considered an independent organisation. The GCR had stations in Hanoi and Saigon intercepting Chinese, British, Burmese and of course DRV radio communications.[6] However, during the early years of the war, the French could not intercept Vietminh communications. The radio stations had low power, and the equipment was of Japanese, French and American origin. Also, the humidity and heat, especially in the North Tonkin area, hindered signals intelligence operations. The Vietminh had set up a network with a head station in Hanoi (before they abandoned the city in December 1946) and outstations in Viet Bac, Hoa Binh and Dong Trieu, Trung Bo (in central Vietnam), Hué and Da Nang. The GCR had located the Vietminh radio nets of Hanoi (the headquarters of Ho Chi Minh) with his military commands as well as with sympathisers in Laos and Thailand.[7]

The Second Bureau of the État-Major Interarmées et Forces Terrestres (EMIFT) was the intelligence agency that directly served the commander in chief; the EMIFT gathered intelligence and analysis from its counterparts, the Second Bureau of the Forces Terrestres du Nord Vietnam and Zone Opérationnelle du Tonkin (FTNV/ZOT), and the Second Bureau of forces in South Vietnam. In addition, the Second Bureau of the Navy and Air Force provided intelligence from their sources. French pilots also flew over South China, bringing back photos to the EMIFT, which showed the Chinese air force deployments and their state of readiness in Yunnan and Kwang Si provinces. The Navy kept the Vietminh's arms smuggling from China and Thailand under close watch. Finally, the commander in chief had his human intelligence agency, the sixth section of the EMIFT, the Service de Renseignement Opérationnel (SRO). The SRO agents were dispatched behind enemy lines.[8] Nonetheless, the SRO was penetrated by a young Vietminh agent in 1949.[9]

***

The Vietminh established the Public Security and Intelligence service, as well as the Ministry of Defence Bureau of Communications and Information, which also handled cryptographic communications. A defector provided the French with information on the cryptographic bureau. The defector revealed that two-thirds of intelligence was sourced through intercepts. Already, in October 1949, Colonel Belleux had attempted in vain to keep his opponents from learning cryptography in the public libraries of Vietnam by ordering them to withhold access to classic books on the subject, such as Baudoin's *Éléments de Cryptographie*. A similar prohibition was also implemented in public libraries in France.[10] The defector spoke of Chinese advisers in the school for cryptography, as well as in the cryptographic bureau. The French mistakenly assumed that also Russian cryptographers were serving alongside the Vietnamese.[11]

The Vietnamese, who before the war had received training in radio communications, telegraphy, maths and even scouting found themselves leading the security apparatus of the Democratic Republic of Vietnam. In 1943, after the Allied landing against the Vichy regime in Madagascar, MI6 called on imprisoned Vietminh nationalists (among them Nguyen Van Ngoc, Tran Hieu – a graduate of the École Pratique Industrielle of Hanoi – and Le Gian) to gather intelligence against the Japanese. They received specialist training in India and were later dispatched to South China. Eventually, Le Gian and Tran Hieu, following US orders and training from the OSS, were parachuted into North Vietnam to provide intelligence on Japanese deployments. Of course, they rejoined the Vietminh and became close associates of Ho Chi Minh. Hieu headed the Ministry of Defence Intelligence Service of the newly established DRV. Le Gian became general director of the Public Security Service. A Japanese colonel who had defected to the Vietminh conducted the first training on intelligence.[12]

The DRV followed French colonial Sûreté patterns in organising the Public Security Service and the Bureau of Security Forces for North Vietnam. The latter had a Scouting Intelligence Unit, a Political Bureau, a Bureau for Legal Administration and a Bureau of Identification.

Initially, only a Scouting Intelligence Service was established in Central Vietnam. In Nam Bo, a National Defence Guard undertook intelligence gathering duties.

The Indochinese Communist Party (ICP) oversaw the establishment and functioning of these services. The key official was Tran Dang Ninh, who led the Control and Inspection Board of the Executive Committee of the ICP's Central Committee. In February 1946, all intelligence services were placed under the Ministry of the Interior; the Vietnamese Public Security Department was placed under Le Gian, who had to report to the Central Committee via Tran Dang Ninh. Vietminh secret services sought to eliminate the presence and the activities of right-wing nationalist parties, the Dai Viet (Greater Vietnam Party), the Viet Nam Quoc Dan Dang (Vietnamese Nationalist Party, VNQDD) and Dong Minh Hoi (Alliance League). In the meantime, aiming to show the nationalist and not the communist image of the DRV, Ho Chi Minh promoted non-communists to government positions. Indicative of his strategy in 1946–7 (at the time when the Vietminh tried unsuccessfully to gain the attention and support of the United States) was the replacement of Le Gian as director of the police by a non-communist. The same applied to Hieu. Both, however, continued developing the security apparatus. Eventually, the new non-communist directors resigned, realising that they were nothing but figureheads. Hieu and Le Gian resumed their duties.

In South Vietnam, intelligence was conducted by the party's Territorial Committee for Nam Bo; the Nam Bo Security Service (for espionage, sabotage and assassination of traitors) was established, covering the Saigon-Cholon area. Another intelligence unit was the Office of Special Affairs, directed by the spy Pham Ngoc Thao. Throughout the war, the Public Security department handled spies in Hanoi and Saigon. Between 1946 and 1953, Tran Quoc Hoan was a key handler in Hanoi; in 1953 he was appointed head of the Ministry of Public Security.

Already in an August 1947 report, Giap blamed military intelligence for failures; he even claimed that it had been infiltrated by French spies. The Bac Kan near-disaster of the raid against Ho Chi Minh's headquarters (discussed in Chapter 3) vindicated his criticism regarding the need for better training of the operatives in urban and rural areas. Giap maintained that the population had to be employed as sources and scouting units to observe and report on the movements and deployments of the opponent.

The leadership soon addressed intelligence reorganisation. On 13 November 1947, representatives of the Ministry of the Interior Public Security (under Le Gian) and the Ministry of Defence Military Intelligence Bureau (under Tran Hieu) agreed to improve coordination of their organisations. They established a new unit called the Public Security Committee on Intelligence (under Public Security), a sub-unit of the police which would continue gathering intelligence in French-occupied cities and areas. The general staff under Giap and his deputy Hoang Van Thai was established on 7 September 1945, based on the French model. It was the destination of all intelligence deemed military or strategic.

By May 1951, Public Security, having lost the war-related intelligence gathering to the Military Intelligence Branch of the general staff, concentrated on the security of the DRV regime. Public Security was assigned to guard, along with the 'people's democratic power', the economy and the army. The same month, a 'strategic intelligence board' was established in the premier's office; among other duties it oversaw operations against the South Vietnamese regime. A strategic intelligence branch operated in the Ministry of Defence, and a Special Intelligence Board was established within the Central Committee, which tasked military intelligence, as well as the Public Security. The South Vietnamese state established its intelligence agency, the Service de Reinseignement (SR), in 1951. The SDECE and the French forces were not happy about it, nor did they offer significant aid. It was feared that the new service would turn against the French who assumed that since they were fighting the war, the Vietnamese SR would soon become the tool of the corrupt nationalist government and their intrigues.[13]

Despite the above-mentioned development of the intelligence machinery throughout the war with the French, the Vietminh did not have a foreign intelligence agency. Thus, in summer 1954, during the negotiations in Geneva no 'research bureau' supported the Vietnamese negotiators. The Russians and the Chinese keenly provided intelligence, advice and persuasion, insisting that the Vietnamese should in effect accept the division of the country, as Ho Chi Minh was himself counselled in Beijing on the eve of the Geneva Conference. The DRV delegates were eventually persuaded.[14]

***

In July 1947, the US vice consul in Hanoi, James O'Sullivan, spoke with an aide of General Salan (now the deputy commander in chief in Indochina); the two discussed intelligence and the role of France and the United States. The French insisted that the Vietminh was a communist organisation and that French intelligence reported the appearance of eight Russians in the border areas; this group, ostensibly, was advising the DRV on the reorganisation of less effective rebel units. The aide warned that if Vietnam turned communist, no democratic rights and freedoms would be afforded to its citizens. O'Sullivan said sarcastically that 'the French Sûreté here gave little evidence of respect for them also'. The general's aide wanted to give a history lesson: Vietnam was a creation of the Japanese, and this was proved by the fact that Japanese joined the Vietminh after World War II. To this, O'Sullivan answered that Germans in the Foreign Legion were fighting for France in Indochina, and that no one had accused France of being an 'Axis creation'. In the case that Japanese would take up senior positions in the Vietminh ranks, 'the French would certainly have [a] great deal more difficulty militarily'.[15]

French colonial officials insisted that the Vietminh were communists. O'Sullivan admitted that there had been 'no recent evidence of high credibility which adds to what was known of [the] character of Vietnam Govt six months ago'. He suspected the French of manipulating intelligence: 'What makes it suspicious is [the] fact [that the] French tried [the] same tactics during [the] months which preceded [the] Haiphong incident in fall of last year.' The group of the 'Russians' was an innocent affair; they were White Russian musicians. In fact, the French consul general in Kunming (China) told the US vice consul there 'that he regarded the report [of Russians helping the Vietminh] as a fabrication of French military intelligence in Indochina'.[16]

The French services exerted strong pressure on the US diplomats because they suspected a US policy of backing the Vietnamese. Charles Reed, the consul in Saigon, remarked on 'the activities in Indochina of the Sûreté and the French Military Security Service, which for example have hinted to consular personnel that any information obtained in the consular establishments should be passed on'.[17]

In September 1947, the chief of the Sûreté returned from Hanoi and paid a visit to Reed. The French official revealed that Emperor Bao Dai had agreed to negotiate with France in order to head a government – but France would not disclose anything, nor would Bao Dai do anything for the time being, so as not to appear like a puppet. He had time to gather some support and gain the people's vote in a referendum. With reference to the intelligence on defections in the Vietminh, the chief of the Sûreté spoke of a 'certain amount of defection from Viet Minh ranks but not enough [to] greatly weaken Ho'. He said that there would be 'no lasting peace solution [for the] FIC [French Indochina] situation without taking Ho into consideration – this [is] why [the] French military hope [an] "unfortunate accident" may happen to Ho.'[18] (In fact, a couple of weeks later, in October 1947, French paratroopers raided Ho Chi Minh's headquarters: see the next chapter.) In 1952, Sûreté officers admitted to British diplomats that 40 per cent of the Vietnamese Hanoi police staff sympathised with the Vietminh.[19]

Meanwhile, the Chinese consul general of Chiang Kai-shek's nationalist regime informed Consul Reed that 'communist agents (including several agents recently arrived from Yunnan) have been stirring up trouble among the thousands of Chinese-made homeless by fires on [the] outskirts of Saigon and yesterday planned demonstration in front of his office with intention [to] create incident with French police'. The Chinese diplomat claimed that French, Chinese and an unconfirmed number of Russian communists 'did not appear to be working together very closely'.[20]

Jefferson Caffery, the US ambassador in Paris, had a meeting with French officials from the Ministry of Foreign Affairs, who claimed that Ho Chi Minh's letter to the French government, dated 20 February 1947, and a 'number of orders and instructions to Vietnam officials recently seized in Indo-China had been examined by [a] number of French handwriting experts who were unanimous and positive in their belief all signatures were forged'. In fact, no one had seen Ho Chi Minh since 20 November 1946; the French intelligence services did not believe in rumours of his assassination, although they could not explain why he had not made an appearance.[21]

The French monitored the Vietminh's broadcasts. One particular broadcast made an impression. Ho Chi Minh issued a statement on the death of Colonels Debes and Gufflet (the chief of staff to General Valluy) who were shot down by Vietminh anti-aircraft fire on 30 March 1947: 'As French they were our friends, as soldiers they were brave, as colonialists they were our opponents. But before God and humanity everyone is a brother and equal. That is why I bow before their souls. I deeply regret that men of valor such as they are sacrificed in this fratricidal war. Otherwise, they would have been very useful in common work between France and Vietnam.'[22]

In his turn, Abbot Moffat at that time the head of the Southeast Asian Affairs Division at the State Department, had been complaining about open source intelligence because of the French censorship which 'is that of a totalitarian regime at its worst'.[23] Despite the censorship, the French could not keep the military's secrets; two years later, in 1949, a very sensitive French general staff report was leaked in Paris. The report argued that the government had to seek peace: the French forces were inadequate to win; Emperor Bao Dai did not have support among the population. The author was none other than General Revers, the chief of the general staff who had visited Indochina in May 1949. He assessed a stalemate which was, in effect, to the advantage of the Vietminh. He maintained that no city or main road was secure from sabotage or ambush and reported that largescale Vietminh operations were launched in the Mekong Delta area. Occasionally, the French forces prevailed but with heavy casualties. The general suggested a partial withdrawal of forces and the evacuation of forts in North Tonkin. Revers's top-secret report was meant for special distribution among top-ranking government officials. In September 1949, the report was leaked, and the Vietminh radio station was able to broadcast part of it.

Another episode drew the interest of the Sûreté. On a Paris bus a Vietnamese student and a French sailor had a fight. Soon the police arrived and discovered a copy of the Revers report in the student's briefcase. The investigation led to another Vietnamese and his apartment where 72 copies of Revers's report were found.[24] The so-called 'general's affair' scandal that ensued, resulted in Revers resigning in December 1949. In October 1950 Trevor-Wilson wrote about the morale of the French forces fighting the Vietminh: 'In our various personal contacts with French Union troops we have not discovered any marked failing of their high state of morale with the possible exception of a few German legionnaires. On the other hand, some of the high-ranking officers, including generals, seem to be taking a somewhat defeatist attitude. We have never seen General Alessandri, usually overoptimistic, in such a depressed state of mind as he is at the moment.'[25]

***

The French secret services played the deception game – and on some occasions very cleverly indeed. In 1948, they created paranoia within the DRV military command. Intelligence was 'leaked' which showed that the secret agent codenamed H122 operated in the upper echelons of the military command. In March of that year, the Public Security Service in Hanoi found a seemingly invaluable French document, 'Report by the Agent codename H122'. Soon it reached the Bureau of Intelligence of the DRV Ministry of Defence. The staff officers read about planned Vietminh operations for that autumn and winter, concluding that this information could come only from a well-connected mole among their ranks in the Viet Bac base high command. It was a matter of time before paranoia would explode, and dozens of 'suspects' would be subjected to cruel interrogations that resulted in forced confessions.

It was reported that within a month 'several hundred military cadres and officers at the regimental level were arrested and interrogated'. Approximately 200 cadres and military personnel and 103 civilians were tortured. In parallel, everyone accused the other of being a French spy. Eventually, many of those interrogated, to avoid further pain, confessed that they were paid agents of the Second Bureau or that they were members of nationalist parties. Tran Dang Ninh, the top security official of the DRV, was called by the Central Committee, and by Ho Chi Minh himself, to search for the elusive secret agent H122.

He concluded that the whole affair was a French deception to demoralise the Vietminh; he stated clearly that there was no such a spy. The party tried in vain to put strict controls on the use of torture during interrogations. A similar paranoia about the existence of spies and nationalists among the Vietminh cadre in South Vietnam was reported in 1949. The fear persisted that nationalists, backed by French arms, had infiltrated Public Security units. The official history of Public Security stated:

In Cho Lon, Nguyen Huu Doc, the Deputy District Public Security Chief, who was personally in command of Area B in Can Duoc district conducted waves of arrests, using brutal torture, rape, and murder in a so-called 'espionage case' that caused unjust suffering for 86 families of innocent civilians.

Similar waves of arrests were made in Tay Ninh. Hundreds of cadres, Party members, civilian supporters, company and battalion-level military commanders were arrested. The arrests even extended into the ranks of Public Security itself, where reconnaissance personnel and investigating officers up to the rank of the Deputy chief of a district public security officer were arrested. A reconnaissance team member who one day went out to arrest someone would suddenly be arrested the very next day. An investigating officer who one day was sitting in his chair conducting interrogations would the next day be forced to stand in that same office to be interrogated himself.[26]

The paranoid hunt for spies cost the Vietminh in South Vietnam legitimacy among the population. The top cadre admitted this: 'It turned out that during this period waves of arrests had been carried out in many provinces that caused us extremely regrettable losses and damage. This was the result of the use of physical violence and torture, forcing people to make statements, putting words in their mouths, and then arresting everyone implicated by the suspects during torture.' The French secret services, having captured relevant documents, were aware that the Vietminh was debating the use of torture in interrogations. This was stated in the July 1949 minutes of the Public Security meeting attended by Diep Ba, Mai Chi Tho and other officials. Mai Chi To was against torture that damaged the image of the party with the harsh treatment of the innocent, turning his family hostile to the Vietminh. Orders were issued to 'harm the health of prisoners as little as possible'. Nonetheless, reports of torture continued to an extent that in 1951 Public Security ordered a stop to its use during interrogations. But this did not affect the situation on the ground. In 1952, more paranoia about the existence of spies among the Vietminh spread in the Saigon-Cholon area; extensive torture of suspects followed. The high command yet again intervened. The Central Bureau for the South of the Vietnam Workers' Party (the successor of the ICP established in 1951) insisted that no spies were found.[27]

After the defeat of Giap at the siege of Na San, the Vietminh defections reached 10,780 in the first quarter of 1953. By the end of the year, though, the trend was reversed, as Giap's forces were moving to the valley of Dien Bien Phu. The desertions to the French were almost nil, and their forces suffered massive desertions of Vietnamese to the Vietminh. The influx of so many deserters in early 1954 made the Vietminh command suspicious, fearing of a French secret plan to infiltrate their ranks with agents posing as deserters. Thus, the standard orders were for deserters to be assigned to agricultural work and not to military units.[28] As we will explore in later chapters, the CIA took advantage of the security paranoia of the DRV intelligence services within their psychological warfare strategy. The agency initiated secret programmes that 'showed' DRV counterintelligence that former North Vietnamese prisoners of war were 'turned' and worked for the United States. In addition to the spies, high-ranking defectors enabled the French to know their opponent better. A commanding officer of the Vietminh political research branch of the Office of Intelligence defected and gave information of Giap's strategy and unit movements.[29]

***

During the war, both opponents employed special methods against each other: the trade of opium, the rise of inflation and the destruction of rice harvest were desperate and failed attempts to support military operations and turn the tables.

The official currency in Indochina was the piaster, issued by the Bank of Indochina. The Vietminh confiscated a large amount of piasters in 1945–6, but when they had to move their government to the mountains they had to find a new currency to be used in DRV territories. They came up with the 'Ho Chi Minh piaster'. The French secret services targeted the new currency. In 1948, the Sûreté was implicated in a plot to transfer confiscated Ho Chi Minh piasters to Hong Kong and exchange them, securing profits. The Sûreté's head explained himself by emphasising that he had to find more money to pay for his informers.[30]

In 1949, the SDECE attempted to cause inflation in the DRV controlled territories by issuing counterfeit Ho Chi Minh piasters. Only a year later, General de Lattre called off the operation, while French intelligence reports claimed that despite the hyperinflation the Vietminh showed flexibility, allowing other currencies to be used in their territories.[31] The Corsican mafia (whose networks operated in Saigon) and the organised Vietnamese criminals, seeking to get quick profits, were also interested in the 'game' of piasters. Meanwhile, the French tried to maintain the piaster as an artificially hard currency, so that the associate states – Laos, Vietnam and Cambodia – would export piasters and keep their imports cheap.

The Hong Kong-based Bank of Communications, employed by the Vietminh and the Chinese communists, was also interested in piasters; the bank had branches in Saigon, Hanoi and Haiphong. In the meantime, Washington had been financing the French military effort. The CIA exercised strong pressure on the French to stop gold and piaster smuggling. After it reached Saigon, gold from Paris that was destined for the Bank of Indochina ended up in the hands of networks that transferred it to Macao; there it was purchased by the Vietminh, who gave it to the Chinese in return for arms. In effect, all were happy: the French bankers (who secured a 50 per cent profit, according to a 1953 French military report), the Vietminh and the Chinese.[32]

Silver piasters were most in demand by the French military, which sought to pay informers venturing into China. In May 1952, the commander of the forces in the sub-section Phongsaly (in North Laos) demanded coins and plates of silver to pay his agents. No one trusted banknotes. Officially, only the Institute of Finance of the Associate States held stocks. General Salan demanded to retrocede the stock on behalf of the military.[33] Ultimately, it was free market economics that dominated the game of the piasters – not ambitious spymasters unaccustomed to finances.

The French assumed that they could cause famine and destroy the DRV financially. Already in 1948, Vietminh propaganda aimed at villagers accused the French (as well as the Khmer) of poisoning the harvest and the stockpiles of food.[34] The country had already suffered a severe famine during and after the Japanese occupation. In 1949, Major W.P. Lunn-Rockliffe, the British military liaison officer in Saigon, remarked of the planned French strategy on rice:

> The French staff have confirmed to me that they are aiming an economic blow at the Vietminh by controlling and blocking the transport of paddy from the Ca Mau peninsula to the Cholon rice-mills. It is well known that the Vietminh largely finance their purchases of arms from abroad by the 'safety money' they extort from the Chinese merchants trading between the paddy areas and their mills in Cholon. If this trade can be cut down to no more than is necessary to feed the Saigon-Cholon area, then, according

to the French staff, the loss of exportable rice will be more than offset by the corresponding loss of revenue to the Vietminh. From the long term point of view it is maintained to be more important to do everything to bring the rebels to heel, prior to full economic recovery, than to continue exporting rice that indirectly finances the Vietminh. The Cau Mau Peninsula has been chosen as the unfortunate area for this experiment as it is furthest away from Cholon, the most easily controlled and contains the strongest Vietminh influence. There is No [emphasis in the original] sure indication as to how long this economic blockade will last although one staff officer remarked that 'he who holds out longest wins.' Obviously it must continue for some months before the effect is felt by the Vietminh.[35]

By December 1949, London was informed that Ho Chi Minh lacked funds. The rice blockade of the French was short-sighted; 'from a security point of view, however, it has been a success, and has deprived the Viet Minh of a considerable source of income, which they previously used to buy in Siam. They are now short of money and arms.'[36]

Both opponents traded in opium. For the French intelligence it was a commodity to sell or pay informers and tribes supporting them. Episodes of the secret trade of opium are abundant in French intelligence files. They show the extent of the lack of funds and the quarrels among the various services to get a portion of the commodity; in 1946 packets of opium were used as a payment among French services.

In September 1950, during operation Chrysalide, one tonne of opium belonging to the Vietminh was confiscated by the French ground forces and the French Navy in Tonkin. Already, the Second Bureau of the general staff had reported in 1948 that the Vietminh was selling opium. The FTNV/ZOT wished to keep all the confiscated opium for itself and clashed with the rest of the services. General Carpentier the chief of staff of all forces in Indochina criticised the attitude of the FTNV/ZOT. In the meantime, French intelligence officers, not having the necessary funds to pay their agents, gave them special permissions to trade in contraband and opium. In November 1952, Colonel Stoeber, the head of the sixth section of the EMIFT, reported that the 'tolerance' of the French to the activities of their agents had ended. Nonetheless, on 18 January the following year, a C-47 Dakota transport landed in Cap

Saint-Jacques in Laos, loaded with one and half tonnes of opium. The opium was divided between the pro-French underground organisation the Binh Xuyen and the GCMA, which held their part in one of their barracks in Saigon. Under 'Operation X' the sale of opium supported the pro-French tribes in Central and North Vietnam.

Another aspect of the war, pertaining mostly to military intelligence, was the employment of children – boys and girls – as spies by both the Vietminh and the French. Given the Vietminh's nationalist call for liberation, the support by their young nationals was a natural reaction against French rule. The French officers never hid their admiration for this source, which provided them with good intelligence. The Adjutant-chef Vandenbergue, an intelligence officer who was personally known to General de Lattre, coordinated the employment of children as spies because he believed that (young local girls, in particular) were clever, charming and that they were trusted by the Vietminh. Children 'observe everything' and 'know what it takes to accomplish a mission because to them spying is just a game'. A 1948 Vietminh circular warned that children hanging around in villages were employed as spies for the French; the children sought to gain information from shepherds, which could be passed on to French intelligence.[37]

***

It was always immensely difficult to track the deployment and movement of the PAVN units which passed through dense jungle. Besides, the weather and the geography did not allow signals intercepts or aircraft on reconnaissance to operate efficiently. Both French military intelligence and Trevor-Wilson with his informers in Hanoi struggled to discover the DRV units' capabilities and the intentions of their commanders.

In May 1950, quoting 'several sources', Trevor-Wilson confirmed that the Vietminh was repairing two roads in the mountains of North Tonkin. Some believed that its headquarters were located at Tuyen Quang. One source claimed that the repairs would be completed by 15 June 1950. General Alessandri and his staff of the Second Bureau of the FTNV/ZOT believed that the Vietminh wanted to transport more food to the areas under its command to feed the starving population. They believed that the Vietminh would be more interested in taking the action to the north. In contrast, Trevor-Wilson reported that the Sûreté ('which rarely sees eye-to-eye with the military') was concerned because it did not consider the SDECE military intelligence officers up to their standards or well-informed of the society and the communities where they operated. Perrier, the head of the Sûreté, sounded alarmed, fearing a largescale surprise attack against the Tonkin Delta and Hanoi within a few months. The Vietminh would be armed with light artillery from China; thus the roads had to accommodate the transport of war supplies. Perrier even feared that there may be Chinese aircraft supporting the Vietminh assault.[38]

Throughout 1950, French intercepts repeatedly showed increasing Chinese aid and reinforcement of the PAVN. In February 1950, the French were informed that about 5,000 Vietminh troops plus artillery were deployed around Pho Lu. Later, in the summer, intercepts were clear of the threat to the strategically important road, Route Coloniale 4 (RC4). On 8 September, the Second Bureau of the FTNV/ZOT warned yet again of Vietminh activity against the RC4.

The eventual destruction of seven battalions at the RC4 was a wake-up call for the French general staff of the newly organised PAVN. Colonel Constans, the commanding officer of the Frontier Zone, opted to evacuate Lan Son, which was under no real threat. The panic of defeat at RC4 left little room for the reassuring intelligence to influence decision-making. The Second Bureau of the FTNV/ZOT claimed that the enemy units were too far from and too tired to reach Lang Son, but Constans ignored this advice.

The PAVN implemented their deception doctrine after the advice of the Chinese. Between January and March 1951 they prepared for an offensive on the eastern edge of the Tonkin Delta. The offensive would materialise in late March and April. They leaked forged documents that pointed to an attack on the north-west delta. The attack would be along the lines of the January 1951 attack against Vinh Yen where the PAVN suffered heavy casualties and eventual defeat. The Second Bureau of the EMFIT closely studied the obtained documents and concluded (as the PAVN hoped that they would) that the attack would be concentrated between Phuc Yen and Son Tay on the west side of the delta. In parallel, DRVN units observed radio silence and employed only phone lines in their communication.

Nonetheless, since 8 February 1951 the Second Bureau had located the deployment of PAVN units moving against Dong Trieu. Staff analysis warned that the attack would take place in mid-March. More solid indications were at hand: PAVN units were observed repairing the road network between Lang Son and Dong Trieu. A noted unit, the 426th Vietminh Independent Intelligence Battalion, was deployed, and it commenced operations north-east of Bac Ninh. Intelligence disclosed that recruits from the 308th Division were dispatched to Kep through the Route Coloniale 1 (RC1). Most significantly, three PAVN deserters were debriefed by French military intelligence. They claimed that the next offensive would take place in the area between Luc Nam and Uong Bi on the eastern side of the delta.

General de Lattre was leaning towards the SRO's conclusion about the veracity of the forged documents. However, the Second Bureau of the FTNV/ZOT estimated that their opponents were interested in Dong Trieu – not Phuc Yen and Son Tay. The SRO had – wrongly – assessed that the 308th division of the Vietminh was marching west and not east. In its turn, the Second Bureau of the northern Tonkin delta sector believed that the 312th division was stationed on the southern slopes of the Tam Dao, north-west of Hanoi.

De Lattre and his deputy, General Salan, remained unsure. French air reconnaissance intelligence followed the PAVN logistics tail and road repairs in the Na Kep-Cao Bang axis in early to mid-March. It was evident that the offensive would take place against Dong Trieu. Air reconnaissance during the night hours showed a significant number of lorries heading to An Chau and Huu Lung, two logistics hubs. The French lacked any indication of activity in the eastern delta. Eventually, the attack against Dong Trieu followed a few days later.

In April and May 1951, the PAVN moved two divisions from the north to the west side of the Tonkin Delta. The French aerial reconnaissance made a bid to locate them, but the dense jungle resulted in yet another surprise attack. General Salan (at that time in Paris) admitted to a 'total surprise' attack against Ninh Binh on 29 May. Colonel Fernand Gambiez of the South Delta sector command did not believe that the PAVN would attack. The Second Bureau's warning about the gathering of enemy forces had gone unheeded.

The French had focused their research on the 308th Division of the PAVN, which they deemed to be the unit that would lead an assault. Key indicators that influenced estimates were that the unit needed recruits and that the Hoa Binh corridor had heavy traffic. In addition, it was observed that the 304th Division moved slowly eastwards. The French anticipated an attack on 15 May. Three days later, the estimate warned of an attack against the provinces Ha Nam, Nam Dinh and Ninh Binh after 25 May. Additional intelligence had come from a valuable source: the deputy commander (intelligence) of the 304th Division had defected to the French. He gave information about the area of the assault and said that the 320th Division would participate.

The defector confessed that the 312th Division was a part of the 320th Division and the 304th Division Group, which would be deployed together. Presumably, the PAVN achieved the surprise by altering the radio call numbers of their divisions, confusing French intelligence, which was trying to determine the exact locations of Divisions 308 and 312. In addition, the 312th kept radio silence while passing the Hoa Binh. On 24 April, the 308th had passed the Clear River; the French did not know. In mid-May, the 308th was beyond the Tu Vu. 'Probably', it was reported, the unit was between the Tam Dao and the Clear River. Staff officers were also unsure about the 102nd Regiment of the 308th Division; some sources alleged that it was following the 312th. On 25 May, an intelligence report claimed that the 308th Division was heading to Hoa Binh and Phu Nho Quan. The PAVN forward high command was located in Hoa Binh. The 308th was not in a position to lead the offensive as the French had expected it. The Second Bureau had 'lost' the 308th by early May. Only by late May did electronic intelligence – and hence the transmissions of the PAVN local commands – establish the deployment of the 308th in the west of the delta. De Lattre was expecting an attack from 25 May onwards.

In their turn, the SDECE intercepted the signals of the 312th Division, which was heading to Nghia Lo in October 1951. The messages revealed that the divisions maintained supplies for only a month and had been encountering severe problems in their movement, falling behind schedule. On 3 October the attack against Nghia Lo failed. The SDECE continued intercepting the messages of the division's headquarters, along with the general headquarters under Giap. The commander of the division avoided reporting on the progress of the operation and was eventually called to report to Giap in person.[39]

In any case, both the French and the Vietnamese made serious radio security mistakes; this allowed each to occasionally have a good understanding of orders given and of movements of units. A French report from January 1952 stated that the 'study of enemy radio is by far our best source of intelligence ... after faltering for a long time, this method of research has at last proved itself.... Certain particularly audacious phases of the battle of Tonkin [after the RC4 disaster] could be carried out only thanks to intelligence produced by listening posts.' Thus, General de Lattre managed to repel the PAVN offensive, while the all-source intelligence received confirmed the existence of Chinese among the PAVN ranks.[40] In April 1953 the GCR used signals emissions to track the movement of the 304th Vietminh division towards Dien Bien Phu.

Meanwhile, the GCR employed mobile direction-finding units which enabled the French general staff to track the deployments of PAVN units in the Tonkin Delta. Thus, the movement of the 42nd Regional Regiment, considered by the French to be an efficient unit, was closely observed in September and October 1951. By the following January, the French general staff had discovered that the PAVN was intercepting French communications.[41] In September 1952, the STR experienced a nasty surprise: the opponent changed the codes overnight while moving against Thailand – leaving the French in the dark. This contributed to the loss of Nghia Lo in 1952. In April 1953, the GCR used signals emissions to track the movement of the 304th Vietminh division towards Dien Bien Phu.[42]

In September 1953 the PAVN fell prey to French signals deception. With operation Pelican, the French aimed to deceive the 320th Division, and to stop them from receiving support from the 304th Division. The 320th Division was about to be attacked as part of another operation, codenamed Mouette. A French naval task force gathered off Haiphong; troops were about to land near Thanh Hoa. French communications, intercepted by the PAVN, made it clear that the landing operation was about to commence. Vietminh spies watched high-rank officers reviewing troops and orders. PAVN prisoners of war were also released, rushing to tell their comrades about the intentions of the French, who were observing the results of their deception.

At a key point, a Vietminh agent's communications were intercepted; he insisted that no French operation was about to take place and that it was all a French ploy. In response, the French spread more rumours about the coming invasion; bombed the road to Thanh

Hoa; printed instructions to their troops on their conduct towards the Catholic communities in the area; and established a second military communications network with 'heavy' traffic to be intercepted by the PAVN. Ultimately, the 304th Division did not support the 320th Division, which suffered heavy casualties during the French attack on 14 October. Just three days later, a regiment of the 304th Division would move to Thanh Hoa to help the 320th.[43]

CHAPTER 3

WITH EXTREME PREJUDICE

Mai Chi Tho, the head of the secret service, the Public Security, admitted: 'In the beginning, we relied heavily on an eye for an eye, impatiently countering [the French and others] with violence. Because of this immaturity, we fell into the traps of the enemy to provoke and divide us. So much blood was spilled, preconceptions hardened, hatred deepened. The front for popular unity and salvation was harmed: we gradually lost people and lost territory.... This immaturity at the beginning of the fight against the French caused us many difficulties, especially from 1949 to 1952.'[1]

The assumption was lethal: to claim political authority you had to kill for it. On 15 May 1945, two months after the Japanese coup, the Vietminh in North Vietnam established the 'Honor Squads to Eliminate Traitors' – reminiscent of Stalin's special detachments, the Smersh ('Death to Spies'), which operated on the Eastern Front. Similar squads were formed in South Vietnam. From late August to September 1945, thousands of Vietminh opponents were murdered. In the south, one of the most prominent victims was Bui Quang Chieu, a noted politician and French citizen. Among the other victims were Thu Thau and Phan Ven Hum; both were Trotskyists – the former a journalist, the latter a politician. Individuals who could form rival political organisations were the most targeted. In Saigon in 1946, assassins made an attempt against another journalist, claiming that he deserved to die because his newspaper supported autonomy for South Vietnam. Printing shops were attacked with grenades. In the fall of 1947, assassination squads murdered journalists working for the newspapers *Soul of the Nation* and

The Masses.[2] Massacres of French citizens, right-wing Vietnamese, colonial forces and Cao Dai and Hoa Hao sect members also paved the way for retaliation. The French military conceded that fighters belonging to the various sects were difficult to control in battle. Ethnic Khmer, fighting for the French, were also responsible for massacres against Vietnamese.[3]

The Vietminh resorted to assassinations of pro-French local officials to impose their authority over territories and villages in North and South Vietnam. Le Van Hien, the finance minister of the DRV in the late 1940s, admitted in his diaries that the DRV government could not even control the various units and local resistance committees. In Central Vietnam, the Vietminh military and civilian officials were at loggerheads; provincial autonomy was the reality. The war had no fronts: in the Mekong Delta the communist theorist Truong Chinh wrote of a 'disorderly war' which required new tactics in comparison to the ones employed by the Vietminh in Central and North Vietnam.[4]

According to the French colonial authorities, in the period between March and early July 1946, 200 prominent Vietnamese were murdered. In 1947, Nguyen Ven Sam, the leader of the National Union Front in the south, and Huynh Phu So, the founder of the Hoa Hao religion, were killed. So had established the Dân Xã (Viet Nam Democratic Socialist Party). So was kidnapped while going to a meeting with the Vietminh. He was tried and executed in Long Xuyen. The same year, the DRV Southern Police condemned at least 900 others to death, accusing them of treason, spying and reactionary ideology.[5] In the Mekong Delta in 1949, French authorities reported 50 kidnappings and 42 assassinations in Tra Vinh Province alone, and another 40 assassinations in Binh Tre. In 1947 and 1948, a Vietminh 'special mobile unit' of women fighters perpetrated grenade attacks on Cathay, Asam and Majestic cinemas.[6]

In February 1946, a group of Khmer in Bic Lieu who supported the French forces arrested and killed communist cadre. Eventually, this group was exterminated.[7] It was admitted later that 'the greatest difficulty after we [the Vietminh] seized power [in Tra Vinh] was that reactionaries incited Khmer to rise and kill [ethnic] Vietnamese cadres'.[8]

In their turn, the French assumed that if Ho Chi Minh and his top lieutenants were killed, the anti-colonial insurgency would collapse. The general staff of the French forces in Indochina conceived a leadership decapitation operation, codenamed Lea. It took months to draft the plan;

in October 1947, the operation would be activated. Intelligence confirmed that Ho Chi Minh, Giap and their other Central Committee members and commanders were in Bac Kan. On 7 October, 17 battalions, armoured vehicles and paratroopers were launched against the Vietminh force there. General Valluy was optimistic, believing in success; he would isolate his opponents before they could withdraw to South China. But the paratroopers could not be deployed on time. It took three flights to take 950 paratroopers into the drop zone. Eventually, a total of 1,100 paratroopers reached the area.

The Vietminh espionage machinery had failed to warn their leader; the agents had useful information two days earlier but had no available means to communicate it. The urgent message about the operation against Ho Chi Minh reached him just as the first paratroopers were getting ready to jump. The DRV leadership evacuated in a matter of minutes before they could be arrested or killed; their units suffered heavy casualties. Nguyen Van To, a senior official, was killed by the paratroopers who ultimately found stacks of secret documents in the headquarters' compounds, which they took to be examined by French intelligence. Nonetheless, within 24 hours Giap had organised a counterattack against the paratroopers, who were expecting the armour units to come to their support: 10 battalions moved from Lang Son to Cao Bang and then to Nguyen Binh and finally to Bac Kan, a 140-mile drive of constant ambushes, and sabotaged roads and bridges. They reached Bac Kan on 13 October and confronted the strong resistance of the regrouped Vietminh. The amphibious force moving in the Clear and Gam Rivers (four battalions) never made it to the battlefield; the rivers made quick movement impossible. On 8 November, Operation Lea was aborted.[9]

Meanwhile, Saigon's public security deteriorated; during the night, grenade explosions and rifle fire were heard near downtown. In the outskirts of the city, nobody wandered around at night. During the day, westerners needed armed escorts to venture outside the city. The French secret services were executing suspected Vietminh cadre, dumping their bodies on street corners and alleys to deter more communists from challenging their authority.[10] *Bandes noires* ('black bands') were employed by the Foreign Legion and other French services; they comprised what Henry Ainley, a British legionnaire heading such a band, described as Vietnamese 'grim-faced, cold-eyed killers'. They were willing to commit any crime to terrorise the Vietminh, as well as the peasants in rural areas.[11] The French hunted down couriers; not all Vietminh networks had radios. A courier carried between 15 and 25 kg of mail, and had to cover 20 to 30 km on foot or 100 to 160 km by bike. The main routes were through the jungle. Exhaustion was common, and they were decimated by malaria, cholera and typhoid. Couriers had to evade checkpoints or hide their identities and parcels when questioned by the ever-suspicious authorities.[12]

On 24 March 1950, Cao Xuan Hoa, a Vietnamese *chef de quartier*, was murdered. A.B. Pirrie, the British Consular Agent in Haiphong, wrote that the victim 'was standing at the doorway of his shop in the rue Admiral Courbet, about 300 yards from the bank, talking to a Frenchman, when a Vietnamien [sic] approached and killed him with two shots from a revolver. The assassin made off in the direction of the Rue Chinoise, and we are reliably informed that two French soldiers witnessed the outrage but made no attempt to interfere.' The same month Caide, an engineer and partner of a company of coal mines, was abducted, possibly by the Vietminh.[13]

A month later, on 28 April 1950, Marcel Marshal Bazin, the head of the Sûreté Federale of Cochinchina, was murdered by the Public Security Service of the South. He had been hunting communists since the 1930s. In 1946–7, together with the Second Bureau of the French general staff in Indochina he had persuaded the religious sects to confront the Vietminh. Bazin's efforts had a serious impact on the Vietminh intelligence networks.[14] Gullion, the US chargé d'affaires, happened to witness the murder:

It was in the morning.... I just walked by the square, and I saw Bazin just about to get in his car, and he was carrying this leather folder. And in front of him was another parked car with some Vietnamese in it. As he started to get into it, this other Vietnamese jumped out of the parked car right in front of him, holding an enormous revolver in both hands, the way they do in American movies now, two-handed, and pumped shots into his belly. I was right across the street from him, a narrow street, and I ducked behind a barber's chair. The assassin got in the car and drove away. The irony of it was that they were expecting some kind of a ceremony, and there was a French squad rehearsing for it, and I remember seeing this fellow go right past them – and he was never found.[15]

On 5 May 1950, the manager and head editor of *Thoi Cuôc* ('The Times') were both murdered.[16] Vietminh agents also killed Major Hans Imfeld, a Second Bureau intelligence officer trained by the British in India during World War II.[17] Meanwhile secret agents Hoang Minh Dao (code number A13) and Nguyen Kim Son (code number A14) posed as influential anti-communists ready to support the militias in Thanh Hoa (in Central Vietnam under DRV rule). In fact, no nationalist group was there at that time; it was a ploy to assess the French plans and deviate any arms cargo. They met with the right-wing nationalists Nguyen Huu Tri, Phan Van Giao and Buu Loc (some had assumed with Bao Dai himself) as well as top French military officers like General Marcel Alessandri and Nguyen De, Bao Dai's close adviser.[18]

The agents received urgent orders from the headquarters of DRV Public Security: the arms transfer to the nationalists had to be blocked. Dao, Son and a young female Vietnamese agent, Nguyen Thi Loi (who posed as the wife of the former) undertook the suicidal mission. They boarded the warship Amyot d'Inville and stayed until the arms were unloaded. Hoang asked the French captain to take his 'wife', who had taken a sleeping pill, back. She carried a suitcase full of explosives. The explosion cost her life, and put the ship out of service for two years. Eventually, the French aborted the plan to support the nationalists in Thanh Hoa.[19]

On 31 July 1951, the Sûreté was surprised by the assassination of Brigadier General Charles Marie Chanson, the commander of South Vietnam. During a public reception in a town south of Saigon, the assassin, a young Vietnamese named Trinh Van Minh, took a grenade from his jacket and released the safety pin as he was approaching the general. H.A. Graves, the British minister in Saigon, described the episode:

[The assassin] rushed from the line of spectators into the group of dignitaries and unloosed a grenade. Some entanglement of the grenade with his clothing prevented the murderer from throwing the weapon and resulted in it being discharged waist high, thus causing greater damage. Thai Lap Thanh [the Vietnamese governor] succumbed at once and General Chanson died soon after from a shrapnel injury to the brain; the assassin survived for some hours but could not be interrogated; nor was his identity established for some days. Two other French officers were severely wounded.[20]

The assassin belonged to the Thanh Nien Bao Quoc Doan (Youth Phalange for the Safeguarding of the Country), which was affiliated with the National Popular Party. Allegedly, he had served in one Vietminh 'assassination committee' before he was captured by the Hoa Hao sect and released after five months. For some time, the security services became suspicious of the role of the Youth Phalange. On 28 July, they stormed its office in Hanoi and arrested the heads of the central and northern committees. The Vietminh waited for five days; when the name of the assassin was released they pronounced him a hero, a 'volunteer to the death'. The chief of the Sûreté resigned after the attack. General de Lattre could not figure out to what extent a nationalist group was associated with the Vietminh or could be infiltrated by them to such an extent that its members plot assassinations.[21]

On 10 August in Saigon, a 'volunteer to the death' was arrested with a grenade in his pocket. He confessed that he was aiming to kill President Tran Van Huu and was sure that his comrades would launch an assassination campaign against high-rank Vietnamese civil servants and military officers. Graves closed his message to the Foreign Office by saying that his informant had no doubts that the Vietminh had ordered him to kill.[22] The British diplomat viewed that there were no clear boundaries between anti-French and nationalists/anti-communist groups. Nonetheless, there was 'no doubt that it [the Phalange] harbours a lot of Vietminh agents and that its members have links with the rebel forces'. General de Lattre was very angry with the death of his old comrade. Graves wrote: '[I]t is not to be expected that he [de Lattre] will switch to gentle persuasion, encouragement and coaxing. And so long as he has a pro-French administration to deal with we conclude that he will go on cracking the whip.'[23]

Provocations with innocent victims were an integral part of the ruthless secret war in Saigon and elsewhere. On 9 January 1952, two car bombs exploded in broad daylight at the Place de Theatre and City Hall, killing and injuring bystanders. The authorities blamed the Vietminh. The Americans spoke about a change in the assassination methods by the communists. The MI6 station and the British legation in Saigon remained sceptical. After a disagreement, warlord General Trình Minh Thế, an autonomous Cao Dai leader, gathered 2,500 of his Cao Dai troops in Tay Ninh near the border with Cambodia. He sought to fight both the French and the communists, and soon broadcasts claimed that he was responsible for the bombings. The Sûreté had no doubt about it. The general looked promising as the 'Third Force' in Vietnam: he could be the influential nationalist between the French, Emperor Bao Dai (considered by many a French puppet) and the Vietminh. The Americans assumed that he should be supported in his bid to consolidate the non-communist Vietnamese.

From Saigon, H.A. Graves wrote to Eden informing him of intelligence reports from MI6 connecting the warlord to the United States:

> One reason for this [the increase in the ranks of Thế's army] may be the support which it is strongly rumoured, he received from certain American elements. At the time of the bombing outrages in Saigon in January, it was realised that the explosives and clock-work devices used were much too ingenious to have been produced by the Cao Dai-ists themselves, and it is also thought that the recent blowing-up of an important bridge on the main My Tho road may have been achieved by Cao Dai-ist irregulars using advanced equipment. It is known that members of American official missions in Saigon make frequent visits to the Tayninh [sic] area [where Thế's forces were based] and it is unfortunately now widely stated in Saigon that the Americans are behind General Thế. Veiled references made by the French to the irresponsible support by the Americans of nationalist groups have, in private conversations with members of my staff, now become direct accusations that the Americans are providing support to General Thế and his men. Incredible as it may seem, I am afraid that there may be a modicum of truth in all this. Members of the American Legation have admitted that their dealings with the sects are bedevilled by their desire to be in a position to use them as the nucleus for guerrilla activity in the event of Indo-China being over-run [by the Chinese] and it has been suggested that the training and equipment which is being provided for such an eventuality has been put by General Thế to premature use. I include this paragraph with considerable reluctance, but I can no

longer ignore the reports which continue to come in from usually reliable sources.[24]

In the early years of the CIA, operations officers were more of the covert action mentality than of the collection effort, which they regarded with slight contempt as a passive affair. Michael Thompson, a CIA operations officer who served in the 1950s and 1960s, remarked in a review article: 'Ambitious junior officers, less gifted ... with narrower professional horizons and their careers still ahead of them, drew from these operations [the secret operations in Albania in 1949, the Soviet Union, Cuba and Indonesia] the erroneous conclusion that engagement in operational activity should be their priority concern: the acquisition of intelligence information was of secondary importance.'[25] Indeed General James Harold 'Jimmy' Doolittle wrote in his famous report to Eisenhower on the efficiency of the CIA under Allen Dulles: 'It is now clear that we are facing an implacable enemy [communism] whose avowed objective is world domination by whatever means and at whatever cost. There are no rules in such a game. Hitherto acceptable norms of human conduct do not apply. If the United States is to survive ... we ... must learn to subvert, sabotage and destroy our enemies by more clever, more sophisticated and more effective methods than those used against us.'[26] Doolittle was describing the way in which young operations officers sent to confront communist-backed insurgencies thought.

Pham Xuan An, a mole of the DRV, witnessed the massacre of 9 January. He remarked later: 'The French G2 [Second Bureau] got a tip that General Thé had planted a bomb. So at the last minute they canceled the parade. Maybe they got the information too late. Maybe they wanted the bomb to go off and embarrass the Americans by having them kill lots of innocent civilians. Anyway, my people were lining the streets, waiting for the parade, when the bomb went off. It shattered the windows in the café Civral and the pharmacy next door. I watched as the police rushed in to help the wounded.'[27]

***

At that time, the world-acclaimed author Graham Greene was staying in Saigon at the invitation of Trevor-Wilson, who was consul general in Hanoi. Trevor-Wilson was receiving information from General Salan: 'He gave me, much later on, when I had become Consul in Hanoi, a complete statement of the extent of French forces in Indochina, long before [the battle] of Dien Bien Phu.'[28]

Trevor-Wilson used to play dice with Greene, and they smoked opium together. He wrote: 'Greene was a very busy man, waiting, for instance, to see Ho Chi Minh or General Giap. Only in the evening was he available to see me. We often played a game of 421 at the local restaurant. This was a game of dice. At other times, we would smoke opium. The ambiance of smoking opium won our hearts at once, the hard couch and leather pillow like a brick – the small lamp glowing on the face of the pipe-maker, as he kneads his little ball of brown opium gum over the flame until it bubbles and is ready to smoke. Some people smoke five times, others twenty and addicts up to one hundred pipes. Opium is good for the respiratory system. Greene smoked five or six pipes: I usually twelve. But you should never smoke opium if you are weak. You must be able to give it up at once. Forever!'[29]

Eventually, de Lattre demanded Trevor-Wilson's recall in 1952. The British official remarked: 'Previously, however, I went back to Hanoi using a visa in my passport which had not been crossed out by the French police, at the request of Graham Greene. I was held up by the security police but eventually de Lattre de Tasigny said I could remain for two weeks. A French Sûreté officer followed me wherever I went. On one sad occasion, he accompanied me to Haiphong where I went to say goodbye to my friends there. I had a passion for unfamiliar bath-houses, and I saw a board advertising a Chinese bath. The security officer took the cubicle next to mine. The Chinese bath includes a massage, and the security officer's heart was too weak to stand it. He passed out and was sent to the hospital, where after a while he was released.'[30]

The Sûreté kept Greene under constant surveillance of, among others, Pham Xuan An. His assignment was to censor Greene's reports. The spy later remarked: 'The French gave us orders to watch Graham Greene very closely. He had worked for British intelligence during World War II. Then he came out to Indochina to cover the war. While he was in Asia, smoking opium and pretending to be a journalist, the Deuxième [i.e. Second] Bureau assured us he was a secret agent in MI6, British intelligence. We were also ordered to watch very closely anyone who worked for the CIA. One day Graham Greene came to the post office to file a story. His report was placed on my desk. It was a long report. "What do I do with this?" I asked my supervisor. "You have to be very careful," he said. "If there are any words you are not sure about, just cross them out. Your English isn't very good, but there's nothing he [Greene] can do about it. He can't argue with you. So just go ahead and cross out the words. Mark it up and then give it to the man who types the telegram. They never give him a chance to argue anyway."[31]

Pham Xuan An admitted that he never talked to Greene: 'I saw him at the post office or down at the Continental [hotel], having an aperitif on the terrace, but if I had started talking to him, I would have got in trouble with the French military security, the OR, the Office des Renseignements. These people were planted everywhere.'[32]

A spy's life is full of ironies. Pham Xuan An was given a gift a few years later from Mills C. Brandes, a CIA officer. It was a book by Greene, *The Quiet American*, which narrated, among others events, the bomb attack on 9 January. Brandes assumed that the novel would help An with his English. When it appeared as a film in 1958, the Vietnamese spy who was working as a journalist reviewed it.[33]

Trevor-Wilson wrote of *The Quiet American* (though afterwards he drew a line through the whole paragraph): 'He [Greene] is, of course, a very thoughtful man and everything in his books had to be absolutely right. He published *The Quiet American* in 1955. The Americans thought that Pyle [the American protagonist], an American diplomat in his novel who died near Saigon did not have any connexion with the American Embassy. I was in England when Graham Greene asked me to telephone to General Salan to ask him if he would be at home next day. General Salan was Governor of Paris and said he would love to see us. When we arrived by plane we asked Salan about Pyle and he said that he knew the man killed in Saigon and looked up his records and then said he was killed at 5.30 p.m. on such and such date. This was confirmation that Greene's statement in his novel was correct.'[34]

The official on whom the character of Alden Pyle was based was Leo Horchstetter, the public affairs director of the US economic aid mission in Saigon – not Colonel Lansdale (as the colonel himself and some others wanted to believe). Horchsetter was 'talkative and gregarious', but for Greene he was the 'quiet American'. In fact Greene had a photo of him with French Colonel Leroy. On the back of the photo he wrote each person's name; for Horchstetter he wrote 'Q.A.', meaning 'quiet American'.[35] Greene admitted: 'I shared a room that night with an American attached to an economic aid mission – the members were assumed by the French, probably correctly, to belong to the CIA. My companion bore no resemblance at all to Pyle, the quiet American of my story – he was a man of greater intelligence and of less innocence, but he lectured me all the long drive back to Saigon on the necessity of finding a "third force" in Vietnam. I had never before come so close to the great American dream which was to bedevil affairs in the East as it was to do in Algeria.'[36]

In 1952 Colonel Edward Lansdale was not in Vietnam, but he authored at least one report suggesting that the 'Third Force' of General Thé had to be supported by Washington – the British intelligence reports on the January 1952 bomb attacks in Saigon and the US connection documented that Washington was already working clandestinely on the 'Third Force'.[37]

****

All sides continued their strategy of targeted killings. In the mid-1960s, the CIA would back a 'pacification' programme, which, as it turned out, had as a component the killing of NLF cadre. On 30 March 1965, CIA Saigon station chief Peer De Silva was almost killed in a Viet Cong terrorist attack that cost the lives of 19 people. Sixty other CIA and embassy employees were wounded. De Silva was standing at the window of his office when he noted a man pushing an old grey Peugeot Sedan on the street. He saw a detonator on the driver's seat. He wrote: 'My world turned to glue and slow motion as my mind told me this car was a bomb.... With the phone still in my hand and without conscious thought, I began falling away from the window and turned as I fell, but I was only halfway to the floor when the car exploded.' He was hit in the eyes, ears and throat. He lost his left eye; two other CIA officers were permanently blinded. A year earlier, while he was on a fact-finding visit, McNamara was targeted with a roadside bomb. The attack was organised by the N-10 sapper battalion responsible for bombings in Saigon.[38]

De Silva argued that the aim of the plan that evolved into the Phoenix programme was 'to bring danger and death to the Vietcong functionaries themselves, especially in the areas where they felt secure. We had obtained descriptions and photographs of known cadres who were functioning as committee chiefs, recruiters, province representatives and heads of raiding parties.' No doubt, 'the Vietcong use of terror was purposeful, precise, and frightful to behold.... [The villagers] would feed them, recruit for them, conceal them, and provide them with all the intelligence the Vietcong needed. .... The Vietcong use of terror within the city of Saigon was frequent, sometimes random, and sometimes carefully planned and executed.'[39] In response, the CIA station 'had recruited really tough groups of individuals, organised in teams of three or four, who were willing and able by virtue of prior residence to go into the areas in which we knew the Vietcong senior cadres were active and to see what could be done to eliminate them'.[40] The groups were first named Counter-Terror Teams (CTTs) and were manned and led by Vietnamese; a CIA adviser accompanied them in the field.

In June 1967, under the overall pacification programme, called Civil Operations and Revolutionary Development Support (CORDS), the CIA initiated the Intelligence Coordination and Exploitation (ICEX) programme. The central component of the counter-terror campaign was established in 1968: the South Vietnamese programme, Phung Hoang (named after a mythical bird somewhat similar to the Phoenix). The US advisory role to the programme was codenamed Phoenix, and the MACV and the CIA were the main agencies seconding advisers, and providing arms, funds and transport. The Phung Hoang programme included committees of the National Police, the Special Branch, the National Police Field Force, the Chieu Hoi Amnesty Programme, the Revolutionary Development cadres (a mostly unarmed propaganda scheme with feeble results, imitating in structure the armed propaganda teams of the Viet Cong), the Military Security Service, the ARVN military intelligence and operations general staff representatives and the Provincial Reconnaissance Units (PRUs), along with other government agencies. The 18-man PRUs were the former Counter-Terror Teams; their actions were loosely coordinated at the province and district levels. The Province Intelligence and Operations Coordination Centers (PIOCC) and the District Intelligence and Operations Coordination Centers (DIOCC) were established. The communist cadre arrested by the PRUs would be brought to the Province Interrogation Centers (PIC) to be questioned. Contract employees of the CIA were also serving in Phoenix. By 1970, more than 700 US advisers were involved with Phoenix.[41] In theory, the intelligence sharing was facilitated with the establishment of a key hub, the Combined Intelligence Center, Vietnam (CICV), which was staffed with more than 500 US intelligence officers and 100 South Vietnamese. The centre had a Political Order of Battle

Section, which kept files on Viet Cong cadre. Nonetheless, the various Vietnamese intelligence services as well as the United States did not often cooperate or coordinate their activities out of fear of giving away their sources and methods.

A National Security Council report from 1968 described the developing situation in the interrogation centres: 'Problems in detention and judicial processing limit Phoenix/Phung Hoang effectiveness... [P]rovincial detention centers are frequently overcrowded, and poor prisoner accounting procedures are the rule rather than the exception. Roughly 60% of the prisoners arrested in 1968 were released.'[42]

In 1969, William Colby of the CIA (indeed, its future director) was assigned to head CORDS. He was informed by Special Branch Adviser Ralph McGehee on Operation Projectile, which had discovered a Viet Cong spy-ring with connections to President Thieu's office (we will look at this in more detail in Chapter 10). But Colby was uninterested in counter-espionage; he wanted statistics on CORDS activities. Among the arrested spies was a close friend of Thieu and his adviser on Catholic affairs. In his turn, Colonel Nguyen Mau, the commander of the Special Branch, focused on counterintelligence and saw Phoenix as an arbitrary arrest scheme.[43] (It should be noted that at that time Colby's relations with Angleton, the counterintelligence chief at Langley, were almost hostile. Angleton warned that DRV services had penetrated South Vietnamese services; allegedly he even blocked Colby's entry into certain CIA offices in Saigon.)[44]

The Special Intelligence Estimate 14-69, distributed on 15 January 1969, said that Phoenix was an 'additional pressure and is directed against that part of the system which the VC [Viet Cong] have long considered crucial. However, it cannot yet be credited with an appreciable countrywide impact on the integrity or general effectiveness of the VC Infrastructure (VCI). About 13,000 members of the VC infrastructure are claimed to have been killed, captured, or induced to defect. This total may include individuals improperly identified as members of the infrastructure; it certainly includes large numbers of low-level cadres who can be replaced fairly easily. The numbers of key cadre eliminated is quite small since they are the most difficult to find.'[45]

The Provisional Reconnaissance Units reached approximately 5,000 men and operated until April 1975; a PRU patrol was usually supported by a SEAL team. By May 1970, 102 US military personnel were advising the PRUs; all PRU advisers reported to the CIA regional officer in charge and the agency's province office for PRU field activities.[46]

On 25 February 1969, a seven-man SEAL team was about to kidnap a communist district committee secretary in the village of Thanh Phong in the Mekong. They assumed that they were being fired on, opening fire indiscriminately (with silencers). They killed 21 villagers, including women and children, who were added to the body count of the 'neutralised' list. The head of the team, Lieutenant Kerrey, was awarded the Bronze Star for the mission.[47] Speaking of the raid in 1998, Kerrey said: 'It's far more than guilt. It's the shame. You can never, can never get away from it. It darkens your day. I thought dying for your country was the worst thing that could happen to you, and I don't think it is. I think killing for your country can be a lot worse. Because that's the memory that haunts.'[48]

News of a 'US sponsored killing campaign' against civilians compelled the CIA and the White House to a defensive stance. General Creighton Abrams, the commander of MACV, distanced the military from the programme, ordering back US military advisers. Ted Shackley, the Saigon chief of station, also tried to distance himself from Phoenix and the PRUs at the time of high media criticism. He noted that the agency should focus more on espionage. Shackley remarked:

> I did not approve of it [the Phoenix], either. Each of the DIOCCs, each of the PIOCCs, each of the PRUs, and each of the provincial interrogation centers [PICs] had its American adviser, a CIA case officer who, I thought, would be better employed in more traditional intelligence pursuits. According to figures I was given in Washington, the PICs were processing a total of twenty-five hundred Vietcong prisoners per month. If this was true, I thought, more operational leads and more intelligence should be coming out. CIA officers who had worked on the program and who I was able to talk to in Washington said they found the activity repugnant. They felt that the dossiers were based on dubious information. And it was obvious that all too frequently, arrest efforts turned into firefights, and more so-called VCI were killed than detained for processing. I raised these points in my farewell interview with Dick Helms (the CIA director) and asked whether, if Phung Hoang must for some reason be allowed to continue, it

could not at least be turned over to the U.S. Army for management. Helms told me, 'Ted, I agree we need to refocus CIA's role in Vietnam. Unfortunately, we can't do that on our own. We are not free agents. A shift in our Vietnam posture would require interdepartmental coordination'.[49]

During the congressional hearings, Colby had no other option but to defend Phoenix. He repeated again and again that the arrest and interrogation of Viet Cong was the aim – not their murder.[50] Senator Clifford Case demanded that he state under oath that Phoenix was not a counter-terror campaign. Colby, angry, replied that he was already under oath, saying evasively: 'There was a counter-terror program, but it has been discarded as a concept.'[51] In July 1969, Colby admitted to General Abrams that 'the figures of those neutralised seemed fairly impressive standing by themselves. But they represent a reduction of only one and one-half percent of the total [estimated] VCI strength each month. And they can replace a good part of that.'[52] Estimates put the 'neutralised' cadre (killed, arrested/interrogated or defected) between 19,000 and 20,000 from 1968 to 1972.[53] Others argued that up to 81,740 communist cadres were neutralised, with 26,369 killed.[54] Colby, while defending the concept of Phoenix, insisted that: 'I have never been highly satisfied with the accuracies of our intelligence on the VCI.'[55] Mike Walsh, a PRU adviser, warned that 'the VCI black list eventually became corrupt. It became a place to put the names of these corrupt [ARVN] senior officers' enemies, to avoid repayment of debt or even to settle a score.'[56]

Confiscated documents showed that the cadre of the NLF and the PAVN were worried about the results of Phoenix and wanted more security measures to protect their ranks.[57] One document from November 1970 said that in the Binh Dinh province 'the number of friends of guerrillas in mountainous and lowland areas and province capitals since the beginning of 1969 to Jun 70 [is] seriously decreased. On the average, it decreased by 42% but decreased 60% or 70% in some areas, and from only 10 to 40% in mountainous districts. The decrease in guerrilla strength is still going on. . . . At present, the number of guerrillas in many villages is very small. In some places, especially in the southern area, there are no guerillas. . . . Only 20 percent of secret guerrillas were operative. The rest dared not to engage in combat activities because they were afraid of being discovered by the enemy or driven out of their areas of operations.'[58]

According to the official history of the PAVN, by the end of 1969 the US and ARVN troops had retaken almost all of the regions of Mekong. 'We were only able to hold our bases in the U Minh Forest, the Plain of Reeds, and a number of isolated liberated base "spots" north of Route 4 and in Cao Lanh district. The enemy established 1,000 new outposts and gained control of an additional one million people.'[59] Nonetheless, in many provinces the insurgency was not dead but resurfaced from 1970s onwards in patterns similar to the past. In the Ding Tuong province, the operations of the guerrillas escalated in 1952–3, after a defeat suffered at the hands of the French; in late 1950s the communists geared up despite President Diem's 'anti-communist denunciation campaign'.[60]

The Viet Cong sought to retaliate against the Provisional Reconnaissance Units. This was not proof of the 'efficiency' of Phoenix but an anticipated response in times of war.[61] What is certain is that the CCT and PRU troopers were *not* honourable and disciplined soldiers. Narcotics smuggling, rapes and other atrocities, as well as false reporting to their seniors and to the Americans, were also in their trade. Tom Martin, a US adviser in CORDS, remarked that the PRUs who wore no uniforms, 'were sort of like the Dirty Dozen. They were recruited from jails and deserters; they were real killers ... they were the ones who started giving rewards for enemy ears and noses and stuff like that.'[62]

Senior adviser Lieutenant Colonel Timothy Gannon wrote in his dispatch on 16 July 1970 about the Vietnamese military's contribution to Phoenix in the province of Darlac: 'I have seen no real evidence of Vietnamese command interest in the program. Inspections by Vietnamese officials are not frequent enough and are largely ceremonial in nature. The Vietnamese are simply going through the motions. The program exists, they are collecting information but they are content to stop there.'[63] In Hau Nghia province, senior adviser Lieutenant Colonel Barlett wrote: 'Phung Hoang is not successful ... although we have a high rate of neutralisation and have achieved it through reaction to intelligence, we have had no success with organised, routine, specific targeting.'[64] In Long An Province, Lieutenant Colonel Robert W. Lockridge summed up his conclusions about the efficiency of Phoenix: 'In almost two years time, I know of only two operations that were truly Phung Hoang [Phoenix] operations. Both were conducted personally by the Province Chief. . . . This in no way implies we did not neutralise VCI. However, those that were neutralised were either accidental or part of a military operation performing another mission.'[65]

In addition, the US advisers warned that high-rank captured Viet Cong paid their way out of prisons. Lieutenant Colonel Linton C. Beasley reported during his tour of duty in Kien Phong province (July 1971– January 1973): 'Implementation [of the Phoenix program] has been characterised by procrastination, improper interrogation, premature release, corruption involving payoff to police and other government officials and intimidation of probably loyal citizens.'[66] Even the Pentagon's statistics showed that of the 10,443 people characterised as 'Viet Cong' and killed between January 1970 and March 1971, only 616 had been identified and targeted by the Phoenix programme.[67]

CHAPTER 4

SPYMASTERS' FEAR

London, Washington and Paris were worried about Mao's intentions in Vietnam. In early February 1950, A.B. Pirrie, the British consular agent in Haiphong, reported that he had learned from a Chinese source that the PAVN had bought essential commodities from the Chinese.[1] There was considerable fear about the spreading of communist propaganda among the youth. An inspector of the BST informed the British that 40 Chinese boy scouts (living with their families in Hanoi) had crossed the border and joined the communists.[2]

As early as summer 1948, the United States assumed that the Vietminh were getting aid from Stalin and Mao; US diplomats wrongly assessed that Ho Chi Minh 'has strayed so little from the Soviet path that he has not given the Kremlin any cause for complaint. The Indo-Chinese communists operating in Viet-Nam are the only ones in South East Asia controlling an organised army and administering extensive territories. Annemites trained in Russia (and a few trained by Chinese communists) are able to manufacture hand grenades, muskets, rifles, pistols, sub-machine guns, bazookas and ammunition of all sorts. A few Soviet technicians are reported to be assisting this work.'[3] It was a hilariously false but alarming report, which came at a time when Stalin was not even interested in South East Asia.

As the Chinese Civil War drew to a close with Mao's victory, Chinese nationalist forces had taken refuge in the Vietnam's south-west provinces bordering China. As a result, there was a considerable delay from mid-1949 to early 1950 in the granting of aid to the PAVN until Mao had defeated the remnants of Chiang Kai-shek's army. In January 1950,

Ho Chi Minh dispatched a close associate, Dinh Manh Chu, to Longzhou and Guangzhou to purchase arms and ammunition. The Chinese Communist Party (CCP) Central Committee had ordered the cadres in Guangxi to 'offer a private welcoming' to Dinh, and to keep his visit secret out of fear of provoking France. In the meantime, Ho Chi Minh's secret visits to Moscow and Beijing brought what he had been asking for since 1945: China, first, followed by the Soviet Union, recognised the Democratic Republic of Vietnam.[4]

In spring 1950, the Chinese Military Advisory Group (CMAG) arrived at PAVN headquarters. Nanning, in China, turned into the main hub of logistics support of food, war materials and medicines.[5] British consular agents and their intelligence staff in Hanoi and Haiphong had been trying to find evidence of the Chinese presence signifying the escalation of the war. Pirrie wrote: 'From a reliable Chinese source I learned that about forty influential Chinese in Haiphong have received a circular letter, posted in Hanoi from a Communist organisation, threatening them with dire consequences if they continue to collaborate politically with the French.'[6] Some communist Chinese taken prisoner in Dong Trieu were transferred to a Chinese refugee camp. About to be lynched by their nationalist compatriots, they were put under guard. Pirrie was informed about the incident and the captivity by 'a usually reliable source'. On 6 July 1950 he reported to the consulate general in Saigon that 'this is the first evidence that has come to my knowledge of active assistance in the way of manpower being given by the Chinese Communists to the Viet Minh'.[7]

In Hanoi, Trevor-Wilson discounted the possibility of any meaningful Chinese interference in Indochina:

> I have read the monthly report from Perrie and would like to make the following comment regarding the suggestion that Chinese Communists have been taken prisoners by the French in the region of Dong Trieu.
>
> I am informed by the Head of the Chinese Affairs Bureau of the French Commissariat that to his knowledge no Chinese Communist soldiers serving with the Viet Minh have been captured.
>
> One Chinese lunatic who had been employed as a coolie by the Chinese Communist Army in China was caught near Dong Trieu

in January, but he proved so stupid that it is probably true that he did not realise where he was.

A few 'local' Chinese, some of them of mixed Tongkinese [sic]/ Chinese blood, were also caught in the area recently, but all were domiciled in the Tongking [sic] and were merely serving as Viet Minh agents.[8]

Colonel Carbonel told Pirrie that he had seen dead enemy soldiers, concluding that they were Chinese, but assumed that they were people living in the border areas helping the PAVN with supplies – nothing more.[9]

On 22 July 1952, after repeated requests by the PAVN for Chinese troops to be dispatched to Vietnam, the Central Military Commission stated that on principle no Chinese soldier could be sent to Vietnam; the PAVN would have to confront French 'imperialism' by themselves. Nonetheless, army units would be stationed near the border as a 'gesture of support'.[10] As we will explore later in this chapter, the deployment of Chinese divisions near the border would lead US intelligence to mistakenly conclude that Mao was seriously considering invading Vietnam on the pattern of the Chinese intervention in Korea. Nevertheless, Zhou Enlai would remark in a conversation with Stalin that, due to Chinese casualties in Korea, Beijing was 'in no condition to get involved in another war' in Vietnam.[11]

In March 1950, the first Vietnamese recruits reached the Chinese training centres in Yunnan and Guangxi. The crack 308th Division (which included the 36th, 88th and 102nd Regiments), and the 209th and 174th Regiments, gathered in Guangxi for training and advice. The Chinese officials named them, for security reasons, 'Guangdong and Guangxi Columns' because, like the inhabitants of Guangdong and Guangxi, the Vietnamese were not fluent in Mandarin Chinese. A military academy for the Vietnamese was established in Yanshan. The 308th Division was provided with the up-to-date weapons and equipment and 'received a warm welcome from the laobaixing [ordinary people] of Yunnan'. In three months, 20,000 Vietnamese troops had been trained by the Chinese. New recruits, students and party cadre arrived in the summer of 1950. Training and advice were also coordinated in other locations in south-west China, including Jingxi, Baise, Dongxing, Liuzhou, Longzhou in Guangxi, Mengzi in Yunnan and on Hainan Island. The Vietnamese Military School in Fengming Village, Yiliang County, was considered the most important training centre for the Vietnamese communist party cadre. For the outsiders, it was the 'Yunnan Military District Intelligence Academy' for the People's Liberation Army officers. The school closed in 1956, having trained more than 10,000 cadets.[12]

In the period April–September 1950, China granted the PAVN 14,000 rifles and pistols, 1,700 machine guns and recoilless rifles, 150 mortars, 60 artillery pieces, 300 anti-tank 'bazooka' weapons, ammunition, radios, medicine, general supplies and 2,800 tonnes of food.[13] The lesser known spects of the Chinese contribution were in intelligence and technical advice with reference to cryptography. In 1950–1, 43 Vietnamese cryptologists, headed by the director of Cryptographic Bureau of the General Staff, were dispatched to China for training. Chinese intelligence advisers were also assigned to PAVN regiments.[14]

Meanwhile, French intelligence had an unexpected source: a high-ranking officer of the DRV general staff defected and provided them with information about the Chinese aid, claiming that the Chinese focused on land warfare in the training of their troops in south-east China and not on naval warfare. The defector had previously worked with Chinese advisers to the PAVN.[15]

***

As the US–Russian tension rose and the war in Indochina escalated, Acheson admitted that there was 'no direct evidence' connecting Ho Chi Minh and the Kremlin. However the Department of State assumed it existed, even though it admitted that it was unable to evaluate the amount of pressure or guidance that Moscow was asserting.[16] The CIA collaboration with the French secret services commenced in 1950 upon the recognition of the DRV by China and the Soviet Union. The French asked for help because Vietnam was now seen as a Cold War battlefield and not simply a colonial adventure. Acheson emphasised that the recognition of the DRV by Moscow was as a surprise. He said: 'The Soviet acknowledgment of this movement [the Vietminh] should remove any illusions as to the "nationalist" nature of Ho Chi Minh's aims and reveal Ho in his true colors as the mortal enemy of native independence in Indochina.' For Acheson, the time of the recognition overshadowed the transfer of sovereignty from France to the governments in Laos (in July 1949), Cambodia (in November 1949) and Vietnam. In a ceremony in Paris, President Vincent Auriol and Emperor Bao Dai concluded the Elysee Accords on 8 March 1949: Vietnam was autonomous, an 'associated state' within the French Union. The Vietnamese state would have its own army, but the accords were only a short-term French solution to take advantage of Bao Dai as a front man against Ho Chi Minh. France kept the sovereign powers of the new state.[17] The United States, which previously had not believed in the political potential of the emperor against the PAVN, was now more favourable. Ho Chi Minh had been giving the United States the benefit of the doubt. From 1945 to 1950 the Vietminh propaganda machine, under Ho's explicit orders, avoided criticising the United States. The Central Committee of the Vietnamese Workers' Party ordered the cadre in 1948: '[W]hen it comes to public matters, it is formally prohibited to write, in any document, newspaper or book, one single word or one single line capable of incurring harmful repercussions on the foreign policy of our government in terms of its relations with the United States of America.'[18]

In the meantime, Charles Yost, the director of the Office of Eastern European Affairs at the State Department, drew parallels with Greece, where a civil war had been taking place since 1946, arguing that the recognition of the DRV by the Soviet Union 'contrasts with the cautious Soviet policy in regard to Greece where, though they supported [Communist General] Markos [Vafiadis] over a long period, they never recognised his regime as a government.' It seemed that the Soviets now wanted to speed up the revolution in South East Asia.[19]

**

US intelligence focused on Mao's intentions. As of January 1950, Chinese units had arrived close to the border with Indochina. The estimates were growing gloomy: 'So far they [the Chinese] have given no indication of desiring to cross that border in organised units, even in pursuit of nationalist forces. However, it seems probable that the Chinese communists will supply Ho Chi Minh with arms and military technicians. We do not know the present degree of cooperation between the PAVN and Mao; presumably, however, this cooperation will grow.' In any case, the French forces could not seal the border to arms smuggling and rebel movements.[20]

In early May 1950, Gullion, the US chargé d'affaires in Saigon, made a number of recommendations for helping the French, as well as the new Republic of Vietnam, to counter the DRV. In the fields of propaganda he wrote of the need for an American author to write a book about Vietnam and the true role of the communists – under the cover of a Vietnamese pen name, of course. He added: 'Psychological warfare committees should be organised informally [in] Saigon with ourselves and British as silent partners. "Black" political warfare should be aggressively pushed – playing on dispersed character Viet Minh promoting discord, defeatism, confusion using all media borrowed or bought – radio pamphlets, press agents word of mouth with all shades of allegiance tailored to fill all target groups. Sponsoring Friends of Vietnam should be organised immediately as well as [a] league for Viet Minh. American experts for these purposes should be assigned [to] Saigon immediately closely geared to military operations.'[21]

In early spring 1950, the CIA established a station with the US legation (and the US embassy from 1952 onwards) in Saigon. A US–French agreement was signed on intelligence matters, but the French remained suspicious of real US intentions. In May and June 1952 Pierre Boursicot, the head of the SDECE in Paris, met with Walter Bedell Smith, the CIA director, his deputy (and future director) Allen Dulles and Frank Wisner, the head of the Office of Policy Coordination. All agreed that the CIA should operate in Indochina through the US diplomatic mission in Saigon. Two CIA officers (three by 1952) were assigned to liaison duties with the SDECE; they would coordinate the exchange of military and diplomatic intelligence on a weekly basis. The SDECE avoided discussing what they considered Vietnamese politics within their sphere of interests. The Americans, however, had not made such a distinction, and many 'misunderstandings' came along the way, especially with reference to the activities of the Office of Police Coordination.[22]

In December 1950, Dean Rusk, the assistant secretary of state, asked British Consul Graves for his opinion on a plan for nationalist Chinese troops to engage in the defence of Tonkin. They would not be considered mercenaries since they would seek to push north to confront Mao's troops. The British official tried to deter the American in the strongest terms, warning him that this kind of a scheme would lead to escalation and general war: 'I could not see any good in the proposal. We thought "limited warfare" would be a mistake. This would be a certain way of passing from limited to unlimited warfare. We should inevitably be drawn into largescale hostilities in China – the most disastrous campaign we could get involved in.' Besides, the Vietnamese always viewed the Chinese with suspicion; after all, they had previously occupied Vietnam. Graves reminded Rusk of a State Department white paper from July 1949, in China, which stated that 'the [Chinese] Nationalist Armies did not have to be defeated; they disintegrated'. Rusk backpedalled. He said that this was not a proposal but a mere suggestion and that every way had to be tested since Indochina was 'the key defence point' of South East Asia.[23]

J.D. Murray, an employee of the Foreign Office, agreed with Graves's report. The United States' idea was 'dangerous and unwise'. The French were treating the Nationalist Chinese troops (which had entered Tonkin after their retreat) correctly, and General de Lattre was careful not to provoke Mao into intervening in Indochina.[24] (On 15 January 1951, a leak to the press showed that the Nationalist Chinese legation in Saigon had asked the French for Chinese troops to be armed and assigned to the defence of Tonkin.)[25]

Meanwhile, military intelligence reports were shared with the US military attaché and the French general staff; in January 1951, General de Lattre established a civil-military security council for Indochina; France's Second Bureau of the general staff of de Lattre coordinated the exchange of information with the United States.[26] Nonetheless, the French were suspicious because close to the CIA were individuals from organisations such as the Committee for a Free Asia, which propagated both anti-communism and anti-colonialism. In fact, de Lattre demanded that Robert Blum, the president of the Committee for a Free Asia, who was also heading the Special Technical and Economic Mission of the US embassy, leave the country.[27]

De Lattre consulted with Eisenhower, then the Supreme Allied Commander of NATO forces, on 17 March 1951. The US general wrote in his diary of the domino effect fear: '[The French] campaign out there [in Indochina] is a draining sore in their side. Yet if they quit and Indochina falls to the Commies, it is easily possible that the entire Southeast Asia and Indonesia will go, soon to be followed by India.'[28]

In any case, the intelligence sharing was never smooth because the French were always trying to keep secrets from the Americans. The year 1952 was deemed the worst period for intelligence cooperation. General

Salan insisted on limited exchange of intelligence to keep up the security of operations; he demanded that French officers report to military security once they had discussed military matters with foreigners. (Besides, Salan remembered the murder of Lieutenant Klotz in 1945 by the Vietminh – and the apathy showed by the OSS team, which proved their neutrality.)

Nonetheless, the CIA needed intelligence. Contacts were cultivated with the Chinese and the Vietnamese, in particular with Colonel (later General) Trinh Minh Thé of the Cao Dai sect. The agency built rapport with Ngo Dinh Nhu, Diem's brother, among others. The Sûreté shadowed the Americans and the group of their Chinese and Vietnamese political contacts. The French soon established that these Vietnamese and Chinese were close to the US consul in Hanoi. According to French intelligence one Chinese was provided with a radio transmitter by the United States. General Salan was furious, and was willing to torpedo the agreement for intelligence cooperation that had been concluded by Bedell-Smith and Boursicot.[29]

Surprisingly, US intelligence kept communicating with the Vietminh via the US legation in Bangkok. The discreet contacts were made by Lieutenant William H. Hunter, the assistant naval attaché, who was an experienced intelligence officer. Other US diplomats also attended the secret talks.[30]

On 29–30 November 1951, the Sûreté in Saigon made a wave of arrests of members of the Cao Dai sect and the underground organisation the Binh Xuyen. Two hundred were arrested, and one killed resisting arrest. The French agents were even supported by armour and troops. General de Lattre authorised the arrests in order to quell the paramilitary secret parties of non-communist Vietnamese.[31]

***

In Saigon, Heath, the head of the US diplomatic mission in Saigon remarked on the US–French collaboration in a discussion with General de Lattre: 'We were receiving good cooperation as regards economic and military intelligence but French studies and info on VM [Vietminh] and Commie activities [in] IC [Indochina] were only partly made available to us.'[32]

The US minister was the target of an assassination plot; he got the first warning from South Vietnamese President Tam on 20 September

1952. On 17 October, he was informed about it and reported that 'the Vietnamese security police had finally captured the principal agent ordered by the VM [Vietminh] to assassinate me and had killed his assistant'. The date for the assassination was set for 1 October, but it was postponed. The principal agent arrived in Saigon on 10 October and was identified by the security police; on the evening of 11 October he entered the garden of the US embassy for reconnaissance and left after a couple of minutes. On 12 October, he was arrested along with a female companion. He was carrying a draft of the ambassador's house; in his room, police found a Sten machine gun, a revolver and three grenades, as well as forged papers. After arrest, he admitted the plot and revealed that another accomplice was about to come to his aid. A security police party went to his village where the suspect was eventually shot.[33]

Despite the agreement of the Service Technique de Recherches (STR) to cooperate with the newly established NSA, in May 1953 Acting Secretary of State Walter Bedell Smith wrote: '[F]or *two years* we have been pressing the French by all channels to take CIA and other competent technical assistant and guidance.'[34] (The agreement's task was gathering signals intelligence from China post-Korean war. In August 1953 Allen Dulles, the CIA director, and Boursicot agreed that an NSA station would be established at Seno Base in Laos.)

The new commander of French forces in Indochina, General Henri Navarre, had realised the extent of the support needed by the United States in the war waged. In mid-1953, he referred to the requirement of upgrading airborne intelligence collection with US aid. He was informed of the top-secret NSA–SDECE agreement. Also, the French wanted more funding to establish and support more counter-guerrilla groups to hunt PAVN fighters in the jungle. The CIA was interested in supporting counter-guerrillas: the initial proposal was first drafted and presented to SDECE in May 1950. The outline of the plan required Vietnamese "irregulars" trained by the Americans. An agreement was reached – only to be shattered by General de Lattre when he took control in December 1950. He feared that the United States was starting to interfere in Indochina. At the Singapore conference with the United States in 1951, he had the CIA expelled from the counter-guerrilla scheme. France eventually established the Groupes Commandos Mixtes Aéroportés (GCMA).[35]

In May 1951, Anglo-American and French intelligence representatives met in Singapore to consult on their intelligence priorities and burden sharing. An agreement was concluded. Nonetheless, in spring 1953 the French complained that Anglo-American intelligence was providing them with 'syntheses or commentaries', out-of-date reports and no current raw intelligence – for example of Chinese decrypts or aerial photos over South China.[36]

***

The United States' biggest fear was a PLA intervention in Indochina (long before the Korean War). A draft report by the National Security Council, dated 27 February 1950, warned of communist plans to take over South East Asia and Indochina – the area deemed under immediate threat. Thus, the 'containment' of the threat in Indochina would save the neighbouring countries from falling like dominoes under communist pressure. More specifically, according to a National Security Council report: 'The presence of Chinese Communist troops along the border of Indochina makes it possible for arms, material and troops to move freely from Communist China to the northern Tonkin are now controlled by Ho Chi Minh. There is already evidence of movement of arms'. Evidently, the French and their colonial and Vietnamese troops could not deter the threat. If Vietnam fell, Thailand and Burma would follow.[37]

General de Lattre played upon the United States' escalating fear, even claiming that: 'Tonkin is the key to Southeast Asia, if Southeast Asia is lost, India will burn like a match, and there will be no barrier to the advance of Communism before Suez and Africa. If the Moslem world were thus engulfed, the Moslems in North Africa would soon fall in line and Europe itself would be outflanked.'[38] By April 1950, French and US intelligence warned of the intentions of the Chinese troops concentrating near the border areas; they expected attacks on Hainan, Formosa and Indochina in the 'near future'. French intelligence reported on Russian-made aircraft being given to the PLA. French aerial reconnaissance located repairs of roads leading from China to Tonkin.[39]

In mid-August, French intelligence insisted that a PAVN attack would take place by the end of September; the assault would be backed 'directly or indirectly' by the Chinese. The French had 'definite information of preparations' in the Chinese border areas. They claimed (incorrectly) that the PAVN had been given tanks and aircraft. France feared the eventual prospect of war with China and was willing to reach an agreement with Mao. Bruce, the US ambassador in Paris, wrote that the French 'recognize the flimsy value of any such commitment [for peace on paper by the Chinese] but are not in mood to neglect even a hundred-to-one shot which might inhibit or delay active Chinese involvement in Indochina.'[40]

The United States offered reassuring intelligence. On 15 August, Acheson contacted the US embassy in Paris with an optimistic conclusion: 'Consensus of intelligence info available indicates that Chi [nese] troop movements have been northward rather than to southern provinces.' The PLA was yet again preparing to invade Taiwan in order to set defences in Manchuria and to be able to aid North Korea; the Korean War commenced after the invasion of the South. In any case, for the secretary of state, the Chinese sought to employ the PAVN as 'puppets to further common goals'.[41]

Nonetheless, the PAVN was gearing up for the autumn assault. Rusk, then assistant secretary of state, reported: 'All indications point to a probable communist offensive against Indochina in late September or early October.' About 100,000 Chinese troops were in the border areas, but the assault would be carried out by the PAVN, armed by China. An estimated 30,000 PAVN troops had been under Chinese training for the last four months. Rusk did not believe in the possibility of a Chinese intervention but wrote that in such a case the dominoes of North Indochina, Burma, Laos and Thailand would simply collapse.[42]

Despite the warning, in North Tonkin the French suffered defeat from the PAVN attack at the Colonial Route 4 which resulted in 7,000 casualties and the destruction of nine battalions. Heath, the US minister in Saigon, feared a 'snowball' effect − a chain reaction to the French defeat on both political and military levels; he thought that the non-communist Vietnamese leaders might seek an agreement with Ho Chi Minh to oust the French. Heath was critical of France: 'If [the] French reveal no better military ... then we must also add deficient French generalship and military intelligence to debit side of ledger for which we seek balancing factors.' Most significantly, 'in spite of our constant warnings, they do not up to present time appear to have grasped full implication of practical disappearance of Chinese border as line of demarcation between Red China and Ho Chi Minh. Moreover, they have shown continuing squeamishness about taking any action which would provoke Chinese Communists, even including necessary high-level aerial reconnaissance. Although [the] French knew and informed Legation months ago that attack on RC4 line is possibly impeding, they neither withdrew nor reinforced their positions. Apparently no one wished to take responsibility for hauling down the flag.'[43] The minister was almost in panic: Washington should consider a military intervention since 'it may be only [a] question of weeks or even days before China overtly participated in this aggression'.[44]

By December 1950, the CIA had estimated 185,000 Chinese troops near the borders with Tonkin. The National Intelligence Estimate submitted was clear: 'Direct intervention by Chinese Communist troops may occur at any time. It may have already begun.' Mao could hold back troops only if he had commitments elsewhere or had to fight anti-communist Chinese.[45] (The Chinese intervention in Korea took place on 25 October 1950, when Chinese 'volunteers' assaulted UN positions near the Sino-Korean border.)

Consul Trevor-Wilson reported from Hanoi that General de Lattre had put the number of Chinese troops from 150,000 to 200,000 within 300 km north of the borders, but he did *not* believe in the prospect of an invasion before February 1951. Trevor-Wilson remarked that the Chinese 4th Army had moved to Manchuria. De Lattre assumed that the new PAVN divisions were better equipped and trained than the Chinese ones in South China.[46]

Describing the battles north-west of Hanoi from 14–18 January 1951, where PAVN units were defeated, the British military attaché in Saigon remarked about the existence of Chinese among PAVN ranks: 'Approximately 250 "volunteer" Chinese prisoners were taken [by the French] and many more dead were found.'[47] On another occasion, that June, after the battle at Phat Diem, the British assistant military attaché in Hanoi reported his 'impression' that the 100 dead soldiers found 'were soldiers with Chinese identification papers in Vietminh uniform'.[48] Interestingly, during the battle the French artillery got tactical intelligence from a Catholic priest in the PAVN controlled area.[49]

On 31 January, the United States urgently asked Britain to confirm a report that it had received, which claimed that 25,000 Chinese troops had now crossed the frontier. Britain replied that it had no relevant information to offer.[50] The United States interpreted any incoming information as an indication of the commencement of the Chinese invasion. On 6 February 1955, Gullion informed Gibbs that 'according to reliable reports 150 soldiers of the Chinese Communist Army had crossed the border into Northern Laos for reconnaissance purposes. It is thought that this may be a prelude to a large scale Chinese attack on the French flank.'[51] This information was discounted by British intelligence; it was claimed that Gullion was referring to a 43-man smuggler group operating in a known smugglers' territory near Thailand.[52]

Brigadier L.F. Field, the British military attaché in Saigon, reported in June, citing an 'absolutely reliable source', that the PAVN had had limited success so far and that it was withdrawing its forces from Laos because of the rainy season; in Laos the Vietminh would concentrate on anti-French propaganda. The secret source revealed that a 'Vietminh agent who recently in SW [south-west] Yunnan to collect [a] small quantity of arms has been ordered to deliver them in Vientiane area'.[53]

A small-scale invasion of Chinese troops in Tonkin occurred on 9 March 1951 when the Chinese troops hunting Chinese nationalist guerrillas raided a military post in Ban Nam Cuong, taking a Thai guard prisoner; soon they would withdraw to China. On 11 March 1955, the communist Chinese pursued some 50 Chinese nationalist rebels. The Ban Nam Cuong garrison retreated and eventually the Chinese communists took 22 Thais and one French officer prisoners. Then they returned to China. France had no intention to escalate, seeking to treat the incidents as insignificant. Heath from Saigon reported that 'the prisoners were removed to China, for purposes of intelligence interrogation'. The Chinese nationalist rebels were disarmed by the French and kept in Phong Tho.[54]

By early spring 1951, the French and US intelligence had information that another PAVN attack was imminent. Already in January another offensive had taken place. Heath commented that General de Lattre's 'preparations seem well in hand and his intelligence on enemy plans unusually complete'. But all wondered whether the Chinese would intervene directly. Heath feared that since Washington had not explicitly warned Beijing for the consequences of intervention, the Chinese leadership might be tempted to dispatch troops alongside the PAVN.[55]

The August 1951 National Intelligence Estimate did not reassure decision makers: 'There are numerous indications of Chinese preparations for greater military support of the Viet Minh, possibly including direct intervention with Chinese communist forces.'[56] In Saigon, Heath had meetings with de Lattre, who believed that the PAVN operation against Vinh-Yen was planned by European officers.[57] But the general was not too worried about a Chinese invasion. In discussions with Acheson and his undersecretaries in Washington on 14 September 1951, de Lattre remarked that the invasion 'would [not] be immediately fatal for the signs of a Chinese aggression would be evident in advance; the French could presumably fight a delaying action, if nothing else'.[58]

Nonetheless, US intelligence remained anxious about Chinese intentions. A memorandum from 19 December 1951 said that in view of the 'ominous character of intelligence reports concerning a Chinese preparation for massive intervention in Indochina' the subject of US policy on Indochina had to be addressed at the National Security Council. Indeed 'intelligence reports emanating from Taipei, Hong Kong, Bangkok, Hanoi and Saigon would indicate that the Chinese Communist capability of effecting a massive intervention in Indochina and perhaps Burma has increased significantly'. Approximately 200,000 Chinese troops were deployed in Guangxi, preparing to intervene as 'volunteers', while the war aid to the PAVN increased. The threat was looming: 'The consensus of intelligence reporting would indicate that action on a large scale against French Union and Vietnam forces in Tonkin may be expected on or about the 28th of December [1951].'[59]Acheson became worried and requested to be informed of France's reaction contingencies, including its plan to bring Indochina to the United Nations.[60]

Freeman Matthews, the deputy undersecretary of state for political affairs, believed in 'the accumulation of intelligence reports of possible Chinese moves against Indochina'. He added that the information had gone public, that de Lattre's health was deteriorating, and that there were 'signs' that the French were contemplating withdrawing from Indochina. General Omar Bradley, Chairman of the Joint Chiefs of Staff (JCS), believed that Indochina was next after Korea: 'It looks as if things might move to a climax there at any time. . . . [Nonetheless] I just don't think we could get our public to go along with the idea of our going into Indochina in a military way.'[61]

France was in a panic. By 22 December, US Ambassador Bruce informed Acheson: 'Prime Minister [of the] French Govt calls attention of US Govt to fact that possibility of Chi{nese} intervention in Indochina appears to be becoming more definite. Analysis of entirety {sic} intelligence reports concerning South China and assistance given [to] Viet Minh by Mao Tse-Tung Govt gives.' There were now 290,000 Chinese troops near the border areas of Vietnam. Roads and communication networks has been repaired and upgraded. War material supplied to the Vietminh by the Chinese had 'vastly increased' in the last three months. French intelligence had concluded that US arms – war booty from Korea – was given to the Vietnamese. France wanted an immediate conference with Britain and the United States to discuss a joint response.[62]

The French government, in order to reach an agreement with the United States on an increase in military aid, as well as to bring the issue to the UN, argued that it was beyond doubt that the Chinese aggression against Indochina was already taking place – albeit clandestinely.[63] Nonetheless, MI6 had intelligence with reference to Chinese intentions. Graves remarked that the 'reports of active Chinese intervention at the end of last month were, as we supposed at the time, exaggerated. Recent secret reports from a reliable source indicate that the Chinese are still thinking in terms of material aid and not in terms of intervention.'[64]

On 4 February 1952, Graves wrote to Eden, telling him that 'throughout 1951 rumors were rife of the imminence of Chinese intervention in Tonking {sic}. In actual fact, although the Chinese did so improve their land communications that massive intervention on their part would no longer be severely limited by logistic factors, they confined themselves to continued and in the last quarter, greatly increased material aid to the Viet Minh, and to provision of training facilities in the shape of [military] schools in China and of specialist training teams in Tonking {sic}. The scale of material aid may be gained from the fact that the Viet Minh have been able to equip or re-group the equivalent of four divisions, and provide for their normal maintenance needs. On the other hand, in spite of numerous reports to the contrary, there is every reason to believe that the only Chinese soldiers who crossed the frontier during the year belonged to the training teams.'[65]

The commitments of the Korean War did not deter Britain from giving France aid. In June and July 1952 the British had sold France war material for its campaign: 100,000 shells for the 25-pounder field guns; 250,000 shells, 60 marine engines, three Dakota transports, nine S.51

helicopters. London provided free of charge: 46,000 rounds of 3.7 mm anti-aircraft ammunition; 383,000 rounds of 75 mm ammunition; 141,000 rounds of howitzer ammunition; 50,000 rounds of 37 mm ammunition.[66] The British military attaché in Saigon boasted confidently that 'Sten guns in Tonking [sic] are as common as umbrellas in Piccadilly.'[67] In July 1952, Minister MacDonald sent a letter to Eden referring to remarks by Jean Letourneau, the French Minister for the Associated States in Indochina, about the aid given to the Chinese: 'The bulk of the supplies were believed to come in by Laokay, and the French Air Force did its best to make the routes difficult to use. He [Letourneau] indicated that bombing was not really of very much effect since the greater part of the supply was being carried out by coolies traveling along jungle tracks which it was very difficult to discover and interdict.'[68]

By spring 1952, there was no fear of an imminent invasion. The National Intelligence Estimate 35/1 discounted any such outcome. The assistant chief of staff of G-2 (Intelligence) of the Department of the army added: 'Although the increased Chinese Communist capabilities in South China suggest preparations for an invasion of Indochina, present evidence does not necessarily indicate that such an invasion is imminent.' The Chinese would not provoke the West's response by dispatching 'volunteers' to Indochina. Besides, the intelligence services did not have 'conclusive evidence' that Chinese served with the PAVN combat units.[69] The Pentagon estimated that the continuing deterioration of the security situation (and not an invasion) was the most likely threat.[70] Acheson, in discussions with his British and French counterparts, was confident: 'Sudden large-scale intervention is probably not likely but increased US aid may be followed by increased Chinese communist aid.' Thus, Beijing should be warned one way or another not to further boost the DRV.[71] The National Intelligence Estimate 35/2, drafted in August 1952 and covering the period until mid-1953, predicted no Chinese invasion irrespective of the outcome of the war in Korea because 'present communist strategy in Indochina is achieving considerable advantage with relatively small risk'.[72]

Positive intelligence about direct Soviet involvement in Vietnam was reported in mid-November 1952. French-Vietnamese reconnaissance patrols discovered significant PAVN stockpiles in Phu Doan: 1,500 Soviet-made shells, four Molotova trucks, US-made arms, and Chinese and Japanese weapons were all found.[73]

The National Intelligence Estimate 91 drafted in June 1953 discounted the possibility of a Chinese intervention; China had the capability but not the intention.[74] The PAVN invasion of Laos was deemed part of a wider communist campaign to destabilise Thailand and exert pressure on the French, isolating them in their defence positions in Tonkin.[75]

In any case, French intelligence was apprehensive regarding the Chinese. In early October, France told the United States that 'indications' showed that the Chinese might support the PAVN with jet fighters. French Ambassador Bonnet was specific: 'From an "absolutely sure" source, it was certain that the Chinese were training Vietminh pilots for both conventional and jet aircraft at the Chinese Communist training center at Nanning in Kwangsi (*Guangxi*) province.... A "good" source had reported that Chinese trained Vietminh jet pilots have recently returned from China.' It was claimed that a wide road near Lagoon could be turned into an emergency airfield. 'A report of doubtful reliability' from Taipei claimed that many Soviet-made MIG fighters were transported to southern China, in a base near the borders.[76]

In 1953, the Chinese Communist Party Central Committee established the Guangxi Foreign Liaison Department to undertake the training and supply of PAVN forces as well as their medical care. The conclusion of the Korean War enabled China to provide the PAVN with more aid.[77] By the end of the year the Joint Intelligence Committee in London estimated: 'At first sight Ho has many of the attributes of Tito. He is not a Soviet creation in the sense that the leaders of Eastern European countries are, and he has so far fought his own battles. He has, however, received much material assistance and encouragement from China and the USSR. His prestige is tremendously high in nationalist circles in Indochina and elsewhere in Asia.'[78]

***

Many consider the Battle of Dien Bien Phu and the French defeat as the turning point of the war which compelled France to plead for a negotiated exit from Indochina. The interpretations of the decisions taken evolve around the thesis that the strategic value of Dien Bien Phu was crucial from the start of the French deployment there. Nonetheless, the historical record shows an *evolution* (almost on a weekly/monthly basis) of the importance attributed to the valley by the United States, Britain and France, as well as by the DRV and China.

General Henri Eugène Navarre chose the valley for the confrontation with the PAVN. He was a veteran of both world wars and since 1937 had specialised in military intelligence. In May 1953, he succeeded Salan as commander of the French forces in Indochina, wanting to block the PAVN's communication/transport routes into Laos. In the same month, Navarre was informed that signals intelligence had broken three PAVN operations codes of planning and logistics, revealing part of his enemy's intentions and the aid that they had been given by China.[79]

Colonel Louis Berteil, commanding the 7th Mobile Group, had drafted Navarre's plan based on the 'hedgehog' concept: air-borne, air-supplied troops would be deployed in key loci, defending Laos and deterring any new PAVN assault or infiltration. The plan followed the precedent set by a base in Na San, which in late 1952 successfully resisted PAVN attacks. Navarre presented his war plan in Paris, aiming to create military conditions that would allow the government to negotiate a satisfactory, honourable solution to the Indochinese affair. No sooner had he submitted the draft when the shock came: someone from the top echelons of the government had leaked to the French press the top-secret minutes of the Committee of National Defence chaired by President Vincent Auriol. Navarre had attended the meeting. The revealing article was printed in the 30 July edition of *France-Observateur*. According to the minutes, Navarre had informed the participants that no offensive operations could take place in North Vietnam between 1953 and 1954; during the same period he would try to consolidate the gains in South Vietnam, and only from late 1954 would he move north with offensive operations. In effect, Ho Chi Minh had secret allies in the French government: officials who did not want to continue with the war and leaked highly sensitive information showing evolving French thinking. Bitterly frustrated, Navarre was convinced that *pourriture* (rot) festered in the government he was serving.[80]

By the end of November 1953, the G-2 of the Joint Chiefs of Staff at the Pentagon had discovered four PAVN infantry divisions moving west from North and Central Vietnam. Two additional divisions and elements of a third were moving along the Son Lai- Lai Chau axis. One division from Central Vietnam was marching towards Central Laos. French intelligence suggested that the PAVN intended to take over the area between the Red River to the north and the Black River to the south, where pro-French Thai tribes were attacking PAVN forces. China managed to get a copy of the Navarre plan. General military adviser Wei Guoqing and general political adviser Luo Guibo presented it to Ho Chi Minh on 27 October 1953, urging him to counter the planned French deployments by consolidating his forces in north-west Vietnam and northern Laos first. To this day, China's source for this information remains unknown; but perhaps the Chinese spy's was based on the *France-Observateur* leak, and/or other leaks by French government officials with their petty-politics motivations.[81]

On 20 November 1953, the French government gave the go-ahead. On 20–1 November, six battalions of Foreign Legion paratroopers and Vietnamese units landed in the valley of Dien Bien Phu, in order to block the PAVN movements and their communication with North Laos. The valley had a significant production of rice and opium. The French forces were unaware that a PAVN heavy weapons unit was training in the valley. Eventually, after a couple of days of fighting, they secured the area and built a base that would eventually house 12,000 personnel.[82]

Setting up an air-supplied-only base in a valley far away from friendly forces, and at the limits of aircraft range, was a faulty, high-risk option. For a veteran intelligence officer, Navarre was unjustifiably optimistic: he did not consider the possibility that the troops would be unable to expand their area of operations beyond the base. He assumed 'elements' of PAVN divisions (rather than the whole) threatened the base. He believed that the PAVN would never have the artillery and anti-aircraft support to isolate the base: that they would never be able to handle the logistical demands of supporting a campaign against it. Simply put, Navarre's plan for Dien Bien Phu proved his disregard for the survival of his French officers, the Foreign Legion and colonial troops.

The general had assumed that he could launch attacks from the base in PAVN-controlled territories. General Cogny, an antagonist of Navarre, chose Colonel de Castries to be the commander of the base. Among his staff, Cogny had a Vietnamese interpreter who later allegedly provided Giap with secret information about the Dien Bien Phu.[83] When he set foot on Dien Bien Phu, de Castries realised that he commanded a static defence and could not do anything about it. It was simply a matter of time (be it one month, three months or more) before the PAVN launched attrition assaults against the base. Companies of paratroopers and colonial forces started patrolling out of the base, but were soon compelled to withdraw with heavy casualties. On the base, the SDECE established a secret intelligence echelon of two French officers, along with some French civilians and Thais. They reported directly to Hanoi and Saigon in parallel with Castries, who only later discovered their existence.[84]

In late 1953 no one in Washington paid attention to Dien Bien Phu. Eisenhower remarked in his memoirs: 'Whatever the reasons the occupation of Dien Bien Phu caused little notice at the time, except to soldiers who were well acquainted with the almost invariable fate of troops invested in an isolated fortress. I instructed both the State and Defense Departments to communicate to their French counterparts my concern as to the move.'[85] In December, Giap decided for battle in the valley. This was well before the French government made a statement (at the Berlin Conference of 25 February 1954) that in May the world powers would meet in Geneva to discuss, among other topics, Indochina.

The Chinese Military Advisory Group urged Giap to launch a 'human wave' assault on Dien Bien Phu before the French entrenched their forces. A few years earlier, the British military attaché in Saigon had remarked about the human wave type of assault: 'The Vietminh attacks were carried out in the manner typical of the Asian hordes. There were [sic] wave after wave of attackers mostly drugged and seemingly quite mad. Some were linked to others by pieces of cord tied to the arms, no doubt to prevent them giving themselves up or deserting. However, French report Vietminh tactics were sound, and there was no lack of fighting qualities.'[86]

The Central Military Commission of the Chinese Communist Party directed Wei Guoqing to tell Giap to opt for a 'steady progress', to isolate pockets of resistance one by one. The Vietnamese general grew increasingly cautious, asking for more aid and focusing on the transfer of artillery. Four anti-aircraft battalions, recently trained in China, were dispatched to Dien Bien Phu.[87] French intelligence had intercepted the signal communications of PAVN units, anticipating a general assault on 25 January 1954. However, Giap cancelled it and waited for his forces to be reinforced with additional units. At the same time, signals intercepts kept the French informed of the gathering of more PAVN forces opposite their base.

On 25 January 1955 in Haiphong, the head of the political branch of the PAVN office of intelligence defected. He claimed that Giap had asked for more forces for the Dien Bien Phu front from the moment the French government announced that the Geneva talks would focus on Indochina. The Chinese offered more in military aid and planning advice to Giap and his staff, who were seeking a victory to present as a fait accompli at the negotiations table.[88]

Before the battle, many notable people visited the base, among them Graham Greene and Vice President Richard Nixon. Artillery and armour (like the medium M24 Chaffee) were brought in. The French hoped that the base could resist an attack well into the autumn and, eventually, prevail causing heavy casualties to the PAVN so that Giap would surrender. The illusion that the heavy casualties would compel the PAVN to abandon the siege would come to haunt the defenders right into their last days.

Navarre was overconfident. But the biggest cause of the French intelligence's critical failure was that, despite signals intercepts and aerial reconnaissance, they were unaware that in January–March 1954 the PAVN transported a large number of 75 mm and 105 mm artillery pieces through almost impassable terrain.

At the Bermuda Conference on 7 December 1953 Indochina was on the agenda. In his discussions with, among others, Premier Joseph Laniel and Foreign Minister Georges Bidault, President Eisenhower showed no concern about Navarre's plan for deployment at Dien Bien Phu. He later consulted with his cabinet secretaries about the developing battle.[89]

France's announcement that Indochina was on the agenda of the Geneva Conference, together with the official adoption of the domino theory by the Eisenhower cabinet, emphasised the value of holding Dien Bien Phu on the eve of the PAVN attack. Meanwhile, the PAVN deceived the French air force. On 26 February a Vietnamese deserter reached the base. He told his interrogators that Giap's headquarters was located two-and-half miles north-east of Dien Bien Phu. On the morning of 27 February, a patrol of Bearcats of the French Air Force bombed the location. 25 years later, Payen, the captain who led the mission, discussed the topic with Chinese generals in China. One of them told him that the deserter was a phony, a Chinese and PAVN ploy to test the reaction of the air force on supporting the base.[90]

The siege commenced on 13 March. The intensity of the artillery bombardment surprised the French although they had anticipated the offensive, and the date and the hour were already known to them. The direct fire of the PAVN batteries annihilated the French. The high-ground outpost, codenamed Beatrice, was taken, shocking de Castries and his staff officers. At Beatrice, casualties reached 500 in the legionnaires' ranks; the PAVN losses outnumbered the French. The Dien Bien Phu base could now be supplied only by parachute drops.

At the 18 March meeting of the National Security Council, Allen Dulles, the CIA director, estimated that the chances of a successful French defence were up to 50 per cent. It was evident that the PAVN attacked Dien Bien Phu in a bid to secure a military victory on the eve of the scheduled conference in Geneva. Eisenhower wanted to be informed if France was employing – as required by operations doctrine – the planes and the napalm incendiary bombs provided by his adminis-tration. He assumed that 'the odds of two to one in numbers were not really very heavily against the French, in view of the fact that they were fighting from prepared and heavily fortified positions'.[91] (In fact, the majority of the French fortifications and defences were neither heavy nor deep enough to withstand artillery bombardment; and the defence positions at Dien Bien Phu were not interconnected.) Dulles was incredulous, typifying the CIA's continuing suspicion towards France. He even went so far as to suggest that 'the pessimistic French reports from Saigon might be designed as a build-up to exaggerate the extent of their final victory'.[92]

Navarre had no doubt that France's announcement that Indochina would be discussed in Geneva had turned the valley into the epicentre of Cold War power politics. The general was given a decrypted PAVN message on 31 March. It read: 'The Geneva conference is a result of the moral weakness of our adversary and his disgust of the war. . . . We must exploit our military successes and the confused military situation in France to demoralise the enemy.'[93]

As more bad news from the base reached Paris and Washington, Eisenhower and his cabinet examined the contingency to intervene militarily to save the French. The operation was codenamed Vulture. Nonetheless, the Congress and Senate leaders, among them future

President Lyndon B. Johnson, exerted strong pressure: the United States had to have an alliance of the committed in this endeavour that would go beyond saving Dien Bien Phu. In a vain bid, Secretary of State John F. Dulles flew to London and Paris; the French, though they sought military aid to save their garrison at Dien Bien Phu, were evidently unwilling to consider future allied operations in Vietnam. Thoughts of employing even tactical atomic weapons were aired (Bidault claimed that Dulles had told him that; Duller later denied making any such reference). The use of atomic weapons was discounted as impractical, and as dangerous – it was feared that their use could escalate the situation into a new world war, with the possible intervention of China and the Soviet Union. Anthony Eden, the British foreign secretary, was against any British involvement in Vietnam and prepared for the Geneva Conference.[94]

Dulles wanted to deter a Chinese intervention in Vietnam; he dispatched US Navy ships, among them the USS *Boxer* and USS *Philippine Sea* – two aircraft carriers with atomic weapons.[95] Their presence, which Chinese intelligence may have been alerted through US leaks, ensured that Beijing would not commit forces in Vietnam. Dulles followed the pattern of an earlier crisis. Later, in 1956, he would disclose his brinkmanship with China from the breakdown of the Panmunjom negotiations (in June 1953) to end the Korean War. He said: 'We had already sent the means to the theater for delivering atomic bombs. This became known to the Chinese through their good intelligence sources and in fact we were not unwilling that they should find out.' Eventually, the truce agreement was concluded at Panmunjom.[96]

But Eisenhower played his own game. He was a shrewd officer and strategist; he understood that military expediency was necessary to save the French garrison. Eisenhower wanted to show that the Americans were eager to help – thus proving to his allies that he was not the one to blame if Giap won. Nonetheless, the president did not want to commit US strategy to helping the French, who (without any consultation with him) had recklessly built the base at Dien Bien Phu. He sought to turn Dien Bien Phu into the issue that would bring the French and the British into full alliance for operations in Indochina and South East Asia. If met, the conditions Eisenhower set for a 'united action' (by the British and the French who would have to agree to a timetable for an independent Vietnam), would guarantee him a cohesive alliance.[97] And if the French and the British disagreed – Eisenhower would sit and wait. He had nothing to lose. Gradually, he would apply more and more pressure; and eventually this would lead to the establishment of the Southeast Asia Treaty Organisation (SEATO), one of the Cold War's failed alliances.[98]

Meanwhile, hoping for a tactical victory, Admiral Radford, the chairman of the Joint Chiefs of Staff, provided the president with a full plan whereby US Navy aircraft carriers would support the bombing of PAVN forces around Dien Bien Phu. By early April, the situation in the base was turning desperate. But Eisenhower wanted Congress to authorise the US reaction; he did not lobby legislators.[99]

During a National Security Council meeting the president was prophetic: 'There was just no sense in even talking about United States forces replacing the French in Indochina. If we did so, the Vietnamese could be expected to transfer their hatred of the French to us. I cannot tell you ... how bitterly opposed I am to such a course of action. This war in Indochina would absorb our troops by divisions!'[100] Like Eisenhower, other top-ranking officers feared the jungle. General J. Lawton Collins (who would serve in Vietnam as a special representative with ambassadorial rank in 1954–5; see Chapter 5) was adamant: 'If we go into Indochina with American forces, we will be there for the long pull. Militarily and politically we would be in up to our necks.' Vice Admiral Arthur C. Davis discounted the possibility of a US 'partial involvement': 'One cannot go over Niagara Falls in a barrel only slightly.'[101]

No doubt US military capability had drawn the attention of allies and enemies alike; on 1 March and 31 March hydrogen bombs were tested at the Bikini Islands in the Pacific. London was angry for not being consulted on the tests beforehand. Eisenhower insisted on taking unilateral action, waiting for Congress to authorise action to save Dien Bien Phu.[102]

In his turn, Mao had taken a personal interest in the siege, and provided more artillery pieces and Katyusha rockets for Giap's forces. On the eve of the fall of Dien Bien Phu, Mao sounded adventurist, urging for the PAVN to attack Luang Prabang in Laos. He wanted an assault against Hanoi to follow in the winter of 1954, or early the next year. Nonetheless, the scheme to bring the war to Laos was annulled by the agreement in Geneva on 21 July.[103]

Despite the policy that no Chinese soldier would fight alongside the PAVN, veteran artillery and military engineers from the Korean War were sent to the trenches to give advice on how to weaken the French defences.[104] The Central Military Commission of the Communist Party of China ordered the Chinese military mission 'not to spare artillery shells'. They sought a 'total victory' to increase the possibility that the tables would be turned in Geneva. On 1 May the final bombardment of Dien Bien Phu commenced.[105]

Meanwhile in Geneva, Eden aimed for a settlement with the Russia and China; however, Dulles snubbed the latter. The British foreign secretary (who co-chaired the conference with Soviet Foreign Secretary Molotov) had to change the venue of his residence, the Beau Rivage Hotel, due to specific fears of eavesdropping devices (Eden spoke of 'gadgets for overhearing others'); he thus moved to the villa Le Reposoir.[106]

During a reception at the villa where the Russian delegate was based, Eden's secretary, Ambassador Evelyn Shuckburgh, sat at the conference table. He leaned back in his chair, which cracked under his weight. 'That is a bad diplomat, to break his host's chair', quipped Eden. But while everybody was laughing, Shuckburgh discovered a microphone beneath the seat.[107] Geneva, too, was a place for spy games.

However, the British and the Americans (and possibly the Soviets) did not know of the commencement of direct French-DRV secret contacts. On 30 April in a hotel in Geneva, French Colonel de Brebisson met with Colonel Han Van Lau of the PAVN, who was a member of the DRV delegation. First they discussed the evacuation of wounded from Dien Bien Phu. The two officers consulted six times, between 30 April and 8 June, also discussing truce terms. Bidault himself had opened a back channel with the China during the Geneva Conference, which ended on 21 July.[108]

The garrison at Dien Bien Phu was decimated. Having endured indescribable horrors and hardships, it was forced to surrender. The NSA overheard the last message from Dien Bien Phu on 7 May; it was the last post of the 31st Combat Engineer Battalion, which, at 5.50 p.m., informed the headquarters in Hanoi: 'We are blowing up everything. Adieu.'[109]

CHAPTER 5

THE COLONEL AND THE MOLE

'I was never relaxed for a minute ... Sooner or later as a spy, you'll be captured. I had to prepare myself to be tortured. This was my likely fate.'[1] Pham Xuan An, codenamed Tran Van Trung (code number Z.21), was one of Ho Chi Minh's most reliable moles. Since 1952 he had evaded US and South Vietnamese counterintelligence, dealing with the mental and psychological pressure of his double life and surviving the wars in Vietnam. His spying produced accurate intelligence that directly benefited Hanoi's strategy. He compiled his reports late at night on an old Hermes typewriter. An was based in Saigon. Every few weeks he would visit the Ho Bo woods, about 20 miles from the city, where the regional headquarters of the Viet Cong were located. The reports were photographed, and the rolls of film were taken by trusted messengers. A special guard transported the rolls from there to Mount Ba Den, and then to Phnom Penh. The route was circuitous; the rolls were flown to Canton. From there they reached the headquarters of Ho Chi Minh and his generals, including Giap, who boasted that with An's reports, 'We are now in the United States' war room!'[2]

An took advantage of the friendship of the overconfident counter-insurgency expert Colonel (later General) Edward Lansdale of the USAF, and of that of his lieutenants, who took it upon themselves to teach the young, eager-to-learn Vietnamese the dark arts of psychological warfare and secret operations. In 1946–7, An was a platoon leader of the Vietminh. The son of a Vietnamese bureaucrat trained by the French, he was eager to show his worth to the Communist Party and contribute to the anti-colonialist struggle. He was considered promising spy material.

The party wanted him to infiltrate the upper echelons of the newly-formed National Army of Vietnam (later the Army of the Republic of Vietnam, or ARVN). An's training in spy tradecraft focused on self-discipline and patience. However, on one occasion on a dock, An punched a Frenchman. At that time, An was working undercover in the post office censor's department under the French intelligence. He received no reward for assaulting the Frenchman; instead he was strongly reprimanded by his handlers. An was cautioned against revealing 'the tail of a patriot':

> He should never forget that an intelligence agent cannot be impatient and egoistic. It's not permissible to act like the boss defending his workers. Having been charged with secret work in the bowels of the enemy, if you show an unwillingness to associate with colleagues, turn down bribes, refuse to go for drinks or flirt with girls, how can you get anything done? Only a Communist guy would be so serious and determined. How can you fight if you show your tail like that?[3]

In 1954, An was called up in the National Army of Vietnam. Only his cousin Captain Pham Xuan Giai could save him from being shot on the battlefield. The ambitious young pro-French officer arranged for An to get a promotion as an adjutant at the G5 Civil Affairs (psychological warfare) office at the National Army of Vietnam headquarters. Giai, the head of the G5, was a Machiavellian type; he had been trained as a military officer by the French, but fought alongside the Vietminh in 1945, only to turn against them in 1946. Eventually, he would plan to take part in a coup against President Diem.[4]

In summer 1953, as the First Indochina War escalated, Colonel Lansdale travelled the country. According to one account he had reached Indochina as early as 1950 in a secret reconnaissance mission. He was not a West Point graduate. His full name was Edward Geary Lansdale, and he was born in Detroit in 1908. He studied at UCLA, where he joined the Reserve Officers' Training Corps. To his instructor there, Lansdale was a 'sane thinker possessed of balanced judgment. Better equipped by temperament for celebrations than actions.'[5] He left before graduating and worked in Los Angeles and San Francisco. His recruitment by the OSS opened new opportunities for him to show his talent. In 1943 he

was commissioned lieutenant, and by the end of the war he was an
acting major heading the intelligence division of the Air Force's
Western Pacific headquarters. He sensed that the Cold War needed
him and did not look to return to civilian life. He stayed in the
Philippines until 1948, investigating war crimes and looking for
prisoners of war. In 1947, he was commissioned captain in the USAF.
In 1950, at the personal request of President Elpidio Quirino, Lansdale
was assigned to the Joint United States Military Assistance Group in
the Philippines to assist the army and organise the intelligence services
to fight the insurrection of the communist guerrilla movement
Hukbalahap. Lansdale, promoting his ideas in paramilitary operations,
psychological war, propaganda and the rehabilitation of captured rebels,
developed a close rapport with the Philippine Secretary of Defence
Ramon Magsaysay, who was named president in December 1953.

On the eve of the fall of Dien Bien Phu in April 1954, the United
States decided to create a parallel to the 'regular' station CIA secret
mission under the official name Saigon Military Mission (SMM). The
plan was that it would help the National Army of Vietnam to stand on
its feet. US funds and French mentality would not suffice to prepare
the Vietnamese regime troops to confront the PAVN successfully. The
necessary expertise in advice and training in special paramilitary and
propaganda subjects would be provided by the SMM, headed by
'assistant air attaché' Colonel Lansdale (who was ostensibly working for
the Military Assistance Advisory Group (MAAG) under General John
'Iron Mike' O'Daniel). Lansdale served in the Air Force, not the CIA, but
the Dulles brothers (the secretary of state and the CIA director) had
created him this special assignment at the CIA in Saigon. Lansdale
would be their man; he would report directly to the CIA director and
not to Emmet McCarthy, the head of the station in Saigon.[6] This
arrangement would have a direct impact on US policy towards Diem (as
we will explore later in this chapter).

At the conclusion of the negotiations in Geneva in July 1954, the
CIA proposed a new scheme of cooperation with SDECE, the French
secret service. Initially the French concurred. Nonetheless, the
aspirations for a close relationship were influenced and eventually
side-lined by the complex South Vietnamese politics and intrigue in
1954–5, with the United States backing Diem, who sought with a
referendum to oust Emperor Bao Dai.[7]

Paul Harwood, an Asian Studies graduate, was Lansdale's counterpart in the 'regular' CIA station in Saigon. He worked for the office of the chief of station, McCarthy. Harwood was in direct contact with the younger brother of Diem, Ngo Dinh Nhu, who was his adviser. Without specific directives – or authorisation – the intelligence officer committed the United States to supporting Diem's bid to become prime minister. Harwood had set the terms for US military training for the South Vietnamese forces and the commitment of the South Vietnamese to resist the PAVN. On behalf of Diem, Nhu accepted. The United States, unwilling to show any hint of abandoning anti-communist allies like Diem (who was also supported by the young Senator John F. Kennedy at that time) did not deviate from Harwood's statements.[8] Indeed, Harwood's initiative was a fine example of an intelligence officer leading policy.

Under Lansdale, Major Lucien Conein was assigned to set up an armed network of agents in North Vietnam. Conein was a decorated OSS veteran who met Giap and Ho Chi Minh back in 1945. The clock was ticking after the conclusion of the Geneva Accords. In October 1954, Hanoi would be handed over to Ho Chi Minh's troops. Conein worked from Hanoi and directed a team in Haiphong; officially, they were providing relief to refugees and helping them reach South Vietnam. Another paramilitary team was hastily established to confront the remaining PAVN troops in South Vietnam. Key members were Army Lieutenant Colonel Raymond Wittmayer, Major Fred Allen and Lieutenant Edward Williams – the only counter-espionage expert available in Lansdale's SMM. Allen managed to deploy a paramilitary team in Haiphong.[9]

Throughout July 1954, Harwood of the 'regular' CIA station pressed the CIA headquarters in Langley for more arms and personnel for stay-behind paramilitary operations in North Vietnam. He believed that the nationalist parties Dai Viet and Vietnam Quoc Dan Dang (VNQDD) could form the political basis as well as the networks for such tasks.[10] In parallel, Navy Lieutenant Edward Bain and Marine Captain Richard Smith supported the clandestine activities of the Saigon Military Mission in all aspects: from personnel and administration to air, land and sea transport. Lansdale's team report read: 'In effect, they (Bain and Smith) became our official smugglers as well as paymasters, housing officers, transportation officers, warehousemen, file clerks, and mess officers.'[11]

Conein was organising a paramilitary group in Tonkin with the collaboration of the Northern Dai Viets, a pro-Bao Dai party. The CIA officer staged funerals and arranged for arms to fill the coffins.[12] Thirteen Vietnamese 'Binhs' (the name assigned to them by Conein) were led out of Haiphong for training. Another armed group for missions in Tonkin was organised in Saigon by General Nguyen Van Vy. By September 1954, Major Allen would undertake their preparation.[13] Conein and Lansdale did not realise on time that Bao Dai and his loyalists like General Vy would confront Diem's regime.

Lansdale tried to find Diem allies with armed groups. He approached General Trinh Minh Thé, who had about 3,000 Cao Dai members under his command. Thé had been implicated in the bombings in Saigon in January 1952; British intelligence insisted at that time (before Lansdale's arrival in Saigon in 1953 and 1954) that the Americans were in league with Cao Dai. Thé was more than grateful for receiving financial support – in the form of US dollars in cash. According to the SMM report, it was US Ambassador Heath who asked for money to be paid to Thé through the SMM.[14]

Hanoi was the key place for psychological warfare. Lansdale needed to win over his superiors; thus he insisted that: 'Think of psychological warfare as a weapon . . . not as propaganda posters, or as surrender leaflets . . . but as a weapon, like artillery or torpedoes, or guided missiles.'[15] Under his direction, the SMM printed and distributed leaflets purportedly signed by the PAVN giving 'instructions' to the inhabitants on how to behave when the city had been taken over by the communists. They detailed what property rights citizens would have and the new conditions of the economy. The leaflets caused panic and according to the SMM report the Ho Chi Min currency was devalued within a couple of days of their distribution. The DRV leadership denounced the leaflets, blaming the French for black propaganda.[16]

Nonetheless, for years the DRV had also employed black propaganda, using it against the Vietnamese to make them resistant to Lansdale's schemes. Since the mid-1940s, DRV propagandists had been accusing the French and their North African colonial troops of murder, rape and cannibalism. Fearful Vietnamese villagers were informed as late as October 1951 that General de Lattre dispatched 'black French cannibals so that they can devour Vietnamese. . . . These cannibals generally wear raincoats in the style that the Germans usually wear, as well as black turbans.' Leaflets informed the villagers that the French 'seized them [the Vietnamese] by the thousands, brought them to the electric ovens, turning yellow skin into black, transforming them into fake "Maroccans" [sic].' Massacres of Vietnamese by French and colonial North African troops and Khmers and retribution against innocent civilians were numerable, shaping the memories and perceptions of the Vietnamese.[17] No doubt local superstitions, sect culture, black propaganda about cannibalism and memories of massacres had an impact on the Vietnamese perception of reality, of good and evil, war and peace.

In Hanoi in the summer of 1954, Lansdale's men already faced trouble. They made a bid to destroy the presses of the largest publishing house in the city, 'but Vietminh security agents already had moved into the plant and frustrated the attempt'.[18] The failed operation was under a Vietnamese codenamed Trieu, who was directed by his case officer Captain Arundel.

Special operations are not always serious; indeed some have a childish logic that one is surprised to find in the thinking of experienced and hard-nosed intelligence officers. Conein's team sought to contaminate the oil supply of the city's buses to destroy their engines. It would be a delayed sabotage since the United States had forbidden direct sabotage in the north out of respect for the Geneva Accords signed a couple of months earlier. Nonetheless, chemical reactions do not spare anyone. The report read: 'The team had a bad moment when contaminating the oil. They had to work quickly at night in an enclosed storage room. Fumes from the contaminant came close to knocking them out. Dizzy and weak-kneed, they covered their faces with handkerchiefs and completed the job.'[19] Conein explained: 'The oil contaminant was delivered in canisters from Japan. When we opened them, the fumes nearly made us pass out while we were at the bus station, but we recovered long enough to fill the tanks and leave. The lumps of coal were also delivered from Japan. The idea was to plant them at railheads and wait for a bang. We were afraid that some guy would come by, steal some coal to heat his home, and get blown to hell. We later got word that some of it exploded inside locomotives.'[20] Throughout autumn 1954, Lansdale sounded optimistic in his messages to CIA Director Dulles: 'If present plans mature the SMM [will] be in position [to] change [the] Indochina picture rapidly.' He needed more personnel; he had at his disposal only two who 'work without supervision'.[21]

On 9 October 1954 Hanoi was evacuated. French and PAVN officers consulted on the road about how to lead the last traffic of French armoured vehicles out of the city. The newsreels show smiling and happy legionnaires in their white kepis together with their non-commissioned officers and soldiers loading chairs and other material on trucks and shouting 'adieu' as their vehicles pass the PAVN detachments, who quietly fix their bayonets and do not even exchange a glance with the legionnaire sentries who are leaving their post.

At that time, Polish and Russian transport ships docked in South Vietnam to carry Vietnamese communists to Tonkin. Arundel and his 'Binh' team prepared a leaflet 'of the Vietminh Resistance Committee'. The team spread the rumour that warm clothes were required because when they reached Tonkin they would be sent to China to be railroad labourers.[22] Lansdale had worked on a project to lure the Catholics from the north to the south; thus, 800,000 Catholic refugees reached the south by land transports and airplanes. Given that Diem was a staunch Catholic and desperately needed a base and functionaries for his bureaucracy, this operation was hugely beneficial to his aspirations to become the sole ruler of South Vietnam.

Lansdale also promoted books as overt propaganda. Navy medical officer Tom Dooley's book about the Catholic refugees, *Deliver Us from Evil* (1956), became a bestseller in the United States. Lansdale helped Dooley write other books about Indochina, showing the public the need for American involvement.[23]

Lansdale confronted the French, who had blocked the US mission from training the National Army of Vietnam. It was evident that France had a double policy: on the one hand, during the battle of Dien Bien Phu it told Eisenhower that a joint US–French action after the battle would not be contemplated, and that it wanted to withdraw from Indochina as soon as possible; on the other hand, though defeated, France sought to use Emperor Bao Dai, the different religious sects and other pro-French elements to rule together with Diem. It was a continuation of the secret support that the French secret services gave organisations such as the Binh Xuyen and the sects Cao Dai and Hoa Hao. If Diem wanted to rule Saigon and Cholon, he had to destroy the Binh Xuyen, whose leader was Bay Vien; Bao Dai had even made him a general. Bao Dai's wealth came from many sources: opium, smuggling, the 'Hall of Mirrors' (the largest brothel in Asia), the Grand Monde casino in Cholon and the Cloche d'Or casino in Saigon. Each paid him a dividend. One of Vien's lieutenants was appointed director-general of the police in Saigon to ensure that the police adapted to the Binh Xuyen's demands. The French underworld obligingly cooperated with the Binh Xuyen, smuggling opium to Marseille.[24]

There is no one with even a superficial knowledge of the Vietnam wars who does not know Daniel Ellsberg. A hawk turned dove, Ellsberg leaked a massive collection of classified studies (called 'the Pentagon Papers' by the media), shaking the Nixon administration to its core. In 1965 he worked under Lansdale in Saigon. For Ellsberg there were 'three Lansdales':

> The first was the Lansdale, who was reputed to have a magical touch with foreigners.... What I saw him do with the Vietnamese – and I learned from him – was to listen to them instead of lecturing or talking down to them, as most Americans did. He treated them respectfully, as though they were adults worthy of his attention.... The second Lansdale who dealt with American bureaucrats often came across as a kind of idiot – a guy with crazy ideas, naive, and simplistic. He was not at all afraid to appear simpleminded to anyone he did not want to reveal himself to, which was ninety-nine out of a hundred people. To journalists, other than a couple he was close to like Robert Shaplen of *The New Yorker*, he was very guarded and careful about what he told them. To put them off, he spoke in the most basic terms about democracy and Vietnamese traditions.... Then there was the third Lansdale you saw only if you were on his team or worked with him closely. After giving a journalist his hayseed routine, he would join us and his mood would change immediately. He would present an analysis of a situation that was filled with shrewd and perceptive, even cynical, detail about who was doing what to whom.[25]

CIA historian Thomas Ahern writes about the attitude of the colonel: 'Lansdale's style reflected more his civilian experience in advertising than it did clandestine technique. His high profile contacts with Diem and various Vietnamese Army officers and sect leaders generated several French efforts, in both Saigon and Paris, to have him withdrawn.'[26] Lansdale's spies had to keep track of the escalating feuds between Diem, his generals and the Binh Xuyen. In September 1954, Secretary of State for Defense Chan ordered the arrests of Captain Giai (An's cousin) and Lieutenant Colonel Lan of the G-6 office for preparing a coup. Charges were laid for 'political terrorism'. Lan and his loyalist paramilitary commandos were accused of 'political terrorism', and Giai of anti-Diem propaganda. Lieutenant Minh, head of the army radio station, was charged for anti-regime propaganda.

Already General Hinh, National Army chief of staff, planned to topple Diem. According to the SMM report: 'Hinh had hinted at such a plot to his American friends, using a silver cigarette box given him by Egypt's Naguib to carry the hint. SMM became thoroughly involved in the tense controversy which followed, due to our Chief's [Lansdale's] closeness to both President Diem and General Hinh. He had met the latter in the Philippines in 1952, was a friend of both Hinh's wife and favorite mistress.' Muhammad Naguib was the Egyptian general who together with Colonel Gamal Abdel Nasser and other members of the 'Free Officers' movement deposed King Farouk in 1952. In fact, the CIA and foremost officer Kermit Roosevelt had supported the end of Farouk's rule.[27]

Lansdale's SMM had been given an explicit warning about a coup:

Finally, we learned that Hinh was close to action; he had selected 26 October [1954] in the morning for an attack on the Presidential Palace. Hinh was counting heavily on Lt-Col Lan's special forces and on Captain Giai, who was running Hinh's secret headquarters at Hinh's home. We invited these two officers to visit the Philippines, on the pretext that we were making an official trip, could take them along and open the way for them to see some inner workings of the fight against Filipino Communists which they probably would never see otherwise. Hinh reluctantly turned down his own invitation.... Lt-Col Lan was a French agent and the temptation to see behind the scenes was too much. He and Giai accompanied SMM officers on the MAAG C-47, which General O'Daniel instantly made available for the operation. 26 October was spent in the Philippines. The attack on the palace didn't come off.[28]

***

The SMM continued training Vietnamese in unconventional warfare and espionage for missions in North Vietnam late into 1954. Plans were prepared for arms caches to be set up in North Vietnam. Minister of Defense Chan and Trinh Minh Thé asked the SMM for more aid in training their troops to support Diem. Lansdale and the CIA agreed to offer more.[29] In January 1955, the US–French training mission, the Training Relations and Instruction Mission (TRIM), was established under the overall command of General Paul Ely. By taking the top positions in TRIM the French sought to exercise control over the National Army, promoting the pro-Bao Dai, pro-French elements. In response, Ambassador Collins and General O'Daniel assigned Lansdale to TRIM. Lansdale grasped the opportunity offered to him, and 'requested authority to coordinate all US civil and military efforts in this National Security work [of TRIM]'. Collins gave Lansdale 'authority to coordinate this work among all US agencies in Vietnam'.[30]

Ely kept Lansdale at arm's length. Indeed, Lansdale had a reputation for being anti-French and anti-colonialist. Comical episodes at conferences were abundant. Although the French officer spoke English, he insisted that Lansdale's remarks be translated into French before replying in French.[31] 'They had a psychotic suspicion of everything I did', Lansdale remarked of the attitude of the French, although he was hardly blameless. Naturally, the French services were watching him and listen in on overheard his phone conversations. Episodes of Lansdale turning against the French are abundant, showing the nature of confrontations between the French and the Americans after Dien Bien Phu. An angry Lansdale turned against the French security services when he received intelligence that French subjects were implicated in bomb attacks against American owned cars. He met with a French colonel he believed responsible for the attacks and demanded a stop to this, warning him that 'you are ten thousand miles from metropolitan France'. The same night grenade attacks took place in front of the houses of French subjects suspected of being involved in the bomb attacks. The French colonel demanded from the US embassy that Lansdale be sent home, implicating him in the attacks – but to no avail.[32] France had realised that Lansdale promoted Diem over their preferences, Emperor Bao Dai and the sects, and the Binh Xuyen.

TRIM activities were connected to the general staff branches and offices: G1 (administration), G2 (military intelligence), G3 (planning and operations), G4 (logistics) and G5 (civil affairs/psychological warfare). Lansdale was assigned to G5; France was not willing to let him have access or contribute in its core advice to the National Army. Lansdale had to advise a staff of Vietnamese officers, three armed propaganda companies, as well as artists and writers. There was also an army radio unit which broadcast to the troops. Lansdale blamed the French for not having a Vietnamese psychological war strategy to defeat the PAVN, but the Vietnamese nationalists had no voice; there was no appeal to Vietnam's independence from a colonial power. In his memoirs he wrote: 'I started an educational effort with the French staff officers I had met. They found my ideas alien and suggested laughingly that I take up smoking opium instead.'[33]

The ambitious Lansdale wanted his advice to be followed. At G5, he found eager-to-learn officers and non-commissioned officers. Among them was Captain Giai, the head of G5, and his cousin Pham Xuan An, Ho Chi Minh's mole who served as an adjutant.[34] An was happy about this outcome, but he kept it to himself: 'When the Americans came to our office with their bad French, there was only one person they could talk to, Giai. And when he was away, I was the only one they could talk to. Soon I was the liaison officer between the Americans and the Vietnamese. First there was Lansdale and then Lansdale's people and then other military officers. I made friends with all sorts of Americans and even their families ... they were my teachers.'[35] Unaware of the average Vietnamese's xenophobic mentality, the Americans assumed that the good manners of their interlocutors showed their intention to cooperate and to get as much advice as possible. The truth, however, was different. Stuart Herrington, a counterintelligence officer assigned to the Phoenix programme in the early 1970s, pointed out: 'The polite smile and the seemingly obsequious behavior of many Vietnamese was a mask that often concealed contempt for the foreigner. One of my more candid counterparts, who had been trained at an American intelligence school in Okinawa, summed up the situation by reminding me that "you can't help it if you are an American, but you should always remember that very few of our people are capable of genuine positive feelings toward you. You must assume that you are not wholly liked and trusted, and not be deceived by the Asian smile."'[36]

In contrast, the overconfident Lansdale believed that good manners only ensured rapport between him and the people he was to advise.

One friend of his said that Lansdale 'was not exactly fluent in Tagalog, but he had a way of sensing what was being said without knowing the words'.[37] Only a superficial understanding of Asian peoples – especially the Filipinos and Vietnamese – was evident in the thinking of many military intelligence officers. The colonel assumed that his Vietnamese interlocutors needed a new way of thinking and dutifully gave An and the rest of the staff at G5 books on intelligence, such as the classic *Strategic Intelligence for American World Policy* of Sherman Kent, the leading analyst of the CIA, and *Psychological Warfare* by Paul Linebarger. He borrowed tactics and strategy concepts from leading British experts such as Brigadier Robert Thompson – who had served in Malaya and would advise the Americans in the early 1960s, eventually meeting with President Kennedy – and from French Colonel Roger Trinquier, who was serving in Indochina at that time and would fight rebels in the Algerian insurgency, promoting torture as a counterinsurgency operational practice.[38]

Office life was dangerous because all were spying on each other. An was constantly aware of this:

> The guy in the office who worked for the CIA was fighting against my cousin (Captain Giai), who worked for the Deuxième Bureau. They were keeping track of each other's activities, reporting back to their bosses on what was happening. But they were good friends. They played around all the time. This is the Vietnamese way, pure Vietnamese. We were thrown together like a bunch of crabs from the world's five oceans. . . . When we weren't spying on each other, we smoked opium and played together as friends. That was just the way things worked. I had to compartmentalize. It was hard. First you do it by reflex, and then, after a long period of time, you become accustomed to it. I always had to be vigilant. My cousin, my boss, was pro-French. So I had to pretend to be on the French side while I was actually against the French. I was also against the interventionists, the Americans while at the same time I was working for them.[39]

Gradually, An was sucked into the darkness of Trinquier's counter-insurgency methods and the opium trade run by the South Vietnamese. The mole was sure that if discovered he would have to endure torture and face death, as described by Trinquier and implemented by the Vietnamese.[40]

A spy who fears and feels insecure takes advice from anyone – especially the enemy. Lansdale owned a large black poodle. He once told An: 'You have to watch the behavior of your dog. They live by instinct. You have to learn to observe what your dog is telling you. He will show you if you have to be vigilant of your guest. Your dog can protect you.' An admitted:

> Lansdale gave me good advice. Soon after Lansdale left Vietnam, I went to the dog market. I saw a beautiful German shepherd for sale. The man who was selling it said, 'This is the dog of Mr Lansdale, chief of intelligence, who has just left the country. This is a very intelligent dog.' I walked around the corner and saw another German shepherd for sale. 'This is Lansdale's dog,' said the owner. That day every German shepherd in the market was 'Lansdale's dog,' and you were supposed to pay more because it was so intelligent. After that, there wasn't a German shepherd in Vietnam that hadn't formerly belonged to Lansdale. An bought a German shepherd which kept him constant company. Late at night, when he had been compiling his secret reports for Hanoi, the dog would growl softly when he heard a patrol moving through the neighborhood. He was very good at warning me in advance when danger was approaching.[41]

The mole was in daily contact with Lansdale's operatives Major Lucien 'Black Luigi' Conein, Mills C. Brandes and Rufus Phillips. Constantly afraid of being discovered, An never let his guard down: 'No, no one knew [that I was a communist], not even Lou Conein, and he knew everything. He was a very good friend. He came here first as a major, working for Lansdale. He had been a French soldier. He swore like a trooper. Whenever we got together for a drink at the Continental, Lou Conein and Bob Shaplen and I, Conein would be swearing in French, Shaplen in English, and I in Vietnamese. It was like hell in a very small place. . . . Lou Conein was always the man the Vietnamese trusted.'[42]

The SDECE had them all under surveillance. The pro-French Captain Giai was aware that a French 'honey trap' had targeted and ensnared Conein. An also knew of this but kept quiet: 'They [the

French secret services] used lots of pretty girls for gathering information. They succeeded in fooling many people. They failed to trap Lansdale and his other men, like Rufus Phillips, who was very handsome, but the French were successful in fooling Lou Conein.' Lansdale, not knowing this, organised his own 'honey trap' network by arranging for English language courses for mistresses of high-ranking officials: one of the students was a mistress of General Hinh, the commander of the National Army.

Long before Sean Connery got his Walther PPK as James Bond 007 in the franchise's first film, *Dr. No*, it was the real spy, An, who was armed with this pistol. An recalled an episode from January 1956 when he and two US colonels visited rural areas for observation. He had a small pistol for protection, given to him by his cousin Giai. It was a Walther 7.65mm 'with a brown handle and a shiny, blue-green barrel. This is what we call a "love pistol." It is designed to be carried in your handbag or in your pocket and removed when it is required to shoot your spouse or her lover. . . . I tied the pistol with a string to my belt loop, so if it fell out of my pocket, I wouldn't lose it.'[43] On seeing the pistol the officers smiled, looking down upon their Vietnamese aide. They believed in their bigger and more powerful .45 Colts, and told An: 'You are the worst soldier we have ever seen in our lives. . . . You are smart, but you have no initiative. What you need is a brain transplant. You need an American brain grafted onto your Vietnamese brain. Then you might be able to go out in the world and accomplish something.'[44] The mole remained silent and did not show his anger.

Prime Minister Diem, feeling that a confrontation between his generals, the Binh Xuyen and the sects was coming, and worried about his personal security, asked the United States for advice and support. Lansdale called President Magsaysay of the Philippines, who dispatched his senior aide and adviser, Colonel Napoleon Valeriano, who was responsible for security. Valeriano reached Saigon in January 1955 with three other officers. Later, Vietnamese officers were sent for training in Manila.[45]

In the meantime, Lieutenant Phillips and an agent codenamed Trieu were working on an almanac which included dark astrological predictions for the DRV leaders and disasters for North Vietnam; it was arranged for these booklets to be smuggled into Haiphong and other locations in North Vietnam. Of course, the same almanac predicted a good future for South Vietnam under Diem. Simply put, it was another childish, dirty trick which took advantage of the superstitions of some of the population.[46]

'The Dragon Lady' was a publisher who accepted the SMM's offer to publish 'a Thomas Paine type series of essays on Vietnamese patriotism' against the Vietminh. The SMM described her as a 'fine Vietnamese girl who has been the mistress of an anti-American French civilian. Despite anti-American remarks by her boyfriend, we had helped her keep her paper from being closed by the government ... and she found it profitable to heed our advice on the editorial content of her paper.'[47]

A team of the SMM remained in Haiphong, planning for arms caches and recruiting agents to stay behind. The city was scheduled to be placed under DRV control in May 1955. In late January all arms was brought from Saigon to the Haiphong, where the Binh paramilitary team was based. Conein had ordered them to enter the city individually. Lansdale's team reported: 'The infiltration was carried out in careful stages over a 30 day period, a successful operation. The Binhs became normal citizens, carrying out every day civil pursuits, on the surface.' For operations in Tonkin, Lansdale had arranged for the Hao team to be supplied with 14 agent radios, 300 carbines, 50 pistols, 300 lb of explosives and ammunition.[48] In mid-April, the Hao team reached Haiphong aboard US Navy ships. They were supplied with more arms, smuggled from Saigon.

For Diem, the situation in Saigon remained precarious. He was determined to deal with the Binh Xuyen and the sects. Lansdale's team feared the ransacking of their headquarters in case of a battle and looting in Saigon: 'SMM personnel guarded the house night and day, for it also contained our major files other than the working file at our Command Post. All files were fixed for instant destruction, automatic weapons and hand grenades distributed to all personnel. It was a strange scene for new personnel just arriving.'[49]

The PAVN deployed in Haiphong on 14 May 1955. The *Canberra Times* reported that army trucks were moving and soldiers were shouting through loudspeakers: 'Every person who collaborated with the French and Vietnamese forces must report immediately to the nearest police station.' The French forces gradually withdrew to the harbour where they accompanied refugees to French landing craft; they were later taken to US Navy transports heading for the south.[50]

Lansdale's team report was self-congratulatory: 'Our Binh and northern Hao teams were in place, completely equipped. It had taken a tremendous amount of hard work to beat the Geneva deadline, to locate, select, train and infiltrate the men of these two teams and have them in place, ready for actions required against the enemy. It would be a hard task to do openly, but this had to be kept secret from the Vietminh, the International Commission with its suspicious French and Poles and Indians, and even friendly Vietnamese.'[51]

With the French ready to leave the south, Diem had to confront disgruntled officers of the National Army, Hoa Hao and Cao Dai sects and their militias, as well as the Binh Xuyen (by now a well-armed underground organisation of 2,500 men who claimed a part of Saigon and Cholon). The sects demanded autonomous areas and cabinet seats.[52] Money played a key part. The sects, which were subsidised by the French, needed some accommodation with Diem, who did not have financial resources to buy their support. Harwood of the 'regular' CIA station, in a secret arrangement with Diem's brother Nhu, brought the prime minister a large amount of money to be spent at his discretion. In September 1954 Diem asked Lansdale for money.

Lansdale negotiated with Cao Dai leader Colonel Trinh Minh Thé, who maintained his own autonomous Cao Dai force. Thé was in contact with Nhu. According to a CIA declassified history, Lansdale 'delivered [not declassified] in greenbacks to Diem, who passed the money on to Nhu for delivery to Thé'. Two days later, on 15 September 1954, Lansdale paid a visit to Thé's headquarters. But Nhu was angry with the whole stance of Lansdale; Thé got the impression that Diem was a US-backed puppet. Lansdale turned against Nhu but was informed by Joe Redick, his CIA interpreter, that 'Nhu was the regular Station's principal contact in the government'.[53]

In the end, Diem accepted some sect members in his cabinet but the confrontation with the Binh Xuyen was not averted. Lansdale believed that the sect ministers were acting under a French plot to destabilise the regime and promote Bao Dai.[54] The Binh Xuyen occupied the Sûreté building in Saigon; besides, the head of the police was also a Binh Xuyen member. Diem planned to take over the building but the French intervened, offering their aid to persuade the occupiers to come out. Ambassador Collins feared a battle in Saigon and advised against the government fighting the Binh Xuyen and the sects. Meanwhile, An got information that Collins was 'close' to a female Vietnamese who worked for French intelligence; she was 'feeding Collins as much anti-Diem spin as possible'. Collins wanted to go to Washington to convince Eisenhower that Diem had to be replaced by Phan Huy Quat, a pro-French leader. Soon An's intelligence on Collins reached Hanoi.[55]

At midnight on 29 March 1955, the Binh Xuyen and large elements of Cao Dai and Hoa Hao turned against the government forces in Saigon and Cholon. Harwood was with Diem in the palace, 'ducking for cover when an explosion rocked the room', as he later recalled. Snipers fired at a military convoy opposite the palace. The commanding officer of the convoy installed a 105 howitzer and fired against the building at point blank.[56]

The firefight ceased at 3.15 a.m., after the intervention of the French commander Commissioner-General Paul Ely; with about 30,000 troops and 400 armoured vehicles he blocked the main roads 'to guard the European quarters'. The Americans and some of the Diem government understood that Ely was effectively protecting the Binh Xuyen.[57] Lansdale was furious. He reported to Washington that the French were acting as if in a protectorate of theirs.[58]

The Vietnamese prime minister stood his ground because the support of Lansdale gave him confidence. Collins feared that eventually the National Army would turn against Diem. Eisenhower and Dulles were angry at the French for backing the opponents of the regime. Lansdale sent reports showing Diem's policies in a positive light. This was in stark contrast to the reporting from Collins.[59] On 20 April, the ambassador returned to Washington and met with the president, eventually persuading him that Diem had to go. Dulles acceded to the ambassador's arguments and assessments, drafting telegrams to the US embassies in Saigon and Paris with the new US policy: Diem was to be replaced by a leader to chosen by Emperor Bao Dai and other leaders. The messages were sent on 27 April at 6 p.m. Washington DC time.[60]

Bao Dai, who was residing in France, called Diem to consult with him and ask him to hand over the army to General Nguyen Van Vy, a supporter of Hinh. Naturally, Diem remained intransigent, confident that he could win over the sects, the Binh Xuyen and eventually the emperor. The next month, Diem once more turned against the Binh Xuyen police chief. Ambassador Collins was not there to stop him. Like Lansdale, Randolph Kidder, the chargé d'affaires, reported that Diem would win over the sects and the Binh Xuyen. Lansdale continued sending messages, bypassing the embassy and the regular CIA station. He got the key decision makers interested in the crisis: George Aurell called Dulles and his brother Allen (the CIA director), Archibald Roosevelt (Wisner's replacement at the CIA headquarters), Under-secretary of State Hoover, and Ken Young, the director of Philippine and Southeast Asian Affairs at the State Department. Eventually, the decision makers changed their minds; the US embassy in Paris got a new directive: do not proceed with the directive of the previous night that the United States and France should replace Diem.[61]

On the afternoon of 28 April, the Diem's palace was hit by mortar rounds coming from Binh Xuyen-controlled areas. Diem protested to General Ely. Harwood had a secret source within the Binh Xuyen: 'Since the fighting in late March the regular Station had been in almost nightly contact with an agent in the Binh Xuyen; [not declassified] he was in a position to provide authoritative tactical information.'[62] Harwood kept Nhu fully informed.

Eisenhower and Dulles realised that they had acted prematurely; orders were issued to burn the telegrams and to abandon the plan for Bao Dai (together with other leaders) to elect a new leader replacing Diem. The French forces abstained from intervening and guarded the European quarters. In a surreal scene, Americans drinking beer and French sipping aperitifs watched the battle unfold from their rooftops and balconies, waiting for a winner. For them it was like a football game. Vietnamese civilians caught in the crossfire died or ended up in hospital. Ely, on seeing that the Binh Xuyen was gradually routed, offered to intervene to save them. He asked Diem for a ceasefire. Naturally, he got a clear *no*; 'it's a fight to the finish', replied Diem. The National Army pursued the retreating Binh Xuyen, but eventually the French force guarding two bridges prevented their annihilation by giving them time to escape. Surprisingly, the French prime minister himself intervened; Edgar Faure stated that Bao Dai's statement for the Vietnamese National Army to be put under Ely's command was right. Diem could not govern.[63]

Ely paid a visit to Kidder, urging a joint action and policy to compel Diem out of power. Before leaving for Washington, Collins had told Ely that the new US policy required that Diem be deposed. At that time, Kidder had no clear instructions of official US policy. He knew that Collins was against Diem, and that Washington was debating on what to do. He remarked years later: 'I was left no choice but to make up my own mind what our policy was, as I would be damned if I was going to say I didn't know.'[64] Expecting to hear Collins' position on Diem, Ely asked Kidder: 'How do you know that [the US policy is not to remove Diem]?' The chargé d'affaires replied: 'General, I know American foreign policy.'[65]

Meanwhile, about 200 men gathered at Saigon's town hall, claiming to be the general assembly of the democratic and revolutionary forces of the nation. There were members of political parties in attendance, as well as some Cao Dai and Hoa Hao members. The key people were Colonel Thé and his Cao Dai fellow General Nguyen Thanh Phuong and General Ngo of the Hoa Hao. The group, blaming French imperialism, demanded that Bao Dai abdicate and that a new government under Diem be formed. It is believed that either Lansdale or Diem staged the gathering.

Eventually, the Hoa Hao abstained from backing the Binh Xuyen. After reading the reports from Saigon, Dulles decided that it was not the right moment to replace Diem, as Collins had demanded and Eisenhower had previously (rather hastily) agreed to with the ambassador. Eventually, the president sided with the secretary of state.[66]

Pressure from the United States compelled France to grant the National Army passage over the bridges, and to hunt down the remaining Binh Xuyen fighters. During the last phase of the fight, Colonel Thé was shot in the back of the head. According to Pham Xuan An, the trigger was pulled by Cao Dai Major Ta Thanh Long on the order of Nhu, the younger brother of Diem. Long was later assigned to the ARVN and undertook security duties in the presidential special military staff. An assumed that the Diem family wanted Thé dead because, as an anti-communist, he could rally non-Catholics around him, challenging the family's authority once the fight for Saigon was over.[67]

The battle for Saigon and Cholon ended with 500 dead and 2,000 wounded. Ambassador Collins, who eventually accepted the fact that Washington would not oust Diem, mistakenly claimed that a new phase of Binh Xuyen insurgency would commence. But the National Army forces dealt with them effectively. Lansdale beat Collins in the 'war' of informing Washington. Howard Simpson, the press officer of the embassy in Saigon, witnessed the crisis. He claimed that Lansdale's 'cables were vibrant accounts of what he had witnessed during the Saigon fighting. The events and conversations he reported backing Diem's actions had an impressive "I was there" quality.'[68]

By the end of May 1955, Hoa Hao generals Ngo, Ba Cut, Soai and Lan Thanh Nguyen declared that they would continue fighting the Saigon government because they had not secured privileges from Diem. Their 16,000 fighters reached the mountains only to be defeated by the ARVN. Their rebellion had failed; Ngo and Thanh Nguyen returned to Saigon to surrender themselves. Ba Cut continued fighting.[69]

Diem dealt the final blow to the authority of Emperor Bao Dai through the referendum of 23 October 1955. The regime employed all the means available to it to intimidate the people; Lansdale provided his psychological warfare expertise. The new US Ambassador G. Frederick Reinhardt did not report electoral fraud. Diem won with a staggering 98.2 per cent share of the vote.[70]

In 1956, Pham Xuan An was about to be discharged after having completed his national service. His handler, Muoi Huong, wanted him to move to the United States as his spy. Hanoi had secured another spy within the echelons of the South Vietnamese general staff; thus An could make the move, 'building' his career as a journalist in the United States. The mole was given some money from Hanoi, while his applications for a scholarship and visa were supported by both the US military attaché in Saigon as well as Tran Kim Tuyen, the head of Diem's secret police.[71] Everybody had faith in the mole.

CHAPTER 6

SECRET SOURCES AND DOUBLE CROSS

The CIA station was expanding its network of secret sources in South Vietnam. Meanwhile, North Vietnam was deemed a lethal, out of bounds area for any kind of clandestine operation. The informers and the security paranoia of the communist regime ensured that Lansdale's stay-behind groups would soon be arrested. Starting in 1960, the CIA, in collaboration with the South Vietnamese special forces, organised new secret missions for intelligence gathering and sabotage. Meanwhile, in South Vietnam the growing hatred of the Vietnamese military against Diem's family's (the Ngos) rule created a complex environment of intrigue which could not be covered by the CIA station's secret sources. The enemies of the regime – and their plots – were multiplying; the CIA officers could not warn about coups. In some instances, intelligence officers turned into messengers and negotiators with plotters and confidential contacts who had an agenda to advance.

Lansdale left Saigon in December 1956. His tenure as a close adviser to Diem had ended, and the CIA decided to close down his parallel station. Al Ulmer, the head of the Far East Division at Langley, arrived in Saigon and made it clear that the CIA's period of 'free-wheeling improvisation' was over. Only one station would operate, concentrating on secret sources. Some functions of the SMM would be divided among the station, the embassy and the US Information Agency, while others would simply be eliminated. Gradually this arrangement would change because the station would examine the potential to implement land reform and other policies to boost the popularity of an authoritarian ruler who cared only about his family's interests. Diem (like the United States government) was unwilling to organise reunification elections as required by the Geneva Accords scheduled for 1956. He was sure that the Vietminh and the DRV leaders would win. For the outgoing Lansdale, Nhu was turning into a 'Mussolini type character who had set up a network of local district controls styled after the Japanese system' (during World War II occupation).[1]

In April 1956, one of Harwood's (the CIA chief of station) operatives recruited a secret source very close to the Ngo family. The reference in the declassified CIA history remains heavily redacted:

> [R]ecruiting [two lines not declassified] as the Diem family dictatorship developed, [not declassifed] came more and more frequently into conflict with the family's determination to absorb all control to itself [two lines not declassified]. Despite [not declassified] quarrels with Nhu and Diem, [not declassified; probably the name of the source] managed to retain their confidence and became an important if sometimes self-interested source on the inner workings of the family and the government.[2]

The secret source also reported on the activities and stance of Diem's youngest brother, Ngo Dinh Can, the governor of Central Vietnam. In mid-1956, secret intelligence reporting revealed that Can had turned against Nhu and information minister Tranh Chanh Thanh in order to rise to power next to Diem, who had (rather unconvincingly) denied that Can had been organising assassination squads.[3]

Greek-American Nicholas Natsios was named chief of station in April 1957. He sought to expand the reach of secret sources, downplaying covert operations. Ulmer sided with Natsios.[4] Born in Lowell, Massachusetts in 1920, Natsios joined the US Army after the Japanese attack on Pearl Harbour. He fought with OSS in North Africa and Italy, being commissioned a captain in military intelligence with assignment in counterintelligence. He graduated with honours from Ohio State University in 1948 and attained a master's in law and diplomacy from the Tufts Fletcher School of Law and Diplomacy and then joined the CIA; he was sent to the CIA station of Thessaloniki, Greece at the time of the civil war.[5]

Natsios wanted committed spies. He insisted on the so-called 'absolutist' policy on secret sources: 'If they hadn't signed on the dotted line, they couldn't be trusted, and the Station wasn't going to use them.' The 'casual informers', Vietnamese of all walks of life, were not the sources Natsios wanted; 'he had seen the Station as too dependent on casual informants'.[6]

The Diem family government's increasingly authoritarian ways made CIA officers uneasy. At that time, no one predicted the demise of Diem and his brothers. Recognising the need for new leadership, Natsios launched a search for contacts and sources in the anti-communist opposition. One politician from the opposition agreed to become a spy: '[Name not declassified] signed an agreement formalising his recruitment of a year earlier.' In addition 'penetration of the [name not declassified] proceeded when [deputy chief of station Douglas] Blaufarb recruited [name not declassified] disenchanted with Ngo Dinh Nhu.' The search for opposition leaders who could be candidates against Diem intensified. The secret policy was to find 'clean people ... pull them together, select the best potential leaders, and then build them up – all behind Nhu's back.'

At that time, the South Vietnamese regime did not have a central intelligence service. Spying on political opponents was done mainly by the Political and Social Studies Service (SEPES), the intelligence section of Nhu's Can Lao Party. The CIA provided funds and resources to the SEPES, but the United States concluded that under its definition it was not an intelligence agency. The SEPES screened the membership for the party, gathered secret funds and confronted dissidents and opponents to the regime. Nhu was not interested in either cooperation with the United States or in launching SEPES secret operations against the DRV. Only 29 out of 219 SEPES employees were assigned to North Vietnam affairs. Darwin Curtis, a station liaison to the SEPES, thought that this connection should not cease, despite its deficiencies, because 'over 50 percent of the [intelligence] we collect on the DRV comes from SEPES sources', the majority being news brought by refugees from the north.

Natsios sought an agreement with Diem that the SEPES would dispatch secret agents for espionage – not sabotage – to North Vietnam. He brought up this issue during a conversation with Tran Trung Dung of the Ministry of Defence. Nhu, Diem's brother, was informed about the scheme and agreed that the loyal Colonel Le Tung would overview the new secret missions. However, no tangible results were reported. Diem and Nhu were not willing to cooperate to the extent the CIA wanted for operations in the north, nor were they willing to assign considerable resources against the DRV. Natsios was also interested in cooperating with the Special Branch of the National Police in investigating the activities of the National Liberation Front of South Vietnam (NLF), aka the Viet Cong. But the South Vietnamese did not agree on joint operations. Diem had declared an 'Anti-Communist Denunciation' campaign seeking to uncover NLF networks. Meanwhile, Lansdale had been in contact with General Mai Huu Xuan of the Military Security Service, an agency which also had counterintelligence duties. He was a former colonial policeman. After being courted by the CIA, he agreed to cooperate in September 1956; however, a few months later, in December, he reconsidered, saying that he had no authority to share intelligence with the United States.[7]

In 1956, the First Observation Group was established for unconventional warfare in the north; it was put under the direct orders of Diem. In 1958, Diem agreed to a joint operation with the CIA to launch agents against Hanoi. Neither scheme paid any dividends. An arrangement that saw the South Vietnamese screening candidates who would receive special CIA training remained in place until the early 1960s. This meant that the PAVN managed to infiltrate the ranks of special missions.[8]

Natsios and Ambassador Elbridge Durbrow discussed the attitude of the Ngo family. The head of the station referred to the 'CIA's contacts – unilateral agents as well as the nearly exclusive relationship with Nhu – [which] provided unique access to the workings of the government.' The ambassador was right in concluding that Diem had not proceeded to socio-economic reforms that would curb the influence of the Viet Cong. There were increasing signs of an evolving feud between Nhu and Can, who wanted Central Vietnam to be under his sole authority. Nhu distrusted the CIA and spied on Blaufarb. The deputy chief of station realised that his Vietnamese driver, provided by Nhu, was fluent in English and French. Most significantly, Diem and Nhu wanted to oust King Sihanouk of Cambodia and funded dissidents there. The CIA station secured 'unequivocal evidence' that Diem was not backing the US policy of expanding the war. Besides, the Diem–CIA distrust was nurtured by gross mishandling. Late in 1955, Diep, who was a former

Vietminh, combed the operations for stay-behind agents, trying to find suitable candidates living already in the DRV. But his eagerness to work with the United States was misunderstood.[9] In late 1956 he met Ulmer, who 'made an extemporaneous and unsuccessful effort to recruit him'. As a result relations cooled considerably.[10]

OSS veteran William Colby, the future CIA director, reached Saigon in February 1959, first of all to work as Natsios's deputy. At that time, the station had a high-level spy and had expanded the network of secret agents. Ahern wrote: 'The 1956 recruitment of [more than half line not declassified] and Natsios' subsequent emphasis on acquiring controlled agents had substantially improved the Station's access to the regime's inner workings.'[11]

In his turn, Nhu feared the French secret services, telling Colby in February that a 'renegade' Frenchman and two high officials at the French Ministry of Foreign Affairs were conspiring against the regime. Four French subjects and about 1,000 agents were arrested. Many confessed of a plot, probably to avoid further torture during the interrogation. The Saigon station informed the United States of the arrests of four French and 20 Vietnamese agents in December 1959. Before long, French Finance Minister Antoine Pinay had negotiated the release of the French with Diem.[12] Colby was informed that files on about 20 Vietnamese recruited by Conein in 1954–5 were held in the two station safes. Colby himself recruited some Vietnamese and Europeans to go to Tchepone, a Laotian town close to the Ho Chi Minh trail, but he was disappointed with the intelligence he received.[13]

Since Lansdale's tour, the stay-behind groups of paramilitaries he had organised were rooted out by the security services of North Vietnam.[14] The paranoia about the regime's security, the fact that no Diem supporters had remained in the north – to assist any spies and saboteurs – ensured that Lansdale's small teams would be arrested sooner or later.

British intelligence translated circulars from the Vietnamese Workers Party Central Committee. A November 1955 Central Committee circular referred to delays in dispatching instructions to echelons of the Vietminh remaining in the south. The quarterly reports to Hanoi were deemed incomplete, most importantly because 'when faced with the enemy's [Diem regime] Communist Subversion Activity Denunciation Campaign, many Regional Committees fail to react or operate under cover.' Even 'theoretical threats by the enemy' forced some cadre to hide.

But the circular also criticised the 'reckless comrades who act haphazardly and get arrested or denounced'. In addition 'with this passive enjoyment of their own security, our agents are still lacking self-criticism and therefore greatly underestimate the enemy. They do not take sufficient elementary precautions in the cause of their activities, the result being that in one locality the enemy arrested 150 persons returning from an earlier evacuation, and several cadres.'[15]

The Central Committee admitted to weak and not particularly effective propaganda among the students and the citizens in the Saigon-Cholon area. There was the assumption that if the communists win over the masses, 'we will manage to bring on our side, with less trouble, and in less time, the Hoa-Hao and the Binh Xuyen'. Both of these organisations showed, for the time being, 'appeasement' and 'conciliation' towards the communist cadre. Thus, it was the Central Committee's view that 'if we did not give them all necessary help we would lose a considerable force in the common struggle against Diem. Moreover, after the liquidation of the Sects the Diem clique would not fail to concentrate all its forces to destroy us.'[16] Reports claimed that Diem was attempting to negotiate with the sects while his troops hunted them out of Saigon. Thus the DRV decided that it 'must devise a plan to keep the civil war lingering on and prevent Diem from solving his internal problems'. The communist strategy had two aims: to influence the average fighter of the sects, and to link his local leader with the communist party ideals for independence. The communists took the position that the country's need for general elections, peace and unification would influence the sects still surviving following Diem's victories.[17]

Another contemporary circular from the Central Committee to Muoi, the head of intelligence, read: 'In order to liquidate spies and ensure the protection of our organisation, it is necessary that we should have at our disposal revolvers as they are easier to handle. Therefore, I suggest that you should provide two revolvers (at the District we already hold one); we also ask you for authority to kill civic action cadres. We would operate in the following way: Try and mix with the cadres [of the regime] during their meetings and exterminate them to the last one; experience has shown us that these cadres leave organisations behind. . . . We hope to carry out this plan during the month of March [1956]. We only lack the means of action — that is to say arms and ammunition. At present, the cadres are stationed at the Dong Market (Bien Hoa).'[18]

A series of spy trials were organised in Hanoi. In December 1957, the DRV police arrested 14 members of a stay-behind ring and charged French Consular Clerk de Bonfils with espionage.[19] De Bonfils left as soon as possible by air, and the French acting delegate-general protested. One should read between the lines of the comment offered by the British consul general in Hanoi: 'The French acting Delegate-General has not revealed to me any knowledge of intelligence activities by de Bonfils beyond reporting items about local opinion gathered in the course of contact with the public. However, it is known that de Bonfils did have Viet Namese [sic] contacts outside the office.' On 20 March, the arrested were put on trial, and 11 were imprisoned. Their leader, Nguyen Quang Hai, was sentenced to death. The French government was further embarrassed because Berlioz, a French Communist Party leader who had returned from a trip to Hanoi, had declared that the delegation-general 'was maintained for espionage purposes'.[20]

US intelligence was informed of developments through an intelligence-sharing scheme with the British consulate general and the French delegation in Hanoi. In April 1959, Britain reported that ten individuals, including a woman and a student, were tried for being CIA agents implicated in sabotage, assassination and black propaganda. They were accused of being a part of a stay-behind group organised by the former US consulate in Hanoi. Their leader was sentenced to death, five were imprisoned, three received suspended sentences and one was acquitted. It was a public trial that 'resembled a rather dull theatrical performance'. US-made weaponry was on display.[21]

Intelligence sharing existed between the British and the French delegations, but it was due to a mistake. The British ambassador in Saigon wrote to London: 'Recently as a result of a misunderstanding on the part of the member of Chancery concerned, we also gave [in addition to the US mission in Saigon] a carefully vetted selection of correspondence [of the British consulate general in Hanoi] covering about three months, to the French.' The French embassy in Saigon replied with a similar batch of reports from their delegation in Hanoi. The material offered was informative; the British and French opinions on the DRV were found to be 'identical' and showed the 'friendly liaison' between the missions in Hanoi. Nonetheless, for security reasons the British ambassador in Saigon did not want this scheme to continue, claiming that there was evidence that the French Ministry of Foreign Affairs 'was to some extent penetrated by Communist sympathisers'. In any case, the British would show to the French some 'suitable' reports from Hanoi 'whenever it seems that a useful exchange of views may result'.[22]

In May 1959, the 559th Transportation Group of the DRV was established to coordinate the dispatch of fighters and war materiel to the south for the support of the Viet Cong. The Ho Chi Minh trail in Laos would eventually become the main logistics pipeline, but it had not yet been created. As early as 1951, General Nguyen Binh, the commander of the PAVN in the south, insisted in a report to the Ministry of Defence on the creation of an overland 'Indochinese Trail' in Laos and Cambodia to support the PAVN with heavy material. At that time the US–French cooperation in the interception of naval traffic and the fear of an escalation to a general war with the United States (the war in Korea was already taking place) made imperative the contingency of establishing new logistics support routes as alternatives to the sea routes.[23] Two years later, in 1961, the upgrade of Hanoi's cryptosystems communications commenced; this process lasted until 1962 when the NSA realised that the high-grade communication cyphers of the DRV, the Communist Party, and the military and diplomatic apparatuses were unbreakable. Thus, the NSA focused on low-level operational communications – about, for example, PAVN and Viet Cong regiments and battalions – in order to offer tactical intelligence support to US commanders in the field.[24]

***

In the meantime, Natsios was expanding the secret sources networks. He warned the US embassy and the military mission that the Viet Cong would attack Tay Ninh province. Indeed, on 26 January 1960, about 200 guerrillas attacked and seized control of the headquarters of an ARVN regiment in Trang Sup in the province. Other attacks also took place during the Tet celebration period, signifying the coming of full-scale war, and showing that the South Vietnamese regime had not broken the communist networks as it had boasted and as General Williams, the commander of Military Assistance and Aid Group, had confidently assumed. For some time Natsios had been insisting that the general initial any CIA estimate he was given. After the attack in Trang Sup the general complained that he had received no warning from the station, so Natsios showed him the reports he had delivered to him earlier, which predicted a major attack in the province. The general had read them and initialled the cover sheet.[25]

Following Natsios's recommendation, Colby took over as head of station in June 1960. Like Natsios, he assumed that the regime needed urgent reform and believed that positive results could come from more cooperation with Diem. The CIA headquarters at Langley wanted 'Lansdale style' psychological operations and civic action to boost the people's support for Diem. The station proposed policies for a free press, land reform and intelligence cooperation with the creation of a central intelligence service. Colby was more optimistic than Natsios regarding Diem's potential to do well by his people and confront the communist guerrillas.[26] Meanwhile, James 'Jesus' Angleton, the head of counter-intelligence at Langley, persuaded Director Allen Dulles to dispatch a counterintelligence team to the Saigon station. Of course, Colby did not like this. The team discovered that Colby was on friendly terms with a French doctor named Vincent Gregoire (the name turned out to be an alias). He was a communist who had sided with the Viet Cong and was later arrested for passing documents to Moscow. Angleton remained silent, not asking Colby for an explanation.[27] Colby did not have access to the intelligence suspecting the doctor of being a GRU agent; thus, he did not know that he had to file reports of his discussions with him. In any case, Angleton suspected everyone, including Colby. The doctor was working for a charity on a six-month visit to Saigon. Only later was it revealed that afterwards the doctor would be recruited by the GRU.[28]

In July 1960, the CIA station informed Langley that the intelligence-gathering of the non-communist opposition to Diem had been 'accelerated'. Throughout the autumn, contacts with army officers, among them General Tran Van Minh, showed the growing dissent against the Ngo family, who continued to rule with authoritarianism and nepotism. Nonetheless, the CIA did not predict the coup attempt on 11 November 1960. Only a pre-dawn movement of military vehicles and gunfire at the presidential palace made intelligence officers rush (like journalists) to cover the unfolding events and contact the mutineers. Colby authorised George Carver, one of his intelligence officers, to talk to Hoang Co Thuy, a Dai Viet politician eager to assume power. Carver was the 'channel' of the station to the rebels. He insisted that they not raid the palace; instead, they should talk with Diem and try to reach a compromise. Carver himself deemed Diem no good and wanted him ousted, but his instructions from the CIA headquarters were to support Diem and to outmanoeuvre the mutineers so that Diem could gain more time. The rebels, among them paratrooper commander Colonel Nguyen Chanh Thi, assumed that the Americans would support them and kept the station informed via two CIA officers that the station had assigned to them. Colby had explicitly told the CIA officer not to be seen by the rebels as maintaining a 'counselling role'. Diem procrastinated, pretending to want a positive outcome. On 12 November his loyal troops arrived, saving his rule. Surprisingly, Nhu's and Diem's suspicion of the Americans grew. They assumed that the US embassy did not give them unqualified support in their hour of crisis, despite the fact that the station had delayed the rebels from storming the palace.[29] In May 1961, Vice President Lyndon B. Johnson visited Saigon, calling Diem 'the Winston Churchill of Southeast Asia'. The regime needed to reform, but American support was seen as unquestionable.[30]

On 27 February 1962, another coup attempt took the CIA by surprise. Two A-1 Skyraiders of the South Vietnam Air Force bombed the presidential palace. Diem and his family survived, leading the president to declare that he had 'divine protection'. One pilot escaped to Cambodia, the other was arrested. Investigations in the air force claimed that the two belonged to no group; they had simply assumed that Diem's assassination would prompt a revolution to oust the regime, which according to them (and other officers not connected to this plot) was not doing enough against the communists. Again Diem and Nhu held the CIA responsible and blamed the US media for anti-regime coverage of the events.[31] In any case, in May 1962, Diem established the Central Intelligence Organization (CIO) – in essence the Vietnamese CIA, something the United States had been pressing for since 1955. Paul Hodges, the station liaison officer with the new agency, was modestly optimistic; but by March 1963 he concluded that the CIO was a ploy of the regime to keep the Americans preoccupied in order to protect the operations of the Police Special Branch.[32]

Colby appeared to remain optimistic about the potential of cooperation, proposing to Nhu that the CIA and the Vietnamese

Special Forces act together to arm Montagnard tribes against the Viet Cong. (But no one should have forgotten the centuries-long animosity which kept the Vietnamese and the non-Vietnamese tribes apart. The Vietnamese called the tribes of the highlands 'moi', which meant savages. The general concept was for the tribes to be armed so as to defend their homes and families from Viet Cong intrusions. In reality, they were merely a nuisance for the guerrillas coming from the Ho Chi Minh trail considerably.)[33] Nhu accepted the offer. US Special Forces personnel were called up to train 'self-defence' teams, which by 1963 would reach 35,000 fighters.[34] Colby's discussions with Nhu led to the evolution of the Strategic Hamlet programme, which was approved by Diem in February 1962; Nhu was placed as head of the committee in March. Colby was also interested in expanding the Citizens' Irregular Defense Group (CIOG) in the High Plateau; US Special Forces teams would arm and train these groups.[35] Essentially, it was the pro-tribe strategy of the French all over again. There were more resources and money available this time, but the fallacies remained: poor, fragmented tribes, suspicious of the regime due to the animosity they had faced from Diem (through his resettlement policies), were being asked to fight the communist guerrillas on his behalf. Most significantly, causing famine continued to be a government strategy; Nhu wanted more defoliation in the Central Highlands, to hit the Viet Cong as well as to compel the tribes to side with the regime.[36]

In January 1963 a CIA agent reported that Nhu was wrong to assume that the strategic hamlets would work. In Lam Dong Province in Central Vietnam the population could not be trusted to support the regime; US/Vietnamese civic action teams always needed an armed escort for protection. Further similar reports came into the station.[37] The same year, the Montagnards rebelled against Saigon, but were soon routed by the ARVN. The Strategic Hamlet programme was falling apart, but Nhu and his lieutenants cooked the data to show that the scheme delivered results.[38]

* * *

Ahern writes that the CIA station 'was everywhere in the spring of 1963. It was the only element of the US Mission to have contacts in all the politically active non-Communist elements in South Vietnamese society. While Richardson continued his meetings with Ngo Dinh

Nhu, junior Station officers were solidifying clandestine links with the opposition.'[39]

Despite US efforts to turn the ARVN into a credible force, in January 1963 the Viet Cong proved that they had the capability and the tactical expertise to defeat the ARVN in conventional warfare. In Ap Bac, a hamlet in the Mekong Delta near My Tho, the Viet Cong almost destroyed an ARVN superior in numerical force.[40] In essence, it was a victory of the Viet Cong because they withdrew unopposed. Their intelligence was supplied by Pham Xuan An, who had returned from the United States, and, keeping his connections with the South Vietnamese intelligence apparatus, had begun working as a correspondent for US media outlets. Tuyen, the head of the CIO, trusted the US-educated An, whom he had helped before his departure for the States. An was in the midst of the enemy's camp. He later disclosed: 'everyone in the CIO considered me one of their own. ... They were my best source for information during the war.'[41]

In 1963, Pham Xuan An was working for Reuters in Saigon. His contacts and briefings from the MACV and the South Vietnamese military ensured he had all the facts regarding new heliborne tactics and methods employed by the ARVN. Muoi Nho, An's handler, disclosed that in 1962 the spy 'sent us twenty-four rolls of film of all plans related to the US Special War strategy ... they included the master plan of the war, the materials concerning the buildup of armed forces, the support of American troops, the strategic hamlet plan, the plan of reoccupying liberated zones and the plan of consolidating the puppet army with American military equipment.'[42]

The Ap Bac hamlet (just 40 miles south-east of Saigon) was the epicentre of the confrontation. On 28 December 1962, US military intelligence located a Viet Cong radio transmitter and estimated that 120 fighters were deployed in the Ap Tan Thoi hamlet. On 2 January 1963, the ARVN forces moved against the hamlet, but on reaching Ap Bac they were attacked by the Viet Cong; 350 entrenched Viet Cong fighters stood against the 7th Infantry Division (1,400 troops) supported by 10 Shawnee helicopters, five Bell UH-1 Hueys, 13 M-113s, artillery and 13 bombers. Guerrillas shooting from treeline-height shot down 14 helicopters. The ARVN troops disembarking from the helicopters were stuck in the rice paddies, becoming easy targets for the guerrillas.

Nick Turner, a war correspondent under whom An was working, remembered: 'I will never forget the look on [An's] face when he burst into the office with the news of Ap Bac ... emphasizing how important it was, even while first reports were starting to come in.'[43] He recalled:

> An was the first reporter to break the news. He fed me the initial story and details that got me to write it. He told me some American helicopters had been shot down and that I should go to Ap Bac. America was not directly involved in the war at this point, so the fact that American helicopters were getting shot down was big news. It was the first major battle of the war. The Communists stood and fought. They inflicted serious damage, shooting down five troop-carrying helicopters, and then they disappeared into the countryside. The story broke in the Western press and was written exactly the way the Communists wanted it written.[44]

Before the battle, An was providing the Viet Cong with information on the tactics to be employed by the US-trained ARVN pilots, commanders and crews. The mole said later: 'They trusted me and gave me the documents ... so I read them all, spoke with American advisors and my friends who were returning from training, and I wrote reports, nothing else. It was easy once I had the documents.... All I did was read their documents, attend briefings, listen to what people were saying, provide my analysis and send the report to the jungle.'[45] The head of DRV intelligence, Mai Chi Tho, was clear: An's intelligence ensured that the Viet Cong was able to devise successful counter tactics.[46] An and the commander of the Viet Cong troops would later receive medals for the battle of Ap Bac.[47]

***

The newly elected President Kennedy insisted on the investment of resources in special warfare; he repeated his 'instructions that we make every possible effort to launch guerrilla operations in North Vietnam territory.' He assumed that he could wage war without the danger of a nuclear confrontation as he had feared during the Cuban Missile Crisis. The Directorate of Operations at Langley and the station in Saigon were put under considerable pressure to organise and conduct an efficient secret war against Hanoi. But espionage needs time. It took a year for the

CIA together with the South Vietnamese to prepare a single secret agent
to go into North Vietnam. His codename remains classified. He crossed
the Ben Hai River before midnight on 5 December 1960. His case
officer, a Vietnamese, was watching the endeavour from behind a bush.
The agent buried the inner tube he had employed and walked into
the darkness. He was given CIA-made documentation which stood
the test of two DRV police checks. He returned to the south that same
night. Then, on 26 March 1961, he returned to the DRV, near the
demilitarised zone, and remained there for four days while he collected
intelligence on small military camps. Eventually, he rode a bus to the
border and returned in the night.

Colby was optimistic, or at the very least he did not voice his
scepticism about the scheme. However, the same is not true of Robert
Myers, a station chief from Cambodia who paid Colby a visit in Saigon.
When Myers was informed of plans to parachute agents into North
Vietnam he predicted that it would fail, reminding Colby of the failure to
dispatch secret agents to China. Colby responded by bringing up the
possibility of establishing safe areas within the sparsely populated DRV
territory. But beyond operations and strategy, he did not have the luxury
of debating a direct order from the president to the CIA.[48]

Colonel Tung, the head of the Presidential Survey Office (later
renamed the Presidential Liaison Office, PLO), and Diem's trusted officer
oversaw the programme of the secret missions to North Vietnam. The
CIA supplied the training; the Vietnamese recruited and transported the
secret agents. The scheme had three distinct phases: Phase I entailed
secret missions for intelligence gathering and sabotage; Phase II had a
propaganda component with leaflets encouraging the populace to revolt;
Phase III required the creation of sustainable, safe areas within the
DRV.[49] (After Diem's fall in November 1963, Colby returned to Saigon.
Among other things, he discussed the black entry programme with
Colonel Thao, one of Tung's lieutenants; the head of station did not
know that Thao was Hanoi's mole.)[50]

The narrative of the black entry operations is based on Ahern's
declassified history *The Way We Do Things*, which quotes contemporary
field reports, the majority of which remain classified. This gives us a clear
view of exactly what was known and how the field officers and the CIA
headquarters assessed the results of their secret campaign. Other studies
include oral history interviews as well as memoirs which, although

detailed, allow for the benefit of hindsight in understanding the competence of the secret war.[51]

In early April 1961, another secret agent was inserted by a fishing junk, landing at Ha Long Bay. He contacted his extended family and with the help of his brother sent back a total of 23 messages with his radio transmitter. After some weeks of silence, he renewed contact explaining that he was in hiding due to the authorities' new security measures. On 17 April, the People's Armed Security Force (PASF) arrested him and his brother for espionage. A fisherman had found his skiff; militia men started interrogating his community. The station was unaware of this development.[52] Throughout the summer of 1961 three secret agents were dispatched. Their traces were lost. On 27 May 1961, a team codenamed CASTOR was dropped by parachute in a non-Vietnamese tribe area in north-west Vietnam.[53] The station did not learn that CASTOR came under enemy control just four days after landing. The team was discovered by a flight radar, as well as by villagers who reported aircraft engine noise. On 2 June, the team codenamed ECHO was parachuted into south-east DRV. Three weeks of silence followed. Exactly three weeks later, ECHO contacted the PLO centre by radio. Its call sign was deemed wrong. The CIA station concluded that nerves combined with the difficulty of evading the militias had caused the error. Other signals followed. In fact, DRV security had arrested the ECHO team. Villagers first spotted their transport aircraft. The station knew nothing about this.[54]

On 29 June another team, codenamed DIDO, was parachuted into Lai Chau province (in north-west DRV). It was apprehended within four weeks, but the CIA station was unaware.[55] Despite growing suspicions, Langley insisted that 'in the absence of "conclusive evidence" of enemy control, all three teams should be supplied'. Langley expressed some doubts after direction-finding analysis showed that CASTOR was transmitting north-east of the team's estimated location. The CIA station in Saigon did not want suspicions raised, insisting that the teams were operating freely but that they were 'hot' due to the increased security measures of the opponent. Nonetheless, by September they concluded that ECHO was of 'dubious' loyalty. The team's signals operator was making mistakes, and the CIA station concluded that 'the radio operator had indeed consciously signalled having come under enemy control {more than half line not declassified}'.[56]

In a ploy designed to test their loyalty, the station suggested that ECHO escape with the aid of an aircraft. The team had reported having lost men to injuries. Eventually, the team was categorised as 'almost as "hot" as CASTOR'. By August, Langley had to admit: 'In all probability ECHO is compromised. DIDO's status is doubtful because of [the team's] complete silence.'

CASTOR was still considered a free team; it was to be informed that it would receive supplies shortly. The Saigon station informed Langley that CASTOR could not provide intelligence while trying to evade the DRV security services. In August, DIDO communicated with the centre but no important intelligence was divulged. The resupply by air was authorised for CASTOR and DIDO. Field officers argued that DIDO's second and third transmissions had provided a 'reasonable explanation' after six weeks of silence. Eventually, the teams were not resupplied for an unstated reason (perhaps poor weather conditions, transport aircraft mechanical problems or communication difficulties).[57]

Referring to CASTOR, ECHO, DIDO and a secret agent operating alone who had reported the recruitment of informants, Langley concluded: 'Lacking firm evidence to the contrary, all four teams appear to be free of DRV control.'[58] In a clear text message from 7 September 1961 ECHO informed the centre that it was 'already arrested'; it repeated the same message next day. But a secret agent codenamed ARES was deemed still operational. He reported that the authorities had discovered his skiff. The station assumed that ARES and his relatives (whom he had approached) were 'hot' under close watch by counterintelligence and in danger of being arrested.[59] The surviving crew of the transport to supply CASTOR were put on trial in Hanoi in November 1961; they had crash-landed on 1 July. They admitted supplying a guerrilla force. It was natural to assume that they had revealed CASTOR to their interrogators. But the station and Langley still believed that CASTOR was free and should be resupplied. Hanoi revealed the capture of ECHO. The tribes were blamed for siding with the enemy. The station optimistically remarked that the secret operations were 'exactly the type [of] harassment' which compelled the DRV security services 'to dissipate its assets on [its] own internal security in remote areas [of North Vietnam] and thus decrease its subversive efforts in South Vietnam'.[60] (But it was the NLF guerrillas who were causing mayhem in the south, not the DRV security services.) Radio broadcasts in Hanoi that demanded vigilance from the population were deemed a nervous reaction to the secret missions. In fact, all communist states wanted their population to be devoted to internal security at all times.

Other commando teams were inserted by fishing junks. In December 1961, the station informed Langley: 'We certainly include OB [Order of Battle intelligence] in specific missions but ... have emphasized potential resistance, contacts with families to build up intel assets, examination of potential harassment targets such as roads, reports of political controls, attitude of population, etc.'[61] This was at least what the White House wanted to read. A team codenamed EUROPA was assigned to create a network of friends in North Vietnam and assess their fighting potential. The station kept aspirations under check: 'We cannot make [a] passionate plea for tremendous strategic potential [in the] EUROPA area ... we can for our presently projected program of one team per month to give us general geographic coverage of North Vietnam.'[62]

In January 1962, DIDO informed the station that it was signalling 'under duress'.[63] On 11 January, Langley dismissed EUROPA's value. On 12 March, EUROPA communicated with the station, reassuring it that it was operational. Transmissions continued. In June the station sent this message to Langley: 'No reason to believe team doubled.'[64] There was an attempt to resupply CASTOR by air. The CIA was intercepting the North Vietnamese communications; there was no sign of alert. But the South Vietnamese DC-4 carrying the supplies crashed due to bad weather. The Americans still believed that CASTOR was still working against the DRV. It was decided that the team codenamed TOURBILLON should join CASTOR and that both should focus more on sabotage.[65]

On 12 March, the ATLAS team landed in Laos close to the border with South DRV. They were discovered and arrested on 5 April. The CIA learned of the failed mission only when the two survivors stood a public trial. The teams DIDO and ECHO transmitted 'repeated danger and/or duress signals'. By early April 1962, the station concluded that both teams had been captured and possibly turned.[66] Another team codenamed REMUS, comprising six Black Thai tribesmen, entered the game on 16 April 1962. It landed in Laos about 15 km north-west of Dien Bien Phu.[67]

McNamara and the Commander-in-Chief of Pacific Command (CINCPAC), Admiral Harry Felt, reached Saigon in May 1962. McNamara put more pressure on the station to increase black entry operations. Colby argued that the missions should remain more intelligence-oriented, telling both that 15 more teams were to be dispatched by mid-summer. McNamara sought for the operations to be undertaken by the Pentagon; he referred cryptically to 'possible larger efforts of [a] military nature'.[68] Meanwhile, the station and the PSO organised the dispatch by parachute of a new team of Hmongs into North Vietnam near the border with Laos; the mission was also to persuade their tribesmen to side with the team against the communist regime.

On 17 May, TOURBILLON, manned with seven commandos, was parachuted into the drop zone arranged with the CASTOR team. The station was unaware that PASF militia lay in wait to apprehend the commandos. However, unexpectedly strong winds swept the paratroopers to other landing locations. Still, within two days TOURBILLON was under DRV control.[69] After 11 days the captured TOURBILLON signals operator transmitted to the centre. Despite the delay, the station assumed that the team was operating freely. The operator claimed that the leader of CASTOR had welcomed them but that an accident cost the life of one man. By late June, the station believed that TOURBILLON was in reconnaissance for operational targets mission.

On 20 May, a five-man commando team (of Hmong and Red Thai) codenamed EROS landed in Thanh Hoa province, east of the Laotian border. The operational plan included its contact with local tribes. Eventually, villagers found abandoned cans of foreign food and reported it to the DRV authorities; the militias and army units started searching. On 20 June, EROS transmitted that its pursuers were close, and that it did not have food and supplies. The station promised supplies, but no drop was made due to bad weather. EROS desperately searched for food while evading the militias. On 2 August, villagers noticed the presence of the team. Again EROS was on the run, transmitting its status. Then silence followed. The station did not know that on 29 September, the PASF killed a commando and arrested another one. Three fled to Laos and joined some hunters, only to be turned over to the PASF.[70]

The White House insisted on more secret operations, and maritime raids were organised. Eighteen South Vietnamese undertook an underwater demolitions course. The station planned an attack against the DRV naval base at Quang Khe, where Swatow-class gunboats were stationed. The US Navy obliged the CIA by dispatching the USS *Catfish*, an old submarine which guarded the gunboats. On 30 June 1962, operation Vulcan commenced. A junk transported four frogmen armed with limpet mines to the mouth of the Gianh River. At least one explosion was reported; a frogman was killed, but the target gunboat did not sink. The junk drew fire from gunboats and sunk – its crew was taken prisoner. Only one frogman survived the raid and returned. The station informed Langley: 'Mission successful, price heavy.'[71]

Nominally, 28 teams were operating in the DRV. The chief of the External Operations Section tried to warn the decision makers to keep their expectations reasonable: 'The possibilities of any large diversion from the DRV effort against South Vietnam are remote. Our operations are at too small a scale and initiated at too late a date to seriously affect DRV aggression against the South.'[72] The Department of State, especially Ambassador Leonard Unger in Vientiane, insisted that the 1962 Geneva Agreements on Laos should be respected and thus that the agency should not deploy teams, supply them or authorise them to go into Laos. TOURBILLON was deemed still active and was ordered not to go to Laos. On 23 August, Lieutenant General Marshall Carter, the acting CIA director, relayed a message from the president to Deputy Director for Plans Thomas Karamessines, which said that the 'highest levels in the Government' authorised escalation of operation against the DRV. There was still no authorisation to go into Laos.[73] Greek-American Karamessines had a paramilitary background; he was an OSS veteran who in the past had served in Greece, and had advised the Greek government to initiate plans against the communist guerrillas during the civil war.

Keen to show that it responded to White House directions, the CIA station in Saigon proposed a sabotage campaign against installations and communication infrastructure. The teams codenamed BOUVIER and JASON would be dispatched to organise 'a large-scale guerrilla force' among the tribes, launch a propaganda campaign with leaflets, and sabotage and ambush enemy forces.[74] CASTOR was still deemed operational. It was a bad time in an intelligence officer's career to remind the decision makers Rusk and McNamara, who were always keen for secret action, that the DRV was not like occupied Europe, where the OSS and SOE agents had been supported by local resistance movements. In North Vietnam the population cooperated with the authorities out of fear, and informed them of suspicious people in their communities.[75]

With reference to Laos, Carter wanted to outmanoeuvre the operations restrictions, but the White House wanted no 'provocative acts'. The station in Saigon intended for the return of DIDO, CASTOR and EROS. CASTOR transmitted excuses not to abide by the order to withdraw, even claiming that it had no knowledge of the border areas with Laos.[76] None of the three secret agents who had landed in May and June contacted the centre. Nonetheless, the station assumed that it was 'premature to conclude' that they were under the control of the enemy. One of the secret agents had sent 44 messages; but he did not employ the prescribed safety signal. In any case, no one 'considered [this] an indication that he has fallen under enemy control'. The station assumed that TOURBILLON and EUROPA continued to operate. TOUR-BILLON transmitted that it destroyed a bridge on 29 July and wanted more supplies. EUROPA also sought supplies and once they were dropped by parachute, confirmed that it had taken possession of them. It was assumed that CASTOR was also operating against the enemy. By the fall of 1962, it was concluded that DIDO and EROS were transmitting under enemy directions.[77]

A team codenamed TARZAN was dispatched in early January 1963 to check whether Hanoi was respecting the Geneva Agreements on the neutrality of Laos. The transmissions of the team had procedural errors, but the operators gave the correct answer when challenged.[78] Langley worried about the radio direction-finding analysis of the transmissions of the secret missions; they all appeared far from the locations they reported they were operating. The station in Saigon was confident that standard security procedures in addition to radio direction-finding analysis seemed to confirm the loyalty of the teams; some argued that an error of just a few miles in triangulation could give the false impression of the team being under enemy control.[79]

Myers, who headed the Far East Division's North Vietnam Task Force, conferred once more with Colby; he argued that the programme should be discontinued because it did not contribute anything meaningful. However, Colby insisted on the value of the black entry operations. On 13 April 1963, the team codenamed PEGASUS (six ethnic Tho agents) was sent to attack the railway line approximately 75 km north-east of Hanoi. Direction-finding analysis of TOUR-BILLON's transmissions showed that the team was now near Canton in south-east China.[80]

In early August 1963, as the internal crisis in South Vietnam escalated and the Kennedy administration examined the possibility of a coup against Diem (we will explore this in more depth in Chapter 7), Colby admitted to Karamessines: 'No intelligence of value has been, nor ... is likely to be, obtained from such operations. ... [We] have never been, nor in a cold war situation are we likely to be, able to conduct small team operations on a wide enough scale for cumulative results.'[81] The head of the Far East Division began arguing for a change of gears that would see the team embarking on psychological operations that could prove more effective against the communist regime. Nonetheless, the black entry programme was not suspended; Colby was about to train and dispatch 46 teams.[82]

In July 1963, a public trial of the arrested team PEGASUS (landed in mid-April) in Hanoi confirmed the failure of their mission. On 14 May, the team JASON had reached North Vietnam. No transmission was received from it. On 29 May, Hanoi announced the capture of PEGASUS and the SEPES-sponsored team LYRE. By mid-June, seven teams were parachuted into the DRV. Just ten days after landing, the team codenamed BELL made radio contact; in reality, however, its members had been arrested within three days of landing, and their transmission was under the direction of their captors. Resupplying for CASTOR, EUROPA and TOURBILLON was organized – the station assumed that they were still operating.[83]

In May 1963, the psychological warfare strategy against Hanoi commenced. Herbert Weisshart, a covert political action specialist, was assigned to the Saigon station to organise a virtual resistance movement, the Sacred Sword of the Patriots League (SSPL). On 11 August, team EASY landed in North Vietnam near the border with Laos, and contacted the centre. On 4 September team SWAN reached Can Bang in North DRV, only to be arrested on the spot; no transmission of the team was reported. Teams BULL and RUBY were also arrested on arrival in October and December 1963.[84]

At a conference in Honolulu, Colby argued that the black entry programme had not produced results: the majority of the teams were under arrest and enemy control; thus it was better to concentrate on psychological warfare, 'infiltrating ideas, rather than agents and explosives'.[85]

McNamara would not listen and assigned the MACV responsibility for black entry operations under Operational Plan (Oplan) 34A; Operation Switchback was the process through which the Pentagon took over the CIA's operations. The military inherited a list of teams, wrongly assumed operational within the DRV. On 1 February 1964, the management of the black entry operations and irregular warfare passed to the Department of Defense; the MACV established the Military Assistance Command Special Operations Group (MACSOG).[86] McNamara insisted on a 'critical mass' to undertake covert operations. Eventually, President Johnson authorised the escalation of the secret war; he signed National Security Action Memorandum 273 on 26 November 1963.[87]

Studying the story of the black entry operations, we conclude that the Saigon station and Langley were put under serious and continuing pressure from the White House (under Kennedy) and from the Pentagon to show 'results' in missions that were simply impossible. Throughout the Vietnam War, the CIA was tasked with secret operations in the DRV, the Strategic Hamlet programme (which also entailed land reform and in effect public administration functions) as well as battle damage assessments and later the Phoenix programme. In the early 1960s, decision makers did not understand 'no, it won't work' as an answer from an intelligence expert. Only in the early 1970s did Helms manage to convince Secretary of State Kissinger (who wanted operations against Hanoi) that the black entry missions from Laos did not produce anything and should cease.[88] By that time the decision makers had become pessimistic about the course that the war was taking, and thus the intelligence experts could voice their disagreements about the feasibility of proposed operations (and eventually avert any new failures of 'missions impossible').

In the early 1960s, it was difficult for Colby and his peers (belonging to the 'can-do' culture of the OSS and early CIA) to understand that although the jungle looked impassable from above, inside it was a human ecosystem with thousands of villages. Thus peasants and tribes who had lived there for centuries were able to report the movements of intruders and to confront them. The CIA-backed paramilitary teams could not sustain themselves; neither by operating with some of their relatives and their communities, nor by establishing their own safe havens. The DRV security services and militias were operating in their environment. The French attempted to employ the tribes against the PAVN and launched many paratrooper missions into the jungle, but eventually lost and withdrew. First the CIA and then the Pentagon followed the same operational concept. Nonetheless, once the White House had insisted that it was interested in something, the bureaucrats had to protect themselves from critics and do what they were asked – no matter how impossible it sounded.

CHAPTER 7

THE SPY AND THE COUP

The 1963 coup and the subsequent escalating military commitment of the United States to support the military rulers of South Vietnam have been the subjects of numerous accounts. They are considered yet another 'turning point' in the wars for Vietnam. This chapter seeks to uncover the role of the 'tip of the spear' of the CIA, Lucien Conein (codename Black Luigi), who was the sole liaison to the group of generals who aimed to topple President Diem. Conein's exploits in Hanoi and Saigon have been presented in the previous chapters. To the Saigon community of journalists he was a 'celebrity' – a known spy. Stories of his alleged secret missions spread among his peers. All assumed that the two fingers he had lost were a painful reminder of a dangerous secret episode in his career. In fact, repairing a car fan had cost him his two fingers.[1] For Colby, at that time the Far East Division head at CIA headquarters in Langley, 'Conein's effectiveness rested on friendships with the Vietnamese that in several cases dated back to his service as an OSS officer in Vietnam in 1945. He was less strong on political substance, and this limited his role essentially to that of the intermediary.'[2]

For years, Diem was at best indifferent towards the misery of the non-Catholic population in the rural areas despite the representations and advice provided by the US embassy, the MAAG, and the CIA station. In Hue on 8 May 1963, a Buddhist demonstration celebrating Buddha's 2,527th birthday turned into a bloodbath; the police and militias loyal to Nhu Diem's brother, one of the first top-secret CIA contacts since the mid-1950s, suppressed the march with extreme violence. Diem's handling of Buddhists was motivated by religious fanaticism. Surprised, CIA station officers contacted Buddhist leader Tri Quang who was described as 'self-confident, dominating, committed, and slippery, but able to make a joke and take one at his own expense'.[3] Meanwhile the deputy chief of station David Smith (one of Lansdale's lieutenants back in the 1950s) believed, without hard intelligence, the rumour that Diem's brother Nhu was thinking about negotiating with the DRV.[4] In May the Buddhists organised more demonstrations in Saigon. One of the most dramatic photos of the 1960s was taken during a demonstration on 11 June when a monk set himself on fire protesting the stance of the regime.

For years the State Department and the CIA had warned that Diem had no respect for human rights, but no one had anticipated this. Kennedy felt he had to address the issue of repression immediately. The United States considered South Vietnam an ally, granting its regime considerable military and economic aid. Despite US recommendations to initiate reforms, the Ngo brothers showed that they simply did not care. The demonstrations grew larger and more violent; Diem declared martial law. On 21 August, Diem's brother Nhu ordered his loyalists (seeking to embarrass the military, he employed loyalists in ARVN uniforms) to assault the largest Buddhist pagodas in South Vietnam. Hundreds of Buddhists were killed, and 1,400 arrested. The statue of the Buddha in the Tu Dam pagoda in Hue was destroyed with explosives.

Two monks from the Xa Loi pagoda escaped into a USAID building in Saigon. Regime loyalists demanded that the Americans hand over the Buddhists. The building was under diplomatic immunity. Foreign Minister Mau talked with the US officials, demanding that they surrender the monks. William Trueheart, Ambassador Nolting's deputy (the ambassador had returned home), stood his ground and asked for orders from Washington. Eventually, he received directions not to put the monks in harm's way and to offer sanctuary – other monks had also found their way to the embassy. Henry Cabot Lodge, the new ambassador, arrived on 22 August while the United States denounced the pagoda raids as a 'direct violation by the Vietnamese government of assurances that it was pursuing a policy of reconciliation with the Buddhists'. The ambassador started lobbying among US government echelons for the need to oust Diem and Nhu because they had caused chaos, something detrimental to the war effort against the Viet Cong.[5]

Pham Xuan An, Hanoi's mole, had been covering the Buddhist protests posing as a journalist. Later he claimed that 'before they burned themselves, the monks would ring me and give me the story first; I knew that someone was going to die. If I reported it to the police, a life would be saved, but this was against the rules. The source had given me the story on condition that I shouldn't reveal it before it happened. These are the ethics of the press. You have to observe them, no matter how tough it may be.'[6]

In early June, the CIA station reported 'indications' that a coup was in the making. On 28 June, the exiled Tran Kim Tuyen, the former head of SEPES, met with a former deputy chief of the CIA station. Tuyen was critical of the regime but said that he did not want to topple it. Nonetheless, other secret sources claimed on that same day that he was involved in coup preparations.[7] There was the Hanoi mole in Tuyen's group playing a leading role: Colonel Pham Ngoc Thao. As the head of a section of the Strategic Hamlet programme, he was successful in fomenting protest among the population by mismanaging the whole scheme. Tuyen's group felt sidelined by Nhu's Can Lao secret party cadre. Thao and Colonel Do Mau, the head of the Military Security Service (MSS), considered the possibility of a coup on 15 July. Conein was informed of this and discouraged Thao's superior officer, General Khiem, who was also thinking of a coup. Tuyen's group consisted of middle-level officers, i.e. captains, majors and colonels. Thao and Mau started planning a coup on 24 October.

Surprisingly, the key plotting generals had no troops to command; consequently, they always felt insecure and sought secret negotiations and reassurances from each other as well as from the United States. Major General Minh ('the Big Minh') was appointed 'Presidential Military Adviser', commanding only three phones as he was fond of saying. Minh was born into a wealthy landowning family. On the eve of World War II, he joined the colonial army and was one of only 50 Vietnamese to be commissioned after graduating from the École Militaire in France. During the 1940s, Imperial Japan invaded Indochina and seized control from France. He was captured and tortured by the Japanese during the occupation. He only had one tooth left in his mouth. During the First Indochina War, he fought with the colonial troops. In 1954, he was arrested by the PAVN but managed to escape by strangling a guard.

During the battle against the Binh Xuyen in 1955, he sided with Diem. Later he attended the Command and General Staff School at Fort Leavenworth in Kansas.

General Don also had no troops because Diem did not trust him. General Nguyen Khanh commanded the 2nd Corps in the Central Highlands; Colonel Nguyen Van Thieu commanded the 5th Division close to Saigon. General Ton That Dinh was approached by the plotters because he commanded the 3rd Corps, deployed around Saigon. He had converted to Catholicism and commanded the military wing of the Cao Lao. The others believed that Diem favoured him. In reality, he had been humiliated in front of many officials by the president when he had wrongly assumed that he would be appointed minister of the interior. The CIA deemed him a 'basic opportunist'.[8]

Diem allowed many high-ranking officers to attend the 4 July reception at the US embassy. Conein was there and conferred with them. Afterwards, they opted to go to a hotel for yet another drink. They trusted Conein. General Don confided that they were planning to oust Diem; Conein lost no time and reported everything to station chief John Richardson and Ambassador Lodge, who directed him to continue keeping track of the military's intentions. The station had realised that the general and the Tuyen group were just two of the ostensibly many groups that were preparing a coup. Can, Colby, now head of the Far East Division at Langley, was against support for Nhu any longer; he hoped that the implementation of the Strategic Hamlet programme would gain the United States some time until a 'Vietnamese Nasser' deposed Diem.[9]

On 23 August, General Don told Conein that he did not know anything about the raids in the pagodas and that everything was done on Nhu's orders. Another top source was Nguyen Dinh Thuan, a high-ranking presidential palace official who told Rufus Phillips (at that time director of USOM's Rural Affairs Division – he had worked with Conein in operations under Lansdale back in the 1950s) that Nhu had ordered the raids, resorting to the martial law provisions. Ahern wrote that 'the Station was as much in the dark as the dissident generals claimed to have been and got no warning regarding the raids'. Richardson was very angry about the treatment of the Buddhists. He feared the impact of any leak that the CIA was in official contact with the generals. Colby proposed to Diem that he 'retire' to Dalat.

But witnessing the growing hatred, Richardson held no illusions, remarking perceptively that 'the Ngo family will be lucky to get out of the country alive' after a coup.[10]

In response to Nhu's attitude and actions, key US decision makers Undersecretary George Ball (who signed on the final page), Averell Harriman at the State Department, Michael Forrestal (an NSC staffer for South East Asia) and Assistant Secretary of State for Far Eastern Affairs Roger A. Hilsman worked on new directions for the ambassador, in case Diem did not replace Nhu. '[W]e must face the possibility that Diem himself cannot be preserved ... [and] tell appropriate military commanders we will give them direct support in any interim period of breakdown [of] central government mechanism.'[11] In his turn, Lansdale proposed that Nhu be given an honorary professorship at Harvard ('Kick him upstairs. Tell him he is an intellectual. Listen to him and give him a job there'), only to receive the angry reply from Harvard economist and Kennedy's ambassador to India, John Galbraith: 'We don't do that at Harvard.'[12]

Ambassador Lodge and his 'country team' (the embassy, the CIA station and the MAAG) were advised to 'urgently examine all possible alternative leadership and make detailed plans as to how we might bring about Diem's replacement if this should become necessary'. There would be no specific instructions, 'but you will also know we will back you to the hilt on actions you take to achieve our objectives'.[13] Kennedy did not object to the cable to the ambassador; Michael Forrestal had already reported to him that officials were drafting the message and asked the president whether he wanted it sent. At an NSC meeting on 26 August 1963 Hilsman stated: 'We are all in agreement that Nhu must go.' 'We just want to be sure' that the coup will succeed, Kennedy was heard to say.[14]

Station chief Richardson admitted to Langley that 'he could not discuss the mechanics of a coup against Diem without conferring with the generals', and thus agreed to a CIA liaison with the plotters. Colby's answer showed that he wanted more: '[The] US must win this affair if it goes into it, and it has already decided to do just that.... In this connection, we are confident you will keep [your] eye on this main ball rather than window dressing of civilian leadership.'[15]

Meanwhile, General Khanh met with Al Spera and another CIA intelligence officer, voicing his discontent with the regime and warning that the president might work out an agreement with North Vietnam. Diem was not willing to find common ground with the Buddhists. Khanh asked for US support in such an event because he and his comrades would turn against the government. The general wanted to know the US stance in advance. Spera asked him about the new government post-coup, only to be surprised by Khanh's response: the military was interested only in fighting the Viet Cong thus 'it was up to the United States to take care of the political part'.[16]

This piece of intelligence was crucial for the United States to realise the increasing burden of its responsibility in South Vietnam after a successful coup. Decision makers in Washington and intelligence officers in Saigon focused only on the generals' plots and their potential for seizing power. Conein spoke with General Khiem, who feared that Nhu had spies among General Don's staff and did not want the general to be briefed by Conein on security grounds. Khiem would arrange a meeting between Conein and Major General Minh. Nonetheless, General Khanh sounded unsure; in his opinion the plotters were not yet ready – they should wait for the evidence of Nhu-DRV contact to emerge.[17]

On 27 August 1963, Conein met with General Khiem. He was informed of the major players in the coup; among them there were many generals, as well as Vice President Nguyen Ngoc Tho. Khiem assured him that a coup would take place within a month; he expressed doubt about the competency of the security arrangements for the contacts between the CIA and the generals. The authority of Conein and Spera to negotiate with the plotters was questioned, and he demanded confirmation that the United States would support them. General Minh insisted that the United States would not hesitate to confront Diem. Colby informed Kennedy and his national security team of all this. The president could not make up his mind, supposing that a coup could not succeed. McNamara and Nolting boosted Kennedy's uncertainty. (The ambassador had met the flamboyant Conein once in Saigon. During a roof garden party, Conein, in order to get a man's attention in the street, had thrown down a flowerpot. Nolting was passing below and was lucky not to have been hit.)[18] The president concluded that 'the generals interested in the coup were not good enough to bring it about', but Kennedy did not retract the 24 August guidance to Lodge.[19]

On 28 August, Richardson reported from Saigon that the confrontation was a matter of time and that 'if the Ngo family wins now, they and Vietnam will stagger on to final defeat at the hands of their own people and the Viet Cong'.[20] That same day, in Washington National Security Adviser McGeorge Bundy took notes during a National Security Council Meeting. The handwritten notes are not always legible and reflect statements and ideas aired – not decisions taken. Among other things, McNamara wondered 'how to make the thing [i.e. the coup] work'. Undersecretary of State George Ball's advice was to 'let it go as it is'. Bundy noted: '[The] worst thing we can do is leave it [the political situation in Saigon] that way.' He also wrote a 'Principle of Action ... we should never encourage them [the South Vietnamese generals] and then let it fail.'[21] Ball stated: 'We must decide now to go through to a successful overthrow of Diem.' Harriman concurred.

Kennedy asked what could be done to boost the generals' forces. Harriman insisted: 'We have lost Vietnam if the coup fails. . . . We have lost the fight in Vietnam and must withdraw if a coup does not take place.'[22] The president remarked: 'We should decide what we can do here or suggest things that can be done in the field which would maximize the chances of the rebel generals. We should ask Ambassador Lodge and General Harkins how we can build up military forces which would carry out a coup. At present, it does not look as if the coup forces could defeat Diem ... the Defense Department [is to] come up with ways of building up the anti-Diem forces in Saigon.'[23] This was a direct order to McNamara. The next day Kennedy admitted that Congress might get 'mad' at him for backing conspiring generals, but said that it would 'be madder if Vietnam goes down the drain'. Kennedy's assessment was severe: 'We're up to our hips in mud out there.'[24]

Back in Saigon, Conein and Spera met with General Khiem, who did not disclose the plans for the coup. Both intelligence officers feared being implicated in a provocation by the regime, but as the discussion evolved they concluded that the generals feared the same: the United States working with Diem against them. When they asked about forming a civilian government after the coup, Khiem gave the troubling answer that the 'US [was] to think what type political leadership should follow'.[25]

Lodge quarrelled with Richardson after realising that Conein and Spera were ordered not to reveal their cards in their talks with the generals. Bui Diem of the Dai Viet party and Brigadier General Le Van Kim, both of who trusted Phillips, aired their views: the generals were still feeling insecure and wanted reassurance that whatever Conein and Spera were telling them came from the ambassador. Phillips consulted with Lodge and got the confirmation Kim wanted. Then he asked Conein to meet with General Khiem 'to discuss the mechanics' of the coup. Lodge even authorised the Station to 'volunteer' in tactical planning.[26]

Nonetheless, fear and panic loomed. A secret source of the station claimed that Nhu was about to arrest the generals, whom he suspected of plotting against him. It was the evening of 30 August. The station officers scrambled to warn the generals. A MAAG officer would be the secret liaison. He was working alongside an ARVN major who was an assistant to General Minh. The MAAG officer did not find the major at his home and called General Kim. Ultimately, Diem and Nhu did not go after their generals. Presumably, it was an erroneous report. Lodge wanted action, but the generals abstained, trying to hide their panic. On 30 August, Khiem informed Lodge via an aide that he was 'too busy' to meet with him. General Harkins met with General Khiem on 31 August only to be informed that the generals did not have the required forces at their disposal and that, what was more, they 'did not feel ready'.[27] That same day, Kim informed Phillips that Nhu knew of the plot and had alerted his special forces. Nonetheless, he claimed that the preparations would continue and blamed the United States for having done nothing to show that it wanted Nhu ousted. Kim questioned Khiem's authority as a spokesman of the plotters. In any case, Richardson informed Langley: 'This particular coup is finished. . . . We did our best and got licked.'[28] Ambassador Lodge instructed the CIA station not to encourage future coup plans directly. The CIA officers in their new discussions with the generals would show only 'an open-minded or sympathetic interest'.[29]

Nhu started publically attacking the agency during early September. The English-language *Times of Vietnam*, Nhu's propaganda outlet, printed an article titled 'CIA Financing Planned Coup d'Etat'. He played a double game when he met with the ambassador, reassuring him that he would withdraw from public life and that the Buddhists would be respected. Nonetheless he mentioned the need for the withdrawal of 'certain US agents' from Vietnam.[30]

Once again a secret source sounded the alarm. On 5 September, the source reported that he had talked with Tran Van Khiem, the brother of Nhu's wife. Allegedly, Khiem showed the source a list of Americans to be assassinated, with Richardson as his top priority. Conein was also included. Khiem must have gotten wind of this and rushed to call Richardson on the phone. He arranged a meeting, trying to reassure him that no assassination list existed and that both were targets just of rumours.[31]

On 4 September, Conein met with Brigadier General Dinh, the military governor of Saigon, who commanded troops vital for the success of a coup. The intelligence officer described him as exultant and ranting. His nervous bodyguards, who carried submachine guns, suspected even Conein. Dinh boasted that at the 'crucial hour' he would become the 'saviour' who would deliver his country from the Viet Cong; he was the one who 'could kill or kidnap anyone in Saigon, including – should there be a move to accommodate the Communists – Diem himself.'[32] He insisted that communist forces were deployed across the capital, even going so far as to claim that John Mecklin, the head of the USIS, was a communist. Dinh asked Conein directly whether he had been working against him, only to be reassured of the agent's good faith. The general's behaviour had no logic. He then called Conein's wife on the phone, congratulating her for having the 'privilege' of talking to him, the military governor. She was more than surprised when an aide of the brigadier later presented her with flowers sent by him. For Conein, who had known Dinh for years, the general was yet another person who appeared determined to turn against Diem.[33]

In the meantime, Al Spera informed the station that General Khiem was afraid that Nhu would enter into negotiations with Hanoi. It should be noted that the NSA never had signals intelligence revealing that Nhu had secretly contacted the DRV.[34] Khiem claimed that General Dinh had told Nhu that a US official offered him 20m piasters to organise a coup. Conein reported that the generals did not know each other's initiatives and plans. Having heard the rumours that he was willing to negotiate with the DRV, Nhu entertained the angst of his generals and some US embassy officials in an interview with journalist Joseph Alsop.[35]

Lodge asked Rusk to tell Kennedy that Major General Edward Lansdale should be sent immediately 'to take charge, under my supervision, of all US relationships with a change of government here'. The ambassador wanted to oust Richardson because he considered him an impediment to his pro-coup policy. The ambassador's request shows that he was missing something vital; Lansdale had always been pro-Diem. Kennedy had already discussed with Lansdale the possibility of an assignment in Saigon that would entail opposing Diem. The major general voiced his disagreement, only for McNamara to become furious with him for disobeying a direct order from the president.[36]

CIA director McCone did not want to hear anything about Lansdale and blocked his assignment to Saigon. According to the director: 'It was not merely Agency experience with Lansdale that made him unacceptable; rather, Lansdale's close association with Diem would make his return to Saigon positively detrimental to US interests unless the object were to seek an understanding with Diem and Nhu using Lansdale as a "friend in court".'[37] The director hoped to become a chief foreign policy adviser to the president. He wanted the agency to focus on intelligence gathering and to abandon any involvement in black operations, including assassinations.[38]

In Saigon the web of intrigue, lies and suspicion was growing, while in Washington Kennedy and his national security team were not sure that the coup was the right option. On 26 September 1963, the chief of the Special Police reported to Diem that he was the target of an assassination plot instigated by the CIA which had at its disposal 'about fifty sabotage and assassination experts [who] had been in Saigon for over three months'. A secret source informed the station of the Special Police chief's claims.[39]

Kennedy had sent General Victor Krulak and Joseph Mendenhall, a senior State Department official, to Saigon. In early September, they returned with their assessments. Krulak insisted that a 'shooting war is still going ahead at an impressive pace'; while Mendenhall talked about the 'breakdown of the civilian government in Saigon' and argued that 'Nhu must go if the war is to be won.' At the meeting Kennedy, frustrated, looked at them both, asking sarcastically: 'Did you two gentlemen visit the same country?'[40] The president finally dispatched McNamara and General Taylor, accompanied by Colby, on a hasty fact-finding visit to Saigon; it was yet another attempt to persuade Diem to break with Nhu.[41]

Conein met General Don at the airport on 2 October (some accounts claim that this was an accidental meeting). The general asked Conein to visit him at Nha Trang. Conein had authorisation to go. Don told him that the generals had prepared a coup, and that General Minh was willing to share the details with Conein; again the generals were asking for assurance of US backing once they took up arms against the regime. On 5 October, Conein met with Minh, who once again wanted to know about US policy in advance. He blamed Diem for leaning towards the communists. In fact, the generals still feared the contingency of the United States turning against them – they wanted reassurances, and for the military and economic aid to continue. Conein (who was warned by Lodge not to be taken in) said that he would relate all their concerns to the station and to the ambassador.

Conein was now the sole liaison between the ever-suspicious plotters and the embassy, the CIA station and the White House. Minh had told him that one of his options was to kill Nhu and Can but not Diem.[42] Kennedy was seriously considering withdrawing the US military personnel from South Vietnam; by 1963 they had reached more than 16,000 in number. He hoped that he could implement his policy if re-elected in 1964; he also hoped that the ARVN could counter the Viet Cong. Nonetheless, in a 5 October meeting he accepted his brother's position not to call for the withdrawal of 1,000 personnel in December to signal the establishment of the US military presence.[43]

Lodge was extremely cautious when he handed Conein his instructions. The intelligence officer would later explain: '[Lodge] would fold a piece of paper and what pertained to you for instructions he would let you read that, and that alone so that you didn't know who was sending it or where it came from. Afterward, he would remark, "Those are the instructions. Do you understand them?" "Yes, sir." "All right, go carry them out."'[44]

Eventually, Lodge had Richardson removed from Saigon. He left on 5 October. The acting chief of station would be David Smith, who on 5 October, told the ambassador that 'we do not set ourselves irrevocably against the assassination plot [against Diem and Nhu], since the other two alternatives mean either a bloodbath in Saigon or a protracted struggle which could rip the Army and the country asunder'.[45] On being informed of these remarks, McCone angrily ordered Smith to tell the ambassador that 'assassination discussions need more careful handling'. He said that the 'best line is no line ... [The White House must have] no responsibility for [the] actions of any of [the] various contending Vietnamese groups ... cannot be in [the] position of stimulating, approving or supporting assassination, but on [the] other hand, we are in no way responsible for stopping every such threat of which we might receive even partial knowledge. We certainly would not favor [the] assassination of Diem ... taking [a] position on this matter opens [the] door too easily for probes of our position. [The White House is] naturally interested in intelligence on any such plan [but it] cannot be in [the] position [of] actively condoning such [a] course of action and thereby engaging our responsibility therefore.'[46]

Conein was kept in the dark. He was informed of McCone's cable only on the eve of the coup. Minh and the generals had the signals they wanted: no US intervention to save Diem; besides the United States had cut aid to the regime – another signal of disfavour.[47] On 8 October, at a meeting with his national security team, Kennedy asked about Conein. The transcript reads as follows:

McNamara: Conein is the man who is the contact with General Minh.

Kennedy: What's his status?

McNamara: He's a former colonel in one of the military services. . . . He's under contract to CIA.

Kennedy: What does he do?

Colby: He's in the MACV, Sir. That's his cover.

Kennedy: He's an American?

McCone: Yes, he's American. He's one of our agents, under cover.

McNamara: He's a colorful figure. He's a Lawrence of Arabia type. He's well known to all the reporters in Vietnam. He's well known to the Vietnamese government. And here he is contacting an individual that's known to be a dissident and a probable coup leader. It's open as though we were announcing it over the radio. To continue this kind of activity just strikes me as absurd.

[. . .]

McCone: Our preference would be to have Conein make only one contact, and then to establish at that time a completely new channel.

[. . .]

Colby: It might be harder for someone who's outside the country even to get anywhere near Minh without arousing more attention than a fellow who lives actually in the country. . . . The advantage of Conein is that he's been working with administrative superiors, working on strategic hamlets, and this and that and the other, and he has natural access to a lot of people.[48]

The next day Washington authorised the ambassador to inform the generals that the United States would not block their bid to seize power. Conein would ask for more details of their plans, but the official policy of the station was not to give opinion or advice thus not directly connecting the United States to the coup.[49]

Meanwhile, a rumour was spreading in Saigon that Nhu and his trusted Colonel Tung were planning for a 'student' demonstration to turn into a raid against the US embassy with the objective of assassinating Lodge and other officials. Lodge wrote to Secretary of State Rusk:

a. If I am assassinated in the way indicated in above reports, the deed will in effect have been done by the [Government of Vietnam], however much the attempt to disguise it, since they will have instigated the mob and will have denied us the police protection which they are totally capable of giving us in view of the very large police force in Saigon which is under their absolute control. This will, therefore, automatically constitute a rupture of diplomatic relations and means that present assumptions underlying US presence here would be false. This will have grave consequences for all Americans in Viet-Nam,

notably as regards evacuation, and there should be fresh
contingency planning to cover this situation.

b. If I am assassinated, a new situation would be created which
might give us a chance to move effectively for a change of
government using methods which would now be rejected by US
and world opinion, but which would then become acceptable ...
Nhu is apparently pleased with his raids on the Buddhist pagodas
last summer and is said to be annoyed with me for having advised
him to leave the country for a while. Also he is reported to be
smoking opium. For all these reasons my associates here, whose
experience antedates mine, consider assassination to be [a] real
possibility. Needless to say, this comes as no surprise, as I realized
the possibility of this when I accepted this post.[50]

McCone deemed Lodge's reaction 'hysterical'.[51] Without suspecting
anything, Nhu once again played the propaganda game, giving another
interview to the *Times of Vietnam*, published on 17 October, stating that
he knew of six CIA officers who conspired against the regime. Ahern
assumed that Nhu must have had some information about the general's
contacts with Conein.[52]

On 23 October, General Don called Conein and asked him to come to
the Joint General Staff headquarters building. He was angry at General
Harkins. He had told him not to proceed with the coup. Colonel
Nguyen Khuong, serving in Dan's staff, had disclosed to a US officer that
the date of the coup would be 'on or about' 27 October. Harkins was
informed of this and warned General Don that the war against the Viet
Cong could afford no distractions. Harkins told Lodge that he had told
Dan to focus on the military operations, not politics; Harkins assumed
that the United States was not in favour of a coup. The ambassador
insisted that according to his instructions from the 'highest levels', the
embassy and the station should not attempt to hinder Diem's and his
family's fall from power. [53]

Don told Conein that Diem was informed about Colonel Khuong's
claims of an upcoming coup; that was why the 5th and 7th Divisions,
crack troops for a coup, had received orders to continue operations
against the guerrillas – it was a way for these troops to remain occupied.
Again the general demanded reassurances from the United States

regarding the conspirators. Conein reported to the station that he had responded with the same lines: Washington 'would not thwart a change of government or deny economic and military assistance'; the new government had to win the people and pursue 'working relationships with the US'.[54] Conein was no pro-Diem American; he could have hinted at US support for a coup even with a nod. We ought to bear in mind, after all, that this was in a series of secret meetings with no note-takers. The discussion continued with Conein (intentionally) questioning the existence of coup plans. It was a ploy of his to test Don who keenly reassured him of contingency plans.[55] Meanwhile Langley advised caution, fearing a trap into which Conein and the station could be provoked by the regime.

Hastily, Harkins requested a meeting with Don at Saigon airport on 24 October at 6.30 a.m. Conein arranged the details. Harkins reassured Don that the United States would not block a change of government. Don wanted to speak to Lodge in person about the coup committee's plans, but no meeting took place. The Vietnamese general met with Conein at a dentist's office in downtown Saigon, telling him that due to security precautions decided by the coup committee, he could not disclose the 'political organisation plan'. He could, however, reveal to Lodge the political-military plans two days before the coup.

Conein offered bait, reminding Don that 'any US endorsement depended on a judgment of the generals' plans'. It was his ploy since no US government was willing to review coup plans (and the station was instructed not to appear in a counselling role, as we mentioned above) and pass judgment on the conspirators who desperately wanted to be taken seriously. By revealing their plans (and being reminded that they need to do so to get US support), Conein and the station were assessing their commitment and organisational capabilities to topple Diem. Don was on the defensive. He replied that the coup would take place 'no later than 2 November'.[56] Conein said that Washington would not condone assassinations. According to Conein, the general replied: 'All right, you don't like it. We won't talk about it anymore.'[57]

Don disclosed that the committee included generals Minh, Pham Xuan Chieu and Kim. Don assumed that the 3rd Corps commander General Dinh would either 'cooperate [with the plotters] or be crushed'. He claimed that the military would install a government of politicians; they would respect human rights, freeing political prisoners – something the Americans wanted to hear. Don warned Conein: the United States should not attempt to impede the coup like they had in 1960. Regarding Diem's future, the committee had decided that 'the entire Ngo family had to be eliminated from the political scene in Vietnam'.[58]

A CIA station secret source infiltrated another coup committee, the Tuyen group. One of the leaders was Pham Ngoc Thao, a Hanoi mole. The Tuyen group claimed that they would attack the president's residency once they had all the ammunition and transport required for the assault. A CIA officer talked to Thao, who said that no action would be taken for now.[59]

Kennedy and his national security team discussed Conein during their 25 October meeting. There was evident fear that the coup machinations, discovered by Diem, would link the plotters to the US government. McCone, as if preparing his audience to blame anything on Conein, now reported that the intelligence officer was 'perfectly overt. . . . He was not an undercover person at all.' McGeorge Bundy found a good opportunity to blame the CIA: 'What we've got to find is a man that really is regarded as highly professional by the agency . . . that also Lodge will take and use as his own. And that man doesn't exist.' McNanamara said: 'We're just like a bunch of amateurs . . . I hate to be associated with this effort, uh, dealing with Conein. He's an unstable person . . . We're dealing through a press-minded ambassador and an unstable, uh, uh, Frenchman.'[60]

Robert Kennedy conferred with the president, who said: 'They want to have a conversation with an American, uh, to understand what the American governmental policy will be'. The conversation continued:

Robert Kennedy: Somebody should really find out where it's going.

President: How they gonna find out unless they have a conversation?

Robert Kennedy: Well, somebody can have the conversation initially.

President: Well, then, he will be the representative of the American government.

Robert Kennedy: Well, I don't know that that's necessarily true. The coup plotters don't have to know where he's from or who he's from.

McGeorge Bundy: They really have to know if they're gonna tell him the coup plans.

Robert Kennedy: Well, I don't know. A person comes in and ... he's not seen around the embassy all the time.

[...]

McGeorge Bundy: But who do [the plotters] think they're talking to?

Robert Kennedy: Well, they just, they think they're talking to somebody that's, uh, probably somehow associated with the United States. But they're not sure. And they can't identify who it is, exactly.

President: I don't think we can set up any satisfactory contact other than Conein between now and November 2nd. There's this reservation about Lodge's conduct, but he's there.... We can't fire him.[61]

Ambassador Lodge informed the White House that the station's stance could be described as 'punctilious' with reference to his instructions. In any case, the ambassador wrote in his cable that Conein could not be replaced – especially not at that moment. The next day, on 25 October, in another message to Bundy, he discounted the possibility of the generals collaborating with Diem to expose the CIA and Washington. If there was a trap, he wrote, the CIA was 'perfectly prepared to have me disavow Conein at any time it may serve the national interest'.[62]

Langley had proposed an arrangement for Conein's meeting to be secretly taped. Smith was negative, fearing the tapes might be discovered by Diem's security services. Furthermore, the CIA Technical Services Division could not provide the operators with such a small device.[63] Lodge's cable led to another meeting. Kennedy met only with his brother Robert, McNamara, Bundy and McCone. The secretary of defense and the director of the CIA clashed over Conein's reports, questioning their accuracy. Again McCone voiced his doubts about the possibility that a coup would bring stability and (accurately) predicted that one coup would generate another, resulting in the chaos that would ensure a Viet Cong victory.[64]

Kennedy asked Bundy to draft a cable to the ambassador, as McCone put it, relating 'our concern over the situation ... [and] urging free and open talks with Diem.' Nonetheless, the outgoing cable read differently: Washington was worried about a failed coup which could expose its role. Thus, no plan with modest chances of success should be condoned by the embassy.[65]

Meanwhile, the station was unaware of Nhu's 'Operation Bravo'. Ahern remarked that 'as the Station later pieced it together', Nhu plotted, ordering Dinh to arrange an assault against the capital by loyalist policemen based in the nearby areas (phase Bravo I). The fake coup would take place on 1 November. Terrorist attacks against US installations and personnel would be organised. In phase Bravo II, troops loyal to the regime under the command of Nhu and Dinh would strike back, rushing the assault, proving that only the Diem regime could be trusted. Operation Bravo also included the assassination of the plotting generals Minh, Don and Kim.[66] (But Nhu did not know that the mole in his plan was Dinh himself, who warned the others.)

On 27 October, Lodge, accompanying Diem on a flight to Dalat, reached the Tan Son Nhut airport in Saigon. There he talked with General Don, confirming Conein's 'good faith' toward the plotters. The ambassador asked him about the date of the coup only to receive a negative reply; this was solely a Vietnamese issue. The next day, Don met with Conein at the same dentist as before. Don said that he believed in the ambassador's assurances and Conein's good faith but insisted that all talk of coup preparations and meetings should stop to preserve security. Conein – on his initiative – asked Don to give him the plans in time for the ambassador to review them before flying to Washington on 31 October. The general answered with an order-of-battle of his forces; the American would get a warning only four hours before the coup. Military aides would facilitate Conein's and Don's communications, ensuring the utmost secrecy. Yet 'nothing would happen in the next two days'.[67]

On 29 October, Colby briefed the president and his national security council on the order of battle of the generals and Diem's forces. Once he concluded that the forces were more or less equal, the option of the coup was questioned by McNamara, General Taylor, McCone and Robert Kennedy. The director of the CIA found yet another opportunity to warn that this coup would not be the only one to take place in South Vietnam.[68] General Taylor accepted that even a successful coup would have an impact on the current operations against the Viet Cong. Rusk and Harriman had doubts about the coup serving US interests. Kennedy now favoured discouraging the Vietnamese generals. But Lodge's cable was clear (and indirectly critical of the new president's stance): '[I] do not think we have the power to delay or discourage a coup.' Kennedy remarked on the 'nerve, if not his [the ambassador's] prudence'. Harkins was still against the coup, claiming that Diem could not be replaced as a credible anti-communist leader.[69] Kennedy wanted more briefings of the opposing forces as well as to know Lodge's and the CIA station's stances towards the generals.[70]

National Security Adviser McGeorge Bundy, on behalf of the National Security Council, sent a message to Lodge: Washington did not assess that 'presently revealed plans give clear prospect of quick results'. Nonetheless, the ambassador had to give more information to General Harkins and Smith; all three officials were to work together to draft a full assessment of the situation. The ambassador replied that he did not agree that Harkins should replace him before flying for Washington – as Kennedy himself had wanted. (Eventually, Lodge would cancel his flight and stay in Saigon.) He gave the White House the latest information about the orders-of-battle, boasting that there were chances of success and that the United States should not stop now.[71]

At the 29 October meeting with his national security team, Kennedy sounded optimistic about the coup forces' bid for victory, despite the fact the estimates of the orders of battle showed that the opposing forces were even: 'I'm sure that's the way it is with every coup. It always looks balanced, until somebody acts. Then support for the coup is forthcoming.' Robert Kennedy insisted that there was no intelligence on the conspirators: 'We have a right to know what the rebel generals are planning. We can't go half way. If the coup fails, Diem will throw us out. [Diem]'s a determined figure who's gonna stick around and, I should think, go down fighting. If [the coup]'s a failure, I would think Diem's gonna tell us to get the hell out of the country ... He's gonna have enough, with his intelligence, to know that there's been these contacts and these conversations, and he's gonna capture these people. They're gonna say the United States was behind it. I would think that we're just going down the road to disaster.'[72]

On 30 October, General Harkins wrote to General Maxwell Taylor, telling him that Don was involved in a coup conspiracy and wondering why the Vietnamese generals had confided their intentions to Conein and not to him. Harkins disagreed with Lodge's aforementioned reply to Bundy; there should be no US involvement in the coup; more information was needed to predict whether it could succeed. The same day, Smith wrote to Helms that 'the chances of survival' of Diem's rule were 'diminishing'. Still, the acting head of station was not certain that the generals would be successful. The quest for more information on the order of battle of the opposing forces continued.[73]

Colby sounded an improbable solution to avoid a coup. He proposed to MacCone that Nhu assumed power with Washington's backing. It was simply illogical given the US hostility toward Nhu, who was known for his 'fascist overtones' and anti-Buddhist policy. Colby claimed that Diem's brother was a 'strong, reasonably well oriented and efficient potential successor'.[74] The 24 August instructions to Lodge focused on first removing Nhu and, if this failed, then removing Diem. Colby was going against established US secret policy but without reasonable arguments for the US to support a man who, among other things, repressed his people and blamed the CIA.[75]

Conein observed the developing situation. Lodge suspected that he did not support the coup. Their relations were not smooth. Allegedly, the ambassador had threatened him that if no coup took place 'he would see to it' that Conein 'never worked another day for the US Government'.[76]

Early in the morning of 1 November, the MACV chief of staff, Major General Richard Stilwell, called his office. Smith told him that no coup would take place. Stilwell had himself interviewed US advisers working with Vietnamese officers who seemed loyal to the regime. Thus, the station would 'protect' itself (according to Stilwell) by not sending back reports predicting a coup. Admiral Harry Felt (the commander in chief of US forces in the Pacific and Far East) visited Saigon the same day. Stilwell was certain that no coup was about to take place. He paid a visit to Diem together with Lodge the same morning. Diem spoke to them of 'junior CIA officers, one of them named Hodges, who were "poisoning [the] atmosphere by spreading rumors of coups about him".'[77] This 'Hodges' had informed his generals that the Seventh Fleet would intervene with a landing of troops in case the government organised a demonstration against the embassy. He also repeated that it was the military that had launched the raids against the pagodas.[78]

Diem mistakenly assumed that he could put pressure on the ambassador by telling him that US agents had instigated the Buddhist protests. Lodge, unwilling to give any hint of the upcoming coup and in order to assuage any suspicions Diem might have, assured him that he would deport any US subject who was implicated in any such scheme. In his turn, Diem sounded proud of Nhu, claiming that his brother 'had no interest in power, he so overflowed with solutions to difficult problems that everyone asked for his advice'. The ambassador assumed that Diem was hinting at a 'package deal.'[79] In any case, both Diem and Lodge continued playing the duplicity game with each other. Diem said to Lodge: 'I know there is going to be a coup attempt, but I don't know who is going to do it.' He wanted to prepare the ambassador for the fake coup about to materialise under operation Bravo. Lodge (having in mind the generals' upcoming coup) reassured him: 'I don't think that there is anything to worry about.'[80]

The station's first report to Langley that day began by saying that the city looked 'more nearly normal than at any time since May 8th [the date of the first Buddhist protest].' But things changed. At 1.30 p.m., Langley received a cable reporting 'red neckerchief troops pouring into Saigon from direction Bien Hoa, presumably marines'.[81]

Conein had been risking his neck for a long time. The plotting generals, who lived in fear of being discovered by Diem, considered him their 'insurance policy'. If they failed, Conein's presence and knowledge would 'connect' the coup attempt with the White House. General Don's aide summoned Conein; the coup was underway – the trusted intelligence liaison rushed to the Joint General Staff building. The dentist in whose office Conein met Don came to the station and asked to see Conein; Don had been calling him but could not find him. General Don's aide reached Conein's house. Conein had hastily dressed in his US colonel uniform (that was Conein's own 'insurance': to be identified as an American officer). The dentist, who had also arrived, told him to 'bring all available money'. According to a CIA contingency, Conein had money in piasters at his home. He took the equivalent of $42,000 in

162   SECRETS AND LIES IN VIETNAM

piasters, stacking them in a briefcase (he had more money available but
it did not fit in only one case). The funds were for food, medical costs and
death benefits for the Vietnamese. Conein also took a .38 revolver and
jumped into a jeep with the well-armed rebel soldiers. He saw a Special
Forces detachment stationed outside his house where his wife and his
three-month-old daughter lived.[82]

Before leaving, he contacted the home of CIA officer Stuart Methven
using a special emergency radio, telling him: 'Bring me some scotch
whisky.' Methven did not understand and told him to break off the
conversation. Conein, angry, shouted again to bring him some whisky
and to relate his 'request' to the embassy. Methven did as he was told.
He wrote in his memoirs 'I learned later that "scotch whisky" was the
signal indicating the coup was in progress.'[83]

Conein later said that if the coup had failed and Diem had discovered
his role, 'I probably would have a very efficient Vietcong incident – in
other words, I would be blown up or assassinated or something like that,
and it would be blamed on the Vietcong.' He reached the headquarters at
about 3.30 p.m. when a heavy firefight was heard around the palace.
General Minh asked him in an aggressive tone: 'What are you doing
here?' Conein told him that he was called by Don. Minh revealed the
generals' trap. They had called him not because they trusted him, as
many would have presumed: 'In case we fail, you're going with us.'
(Later, Conein concluded: 'I was part and parcel of the whole conspiracy,
so if something went wrong, they would go down the drain with me.
We were all going down the drain together.')[84]

Station intelligence officers scrambled in the streets to report on the
movement of troops and their raids on the regime's buildings. Conein
informed Smith of the arrest of regime officers, among them Colonel Le
Quang Tung, the commander of the Special Forces as well as the
commanders of the Marines, the Air Force and the Civil Guard. The
chief of the Navy was killed in the morning in a 'premature action'.[85]
Colonel Tung and Major Trieu, Diem's trusted officers, were arrested and
executed by Captain Nhung, the bodyguard of General Minh.[86]

There was an exchange of fire at the presidential palace, intelligence
officers reported. One, at high risk, approached and counted about 200
of the generals' troops at the palace. Another station officer spoke of 35
armoured vehicles being present. Conein reported to the station that the
mutineers wanted to reach Diem by phone to ask him to surrender, in

order to avoid a bloodbath. Drawing on the memories of the 1960 coup attempt, when the rebels were outmanoeuvred and lost precious time before the arrival of loyalist troops to back Diem, they were intending to get a 'yes or no' answer, not to negotiate with him.

Nhu and Diem had relaxed their guard, believing that the fake coup was underway; but their sentries noted that the troops entering Saigon were not friendly and wore identification: red scarves.[87]

At one point, the generals were listening to government broadcasts that the coup plotters had been arrested. It was a propaganda ploy of Diem. An air attack against the palace was underway. It looked like the mutineers had prevailed in the military units and by mid-afternoon they commenced talking with Conein about politics; anti-regime political leaders were already at the JGS. The general repeated to Conein that the new government would solely comprise civilians.

Nonetheless, serious confusion ruled. The US embassy reported, without citing their source, that the generals wanted the embassy to be an intermediary and to present Diem with their ultimatum. Conein said that Minh and Nhu spoke on the phone; Minh threatened Diem with a 'massive air bombardment'. General Dinh picked up the phone and threatened Nhu, swearing at him and his brother. A Vietnamese officer told Conein that Dinh wanted Nhu to realise that his trusted general 'was no longer leading a phony coup but had joined a genuine rebellion'.[88]

At 4 p.m. on 1 November 1963, Diem called Ambassador Lodge. The president shouted in French so loudly that the ambassador's aides could hear him clearly:

President Diem: Some military units have begun a rebellion, and I want to know what the attitude of the US is?

Ambassador: I have heard some shooting but, of course, am not acquainted with all the facts. I do not feel well enough informed at this time to be able to tell you. Remember, it is 4:30 A.M. in Washington, and the United States Government cannot possibly have an official view at this time.

President Diem: You must have some idea. I am, after all, the Chief of State. I have always tried to do my duty and want now to do what duty and good sense require. I believe in duty, above all.

Ambassador: You have certainly done your duty. I told you only this morning how much I admire your courage and the great contributions you have made to your country's well being. No one can take from you the credit for all that you have accomplished. Now I am very worried about your physical safety. It has been reported to me that those in charge of the current activity against you offer both you and your brother safe conduct out of the country if you resign. Had your heard this?

President Diem: No. [*And then after a pause:*] You have my telephone number.

Ambassador: Yes, and you have mine. If I can do anything at all to insure your personal safety, please call me at once.[89]

According to Lodge's aide Frederick Flott, the ambassador made Diem an offer: a limousine with US flags and one of his staff would reach the palace, persuade the troops gathered outside to be allowed in, and take Diem and Nhu to the airport to be taken safely abroad. Flott would be the one to accompany them. However, Diem misunderstood, thinking that the ambassador would send troops to confront the mutineers.[90]

According to a US embassy official, the conversation also entailed this exchange:

Ambassador: Well, you are a chief of state. I cannot give you advice, but personally, and as a friend, and as somebody who is concerned about your health, my suggestion would be you think seriously of getting away. Now, if I can be of any help on that, I'm prepared to send my driver with an officer of mine to escort you to safety. And we can get you on my jet aircraft, and I'm sure I can deliver on that. One of my officers will ride in the front seat of my limousine with the chauffeur.

President Diem: No, I cannot agree to fleeing, because this is all a tempest in a teapot; it's a couple of hothead generals who don't speak for the army, and I know that the real troops are loyal to me and will soon have this all straightened out.

Ambassador: Well, Mr President, that is your decision, certainly. I cannot advise you one way or the other. But as I've said, if I can ever be of any assistance in looking after your security, I would certainly do so.

President Diem: Well, I want you to tell Washington that this is being done and that I want them to land the BLTs [Battalion Landing Teams], the two marine BLTs on the aircraft carriers offshore. I want them to land and protect the palace.[91]

Diem's bodyguard, who survived the coup, would claim years later that Diem also added, shouting: 'Mr Ambassador, do you realize who you are talking to? I would like you to know that you are talking to the president of an independent and sovereign nation. I will only leave this country if it is the wish of my people. I will never leave according to the request of rebellious generals or of an American ambassador. The US government must take full responsibility before the world for this miserable matter.'[92]

Conein informed the station that General Minh called Diem on the phone at about 5 p.m. Eventually, Diem stopped their adversarial conversation. The general informed Conein that an air attack against the presidential palace was about to be launched. At about 7 p.m., Minh presented Diem with a new ultimatum: he had to surrender, or else he would 'blast him off the face of the earth'.[93]

Conein was asked to contact the Buddhist leader Thich Tri Quang, who had been living at the US embassy since the pagoda crisis. The generals intended to appoint him as a Buddhist adviser in their government.[94] At 8.20 p.m., some 105 mm artillery pieces were fired at the palace. General Minh unleashed an infantry battalion with armour support against the palace. In the meantime, General Kim informed Conein of the committee's resolution to establish a military junta before forming a civilian government. Conein concluded that Minh was the leader who headed the committee.[95]

Generals Don and Khiem informed Conein of phone discussions with Diem and asked him whether he could find a US aircraft to take the president and his brother out of the country. The intelligence officer asked the embassy. Smith replied that France would grant Diem asylum, but that it would take 24 hours for an aircraft to reach Saigon and then to fly directly to Paris. Conein informed the generals. The president ordered his loyalists to cease fire.[96] Conein drove to the embassy. He received clear orders to put pressure on the generals to see that the Ngos would not be harmed and that labour leader Tran Quan Buu would not be arrested.[97]

At 6.20 a.m. on 2 November Diem phoned Don, who had remained at the JGS. He offered his surrender in return for being allowed to leave the country. He wanted the general's promise. (However, he was fooling them too, seeking to buy time: he had escaped with his brother via an underground tunnel and was calling them from a safe house; the generals assumed that he was still in the palace and the station did not know of this development.) General Minh did not want to wait for the aircraft for Diem; at 6.30 a.m. Minh left for the palace, seeking to be the one to accept Diem's surrender in person.

Meanwhile, Colonel Thao, Hanoi's mole who had openly sided with Minh, interrogated a captured palace officer, who revealed that the Ngos had escaped via a tunnel. Thao finally reached the safe house (the residency of a Chinese merchant). Diem and Nhu saw him and fled to the nearby church of St Francis Xavier. The church was full of people for All Souls' Day. The exhausted Nhu and Diem were in civilian clothes, but an informer saw them in the courtyard and called the military. Soon Minh's jeeps and armour arrived, commanded by a personal enemy of Diem, the pro-French General Mai Huu Xuan.[98] It is not clear whether the mole himself had alerted Minh of the Ngos' presence.

Lodge's aide Colonel Mike Dunn witnessed Diem's last call to the ambassador at around 7 a.m. on 2 November. Diem and Nhu were about to surrender and, with Minh's agreement, they were to be transported to the airport. Dunn offered to go with them to protect them. But the ambassador said: 'We just can't get that involved.'[99]

It was 8 a.m. An intelligence officer from the station remained close to the palace and reported that the troops seemed to be waiting for Diem and Nhu to come out. Two hours passed without any developments. He then understood that they had both fled. Langley called, frantically asking for more information about the whereabouts of the Ngos. At about 11 a.m., Conein drove to the JGS headquarters. Minh was there, having returned from the palace. He told Conein that both brothers were dead; they had 'committed suicide in a Catholic church'.

Conein hit back: 'Someone had better construct a more plausible story.'[100] Conein asked where the bodies of Diem and Nhu were, only to be informed that they had been transported behind the JGS building.

Conein informed the station. At midday, the station informed Langley that the Ngo brothers were 'probably dead'. Smith concluded that there was now a new regime in Saigon, remarking that people 'poured into the streets in [an] exhilarated mood,' offering food to the soldiers. The headquarters of Madame Nhu's Women's Solidarity Movement was set on fire.[101] Minh, Don and Kim each asked Conein separately to see Diem's and Nhu's bodies for themselves. The intelligence officer said no. He was nervous that the 'generals would think he [was] taking grisly relish in his part' in the coup.[102] He shot back with a sarcastic remark when Minh asked him why he did not want to see the dead bodies of Diem and Nhu: 'Well, if by chance one of a million of the people believe you that they committed suicide in Church, and I see that they have not committed suicide, and I know differently, then if it ever leaks out, I am in trouble.'[103] He drove back to the embassy and sent a cable on the Ngos' demise.

CIA Director McCone was about to meet with Kennedy and still needed more information on the brothers' deaths. He commented on Conein's reaction to the generals' 'offer' to show him the dead bodies. Kennedy was informed of the Ngos' deaths and could not hide his surprise. According to Maxwell Taylor, on hearing the news Kennedy 'leaped to his feet and rushed from the room with a look of shock and dismay on his face which I had never seen before'.[104] The president asked McCone to ensure the safe passage of Nhu's children to Europe. Eventually, they reached Rome safely.[105] Can Ngo, Diem's brother, asked for asylum at the US consulate in Hue; no asylum was granted after Minh's assurance that Can would be tried and that clemency would be possible. Conein handed Can (whom Lodge considered 'a reprehensible figure who deserves all the loathing which he now receives') over to the new regime. (Can was tried for murder; during the trial he suffered a heart attack, and his diabetes condition became grave. He was sentenced to death.[106])

Now Kennedy, showing remorse, admitted that the 24 August instructions to Lodge had 'encouraged Lodge along a course to which he was in any case inclined'.[107] The murder of the Ngos dominated the post-coup discussions at the White House:

McCone: I would suggest that we not get into, into this story [of the killings].

Bundy: What happens if we now ask to see the bodies, and there were a couple of bullets in the back of them, in the back of this kind? We don't gain much by that.

President: If Big Minh ordered the execution, then, then, uh, I don't know. Do we think he meant to?

Hilsman: There's some suspicion.

Bundy: Some think he did.

Hilsman: Some think he did.

President: Pretty stupid.

[. . .]

President: What are we gonna say about the, uh, death of Diem and Nhu? We're not gonna say anything, right? We've already got an unfortunate event. Nonetheless, it'd be regrettable if it were ascribed, unless the evidence is clear if it were ascribed to Big Minh and the responsible council of generals. I don't want it wrapped around him if we can help it.

Hilsman: The information's gonna come out. It's gonna come out in the next forty-eight hours.

President: His role may not. I'm sure Lodge must be aware that this is an unfortunate matter, and I suppose next they're gonna make every effort to disassociate Big Minh and Conein. . . . If there was not responsibility on his [Minh's] part, that should be made clear.'

Hilsman: In other words, get a story and stick to it.

Bundy: Got it.

President: It ought to be a true story if possible.[108]

The next day, an occasional source of the station presented his CIA case
officer with photographs of the brothers' bodies in an armoured vehicle.
The station sent this cable to Lieutenant General Gordon Blake, the
NSA Director:

> Critic. Young Vietnamese Saigon businessman who [is] CAS
> casual source exhibited set of snapshots morning 3 Nov which
> showed Dinh Diem and Ngo Dinh Nhu covered with blood,
> apparently bullet-riddled, lying dead on floor of armored vehicle
> with hands tied behind them. Source claims pictures given to him
> by the actual photographer who member of coup forces.[109]

Minh and the other generals wanted the United States to have hard
evidence of the Ngos' deaths. Conein had declined to see the bodies.
By 12 November, the CIA had no conclusive intelligence on the actual
conditions of the brothers' deaths: 'On the basis of available information,
our best judgment is that Diem and Nhu may well have been killed by a
junior officer or enlisted personnel acting unilaterally, possibly provoked
by the captives' haughtiness. It is possible, however, that General Dinh
or some other senior officer may have ordered their execution. In any
case, it seems likely that Diem and Nhu never reached the JGS alive.'[110]
     Subsequent CIA investigations concluded that it was Minh who
took the decision to murder the Ngo brothers. Conein said: 'We
knew ... within a matter of hours exactly what happened, and I reported
it, and it was reported back here [in Washington] at headquarters exactly
what happened. ... I have it on very good authority of very many people
that Big Minh gave the order.'[111] Other reports pointed the finger at
General Xuan, the coup committee, and the officer in command of the
detail which was assigned to take them to the airport. All post-coup
reports identified the murderer, Captain Nhung, one of Minh's
bodyguards. The general had made a gesture to him using his two
fingers; it was the sign of the kill.[112]
     This chapter has showed that neither the White House, the US
embassy, the CIA station nor the divided Vietnamese generals had
seriously discussed the subject of sustainable political arrangements after
Diem's fall. The sole task of first deciding and then working for regime
change was daunting to Kennedy and all of his national security team,
diplomats and intelligence officers in Saigon and absorbed their time and

thinking. The coup was not a guaranteed success, as everyone had assumed after 2 November. The 24 August cable to Lodge was never retracted.

Conein had turned from Lansdale's secret warrior into a sole liaison and hostage to the generals. He was the one who had been risking his life before, during and after the coup. No one would thank him, and Washington and Lodge would disassociate themselves from him in case the generals failed. The evidence shows that the coup was entirely a Vietnamese affair; the US role was essentially marginal. Kennedy and his national security team may have been discussing a coup for months (and Lodge may have been arguing with Washington on the merits of toppling Diem) but secrecy undermined Washington's credibility in the eyes of the conspirators, who feared being discovered; they were also suspicious of the United States' real motives towards them. The secretive generals did not want a trusted liaison, but a *hostage* – Conein – to connect them with official US policy and the US embassy in case Diem and Nhu uncovered their plot. Throughout the autumn of 1963, they had heard only the line that the United States would not hinder a regime change, and that aid to the current regime was being cut off; nothing more.

By the afternoon of 2 November, the United States was satisfied that no civil war had broken out. The generals were in control of the situation, and on 5 November they announced that the new government would have 'a military committee' chaired by Minh, and a civilian's cabinet with Buddhist Nguyen Ngoc Tho as prime minister (he was vice president under Diem). General Don was appointed minister of defence, and General Dinh led the Ministry of Security (formerly Interior). On 8 November, the United States formally recognised the new government. On 22 November, Kennedy was assassinated by a sniper in Dallas. On 30 January 1964, General Khanh deposed General *Minh*. Khanh's coup surprised the CIA station.[113] McCone was right when he predicted that a succession of coups would take place. The now Major *Nhung*, who had killed the Ngos and Tung, was executed with a shot in the back of the head.

Pham Xuan An, the Hanoi mole, admitted that he was surprised by the coup against Diem. He said that at that time his handlers assumed that the coup signified the US intention to abandon South Vietnam. An claimed that he told his superiors then: 'No way, they are coming, and you better get ready for a big war.'[114]

In his turn, General Khanh was planning to secretly contact the NLF. An was informed of this by Conein himself. One day Conein was on a helicopter with Khanh and trapped him into revealing the possibility of negotiating with the NLF. The general aired his views in favour of such an initial. Later, the CIA intelligence officer, feeling betrayed, started shouting at An in his characteristic style: 'An, get your wife and family, pack up, and get out of here. All is lost. Your country is going to fall into the Communists' hands very soon. It is worse than I ever thought, Khanh is in bed with the NLF.' An recalled: 'I never saw Lou Conein that angry in his life, but he was seriously worried about me and my family ... when he calmed down he concluded that Khanh would not get support for a settlement with the NLF.'[115]

In any case, Conein would soon find himself in more trouble. One night in Saigon in August 1964, a couple of US Army armoured vehicles drove alone – without the usual South Vietnamese military police escort – to a pier in order to be loaded onto a transport heading for a Republic of Vietnam port in the north of the country. The vehicles stopped in front of the headquarters of the Republic of Vietnam Navy where Khanh was staying for the night in secret. Staring out of the window, Khanh saw the armour and feared that a US-backed coup had been launched against his rule. He called the US ambassador, who, in his turn, asked Conein via the CIA station chief to see what was going on. The next morning many in the hierarchy of the South Vietnamese armed forces would mistakenly conclude that the coup attempt was the CIA's move against Khanh. Conein was held responsible for implicating the agency in this and was ousted from Saigon by Lodge.[116]

CHAPTER 8

DISTORTIONS AND ESCALATION

In 1963, Le Duan, the first secretary of the Vietnamese Workers' Party (VWP), a leader from the south who since 1954 had insisted on Hanoi continuing the fight against the ARVN and the US advisers, succeeded in getting the 9th Central Committee Plenum to pass Resolution Nine, which included a secret part titled 'Strive to Struggle, Rush forward to win new Victories in the South'. It prescribed the escalation of war in South Vietnam with the introduction of more Viet Cong fighters to fight for total victory; the aim was the fast 'annihilation' of the ARVN before any meaningful US intervention to save them.[1] The secret document envisioned the direct participation of PAVN forces ('This armed struggle must follow the rules of war [and involve] main forces').[2] Resolution Nine was in effect a secret declaration of war. Hanoi was aware that Moscow would not agree with this strategy.[3]

The political crises in South Vietnam with the coup against Diem and the new coup of February 1964 convinced Hanoi that the regime was unstable, and thus that before any US military intervention, the communists' escalated operations would lead to the fall of Saigon's generals. Nonetheless, Le Duan and his loyalists, who purged 'dissidents' and moderates within the government and party, underestimated the capabilities of the United States, concluding that it would not be able 'to commit the full force of US military might to the Vietnam War'. Hanoi wrongly predicted that even if an intervention were to take place it would be limited and thus the US military would show itself unable to change the course of the eventual collapse of the South Vietnamese regime. In addition, the DRV leadership assumed that Moscow and

Beijing would exercise pressure on Washington not to escalate. A time window, opened by the diplomatic exchanges and consultations of the great powers, would give the PAVN the opportunity to destroy the South Vietnamese forces. In any case, Moscow sounded as though it did not believe in the potential for Hanoi's victory, fearing also the use of nuclear weapons by the United States. Le Duan confidently discounted such an outcome: the party's theoretical journal, *Hoc tap*, insisted that the United States was interested in colonies in order to sell its products; thus, it would never 'seize a piece of land which had been contaminated by nuclear fallout'.[4] Throughout winter, spring and summer 1964 Hanoi escalated, while not committing PAVN forces, seeking to show to all that they were respecting the Geneva Agreements of 1954.

Meanwhile, MACSOG and the US Navy were conducting intelligence gathering, as well as providing support to South Vietnamese raids and coastal bombings of PAVN installations. The maritime signals intelligence missions under the codename Desoto harassed and provoked the North Vietnamese forces.

Hanoi had opted for escalation of the insurgency, not restricted to land. On the evening of 29 December 1963, two Viet Cong sappers attached 80 kg of explosives to the hull of USNS Core (a World War II Bogue-class escort aircraft carrier) in the port of Saigon. The bomb did not explode. In order to ensure total secrecy of the failed mission, the commandos returned and took it out. On 2 May 1964, the same team of sappers organised another attack; the sappers infiltrated the USNS Card (they assumed she was the Core) in the port of Saigon. The carrier was a military transport (bringing heavy artillery pieces, armoured personnel carriers, aircraft, helicopters and ammunition for the ARVN). Under the cover of darkness the two sappers placed two mines on her hull and escaped safely. The explosions created a hole 3.7 metres long and 0.91 metres high on the starboard. Five civilian crew members were killed. The Card sank 48 feet. Michael V. Forrestal wrote to Bundy, the special assistant for National Security Affairs, saying that 'probably both Lodge and Khanh are somewhat shaken by events of the last few days.'[5] After 17 days the Card was refloated, and towed to the Philippines for repairs. (On 20 October 1964, the DRV released a postage stamp commemorating the raid against Card: 'Aircraft Carrier of America sunk in the Harbor of Saigon.' The Card returned to active service on 11 December.)[6]

On 2 August 1964, the destroyer USS *Maddox* was attacked by three DRV Navy torpedo boats while it was on a Desoto mission. The USS *Maddox* was steaming three to four miles inside the 12-mile limit claimed by the DRV. The commander of the warship had received a prompt warning of DRV intentions on 1 August (but did not receive another relevant message on 2 August). The NSA had tracked the command, control communication and intelligence activities of the DRV local naval headquarters.[7] Four F-8 Corsairs were dispatched to support the warship; all three torpedo boats were damaged, and four Vietnamese sailors were killed. The White House remained calm. President Johnson ordered that the destroyers USS *Maddox* and USS *Turner Joy* continue their signal intelligence operations; however, in parallel, South Vietnamese boats raided DRV installations. Hanoi wrongly assessed that all these operations were coordinated.

On 4 August, USS *Maddox* and USS *Turner Joy* continued operating together. The USS *Maddox* received wrong signals intelligence warnings to the effect that an attack against the Desoto mission that evening was deemed 'possible'. The warning originated from the USMC intercept base at Phu Bei.[8] (Phu Bai reported three hours later – during the 'battle' – that the DRV boats in question had been towed to Haiphong for repairs; this was not reported to the *Maddox*.)[9]

Captain John Herrick, the commander of USS *Maddox*, and her crew were put on war footage, operationally and mentally. After 8 p.m. the ship's radars spotted two surface contacts and three air contacts 40–45 miles north-east, about 100–110 miles from DRV coasts. USS *Ticonderoga* dispatched four Skyraiders to provide cover for the warships.

The weather conditions were bad. At 8.45 p.m. the surface contacts were gone – lost about 27 miles from the *Maddox*. At 9.08 p.m. radars reported one surface contact and later others, 15 miles south-west, all contacts moving against the destroyers at 30 knots. The Skyraider pilots did not locate the boats but reported seeing the wakes. At 9.31 p.m. the surface contacts disappeared from the radar screens. At 9.34 p.m. a surface contact, a boat coming from the east, was spotted moving against the USS *Maddox* at 40 knots; it was only 9,800 yards away. *Turner Joy* located another surface contact but some claimed that it was the same spotted by *Maddox*. At 9.37 p.m. the surface contact was 6,200 yards away from *Maddox*; then it turned to the south. *Maddox* assumed that the turn was after launching a torpedo; the sonar operator reported hearing a noise spike but it did not refer to a torpedo.[10]

Turner Joy did not report anything similar. At 9.40 p.m. Captain Herrick informed the 7th Fleet headquarters that he had opened fire to protect his ship against enemy attack. Before *Maddox*, *Turner Joy* had opened fire against the surface contacts deemed to be patrol/torpedo boats. But radar operators could not keep track of their targets. At 9,000 yards the surface contact targeted by *Maddox* disappeared. *Turner Joy's* target disappeared 4,000 yards away. At 10.01 p.m. surface contacts from the west were spotted.

Both ships opened massive salvos, assuming that 13 DRV boats were attacking them and that at least two torpedoes had been launched against them. US Navy pilots said that they had not seen the enemy below. At 11.35 p.m. Herrick considered the battle over and reported that two enemy boats had been sunk and others damaged.[11] Both ships had been manoeuvring to evade the torpedoes; this confused their sonar operators who, hearing the noise of the wakes, assumed an attack and reported it to their commanders.[12] When Herrick realised this, he sent a cable expressing his doubts about whether a battle with the enemy had taken place, mentioning 'an apparent attempted ambush at [the] beginning'.[13]

Already, since the first message from Herrick (that he was expecting an attack), McNamara had called Johnson, informing him of the 'imminent attack' against the warships. Later, the message that the warships were 'under attack' reached him. The secretary of defense exchanged messages with Admiral Ulysses Simpson Grant Sharp, the head of the Pacific Command, who voiced doubts about the second Tonkin incident. The secretary of defense seized upon an NSA intercept and translation of a message of an unidentified DRV naval command, which said that the DRV 'shot down two planes in the battle area ... we had sacrificed two ships and all the rest are okay ... the enemy ship could also have been damaged.' The NSA analysis also assumed that it was a post-action report from 4 August. The sceptics did not doubt that the attack took place; however, as Hanyok put it, they did wonder 'that the intercept time (1550 – Zulu Time – or 1559Z) of the "after action" intercept coincided with the time frame of the attack on the two destroyers: an analytic "coin toss" was made and the translation went out which was interpreted as supporting the validity of the second attack.'

The connection between the intercept and the 'attack' was inferred but it was not clear and direct.[14]

Despite the public stance of Johnson and NcNamara, many high-ranking officials at the CIA and the Pentagon doubted that the second incident had been real. In contrast, pilots and the ships' crews in post-action interviews insisted that the DRV boats attack was real.[15] At a conference with the joint chiefs of staff, McNamara concluded that there was no doubt that a battle had taken place. But in fact, the NSA intercept of the DRV communication referred to the 2 August engagement, not the 4 August. Now it was too late for Herrick. Misidentified wakes and ship manoeuvres were turned into the basis for military strategy against the DRV.[16]

A few days later, Johnson said about Tonkin: 'Hell those damn, stupid sailors were just shooting at flying fish.'[17] Simply put, top decision makers were exposed to real-time tactical intelligence. The mistakes of low-rank sonar and radio specialists and the uncritical acceptance of their findings by US Navy commanders led to a comic incident of two warships fighting with shadows. The commanders cabled Washington real-time tactical intelligence, which was rushed into the White House by a dangerously overconfident McNamara. Captain Herrick wrongly presumed that he had the luxury of airing his doubts later about the 'incident'. On 7 August, Congress voted for the Bay of Tonkin Resolution (officially called the Southeast Asia Resolution), which allowed for more US military involvement in the support of South Vietnam. The moment Johnson heard that Congress had voted for the resolution he told an aide that it was 'like Grandma's nightshirt. It covers everything.'[18]

Surprisingly, Mao Tse-tung had accurate intelligence of what had really happened. On 13 August, he met with Le Duan in Beijing for a consultation on the crisis and told him that the 4 August incident 'was not an intentional attack by the Americans [but was caused by] the Americans' mistaken judgment, based on wrong information'.[19]

On 18 September in the Gulf of Tonkin, during yet another Desoto mission, destroyers USS *Morton* and *Richard S. Edwards* received an intercepted message from the NSA; it warned them of a DRV naval command to its ships, and to be cautious of provocations of South Vietnamese raiding parties and US warships. The DRV ships were explicitly ordered to 'avoid provocation' and to deploy in defensive positions while keeping track of US vessels. Nonetheless, at 5.29 p.m., the radars of the two destroyers showed that surface contacts were following them. The US commanders opted for evasive manoeuvres. About 55 minutes later, after USS *Morton* had fired a warning shot, both ships opened fire against the five surface contacts seen in their radar screen. The salvos continued for about an hour. The surface contacts did not respond, and just continued to follow at a speed curiously matching the destroyers'. The radars showed more than five vessels. Eventually, *Morton* and *Richard S. Edwards* would report back that they had sunk five enemy vessels. The Pentagon ordered a search for debris which produced nothing. Plans for retaliation were examined but Johnson did not authorise them; ultimately, there was no retaliation despite the Gulf of Tonkin Resolution in hand. The Desoto missions were discontinued.[20] The Bay of Tonkin *non*-incident of 4 August (and of 18 September) was no conspiracy, and it is arguable whether it was a turning point in the US involvement in Vietnam. Johnson did not employ the Bay of Tonkin resolution; he was still hesitant.

The DRV leadership took the US claims for a naval battle on 4 August and the retaliatory bombings of the next day as 'unprovoked aggression'. Responding to Le Duan's proposal, the Central Committee authorised the introduction of regular PAVN troops into the conflict. The main objective was a quick victory before the anticipated US intervention to help Saigon. In the 25–9 September session of the Politburo the strategy was made clear: to 'take advantage of this opportune time to try and defeat completely the puppet army before American forces intervened'.[21] In the immediate wake of the Bay of Tonkin episodes, China offered more weapons and aircraft, making Le Duan confident of his choices based on Resolution Nine. On 16 October 1964, China tested its first nuclear weapon; in the eyes of the DRV leadership this showed their closest ally's ability to deter the aggression of the United States.[22]

***

On 1 November 1964, the Viet Cong attacked the airbase at Bien Hoa. On 20 November, the elements of the 325th PAVN division (the 18th, 95th and 101st regiments) departed for South Vietnam.[23] On 6 December, the PAVN and the Viet Cong, under a coordinated plan, successfully attacked ARVN forces at An Lao. In Saigon on Christmas

Eve 1964, two Viet Cong fighters attacked the US officers' quarters with a car bomb (two Americans died and 60 were wounded, including South Vietnamese). In the early hours of 7 February 1965, Camp Holloway near Pleiku was attacked. Eventually, the Viet Cong withdrew leaving eight US soldiers dead and another 126 wounded; 10 aircraft were destroyed and 15 were damaged. Johnson initiated, in full scale and scope, the air bombing of the Ho Chi Minh trail under Operation Rolling Thunder (2 March 1965–2 November 1968), which bore no strategic results. The US ground deployments escalated with the USMC landing at Danang on 8 March, initially to protect US bases and eventually to 'search and destroy' enemy units. China, anxious about an escalation similar to the war in Korea, issued a secret warning; on 2 April, Premier Zhou Enlai asked President Ayub Khan of Pakistan to inform Johnson that China would not get militarily involved in Vietnam and would not provoke the United States unless it attacked his country directly. In such a case, a total war was a certainty. Johnson took serious care that Rolling Thunder bombings did not provoke China.[24]

***

In the meantime, the post-Diem governments of Saigon remained unstable, with generals competing for power and widespread corruption. Pham Ngoc Thao, like Pham Xuan An, was a top Hanoi spy who had benefited from Tuyen's patronage and had turned into an influential mole within the military and the Strategic Hamlet programme. By late December 1964, Thao suspected junta leader General Khanh of wanting him dead out of fear that, together with the United States, he and General Khiem had conspired against him. Thao went into hiding and started organising his own coup; among others, he recruited the remaining Diemists. He was aware that other generals, like Air Marshal Nguyen Cao Ky, were also plotting their own coups. Thus in order to survive, he hastened his own preparations. Thao kept contact with the CIA station. On 19 February 1965, Thao launched his coup. General Khanh escaped from his surrounded house. In the early hours of 20 February, regime forces reached Saigon, among them the 7th Airborne Brigade which had sided with Ky. Thao narrowly escaped. In May, together with General Phat, he was sentenced to death in absentia. Thao was a wanted man with a $30,000 bounty. He was reported dead on 16 July. According to Pham Xuan An, Thao was finally arrested and tortured: 'They crushed his testicles. Then they strangled him. This was done by General Loan.' Loan was the chief of police who had shot a Viet Cong in the head in front of the cameras during the 1968 Tet offensive.[25] General Thieu, the former commander of IV Corps, formed a junta with Air Marshal Ky. Eventually, they would antagonise each other and in 1967, Thieu, with US support, was elected president of the Republic of Vietnam.

***

The USAF bombed the Ho Chi Minh trail but there was no serious impact on the logistics traffic of the PAVN; for example, within 24 hours of a devastating bombing by B-52s on 12 April 1966, PAVN forces were moving through the targeted segments of the trail. Less than two weeks later a second bombing sortie followed. After 18 hours, the specific segment was hosting logistics traffic.[26] In addition, prompt tactical intelligence ensured the PAVN immediate reaction within hours of a US Special Forces deployment near the trail. By the end of 1968, 'some of them [US Special Forces missions] did not get to stay but it was a touch and go'.[27] Next year the enemy presence was wider. Colonel Jack 'the Iceman' Isler, the chief of Operational Plan 35, admitted that the Special Forces teams remained near the trail and the surrounding area for 'no more than two days. Many times it was six hours. . . . There were so many NVN (North Vietnamese) security forces out there, our teams would just run into them.'[28]

In 1966, retired General Lansdale returned to Saigon as a special assistant to the embassy. He remained until 1968, becoming disillusioned with the junta. Like the other US officials, he urged in vain for democratic reforms. In September 1967, Lansdale told Ambassador Bunker about his conversation with the soon-to-be-elected President Thieu: 'We then talked about the evolution of political parties, including the part played in this process by both the Senate and the Lower House. I stressed the attitude the new President would have to take, to encourage the emergence into public life of the present clandestine concept of political organizations in Viet Nam, and the growth of various groups into more unified national parties that had structures in villages and precincts. I asked about the composition of his Administration, if he becomes President. Thieu laughed and said, "go ahead and give me a lecture about a broadly based Government".

He explained that "this is what Americans talk to me about".[29] Lansdale must have sounded naive to a man who belonged to a long tradition of bloody coups and counter-coups.

***

Meanwhile, Pham Xuan An, was working for the United Press International (UPI) correspondent Ray Herndon, who wondered where An was going with the car he had borrowed from him. Herndon remarked that An 'seemed to show up in too many places at once and be too interested in observing what was happening. Of course, our side was spying on us too. The CIA put an agent named Don Larrimore on our staff. I caught him once inside my apartment riffling through my telephone book. So we were suspicious of everybody, An included.'[30] Foreign correspondent Turner claimed that 'no one seemed to believe that An was a security risk, and I wasn't going to mention it to British or American intelligence. I was afraid they would clam up and not talk to me anymore. . . . They regarded me as representing a British outfit, and I wasn't treated as well as if I had been in American news.'[31]

An had to go to the Cu Chi tunnels for new instructions and debriefing. He experienced being caught in the crossfire. The last time he went there was in 1966; afterwards, the deployment of the 25th Infantry Division made it impossible for him to approach the area. Thus, he employed a secret messenger.[32] The mole knew where the captured Viet Cong documents were being examined. Special Branch Criminal Investigation Department translated them into English. The CIO and the Vietnamese military intelligence, once they had them, kept An informed in order to have his input. In his press articles he wrote of 'reliable sources'. He had access to interrogation reports, among them ones from Viet Cong defectors. After the Tet offensive, Tran Van Dac (codename Tam Ha), a DRV spy who was also a commissar, defected. He had access to the plans for the second phase of Tet offensive. Tu Cang, who headed DRV intelligence in South Vietnam, had to go to Saigon; An picked him up. Together they approached a military base in the suburbs of the capital. Cang was asked to stay in the car. An went inside the base to search for the 'story'; eventually he got out with some documents: photocopies of Dac's debriefing. Indeed, the defector had revealed details of strategy, tactics, intentions, names of senior NLF commanders and the locations of regional headquarters.[33]

Thuong was one of An's secret couriers, who, despite elaborate security measures, knew of many people in the network supporting the mole. He held fake identification cards, among them of an ARVN captain, a farmer and a Special Branch secret agent (this was his 'last resort' in case he was stopped by a policeman). In 1969, a defector disclosed that Thuong was a secret NLF courier. After 15 years in secret missions, he was arrested by a detachment supported by a helicopter. From the loudspeaker they called him by his codename and urged him to defect. He fired with his pistol at the helicopter and, according to his account, the helicopter crashed and exploded. The ARVN paratroopers hunted him down; he hid some secret documents (one of them identified An as a spy; among the files was one of his reports written in secret ink) and US dollars he had on him and tried to escape. He hid in a bunker but his pursuers employed smoking gas; he was arrested and an effort was made to persuade him to defect and reveal anything that he knew. The paratroopers did not find the documents. Thuong did not cooperate with his captors. He was tortured and insisted that it was the Koreans and Americans who cut off both his legs. After the Paris Peace Accords he was released.[34]

***

In Hanoi, Le Duan and General Van Tien Dung pressed for a general offensive which (they anticipated) would lead immediately to an uprising against the regime. Both leaders believed that the mayhem of war during a presidential election year in the United States would compel Washington to negotiate with the DRV.[35] General Giap and the ailing Ho Chi Minh initially remained hesitant, believing this to be a high risk plan. General Van Tien Dung, the head of the general staff, was strongly in favour of moving forward with the offensive and the general uprising, having assigned the planning to the Military Operations Command in September 1967. Already in June 1967, the Politburo passed a resolution for a major offensive in urban centres. During meetings in late October and early December 1967, the Politburo examined the exact timing of the attack. At the October meeting, the top party cadre 'realized it was possible to carry out the plan earlier than we had initially planned. To achieve the element of surprise, the Politburo decided to launch the General Offensive during Tet 1968.' Le Duan did not attend the meeting (he was in Moscow);

neither did Ho Chi Minh and General Giap. The plans for the offensive were kept secret from the Russians, who in Vietnamese eyes looked more interested in negotiating peace between the DRV and Saigon. Indeed, by the end of 1967, the Soviet ambassador in Hanoi was being watched by DRV security; some suspected that he sided with dissidents among the top cadre. On 25 October 1967, the COSVN issued the Quang Trung Resolution for the general offensive and uprising.[36]

The offensive against 90 cities and villages in South Vietnam commenced on 31 January 1968, setting the whole country ablaze. Eventually, the Viet Cong lost the battle and their ranks were decimated, with casualties reaching 40,000. The MACV and ARVN established their control in South Vietnamese cities and provinces. In political terms, Hanoi lost because the anticipated uprising had not materialised. In strategic terms, Washington lost the willingness to fight further for Vietnam. President Johnson announced that bombings would halt, as well as his withdrawal of candidacy from the presidential election and his intention to negotiate with the DRV. General Westmoreland, the head of the MACV, who boasted that the US had been winning the war since 1964, found himself on the defensive. Criticism mounted from the media, from Congress and from the public.

The General Offensive/Uprising was divided into three phases. Phase I entailed a conventional attack, with a focus on the USMC base in Khe Sanh in order to draw the attention of the MACV, as if the United States faced a siege similar to France at Dien Bien Phu (during the nine-week battle the PAVN lost between 8,000 and 10,000 troops in the effort against Khe Sanh). Phase II included the attacks against cities and villages to cripple government control and to cause an uprising. Phase III focused on a post-general uprising situation where US forces would be under siege in South Vietnam. Hanoi would have achieved the 'decisive victory' and at the coming negotiations the United States would concede to withdraw from Vietnam.

US intelligence was not aware of the phases of the Tet offensive: Phase I was initiated in Con Thien (south of the demilitarised zone), where in September 1967 PAVN forces had attacked a USMC base. Westmoreland found an opportunity to avert a siege by bombing the attackers, who, by October, withdrew with heavy casualties. In addition, the PAVN attack at Song Be failed.

Signals intelligence showed PAVN units concentrated in Western Kontum province. Redeploying his forces, Westmoreland was ready for yet another fight. By the end of 1967, the PAVN was losing the battles in the border areas. US military intelligence found documents of the B-3 Front Command (Central Highlands); among them, one order of the winter-spring campaign read: 'To annihilate a major US unit in order to force the enemy to deploy more troops ... to improve [PAVN] troop combat techniques. ... To destroy an enemy unit and liberate an area and strengthen the base area ... to effect close coordination of battles throughout South Vietnam'.[37] MACV general staff officers could not believe that Hanoi had the capabilities for attacks in South Vietnam. Given the (wrongly calculated) losses of the PAVN and Viet Cong in 1967, the plan for a countrywide wave of attacks sounded illogical, bordering on party propaganda. One intelligence officer claimed: '[Even] if we had gotten the whole battle plan, it would have not been believed. It would have not been credible to us.'[38]

Since late October 1967, NSA signals intelligence indicated concentration of enemy forces around Khe Sanh, the USMC base. On 19 November, troops of the 101st Airborne Division recovered PAVN documents; among them a notebook of a political officer of the PAVN. The entries covered news of the US policy; there were some notes from staff briefings about coordinating a general attack and a Vietnamese uprising against the Saigon regime. The conclusion sounded more like propaganda than a factual report: 'Central Headquarters concludes that the direct revolution has come and that the opportunity for a general offensive and general uprising is within reach.'[39]

In early January, more PAVN forces gathered around Khe Sanh. It seemed that the base was the linchpin of ensuing major action. On 7 January, Westmoreland informed the White House that 'the enemy's current dispositions indicate that his main effort will be made in northern I CTZ [Corps Territorial Zone]'.[40] A rumour spread: General Giap himself paid a visit to his forces opposite the US base; the general, ready for another siege, observed the American positions.[41] Westmoreland was thinking in terms of the Dien Bien Phu siege. (Major General George Keegan, the commander of the 7th Air Force, even called eight French field officers who had served in Dien Bien Phu during the 1954 battle to advise him; he framed the coming battle as an exact repeat of the past one.)[42]

The command of the USMC base did not believe that a large force had gathered opposite them; however, on 20 January a PAVN messenger was captured and revealed the coming attack the next day. On 21 January the attack commenced; it was repelled, but the destruction of ammunition and fuel depots compelled the MACV to organise the airlift of war supplies since the base was now cut off. General Wheeler (the chairman of the Joint Chiefs of Staff) sent his assessment to Westmoreland: Khe Sanh was an opportunity or a possible disaster – an opportunity to carpet bomb the PAVN forces; or a disaster of a prolonged siege similar to Dien Bien Phu.[43] The US media rushed to call the marines a 'doomed garrison', reinforcing the media-savvy Westmoreland's perception of Dien Bien Phu. President Johnson had a model of the base at the White House, checking on the support provided to the marines and the battle updates. In his heavy Texan accent, the concerned president told Wheeler: 'I don't want no damn Dinbinphoo'.[44]

That same day, the NSA located a forward headquarters 10 km from Hue signalling to three PAVN regiments. It was also noted that the 2nd PAVN Division and subordinate units were moving to the coastal regions of Quang Ngai, Phu Yen, Khanh Hoa and other provinces.[45]

Westmoreland expected that any attack in other sectors and areas would result in delaying the reinforcement of Khe Sanh. Meanwhile, the NSA intercepted the communications of the PAVN B-3 Front Command (Central Highlands) and units, which were moving south via Laos and Cambodia. On 20 January, ARVN forces captured documents that revealed plans to attack the cities of Qui Nhom and Ban Me Thuot.[46]

The intercepted messages and traffic of PAVN and Viet Cong units referred to new weaponry, special tasks for units and propaganda, and command prescriptions for security measures. There was also mention of N-Day (literally speaking D-Day). In his major declassified study of the NSA in Vietnam, Hanyok points out that from 25 January onwards the NSA reports of intercepted PAVN/Viet Cong communications made no special reference to any new-type weaponry of the enemy. The command prescriptions for operational security sounded standard and usual. Signals intelligence did not disclose special assault Viet Cong units, nor any missions of theirs. Few cities were mentioned as targets in the reporting from signals intelligence. The reports of warning referred to cities and locations near Khe Sanh, the demilitarised zone, Danang and the western Central Highlands. Planned enemy activities in Nam Bo and Bien Hoa were deemed 'possibly related' to the activities in the north of the country. The provinces near Saigon and the Mekong were not mentioned in any report.[47]

The first NSA report claimed that the N-Day would be on 25–6 January; a later report claimed that the attack would commence on 29 January or 'shortly thereafter'. Follow-up NSA report No. 5 (from 25 January) referred to an intercepted communication of an element of the 1st PAVN division to an unidentified subordinate unit that the attack would commence 'as soon as possible but no later than 0030 hours (Golf) on 30 January'.[48] N-Day was not mentioned in the communications of subordinate units to B-3.

On 25 January, the Army Security Agency (ASA) base at Pleiku intercepted a message to an element of the 1st PAVN Division, which read: 'N-Day could be moved to an earlier date than previously established. It will be reported later.'[49] On 25 January at 11.32 p.m. (Zulu time), the NSA distributed a report titled 'Coordinated Vietnamese Communist Offensive Evidenced in South Vietnam'. This paper claimed that 'the bulk of the SIGINT evidence indicates the most critical areas to be in the northern half of the country. . . . [There is] some additional evidence that Communist units in the Nam Bo may also be involved.'[50] Following reports focused the interest on the PAVN with reference to Khe Sanh, Hue and the highlands.[51]

The traffic analysis of signals among many low-level PAVN/NLF units and direction-finding analysis showed them redeploying and moving through rural areas of South Vietnam. Nonetheless, NSA analysts could not discern the overall intentions of Hanoi. In effect and having in mind the inaccessibly of high grade communications of the PAVN, the abundant tactical information blurred the picture of Giap's plan for South Vietnam.[52] Hanyok puts emphasis on the fact that there is no evidence that the NSA issued any warning or alert about a general offensive on the eve of the attacks to any signals intelligence agencies and bases (the National Security Agency Representative in Vietnam, the 509th ASA Group, operational units of MACV or the 7th Air Force).[53]

The 'premature attacks' (termed as such with the benefit of hindsight) in the southern Central Highlands occurred on 30 January. After the attacks, Westmoreland put his troops on alert.[54] On the eve of the Tet Offensive, ARVN military intelligence interrogated a captured Viet

Cong who revealed information about a coming attack; however, this was too little too late to ring the alarm bell to the extent of preparing MACV for the coming largescale attacks.[55]

Evidently, the PAVN and the Viet Cong had readjusted their N-Day (something unknown to the NSA at that time). Due to communication problems some units commenced the attack on 30 January without knowing the final order for 31 January.[56] Hanyok writes that 'the evidence for a change in the attack date exists in both SIGINT and collateral intelligence sources. [Half of line not declassified] briefing in the middle of February carried the information that a document captured on 9 February indicated that the date of the initiation of the offensive had been postponed shortly before it began, but no date is specified.'[57]

A total of five battalions (4,000 troops) were deployed inside Saigon in small teams, some in ARVN uniforms. They were armed from secret caches (allegedly many weapons were buried during fake funerals at the cemetery the previous weeks – the same method Lansdale had employed in arming stay-behind teams in the DRV back in the 1950s). In Saigon the Viet Cong was supported by 325 'loyal families' which had located 400 places for their fighters.[58] In Cholon at the Chinese quarter of the city at the Phut To racetrack, the Viet Cong set up its command post.[59]

The 30 January intelligence summary of the DIA claimed that 'indications point to N-Day being scheduled in the Tet period, but it still seems likely that the Communists would wait until after the holiday to carry out a plan.' A few hours later, on the night of 30–1 January (29–30 January in Washington), all PAVN/Viet Cong communications abruptly ceased. US Army signals specialist David Parks, serving at that time in Bien Hoa airbase, near Saigon, remarked: 'About midnight. Every VC/NVN (PAVN) radio in the country went silent. . . . It was the damnedest thing I ever didn't hear. Complete radio silence.'[60]

At 3 a.m. on 31 January, the Tet Offensive commenced. In Saigon, Vietnamese fighters attacked the presidential palace, military and government buildings as well as the US embassy (at that time only four US personnel were inside) where they managed to reach the first floor before being pushed back.[61] Viet Cong fighters indiscriminately murdered Vietnamese government officials and employees as well as foreigners in the cities and villages.[62]

The full-scale hostilities started to be reported by NSA by the night of 1 February (this report followed the report No. 15 of 25 January).[63] In Washington, the attacks were interpreted as a sideshow of the Khe Sanh battle. When National Security Adviser Walter Rostow informed Johnson of mortar fire and of the raid on the US embassy in Saigon, McNamara insisted that 'the answer to these mortar attacks is success at Khe Sanh'.[64] Westmoreland reassured Wheeler that the offensive sought to divert attention from the battles in the north of the country. The CIA estimated that the attacks were simply 'harassments'; the DIA followed the same line, arguing that the attacks from 31 January aimed to block reinforcements to the USMC base. At a press conference, Westmoreland claimed that the enemy campaign had three phases: a. the attacks in the Highlands, the borders with Cambodia and the Mekong to divert US attention; b. the attacks against main cities; and c. the upcoming push against Khe Sanh and the wider north region.[65] By March, signals intelligence showed that two PAVN divisions were withdrawing from the siege of the marines base.[66] In April, units reached Khe Sanh to relieve the defenders. That month the United States decided to abandon the base.

The operational security of the PAVN and the Viet Cong structures prevented the NSA from intercepting vital exchanges which would have disclosed the aim and magnitude of the Tet Offensive as it materialised.[67] 'N-Day' was a term overheard only in the communications of B-3 Front Headquarters and by no other unit or commander.[68] In early January 1968, NLF-captured documents claimed that the winter-spring campaign constituted a 'historical phase' in the war for a decisive victory. The CIA station believed in the value of the documents in predicting Hanoi's intentions. Nonetheless, Langley saw the documents more as propaganda to indoctrinate the NLF fighters than as a credible source on which to base an estimate.[69] Analysts at the CIA headquarters assumed that it made little sense for the NLF to attack because a general uprising was not possible and thus Hanoi estimated (as the CIA analysts assumed) that a general offensive would only result in defeat and heavy casualties. It was argued that the authors of the captured documents wanted to convince the communist cadre that an (elusive) decisive victory was possible. Langley believed that after the traditional Tet truce (observed by the NLF in the past), the PAVN and NLF could proceed to an 'unprecedentedly massive offensive along more traditional, post-Tet lines, involving widespread assaults on allied military bases, airfields, command posts, outposts, and pacified hamlets, combined with an effort to culminate the siege at Khe Sanh with a victory'.[70]

***

Back in late 1967, the 40-year-old spymaster Major Tu Cang, a graduate of the colonial lycée of Saigon who always carried two K-54 pistols (Chinese copies of the Soviet type Tokarev TT-33), reached Saigon and informed Pham Xuan An of the requirement to collect intelligence of primary military and political targets in Saigon. In preparation for the Tet offensive, both drove around in a Renault 4CV and did reconnaissance. Eventually, Tu Cang and An agreed on 20 key targets in Saigon, among them the presidential palace and the US embassy.[71]

At 2.48 a.m. on 31 January 1968, Tu Cang headed a 17-man commando team that raided the presidential palace. Fifteen lost their lives. Tu Cang fled to a block of flats and fired against the guards and ARVN troops; he claims that he fired and killed two US officers.[72] He hid in the apartment of Tam Thao (a secret communist agent), who persuaded the soldiers that she did not belong to the communist cause. Tu Cang was saved. Later the same morning, together with An they drove around the city observing the results of the failed Viet Cong attack.[73]

Westmoreland found himself isolated, following the battle by phone: 'By my Marine aide talking to the Marine guard inside the embassy and by my numerous telephone conversations with the US Army MP [military police] command, I was able to follow the course of the battle and direct action.'[74] The general reached the embassy by mid-morning, when the attackers had all been killed. In a hasty press conference, he insisted that all the attacks were diversionary and that the centre of gravity was in Khe Sanh.[75] Later at the MACV headquarters he directed the response. However, the headquarters were no fortified wartime command post. Westmoreland could not return to his residence. 'It was humiliating ... he couldn't get out of his own headquarters', remarked Zeb Bradford, a field officer and Westmoreland's aide de camp. 'The mood was grim, even despondent' among the top ranking officers; 'the doom was made complete when a stray bullet smashed through a window in the room where the generals were eating. With as much dignity as possible these senior officers had to evacuate themselves to a safer part of the building', added Bradford.[76] Westmoreland could not stay at his own office because of sniper fire. Senior officers remained at the

MACV headquarters throughout the Tet offensive. Bradford remembered hearing Westmoreland say in despair: 'Everything I have worked for is lost. It's all been a failure.'[77] Colonel Fred Schoomaker heard the president shouting on the phone to Westmoreland: 'What the hell is going on out there?!! You just told Congress light at the end of the tunnel and all that!!!'[78]

During the battles, the Pentagon had panicked to such an extent that General Wheeler asked Westmoreland 'whether tactical nuclear weapons should be used'. He asked for a list of targets. Westmoreland wanted to keep his options open but did not want right now to employ nuclear weapons, replying: 'I visualize that either tactical nuclear weapons or chemical agents would be active candidates for employment.'[79] He ordered a secret staff team to examine the use of tactical nuclear weapons. Eventually, Washington feared this would leak to the press and ordered him to stop everything related.[80]

Meanwhile, the KGB supplied the Kremlin with top-secret intelligence: while the Tet battles raged and despite propaganda, Hanoi was seriously contemplating a political negotiation and settlement with the United States. Further intelligence on Hanoi's evolving stance and debates among leaders was leaked to the KGB, probably by a secret source within the Politburo which examined diplomatic strategy between 2 and 6 April.[81]

Westmoreland was right when he wrote to Wheeler that the offensive dealt 'a psychological blow, possibly greater in Washington than in South Vietnam'.[82] On 31 March, Johnson surprised everyone by stating that he would not run for a second term, also announcing a partial halt to the bombing campaign. In May, Hanoi conceded that negotiations could start in Paris. In June, Westmoreland returned to Washington; General Creighton Abrams, his replacement, promoted a 'one war' concept: he planned the 'Vietnamisation' of the war, assigning to the ARVN the burden of counter-insurgency. (The 'Vietnamisation' was a concept first introduced by the French with the establishment of the National Army of Vietnam.)

Tu Cang spoke of his conversations with An in Saigon: 'We held Party meetings and discussed work in luxurious restaurants where the tables were placed far from each other, and no one could overhear what we were saying. An always brought his dog with him. It was a very intelligent dog that understood foreign languages, and people were afraid of it.'[83] He claimed that the attacks against the palace and the US embassy were 'faints' to draw more enemy troops into the city. In those days, Tu Cang reported that the Tet Offensive would not lead to military victory but would have a 'political and psychological impact' in Washington and Saigon.[84] Later, An concluded that it was the Tet Offensive which compelled Washington to sit at the negotiations table.[85] Tu Cang explained: 'The Tet Offensive had three goals: to take over Saigon, to kill the puppet forces, and to make a big noise. For the first goal, we failed. For the second goal, we failed. Only for the third goal did we succeed.'[86] On 4 May, the second phase of the Tet Offensive was initiated; attacks against 119 bases, towns and cities took place.[87] An claims that after the Tet Offensive he was approached by the CIA station to work for them, turning from journalist to a farmer in a plantation in Tay Nonh, a Viet Cong-infiltrated area. He declined the offer to work as a double agent, but did not inform Hanoi of the CIA's approach.[88]

According to the Field Service Regulations, Operations, FM 100-5 manual (Department of the Army, 1962, pp. 46–8) the principles of war were: a 'clearly defined, decisive and attainable' objective, employment of mass of force, economy of force, manoeuvre, unity of command, security, surprise and simplicity of the war plan. There was the assumption that one way or another enemy commanders (as actors seeking to minimise risk and increase their chances of victory) would abide by these principles. Nonetheless, the Tet Offensive had an indisputably unorthodox component (i.e. a mass guerrilla-type activity against 90 main targets in villages and cities). Giap and his fellow generals did not concentrate on a few targets, did not spare troops, did not care about casualties and full logistics support for their troops. Hanoi aimed for a high-risk revolutionary war the US staff officers simply could not imagine.

CHAPTER 9

MOLEHUNT AND SPIES IN THE VIET CONG

The Viet Cong adapted more and more to the battlefield and invented countermeasures to get early warning of bombings and raids against the Ho Chi Minh Trail and their bases. Successful interception of US tactical signals ensured this. On 20 December 1969, troops of the 1st US Infantry Division raided a command post 4 km north of Ben Suc, capturing 12 soldiers. The Americans discovered large stacks of documents, as well as communications equipment (among them three US Army FM radios of the AN/PRC-25/77 types, one Chinese Communist AM receiver, seven Sony transistor radios, one Panasonic receiver, one homemade receiver and one homemade transmitter). This equipment (within their range) ensured to their operators the interception of US tactical communications. The prisoners of war confessed that English linguists were attached to their cadre for the speedy exploitation of intelligence. The confiscated documents included training manuals for the communication equipment and instructions for monitoring enemy communications. The Viet Cong intelligence cadre informed their guerrillas specifically about the communication procedures of the 1st Infantry Division, 1st Cavalry Division, 4th Infantry Division, 25th Infantry Division, 11th Armored Cavalry Regiment, 5th Vietnamese Division and the various US Military Assistance Command teams. They also focused on intercepting the signals that informed the US and ARVN forces prior to B-52 bombing campaigns, which informed the US and ARVN forces enabling them to stay out of the targeting boxes. In parallel, the NLF signals intelligence jammed US and ARVN radio frequencies and signalled false messages in order to cause friendly fire incidents.[1] General Abrams, Westmoreland's successor, was informed of the findings of the raid and was presented with some of the captured documents. He simply admitted: 'This work is really rather startling; the attention to detail, complete accuracy, and thorough professionalism is amazing. These guys are reading our mail, and everyone will be informed that they are.'[2] Meanwhile, Hanoi's spymasters developed more secret sources – moles in South Vietnam – while Saigon and other cities continued to be the targets of NFL terrorist attacks.

One US agency assigned with counterintelligence duties was the Office of Naval Intelligence (ONI) in Vietnam; it was based in Saigon and manned with special agents who investigated crimes involving US military personnel. In 1967, Vietnamese Navy Security, which cooperated with ONI, arrested a Vietnamese port employee who had in his possession two Soviet-made grenades. He confessed to working under the orders of the NLF to destroy 'something' on the port with the first grenade, and with the second to attack a bar where Americans gathered. He said that all his family was living in NLF-controlled areas and that the Viet Cong demanded that he prove his 'loyalty' to its cause. The US naval intelligence agents made a bid to recruit him as a double agent: it was arranged for a 'safe' (and spectacular) explosion to take place in the port as well as a grenade to be 'discovered' in a bar; thus the would-be-saboteur would have proven his worth to his handlers. The local press showed interest in these two episodes of NLF 'complicity'. Nonetheless, the port employee was not willing to act as a double agent, fearing for his family.[3]

***

Vu Ngoc Nha was a top Hanoi mole; he was recruited in 1955 and ordered to infiltrate the government echelons. He soon became an aide to Diem and later to General Nguyen Van Thieu, who became president of the Republic of Vietnam. Gradually, Nha established a spy-ring. During the 1968 Tet Offensive raid against the presidential palace, Nha was inside; his co-conspirators sought Thieu to kill him, but the president was not there. In the chaos, Nha assumed that if the guards found wine they would get drunk and would no longer pose any significant resistance. He opened the wine cellar. Eventually some soldiers drank wine: it made them fearless.[4]

Nha secured vital intelligence from Huynh Van Trong, a special assistant for political affairs to Thieu. By July 1969 under Operation Projectile, the South Vietnamese Special Branch amassed information against Trong and Vu Ngoc Nha; they knew that Nha had been working for the strategic intelligence unit of the Central Office for South Vietnam (COSVN) of the DRV. Thieu was informed 24 hours in advance. The Special Branch arrested the spy-ring comprised of more than 100 members. Nha was arrested in Saigon on 16 July 1969; incriminating evidence – including documents, letters and microfilm – was discovered at his home. In an interview in 2001, Nha said that he and Thieu 'discussed not only matters of national importance, but also talked over his family's affairs. . . . Some things were known only by him and me. He even gave me the key to his room.' Nha had information on the Thieu-Nixon meeting in June 1969 as well as of the negotiation strategy of South Vietnam in the Paris conference. Intelligence of ARVN psychological operations was also revealed to Hanoi. He was brutally tortured. Eventually he was released in the prisoner exchange after the Paris Accords in 1973. After 1975, Nha was named a major general of PAVN.[5]

On 2 September 1969 the 79-year-old Ho Chi Minh died from heart failure. His death was kept secret for two days so that the announcement did not to coincide with the anniversary of the founding of the DRV.

In Dalat in October 1969, the CIA conducted yet another counterespionage operation. This time operative Antonio Mendez (who in 1980 would exfiltrate from Iran six US foreign service officers posing as a Canadian film crew scouting locations for the shooting of *Argo*, a science fiction film) was called to debrief a Viet Cong defector (with the help of an interpreter), a woman in her early twenties. She used to be a cook in a safe house where intelligence personnel were stationed – intelligence officers who, with their agents, penetrated the ARVN and the South Vietnamese regime. Their real names were kept secret from her. But she had 'a near-photographic memory'. Mendez, being also an artist who had contributed to the drafting of police sketches on other occasions for the South Vietnamese security services, realised that the woman was a key source: she had 'a romantic streak, a quality discouraged by the Viet Cong. To amuse herself, she had created fantasy tales for each of the several dozen people who had passed through the safe house en route to Saigon over the years. These tales were her mental cues for recalling their exact appearance and mannerisms. . . . Ming [the defector's codename] would patiently describe the fantasy image she had created for each real person. Then we would study albums with hundreds of photographs of Northern and Southern Vietnamese, and she would select certain features shared by the subject of her fantasy and the people in the photographs. . . . Although it occurred to me that she could have been nothing more than an excellent storyteller with a vivid imagination, I did not think so by the end – her descriptions were simply too detailed and consistent.'[6] After a couple of days the portraits (face-on and profile) of 26 intelligence officers and operatives emerged and were handed over to South Vietnamese counterintelligence; with the help of the portraits, 13 people were arrested who eventually admitted to being members of the Viet Cong. Most were arrested for the act of espionage or carrying intelligence-gathering equipment. Their agents had infiltrated the US community houses of Saigon, working as trusted servants and employees.[7]

That same year, another top spy was discovered, initially by a policeman who, while checking the identity papers of a passerby at a checkpoint in the Mekong Delta, concluded that his Vietnamese accent was foreign for a man supposedly living in the area. The initial interrogation showed a cultivated, self-confident man. The police suspected him of being a high-ranking communist spy and handed him over to the National Interrogation Center (NIC). There the interrogators realised that they had in front of them Tran Ngoc Hien, a NLF officer, probably a colonel. Hien played for time, seeking to avoid to be handed over to the CIO and hoping that his arrest would alert his network to take security measures which would give time for other members of the ring to evade identification. Shackley, the CIA station chief, wrote that 'as the psychological intensity of our interrogation stepped up, Hien would peel back levels of knowledge and tell us just enough to keep the game going'. He was more willing to talk politics than intelligence; however, eventually he talked about his brother Tran Ngoc Chau in South Vietnam whom he had contacted. He was a former colonel, now a representative in the National Assembly for the Kien Hoa province, and had criticised President Thieu for corruption. When he reached Saigon in 1965, Hien sought to employ his brother as an agent of influence as well as a backchannel to the United States. Chau was noncommittal in their several meetings. On the eve of the October 1967 elections, Chau sounded out his brother for support, money and voters. Hien replied that money could not be provided at such a short notice. Shackley wrote: 'In that delicate exchange of nuances for which the Vietnamese and their language are famous, Hien understood Chau to be asking for help, both in money and in votes from secret Vietcong cadres. There was not enough time, Hien said, to get Chau money, but he did report Chau's desire for help in getting out the vote. Hien claimed he did not know what, if anything, his superiors had done about it, but he added slyly it was interesting that Chau had won his National Assembly seat by a wide majority. His interrogators were left to draw whatever conclusions from this clever gambit that they wished.'[8]

Thieu was informed of the claims by Hien and arranged for Chau to be questioned. Chau confessed that he had met with his brother; he claimed that he was exploring the possibility of him becoming a secret channel for US–Viet Cong communications. He said that he had told the United States of this. General Binh, the head of CIO, asked Shackley about it.[9] The station chief replied that he would review the CIA files, but eventually he admitted that 'the result of this exercise was inconclusive. We found no evidence that Chau had ever acted under CIA control or direction to open a channel to the other side or that he had ever told us he had a brother who was a senior NLF cadre. Chau, however, had in fact told several of his CIA contacts that members of his family were in North Vietnam. The embassy did its own file check, and the results were the same.' Nonetheless, 'one CIA officer did recall a brief exchange of views with Chau on opening a link to the other side. Nothing had ever come of it, we said, and we denied knowing anything about any part Hien might have played in an attempt to set up a channel to the NLF or Hanoi.'[10]

Thieu was becoming suspicious of the US role in the affair. In January 1970, an operative of Colby who was working on the Phoenix programme took Chau to a helicopter pad in Saigon. The retired Colonel John Paul Vann (the noted paramilitary expert who was serving in CORDS) arranged for Chau to reach the Mekong Delta; others claimed that Chau was with a US officer in Can Tho because he planned to leave the country. Eventually, Chau returned to Saigon and hid out in the home of Keyes Beech, a correspondent for the *Chicago Daily News*. When station chief Shackley was invited for lunch at Beech's, he suspected that Chau was there. The station chief could not ignore the CIO's and Thieu's suspicion that Beech was harbouring Chau. Beech asked Shackley whether he would like to meet with Chau; the station chief responded coyly: 'The CIA owed Chau nothing, I said. He had not been an agent, we had not guided his dialog with Hien, and as Chau had freewheeled on this matter, he had to be prepared to defend himself against President Thieu's interpretation of the law.'[11]

A few days later, Beech told Shackley that Chau was at his place when they had had lunch. Shackley was furious: 'At that, I blew up and said I felt that Beech had betrayed my trust. By having Chau at his residence while I was there, it looked like Beech was setting me up for a problem with the GVN, the media, and Chau ... there was an exchange of incivilities, which I'm sure he eventually came to regret as much as I did.'[12]

On 25 February 1970, a military court tried Chau in absentia; he was sentenced in 20 years' imprisonment. Chau did not hide further. The next day he was arrested at the National Assembly. On the eve of the fall of Saigon he was released, only to be imprisoned again by the North Vietnamese. Eventually, both brothers survived the war.[13]

***

Agent recruitment was always a problematic affair in Vietnam; CIA intelligence officers could neither apply basic tradecraft nor their experience from elsewhere. A lack of officers fluent in Vietnamese and with a broader education on Vietnamese culture made the CIA reliant on the Special Branch. The Vietnamese officers of the Special Branch conducted street surveillance and provided 'leads' to their CIA counterparts. But the Special Branch did not always act in bona fide. Many cases of phony agents were uncovered by polygraph tests. In many instances, the Special Branch officers were just arresting ordinary civilians and compelling them to 'admit' to the CIA that they were Viet Cong cadre. These civilians admitted later in polygraph tests that they had nothing to do with the NLF.[14] In other cases, the Special Branch gave them fake NLF documents to support their scenario. By unveiling phony agents, the polygraph tests enraged the CIA case officers. They had desperately wanted to show recruitments. Soon it was discovered that the 'NLF cadre' were unable to answer questions as simple as what was their party name (in the NLF all had an alias) and who had sponsored him or her to enter the party (each recruit had to be sponsored by two party members).[15] John F. Sullivan, who served as a CIA polygraph expert in Vietnam from 1970 to 1975, wrote:

One of the more interesting aspects of Vietnamese operations was that many polygraph subjects 'passed' when responding to questions about the information they were providing but invariably failed on questions about being VC [Viet Cong] or of having direct contact with the VC. Because the authentification process required that sources actually be VC or have direct contact with the VC, Special Branch case officers were telling their informants to claim that they were VC. In many provinces, the VC operated pretty openly, and the local people knew about them. Special Branch case officers in many of the provinces knew the identities of local VC and were aware of their activities. However, an accommodation (we won't bother you if you don't bother us) had been reached between the Special Branch and the VC, and no arrests were made. The Special Branch could thus get good information on the VC without dealing directly with them, but it could not get the CIA to accept the information.[16]

Sullivan remarked: 'Some CIA case officers knew from the start that recruiting VC was a figment of Shackley's imagination, and they faked it. Others, less cynical, actually tried to get with the program and ended up disillusioned. Shackley recognised that regardless of how corrupt or inept the Special Branch was, the CIA could not run operations without it. . . . The Special Branch ran its operations through multiple cutouts whose salaries we paid, and it was rare for one of our case officers to meet face-to-face with a source.'[17]

A 25-year-old female secret agent codenamed Violet 2 put the CIA station in a very awkward position. An eager case officer surpassing the ranks informed Shackley that he had recruited 'a VC security cadre in Kien Hoa province'. Violet 1, her brother, was also an 'agent' of the CIA. Violet 2's first polygraph test showed that she was in good faith. She started feeding the CIA with accurate military intelligence via the Special Branch. Her information led to 209 disseminated reports. The chief of station had taken personal interest in her case, praising her recruitment. Nonetheless, doubts were raised in the CIA ranks. Pressure for a new polygraph test for Violet 1 and Violet 2 resulted, and eventually in July 1971 both were tested − but separately in a Saigon safe house. Her brother revealed that Violet 2 was married to Special Branch Captain Dinh. When she heard what her brother had told the

CIA, she turned on him. Eventually, she admitted that she was not a Viet Cong officer; the whole thing had been faked by the Special Branch seeking money from the CIA to support this operation. Shackley was embarrassed: the 209 reports had no value because they did not derive from a secret source in the enemy camp. Until proved a fake, Violet 2 was second only to Fireball in information development.[18]

The spy codenamed Fireball was recruited in 1969; he provided the CIA with accurate intelligence, however doubts were expressed by some CIA officers and Vietnamese interpreters who attended his debriefings. It was discovered that Fireball had worked for the Special Branch, the Military Security Service and the US Army before he started cooperating with the CIA, and that he had not told this to his CIA handlers. Since 1969, he had been handled in a joint CIA–Special Branch programme.[19] Until the fall of Saigon, Fireball was considered the CIA's top secret source.

Despite daily frustrations the CIA continued trying to recruit spies. After the Paris Peace Accords in 1973, an ICCS member of a communist country made an offer and was recruited as a secret source. He was polygraphed in a safe house in Cholon. Nonetheless, a rather comic incident occurred: Sullivan, the spy and his CIA case officer found another CIA officer making love with a Vietnamese woman. The ICCS delegate 'seemed more confused than anything else'. In any case, the polygraph test showed that the ICCS member was a bona fide would-be spy.[20] Sullivan, who had witnessed the incident, later wrote:

> The fact that a safe house set aside for an interview with a very sensitive source was being used as a love nest was a concern, and it did not speak well of the operational security of Saigon Station. In fact, operational security, as I had known and practiced it prior to Vietnam, was nonexistent. On one occasion, I tested an asset in a safe house and deemed him deceptive. The case officer told me that he wanted to talk to the asset for a while and asked me to leave the safe-house keys with him. I gave him the keys and told him to drop them off in my office. When I got back to the Duc [a hotel where CIA personnel socialised] that night, the desk clerk called to me, 'Mr John, [a] man leave these keys for you.' A tag with the address of the safe house was on the key ring. I could not believe the case officer had done that. I brought this up with Barry and O'Leary [CIA officers], both of whom thought it was no big deal.[21]

Unreliable secret sources were abundant. On one occasion in Military Region 3, Sullivan visited a hotel to interview a spy. He and his case officer waited for two hours in a room but the spy did not appear. The next day he made contact, offering his excuse: he had entered the hotel but could not resist the charms of a prostitute and spent the night with her. Sullivan confessed: 'I have heard a lot of excuses by assets who missed or were late for meetings, but that was a first.'[22]

On another occasion, CIA signals intelligence experts intercepted a message from a 'sophisticated Soviet transmitter'. The signal was located in the house of a French teacher in Saigon. The station made a bid to recruit him. Tom Karamassines, the Deputy Director for Plans, was informed since this case involved the Soviet Union. According to biographical information the French national had served with French army signals during World War II. Initially, the Frenchman denied working for an intelligence service. He was polygraphed and the conclusion was that he was lying. After a second meeting the Frenchman declined to work for the CIA. After the meeting the CIA communications experts intercepted signals from the same transmitter but from a different location. Evidently, he had warned his Soviet handlers; two CIA officers, Sullivan and his prospective case officer, were exposed to the KGB. Only later was it revealed that he was a GRU agent who was eventually arrested by French police while making contact with another GRU officer in Marseille, France.[23]

***

In 1971 under the 'Vietnamisation' scheme of the war, the CIA station in Saigon played an instrumental part in the launching of operation Lam Son 719, an ARVN attack with US logistics and air support against Viet Cong routes from Laos, west of the demilitarised zone. The MACV had agreed for an early 1971 operation but President Thieu repeatedly cancelled the date of attack. General Abrams, the MACV commander, was angry about losing the element of surprise and about being informed that the replies of the ARVN general staff did not 'make sense'. Shackley was called to investigate. He wrote in his memoirs that 'drawing on a few well-placed sources, I was able to tell Ambassador Bunker and General Abrams within a matter of hours that the launch dates selected thus far for Operation Lam Son 719 had been declared by President Thieu to be "inauspicious".... Thieu's astrologer told him the stars weren't properly aligned for such an undertaking.' At the meeting with Abrams, Bunker and Shackley 'a stunned silence was finally broken with a mild comment from Bunker to the effect that incidents like this underscored Vietnamese–American cultural differences and complicated the running of the war. Abrams then asked half-seriously, "Can't we influence the astrologer?".'[24]

The chief of station contacted General Tri, informing him of the trouble with the astrologer. The general suggested 'talking' to him. Shackley agreed, giving the astrologer the suggested dates, calling for him 'to align his stars and dates with MACV's plans'. Tri replied that this could be done 'for just a small consultation fee'. The general was given the dates MACV was interested in for the launch of the operation. In the evening, Shackley was informed that the general accepted his 'invitation' for lunch on 8 February. The next morning 'a sensitive intelligence source' in the palace confirmed that after consulting with his astrologer Thieu had decided that 8 February was the best day for Operation Lam Son 719 to commence.[25] Nonetheless, by 25 March the ARVN forces withdrew back to Vietnam; no significant results were achieved from the much-sought operation, although Abrams insisted on its continuation. In any case, the PAVN had now taken the initiative.

In the meantime, the CIA station prepared for covert assistance for President Thieu for the October 1971 elections. The CIA station would support Thieu and boost two to four political parties and 20 politicians 'who will be responsive to CIA covert direction' to be elected in the Lower House. The station claimed that 'for contingency purposes, however, some of them would be in the opposition camp. These individuals, after their election, would be used to collect political intelligence from key GVN ministries or political parties. In addition, they would simultaneously function as agents of influence in both the Thieu and the opposition camps in order to have a positive impact on Lower House legislation and South Vietnamese political events which are of policy concern to the United States.' In parallel, 'Our Vietnam Station would spend up to [amount not declassified] in order to recruit or infiltrate one or two persons into "Big" Minh's entourage. This would be done for the purposes of obtaining intelligence information on Minh's campaign activities, possibly as a basis for designing counter-activities in support of President Thieu's campaign, and of having agents of influence close to Minh in case he wins the elections.' In any case, 'we would not want to reveal to him [Thieu] our support for specific Lower House candidates. First, our support to these candidates will be very limited, and if Thieu were knowledgeable of our support he might well deny these candidates his own financial support which many of them may require. Secondly, our support in several cases would go to opposition candidates for the purposes indicated previously, and Thieu obviously should not have knowledge of this activity.' In January 1971, Ambassador Bunker in Saigon approved the proposals of the station. On 4 February the 40 Committee (which was the supervisory group established 'to approve, oversee, and control' covert operations, under the chairmanship of the National Security Adviser) authorised them.[26]

***

A Viet Cong with a fourth-grade education was competing with his CIA interrogator, Frank Snepp, a Columbia University graduate, who remarked: 'The nose and jaw are something of out of a Joe Palooka cartoon, but the spirit is gentle, simplistic. . . . The Viet Cong apparently let his wife die in childbirth, and we're exploiting the aftershock. He's ready to betray all his former comrades. You watch him across the chipped black enamel of the interrogation table and wonder what hopelessness feels like. But there he is, meticulously charting Communist plans, exposing his friends, taking some apparent pride when you recite his dissertation back to him to check for errors. And when the session's over he grasps your hand with both of his. Grateful for something, maybe only for having nothing at all to do, nothing more to rationalize.'[27] Snepp would interrogate dozens of arrested Viet Cong members and defectors, among them the infamous Nguyen Tai.

Nguyen Tai was a spy who had operated against the French. He took over as director of the counterespionage KG-2 Political Security Department II in the Ministry of Public Security in 1961. It was claimed that he had persecuted his own father for anti-communist statements. He was in charge of espionage operations as well as counterintelligence against the Vietnamese spies/commandos sent by the CIA and MACSOG in the early and mid-1960s. Tai was involved also in the persecution of senior party cadre 'revisionists', pro-Soviet and pro-Giap officials who had turned against First Secretary Le Duan. In 1964, Nguyen Tai was dispatched to South Vietnam. Two years later he headed the security section of Saigon-Gia Dinh party committee; his orders were to 'exploit every opportunity to kill enemy leaders and vicious thugs, to intensify our political attacks aimed at spreading fear and confusion among the enemy's ranks, and to properly carry out the task of recruiting supporters among the lower ranks of the police.'[28] He organised assassination attempts against General Kiem and Vice President Tran Van Huong (both of whom were eventually wounded), and against other officials and Viet Cong defectors. In 1969, Tai transferred his network to the Mekong Delta for extra security. In December 1970, he was arrested on his way to a meeting. He was found to be carrying falsified documents.

Almost immediately he initiated his counter-interrogation strategy, 'admitting' after a beating that he was a captain of the PAVN who had just entered South Vietnam. As the beating continued, he claimed that he was a secret military intelligence agent sent to establish legal credentials before leaving for France on his espionage mission. He said that he had yet to receive information about his final objective from France. His overall strategy was first to allow himself to be maltreated, then to show that he was breaking, and afterwards to give the interrogator something. He sought to protect his real identity and mission, his headquarters and his network in the delta. While taking advantage of the ego of his brutal interrogator, he played for time as his ring went further underground. Tai had attracted attention by disclosing that he was with military intelligence and was sent to the National Interrogation Center (NIC) to be questioned by CIA and CIO officers.[29]

At the NIC, Tai appeared cooperative to his captors and insisted on his espionage mission to France. When asked about PAVN military intelligence he confirmed only known information to the CIA and CIO, since he was more or less aware of what Viet Cong defectors had already revealed. Meanwhile, members of his network in Saigon sent an agent to find out what Tai had been telling his interrogators. They supplied the agent with the alias in Tai's falsified documents, the date and place of his arrest so as to find some clues in the CIO database. South Vietnamese counterintelligence arrested the agent. Eventually, he confessed his identity, that he worked for Public Security and that he was trying to find an arrested military intelligence officer. The interrogators wondered why a Public Security agent was interested in a military intelligence officer, a member of a different organisation. In any case, the CIA was already suspicious of the real identity of Tai and submitted him to a polygraph test. Afterwards, an American interrogator took over. But later the CIO continued the interrogation. They used electric shock, as well as beating and 'Chinese water torture'. Tai did not break.

Meanwhile, captured Public Security agents and defectors were shown a photograph of Tai. Some revealed vital information about the man in the photo: he was the head of the Saigon-Gia Dinh Security Section. The informers were presented to him. One was a female agent who had bombed the national police headquarters on Tai's orders. Tai, who hit back in the interrogations, still cut such an intimidating figure that one of the agents, allegedly, committed suicide later.

The South Vietnamese told Tai that a prisoner exchange was considered only for high-ranking captives. He had only to disclose his rank, nothing else, in order to return to Hanoi. They had found revealing documents, as well as photographs of him in a security detail for Ho Chi Minh on his visit to Indonesia. Eventually, he wrote in his statement: 'My true name is Nguyen Tai, alias Tu Trong, and I am a colonel in the National Liberation Front of South Vietnam.' Of course, betrayal followed. The interrogators demanded personal details. He replied negatively and new torture sessions commenced lasting more than six months. He tried to commit suicide but was thwarted.

Some wanted Tai back. On 9 October 1971, US Army Sergeant John Sexton was freed without any DRV–CIA arrangement; he was given a note from Tran Bach Dang, the secretary of the Saigon-Gia Dinh party committee, who since August 1967 had voiced his intentions to initiate secret negotiations on prisoners with the United States. A secret exchange took place in December 1967. But there was no follow-up. In 1971, Dang proposed through Sexton to exchange Tai and another communist prisoner, Le Van Hoai, for Douglas Ramsey, a Vietnamese-speaking State Department officer captured in 1966. The negotiations led to nowhere because President Thieu, the CIA and the embassy all wanted to exchange Ramsey for Hoai only. The CIA insisted on special reciprocity: top intelligence officer for top intelligence officer. (Secret negotiations for release of intelligence operatives took place on several occasions during the war.)[30]

Tai remained in US custody to be yet again interrogated. He was locked in an air conditioned white cell; he was isolated; the aim was for him to feel disoriented. He was interrogated by Peter Kapusta, a CIA Soviet/Eastern Europe counterintelligence officer close to Angleton. Another interrogator was Frank Snepp. In his memoirs *Doi Mat Voi CIA My (Face to Face with the CIA)*, Tai indicated that once he realised that he had been turned over to the Americans, he played for time; he waited for the war to end and was not negative as he had been with the South Vietnamese interrogators: 'I will answer questions and try to stretch out the questioning to wait for the war to end. I will answer questions but I won't volunteer anything. The answers I give may be totally incorrect, but I will stubbornly insist that I am right.' He further wrote: 'I had always been firmly opposed to the desires of our propaganda agencies to discuss secret matters in the public media.... Now, because the "Security of the Fatherland" radio program had openly talked about the [Ministry's] "Review of Public Security Service Operations," I was forced to give them [the Americans] some kind of answer.'[31]

The United States had to talk to the prisoner through a South Vietnamese interrogator, usually a female employee. Snepp, who took over from Kapusta, did not use the interpreter, waiting for Tai to speak. (Tai feared that a totally US-controlled custody would ensure that no intelligence of his whereabouts would reach Hanoi. His secret desire was to prove to Hanoi that he was resisting and did not reveal any vital intelligence about his espionage network.) Thus he played the game: he could not understand anything Snepp was telling him and he 'needed' the Vietnamese interpreter (hoping that the interpreter would leak something). Eventually, Snepp asked for a Vietnamese interpreter. Snepp wrote that slowly Tai's weak points emerged. He feared the air conditioned cool temperature. The known fact that he had persecuted his own father 'no matter what the rationale, could only have been traumatic' Snepp concluded, further remarking that if we 'persuade him of the falseness of any one of these premises the whole personality would begin to crumble'. Tai showed nostalgia for his family. At one moment he told his interrogator: 'I cannot think about my wife and children.... The only way I can survive this is by putting all such hope aside. Then there are no illusions or disappointments.' Snepp wrote that Tai 'inadvertently let slip one detail after another in his helpless grasping after the one hope he knew he could not afford.... My superiors seemed satisfied.' In parallel, he interrogated Hoai and Nam Quyet (Dang was also interested in his release). Hoai disclosed information; Quyet, however, when questioned 'would lapse into a fit of coughing, thereby tearing open tubercular scars in his lungs and throat. As the interrogation continued, blood would begin oozing from his nose and mouth. He couldn't resist spitting mouthfuls at me.'[32]

The Paris Peace Accords signed on 27 January 1973 opened the way for a prisoner exchange. The CIO was furious at Snepp because he had told Tai of the prisoner exchange, thus giving him hope to hold on. Tai continued being detained in the white cell and was turned over to the CIO. According to Snepp, Tai's execution was ordered on the eve of the fall of Saigon, following a suggestion of a senior CIA official 'that it would be useful if he "disappeared"'.[33] A plan was discussed to throw Tai from a plane into the South China Sea. While all CIO officers sought to flee, those who were ordered to execute him decided otherwise, fearing reprisals by the advancing PAVN. Snepp assumed that he had been killed, but Tai was handed over to his comrades. In the fall of 1975, he returned to Hanoi (only in June 2002 was he named 'Hero of the People's Armed Forces').[34]

There could not be any doubt that Tai's ability to hold out for so long in revealing anything about himself allowed his secret organisation to readjust itself while the war was reaching its final phase. While he worked hard to survive, Dang and other intelligence leaders, in seeking a prisoner exchange and attempting to learn whether Tai had revealed anything, effectively confirmed his value in the eyes of the CIO and the CIA. Eventually, Dang was accused by Hanoi of acting independently in various areas and was removed from his position on the eve of final victory.[35]

***

The DRV's paranoia and security precautions were extensive. The Sacred Sword of the Patriots League (SSPL) was a scheme initiated by the CIA in 1963 and further implemented by MACSOG until 1968; it was completely abolished after the Paris Peace Accords. The main concept was to boost the security paranoia of the communist regime. Under this scheme, North Vietnamese were abducted and trained in paramilitary warfare. Their instructors persuaded them that they were trained by the SSPL with the aim to depose the communist regime once sent back. The CIA wanted the trained commandos to be arrested by the Public Security and then, under interrogation, to confess to their captors that the SSPL was acting against them. The information from the interrogations would be corroborated by leaflets as well as radio broadcasts calling for SSPL members to coordinate their sabotage and raids. The SSPL was based on a popular fifteenth-century

Vietnamese myth. Emperor Le Loi led a revolt against the Chinese employing mainly guerrilla tactics. His legendary sword, after the battle, was taken and kept by a lake turtle. Le Loi accepted that he needed the sword only to fight and thus the weapon was entrusted to the turtle which lived in the Lake of the Returned Sword. The SSPL maintained an anti-Chinese identity trying to stir up antagonism between Vietnamese nationalism and the Chinese role of advice and support. The SSPL was established by Le Loi admirer Le Quoc Hung in 1953, and by 1961 numbered 10,000 fighters.

The CIA forged letters to North Vietnamese officials and loyalists (implicating them in SSPL activities) in order to draw the suspicion of DRV counterintelligence. One PAVN general who received a forged letter 'was inexplicably relieved of his divisional campaign and recalled to Hanoi'.[36] Ultimately, the SSPL scheme did not turn into a big propaganda war because Washington did not want to destabilise the communist regime. Decision makers feared the escalation of the war in the south as well as a direct Chinese military intervention in support of Hanoi in the case of an insurrection in the DRV.[37]

***

DRV secret services took advantage of the growing anti-war movement and focused their efforts on Paris and other European cities where protests were huge. Jane Fonda, an ardent supporter of the anti-war movement, paid a visit to Hanoi in the summer of 1972. Ho Nam (real name: Hoang Gia Huy), a Public Security officer of the A13 Department/Foreign Intelligence Directorate working in Paris under the cover of a DRV consular officer, met Fonda and dealt with her visa request. Ho Nam said that after Fonda had left Hanoi, she called him from Bangkok and asked him to meet her at the Paris airport; he claimed that the meeting with her took place. Ho Nam boasted about his activities in Paris: 'I was able to select and recruit a network that worked actively and supplied us with important information that helped to reduce our casualties and to gain victory.' Merle Pribbenow, a former CIA officer, does not claim that Fonda spied for the DRV, but does suspect that Ho Nam and other DRV officers took advantage of her anti-war feelings and that they employed her as an 'access agent' or 'social broker' with other people who either had access to classified intelligence or could act in propaganda schemes.[38]

***

The CIA bases in the country were trying to make use of thousands of NLF defectors arrested and imprisoned by the agency before they were handed over to the ARVN and the South Vietnamese security services. Mainly, the defectors wanted protection from their compatriots and were not willing to provide the United States with valuable intelligence. The game of procrastination (and giving as little as possible in order for the Americans not to lose interest in their case) was on.[39] Nonetheless, party cadres who had defected were deemed of high intelligence value. The three major interconnected factors that influenced an NLF cadre to spy on his organisation were: family ties, money and a growing disillusionment with the DRV war effort after the 1968 Tet Offensive.

Of particular importance was the case of the defection of the party secretary Ba Tung from An Tinh village. In CIA custody he revealed that he had defected because he had taken revenge for the rape of one of his liaisons, a 15-year-old girl. She was raped by an NLF guerrilla. Without much thinking Tung ordered him executed. Only later did he realise that the guerrilla was the nephew of the district chief of security of the Trang Bang. Ba Tung escaped to the other side to save himself. The CIA arranged quickly to exfiltrate his wife and children. Gradually, a rapport was built with this high-ranking defector to the extent that he would point out several COSVN cadres among captured Vietnamese. He also elaborated on the structure of his organisation in the district he used to operate. Orrin DeForest, Tung's chief handler (a CIA operative with a police background who was trained by the Japanese secret services in the 1950s), debriefed Ba Tung and participated in the raid at An Tinh where Ba Tung identified NLF cadres. DeForest wrote later: 'I watched Ba Tung during the whole operation. I hardly could believe what he was doing. He could have picked out three, or seven, or ten – we would have been happy with anything we got. But he turned over almost a third of the entire village structure: twenty six legals and two bunker dwellers.'[40]

Ba Tung also pinpointed the headquarters of the N-10 Sapper battalion outside the hamlet of An Thanh; it was located in the jungle, less than a mile from the government's Trang Bang district headquarters. ARVN forces raided the headquarters and killed everyone – including Colonel Nam Cuong, the commander – except for a single female courier. The documents recovered, which comprised directives, orders, manuals and target lists, were described as 'gold'.[41]

Between 1968 and 1975 the CIA maintained at least three high-level spies within the NLF in Military District III, all of whom were handled by DeForest and his associates. The spy codenamed Forcie, and later the Reaper, was a high-ranking communist cadre with access to COSVN directives. His extended family had played a part in his turning. One of his uncles held high rank in the ARVN security services and tried to come into contact with his nephew. The uncle had once belonged to the Vietminh and had fought against the French. Family pressure reached a peak when he was informed that his mother had died. Already (but gradually), the Reaper had started feeding the CIA accurate intelligence.[42] DeForest wrote that by April 1969 the Reaper 'was giving us consistently good information on Viet Cong intentions and capabilities. But developing him had been a fluke, a result of fortuitous personal connections, and I for one didn't see where any other spies might come from.'[43]

Soon enough, however, another great opportunity arose for the CIA. Frustrated with the war, a Viet Cong captain, fearing the final victory of South Vietnam, defected and was held in a CIA interrogation centre. There he confided that he had a friend remaining in the NLF ranks. The CIA handlers convinced the defector to contact his friend's aunt who had raised him. He knew that his friend was visiting her. The CIA provided the defector with 25,000 piasters to be offered to the aunt; it would be the first instalment of a monthly payment, in return her cooperation and that of her nephew. Soon the aunt was on the CIA's side. The defector met with his friend, telling him that it was the United States that had freed him and given him money to live. His friend agreed to work for the CIA (not the South Vietnamese intelligence). As guided by DeForest and his associates, the defector asked his friend for a proof of honesty. He surprised him offering to blow up an NLF ammunition cache in Long Kanh. Indeed, he arranged for the explosion which took the nearby ARVN forces wholly by surprise.[44]

The next day he left a message at the arranged dead drop site: 'I blew it up – Are you happy now?' His codename was changed from Piano to Mad Bomber. As a member of the communist party the Mad Bomber had access to all directives in Subregion Five (subordinate to General Tra's Security Section in COSVN). Subregion Five was composed of

Long Khanh, Bien Hoa, Binh Duong and parts of Phuoc Long and Binh Long. The Mad Bomber took notes and passed the information in dead drops once a week (he hid the messages in a hollow at the bottom of a tree trunk outside a small hamlet). His intelligence was confirmed with information furnished by the Reaper.[45]

One NLF cadre who had defected, Cuu Long, was freed (kept though under CIA surveillance) and managed to turn his Viet Cong former lover into spy for the United States. She was an agent handler of the NLF Military Proselytizing section, and was now having an affair with a COSVN security chief (something known to the CIA). Her cover was as a black-marketer of cigarettes (thus she could visit Bien Hoa at will). Under close CIA surveillance, Cuu Long met with her.[46] Cuu Long, showing himself well-treated by the Americans, offered her money to support her and her mother and played on the nostalgia of former lovers. DeForest wrote: 'Cuu Long, a former security officer himself, conducted the proceedings as if he were Clark Gable.'[47] Eventually, he offered her work with the CIA. She looked worried. He calmed her down and told her that it was solely a CIA operation without the involvement of South Vietnamese intelligence. Money was a major incentive. She was disillusioned with the course of the war for the NLF. DeForest remarked: 'Listening to a translation of the tapes, I had the sense that I was in the presence of an agent who was very close to going over the line, and that we had given her the opportunity to do something she might have eventually done anyway. It's not that uncommon an occurrence, certainly it isn't exclusively Vietnamese.'[48]

Eventually, during her meeting with her former lover, the woman agreed to spy for the United States. DeForest and his associates codenamed her Goldmother (because of two thin golden 'luong' that dangled from a string between her breasts). Once a week, the Goldmother visited the safe house at 15 Cong Ly in Bien Hoa, and provided intelligence; among other information, she gave the names of 11 NLF agents who were part of her network. She continued 'running' her network of spies targeting the 5th ARVN division barracks. There, her most important source of intelligence was a logistics colonel, who informed her of the preparations for various operations. The CIA handler had decided not to neutralise her network. DeForest felt confident: 'Knowing what information she was reporting back gave us a way of offsetting any real damage, as well as the means to plant false information if ever there was a serious need. But the intelligence she was supplying to her supervisors was not nearly as important as what she was giving us, which was nothing less than a fairly detailed outline of all subregional military activity one week – sometimes two weeks – in advance.'[49]

Meanwhile in the spring of 1972, intelligence from secret sources, among them the Mad Bomber and the Reaper, showed that the PAVN and COSVN had no intention of advancing against Saigon, seeking the destruction of the ARVN.[50] By early September the CIA field officers (who possessed relevant intelligence), like DeForest, had concluded that the DRV negotiators wanted to reach an agreement with Kissinger by the end of October. Instructions and directives were issued to COSVN to grab as much land as possible. The operations were of high risk and resulted in heavy casualties. The NLF rushed against time. Agents reported the fast land-grab strategy, while defectors confirmed it. On 27 October 1972, the Mad Bomber reported that the H-1 Batallion was about to attack the village of Song Phu in Binh Duong (south of Phu Cuong City). The attack would take place the following morning. If they had succeeded, they would have deployed forces very close to Saigon. The Mad Bomber's intelligence was forwarded to the ARVN. A-1 bombers flew over the location at 6 a.m. The NLF was about to attack when it was bombed and forced to withdraw.[51]

While Kissinger had been negotiating with the DRV representatives in Paris, the Reaper and the Mad Bomber disclosed COSVN Resolution 20. The resolution distributed to the cadre was clear: the damage done to the COSVN capabilities was great and there was no other option but to start rebuilding the organisation and enhance its security. More intelligence came from the defection of a high-ranking political officer, Mai Thi Trang, who had direct knowledge of the resolution with reference to each province. He reported the despair among cadre and fighters and the lack of man power.[52] Even when the Paris agreement was signed, COSVN fighters feared that victory was not near; their capabilities had been obliterated while the North Vietnamese cadre and officers ruled their organisation. In fact, during the negotiations, and after the conclusion of the agreement in Paris, defectors were numerous because most of them assumed that the accords ensured only the continuance of the war. When the talks were suspended in December 1972 (and the 'Linebacker II' 11-day bombing commenced), the defectors (about 300 per month) knew nothing of importance to disclose to the CIA to illuminate Hanoi's thinking.[53]

In parallel, the CIA watched money ebb from Saigon to banks in Hong Kong; South Vietnamese officials were transferring their wealth. Meanwhile, the COSVN secret financial agents made sure to transfer money to their assets. DeForest estimated that he could discern the PAVN and NLF intentions by keeping an eye on their money couriers. In addition, the CIA bought cheap piasters in Hong Kong (piasters brought in by the South Vietnamese) and used them to pay agents in Vietnam; by dumping piasters in Hong Kong the South Vietnamese had been losing almost 50 per cent of their value.[54]

Under this surveillance scheme, the NLF's top money courier in the south was apprehended in mid-1973. Because of his old age he was dubbed the Grandpa. Realising that the CIA knew of his dealings, he agreed to work for the agency. Grandpa revealed the names of 12 Viet Cong couriers. The CIA wanted him to find the contact in Saigon who provided the funds which were eventually handed over to the NLF. Grandpa was debriefed every couple of weeks in the safe house where Goldmother also reported.[55] According to DeForest: 'Grandpa was reporting Grade A information right from the start.'[56] The Mad Bomber had failed two lie detector tests and, despite DeForest's protests, he was abandoned; payments to him and his aunt were discontinued. DeForest wrote that this came after three years of 'faultless intelligence'.[57] In December 1973, Goldmother warned of a sapper attack against the largest oil reserves depot in the Nha Be peninsula (south of Saigon), but the sabotage was not averted.[58]

CHAPTER 10

MS DAPHNE PARK, MI6 AND SOVIET ESPIONAGE

The British consulate general in Hanoi had operated since 1946 (it was opened by Trevor-Wilson) without any recognition of the DRV. Nonetheless, Ho Chi Minh and his party lieutenants were never willing to oust the British despite their close alliance with the United States. In the 1968–70 consulate general reports appears the 'usual Vietnamese source' who provided information on general conditions, including public security. Other sources of information cited were members of the international diplomatic community, with key interlocutors among the Polish, Czechs, Indonesians and French. Subjects of military intelligence were reported by 'competent' or 'qualified Western observers' (pointing to French intelligence officers in Hanoi). The evolving confrontation between the Russians and the Chinese in Hanoi, due to their countries' war over the borders with Mongolia (between 2 March and 11 September 1969), was also of great interest to Britain.

Interestingly, there were Arab sources – presumably diplomats – disclosing (fragmented) information. Her Majesty's Consul Hirst wrote to the FCO on 14 February 1969 that Arab sources claimed that the road to Haiphong was repaired after the bombing. In addition, they confirmed (backing up Indonesian sources) that Czech and East German technicians were helping with the construction of a power plant in Hanoi.[1]

On 25 March 1969, Philo, the new consul, wrote that 'qualified Western observers' had noticed troops in Hanoi. In addition, he reported that the Indonesian consul 'has heard from the Russians that they have been advised by the Vietnamese authorities to take precautions against a possible Chinese-provoked incident and that the guard on the Russian Embassy have been strengthened. According to the French, the road past the Russian embassy is now closed to Vietnamese, so it was after the Chinese incident last October.'[2] Apparently, Western observers had also seen a train transport loaded with twenty-four 122 mm guns, destined for the south.[3] The communist regime deployed troops within the city and workers militias were regularly drilling in public view. Philo remarked on 16 May: 'The defence group of the local factory was being instructed this week in the construction of a booby trap dug in the ground almost beside the front gate of our office building. The hole has now been filled in: we continue to walk delicately.'[4]

The consulate reported of a 'reliable Western source' who, on 28 May, 'overheard a conversation between two somewhat boisterous Polish technicians' and the United Arab Republic chargé d'affaires; the DRV authorities wanted the technicians to sign an agreement that the Polish government would pay for the replacement parts for the power plant. When the two refused, arguing that they had no such authority to bind their government and that there was no such initial agreement, the DRV officials protested to the Polish embassy and eventually the technicians were ordered to leave Hanoi.[5]

In June 1969, the glass display case of the Chinese embassy, a spot for anti-Soviet propaganda posters, was smashed. The DRV police took new security measures, prohibiting traffic in front of the embassy. According to 'a Western observer' there was a rumour that young Russian embassy employees were responsible for the damage done.[6]

Interestingly, 'a qualified Czech colleague' who was in the Vinh area told the British that the anti-aircraft artillery and troops had been reduced. Few guns and troops were seen on bridges; 'there are now few guns to be seen except at key points such as bridges, and although barrack buildings had been destroyed, troops move back into the barracks'.[7]

The French delegate-general informed his British counterpart about the reception for the 1 May celebration, which lasted for less than an hour. The French assumed that the short reception was due to the 'feebleness of Ho Chi Minh, who makes a compulsory appearance at this occasion. Ho did not speak or show any animation, whereas last year (according to the French) he had joked and been in good spirits. He left the meeting before the end and as he walked feebly away he was followed by someone who appeared to be ready to catch him in case he fell.'[8] A month later, on 1 June, Ho appeared at the International Children's Day ceremony giving insignias to pupils.[9] On 3 July, the Czech ambassador informed the British consul that two Chinese doctors were treating Ho, who was weak 'due to his age', not because of a particular illness.[10] On the morning of 2 September, the 79-year-old Ho Chi Minh died of heart failure. Since the 1920s he had fought for an independent Vietnam but did not live to see the end of the wars.

In October, Daphne Park of MI6 was named consul in Hanoi for 1969–70. She was a shrewd intelligence officer who had entered the world of espionage during World War II. Born in South Africa, she grew up in poverty in Tanganyika. She joined the SOE, training French resistance fighters, and on the end of the war led a Field Intelligence Agency technical detachment in Vienna, looking for former Nazi scientists. Park witnessed the kidnapping campaign of scientists and civilians by Soviet intelligence. In 1948, MI6 admitted Park into the officer ranks, where she was the only woman. She was assigned the task of managing the desk for the stay-behind network in Germany, Austria and Switzerland; she was the point of contact for the MI6 stations.[11] Later, she was sent to Moscow and to Leopoldville in the Congo, where she met the nationalist leader Patrice Lumumba of the National Congolese Movement (soon-to-become prime minister), as well as members of the Central Committee of his party.[12]

Daphne Park disagreed with CIA station chief Natsios' methods about committing in writing the recruited spies (see also Chapter 6). She remarked: 'I never said "Will you work for SIS?" I never needed to say I was an intelligence officer, and I never did. And I never recruited anybody in that way. I never sat down and said, "Sign on the dotted line and I'm going to pay you tuppence." It was understood that I had power. . . . I never said to them, "Please tell me a secret." I talked to them until they told me a secret.'[13] Next to spies, confidential contacts and agents of influence working for their governments were judged by Park as valuable interlocutors. She was confident that her non-'sexy' looks helped her intelligence gathering: 'It's been a huge advantage during my professional career that I've always looked like a cheerful, fat missionary. . . . It wouldn't be any use if you went around looking sinister, would it?'[14] Park sided with the MI6 officers who argued in favour of covert political action to topple foreign governments – all in disagreement with the ever-cautious director Dick White, who aimed for intelligence gathering exclusively. She wanted MI6 to have contacts with promising dissident politicians.[15] Indeed, in the Congo her most important contact was Damian Kandolo, the aide de camp of Lumumba, who turned against him. In fact, Park had once saved Kandolo by hiding him in her car.[16] Eisenhower and Allen Dulles, the CIA director, feared that Lumumba was opening the way for Soviet involvement in the Congo; soon, London and MI6 were convinced of the necessity to eliminate him, and he was arrested and executed by rebel troops on 17 January 1961.[17]

Describing her first images of Hanoi, Park said that 'buffaloes grazed on the grass in front of the Consulate-General, the factory defence militia practiced unarmed combat and grenade throwing there, an occasional battered cyclo-pousse creaked past carrying a family and its chattels, and at night the bats swooped and the cicada were noisy.'[18] At that time, a flu epidemic had claimed the lives of about 1,000 children. The Hungarian official, who talked to the mayor of Hanoi (who was a doctor), informed the British that the virus 'attacked the haemoglobin in the blood' so that bleeding could not be stopped.[19] However, Park reported by the end of October that the epidemic was gradually easing.[20]

The consul was followed all the time by DRV counterintelligence. She applied for a bicycle but the response of the Hanoi Municipal Bureau was negative 'on the grounds of the heavy (bicycle) traffic here, and their natural solicitous concern for my safety in view of the importance they attach to the volume of official business we transact', Park wrote to London. 'I suggested that a happy solution might be for me to order a tandem bicycle and leave the skilled front-seat driving through the dangerous traffic to a Vietnamese. After a brief pause, they replied that alas, tandems are forbidden in the DRV!'[21]

Park wrote of her living conditions: 'The Residence was formerly a house of ill-fame. Handkerchiefs are boiled in the saucepans, other dirty clothes in the dustbin. When the household cat disappeared, opinion was divided whether she had been eaten by the neighbours or the rats. When even more water than usual flooded the bathroom floor, and even less (though more noisome) water came from the tap, and the plumbers eventually came, they withdrew for three days to attend cadre meetings before removing the dead rats they found in the pipes. No rodent extermination service exists because, officially, rats have been eliminated.'[22] In addition, 'the major-domo at the Residence has been at some earlier time an inmate of a mental institution; the misfortune is that he was ever released. Nearly every necessity of life must be imported, though only upon receipt, after some months, of import permits listing each jar of herbs, each bundle of toothpicks. The Director of Customs has sometimes refused a permit, or proposed to allow in only part of the order, on the ground that Her Majesty's Representative "has had enough this year" and does not need it. The presents most prized by local staff, when they dare to accept them, are razor blades, bicycle repair outfits, bottles (empty) and Aspro [a brand name for aspirin].'[23]

Besides, 'the disagreeable and restrictive features of life in North Viet-Nam which I have cited are no more than incidental though they wear away time, temper and sometimes health. The real hardship lies in the fact that, surrounded by Viet-Namese, we can know none of them. It is in part of our non-recognition of North Viet-Nam which creates this special vacuum round us, and it is a wise policy which limits our tour here to a year: it might be difficult to report objectively for longer.'[24]

In any case, 'the unconsciously arrogant reserve which the Viet-Namese display at home, even towards their friends, will be increasingly reinforced by the defensive security processes of a Communist society'.[25] The diplomats from communist states 'at first merely baffled by the bland unpenetrability [sic] of the Viet-Namese, soon find it hard to conceal resentment at being taken for granted. Like the large, damp, crumbling crates of machinery from Eastern Europe, which lie month after month in marshalling yards or at the roadside, they stand about in bulky, awkward groups, and the whole colonial effect is absurdly enhanced by the pith helmets still favoured by so many Viet-Namese.' The Polish ambassador, like many foreign communist officials, assumed that the history and philosophy of Vietnam were a 'sub-division of Chinese studies, and Polish sinologues [sic] see everything Viet-Namese through a distorting mirror'. Contact between communist officials and Vietnamese educated in their countries was forbidden. Only when the Vietnamese wanted something, did meetings with diplomats of socialist states take place.[26]

Life for the ordinary Vietnamese was more than miserable: 'Diplomats and foreigners, driving to and from receptions, cease very soon to see them except as cyclists bent on suicide. Living in Limbo, we are nearer to them, for we walk far more, and especially at night when the children who in daylight pursue us shrieking Lien Xo [Russian], and leave us black and blue with inquisitive pinches, are gathered round the family brazier on the pavement, eating their rice, or are already asleep. Young and old, like battered bundles, sleep in the hottest months on the steps of the Ministry of Foreign Trade, on the pavement, in doorways, anywhere out of the stifling courtyards and the houses where they live, a family to each room. The rats run over them as they sleep, fight over scraps of garbage, and sometimes drown in the water which gathers in the open concrete shelter-holes; and at flood time when the drains overflow and the streets for a while are two or three feet deep in rushing water, they swim along in the brown muddy flood with leaves, twigs and rubbish. There are rats even in the cinema.'[27] In any case 'only a very strong and enduring people could survive, and with such pride and energy, the unremitting struggle that must be needed merely to stay alive in North Viet-Nam'.[28]

Park concluded her valedictory dispatch in October 1970: 'A new kitten appeared at the Residence this month and may one day kill rats if it survives. We have moved a few steps out of Limbo for we have been allowed to travel, and perhaps even hell is a little less hot than before. The children are back from the country, and Hanoi is a year further from the war I do not yet know, and neither do the Viet-Namese, whether that means they are a year nearer to peace.'[29] On 27 June 1970 Park wrote to the FCO: 'Nothing has happened to make our situation worse in the last nine months though no-one could describe it as favourable or normal. There have been incidents which the North Vietnamese could have exploited to be beastly, and they have not done so. There have also been occasions when they have made small, unexpected concessions. But the main issues are unchanged. We have no outward ciphers and no freedom of movement and are limited to a staff of two; and we are of course barred from all contact with Vietnamese other than the appropriate members of the External Affairs Bureau.'[30]

***

Meanwhile, in South Vietnam MI6 personnel as well as British Special Forces were working with the United States. The Government Communications Headquarters (GCHQ), which had stations in Hong

Kong and other South East Asian locations, was trying to intercept and decipher DRV military and diplomatic communications. In any case, the DRV ciphers were deemed 'notoriously secure'.[31]

Eventually, a vital piece of intelligence came from Soviet intercepts. GCHQ intercepted a discussion of Nikolay Firyubin, the deputy foreign minister, who was reporting from Delhi. Kissinger was informed of the intercept by British Ambassador John Freeman on 20 July 1970. Moscow wanted 'a negotiated end to the war in the not very distant future'. It would not block and call for an international summit on Vietnam.[32] The top Soviet diplomat had informed the Indian government that on two previous occasions the United States and the DRV had attempted but failed to reach an agreement out of suspicion of each other. Kissinger noted that this was known to very few people in the White House. The national security adviser concluded that the intercept was 'insufficient evidence' to map Soviet intentions. To Freeman he sounded sure that military escalation would compel the DRV to move towards the negotiating table. During this period, both the NSA and GCHQ had admitted their inability to intercept and decipher high-grade Soviet communications. The intercept offered by GCHQ was the result of patience and luck while it hoped for an indiscretion of the opponent.[33]

Back in London, Sir Dick White, the chief of MI6, came to understand the youth's moral condemnation of the United States for its intervention in Vietnam, as well as the public's perception of his profession, which had lost the romantic and noble image of World War II.[34]

***

The DRV Public Security's SIGINT units intercepted the radio communications of the National Police and Special Branch in Saigon. The Viet Cong had recruited moles in the communications departments of the police services. In parallel, the communications network of the French Foreign Ministry with their consulate in Hanoi (the net P6Z) was targeted. A DRV General later admitted that intercepts provided 'a great deal of important information that would have been difficult for human intelligence sources to obtain and that enabled us to discover the plans of big powers and hostile nations regarding efforts to settle the war on the battlefield as well as to settle the war at the conference table'. Pribbenow is certain that the technical aid for deciphering French cables came from the Soviet Union.[35] Meanwhile, in Hanoi a top-secret operation under the codename B12/MM was conducted by Public Security targeting a foreign diplomatic mission. It was an operation which produced 'accurate, objective' intelligence of US diplomacy and strategy and other 'big countries'; the information also covered the Paris Peace Conference consultations. The Public Security officer who headed the operation remarked in articles in 2009–10 that he had recruited a mole, an employee of the (unnamed) diplomatic establishment. The mole created 'a break-through that allowed the successful implementation of the plan'. Pribbenow writes that 'there is evidence that the Vietnamese may have indeed penetrated the French diplomatic facility in Hanoi and perhaps even recruited a French code clerk'.[36]

It was in the field of signals intelligence that the DRV intelligence services asked for Soviet advice and aid. In 1955, the Ministry of Public Security asked the KGB for electronic equipment for radio intercepting. The KGB dispatched advisers who together with their Vietnamese counterparts mapped the best sites for signals intelligence and trained personnel. Four years later, in 1959, the Ministry of Public Security asked the KGB for help in setting up a wide-scale 'radio counter-espionage and radio intelligence program'. Again, Russia provided advisers and equipment. The Vietnamese codenamed this programme 'Vostok'. It comprised radio counter-espionage, radio intelligence and secure communications. The Public Security wanted to detect enemy radio broadcasts and arrest the South Vietnamese operatives dispatched by the CIA; this was the task of the radio counter-espionage, which also involved the monitoring and decipher-ing of messages of DRV spies, as well as the messages of double-agents controlled by the Public Security. Under the radio intelligence operations, the diplomatic and domestic communications of South Vietnam and other countries were intercepted and decoded. The then-retired General Nguyen Huu Nhan of the Public Security, who had headed the Public Security signals intelligence unit, claimed that the radio counter-espionage programme uncovered CIA-supported com-mando teams in the period 1961–8. A spy who was using high-speed communications equipment was located and arrested. After 1965, the Public Security asked for more aid from the KGB and the Polish intelligence services, in particular for electronic equipment, including mobile radio direction-finding vehicles. The Russians and the Polish upgraded the intelligence capabilities of the Vietnamese to track down enemy commandos.[37]

DRV intelligence began cooperating in training with the Stasi (the East German secret service). The first contacts took place in 1957. Two years later, Vietnamese intelligence officials consulted with their German counterparts in East Berlin. In 1960, Minister of Public Security Tran Quoc Hoan discussed with his counterpart in East Berlin the modernisation of the North Vietnamese security and police. By 1965, the DRV upgraded its technical surveillance departments for counterespionage. In December 1965, Nguyen Minh Tien, the head of the North Vietnamese Technical Operations Sector, discussed with officers of the Stasi Technical Operations Sector methods and techniques for the fabrication of documents. In 1967, the Stasi commenced training Vietnamese intelligence officers and Hanoi was supplied with surveillance and telecommunications equipment. East German intelligence officers were deployed in Hanoi, helping their counterparts to list 'negative elements' as well as expand the networks of DRV informants. Meanwhile, Hungary and Czechoslovakia contributed by developing Hanoi's security apparatus.[38]

The GRU worked in parallel with the KGB and convinced its Vietnamese counterparts to be granted access to the remains of downed US aircraft – among the equipment found, inspected and eventually given to the GRU was the entire cockpit of a downed F-111. Some GRU and the Soviet Air Defense officers attended the interrogations of US prisoners of war. The KGB provided the DRV security training for interrogations.[39] In spring 1967, Moscow and Hanoi concluded an agreement on electronic intelligence (ELINT). Russian specialists with advanced equipment were sent to work with their Vietnamese counterparts on jamming US communications. The DRV Ministry of Defense asked for GRU's aid in breaking US military communications codes. In addition, Vietnamese and Russian experts interrogated captured US pilots for technical information.[40] With the help of the Russians, in 1968 the Ministry of Defense established the 8th Jamming Reconnaissance Battalion aiming at B-52 bombers; according to post-war Vietnamese literature, this battalion played a significant role during the air bombing operations Linebacker I and II of Christmas 1972.[41]

· According to a senior Public Security officer who had served in South Vietnam, by 1972 the warning of coming B-52 bombings provided to the Viet Cong included the date, time and location of the attacks. Meanwhile, Soviet Navy electronic intelligence collection trawlers steaming in the South China Sea and off the coast of Guam shadowed US aircraft carriers and B-52 flights to North Vietnam. However, it is not certain that the Russians shared the intelligence gathered with Hanoi.[42]

Nonetheless, other accounts show that the Soviets had limited access to either US prisoners of war under interrogation or captured US military technology to the extent that KGB chairman Vladimir Semichastny voiced his discontent with the attitude of the Vietnamese. DRV security officials inhibited the access of Soviet intelligence officers to captured Americans, viewing the Soviets with extreme suspicion. In fact, in March 1965, Zhou Enlai had warned Ho Chi Minh that the Soviet advisers and training personnel were involved in espionage and subversion while working with the allied communist regimes in Cuba, China and North Korea.[43] In 1968, the remarks of a Vietnamese journalist to the correspondent of *Izvestia* reached the Central Committee of the CPSU in Moscow. The journalist had asked playfully: 'Do you know what is the Soviet Union's share of the total assistance received by Vietnam and what is the share of Soviet political influence there (if the latter can be measured in percentages)? The figures are, respectively, 75–80 per cent and 4–8 per cent.'[44]

In a speech to a top-secret Public Security conference in 1971, Minister of Public Security Tran Quoc Hoan advised: 'There are some of our [socialist] "brothers" who come to our country to conduct intelligence activities. We must immediately set up a case file, just as if it is a regular counter-espionage case, but the question in this case is whether we should let this case run for a long time or not, because if we let it become a long-term, protracted case, it will cause us political problems and usually it will only result in a waste of our resources. In this case, we should skilfully and flexibly immediately cut off all contacts and connections that are not to our advantage. You need to look at how the Americans do it; they are very practical. One day they attack a problem one way, and the next they attack it in another. Otherwise, one can easily be put on the defensive. . .'[45]

The DRV leadership's confidence in Moscow was shaken by the so-called 'Anti-Party Affair'. From the summer of 1967 to early 1968, dozens of party cadre were arrested and charged with being 'lackeys of a foreign power'. Specifically, they were accused of supporting Moscow's strategy and aims for the DRV not to escalate the war, and of opposing the 'pro-Chinese' stance of Hanoi. Soviet intelligence officers found themselves followed all the time and their movements restricted; one Soviet diplomat was expelled.[46]

In the end, despite extensive counterintelligence, Hanoi was unaware that by 1975 the KGB residency was exploiting a network of 25 agents and 60 confidential contacts, all focusing on the DRV military and intelligence structures as well as the border areas of China. The KGB had recruited a senior intelligence officer under the codename Isayeyev, probably while he was serving in Moscow. He provided intelligence about the personnel of the DRV security and intelligence services, but always broke contact while in Hanoi out of fear of being discovered.[47] In any case, KGB 'active measures' in black propaganda boosted the image of Hanoi fighting the United States. In 1968, the KGB fabricated a letter from Gordon Goldstein of the Office of Naval Research 'revealing' US biological weapons deployed in South Vietnam and Thailand. The 'news' was picked up by the press in South East Asia and India, which concluded that the US Army was conducting biological warfare against Hanoi by spreading diseases.[48]

Oleg Kalugin, a former KGB general, wrote in his memoirs that in the early 1970s the KGB liaison in Hanoi was ordered to contact the DRV intelligence to allow for US prisoners of war to be recruited by the KGB. Nonetheless, the cooperation of the DRV intelligence was limited: 'For half a year, we received no answer from Hanoi. Finally, the Vietnamese said we could send a KGB representative to Hanoi. I sent one of my subordinates, Oleg Nechiporenko, who was permitted to see transcripts of some interrogations of American prisoners. From those documents, he focused on several POWs (Prisoners of War) as possible recruits. On that trip, however, the Vietnamese did not permit Nechiporenko to interview the Americans, and he returned to Moscow empty-handed. In 1973 or 1974, when all American prisoners supposedly had been repatriated, the Vietnamese again contacted us and said we could send a representative to Hanoi. Nechiporenko returned and stayed at least a month. This time he was allowed to question a CIA agent and two American pilots. The CIA officer gave us some information on his agency and even told Nechiporenko he would cooperate with us when he returned to America. Nechiporenko flew back to Moscow, and the CIA man apparently returned to the United States. But in 1975 or 1976, when KGB officers in Washington attempted to contact him, he was nowhere to be found.'[49]

In January 1992, the DRV surprised Washington, admitting that the KGB interrogated at least one American prisoner of war in January 1973. General Kalugin testified before the Senate Select Committee on POW-MIA affairs that the KGB had questioned Americans in Vietnam as late as 1975–8. The DRV government announced that the American interrogated by the KGB was Eugene Andre Weaver, who was taken prisoner on 31 January 1968 in Hue during the first day of the Tet Offensive. Weaver (a former B-17 bomber pilot during World War II) was a CIA adviser to CORDS. His capture was filmed by the PAVN and was later presented on a CBS evening news broadcast. Weaver tried to keep secret his CIA identity, but a Viet Cong guard recognised him because earlier Weaver had interrogated him. Eventually, he was released on 16 March 1973.[50]

CHAPTER 11

THE DOUBLE AGENT GAMES
OF THE WHITE HOUSE

Richard Nixon and Henry Kissinger, his national security adviser and
from September 1973 his secretary of state, are viewed by historians as a
team in foreign policy making. Aristotle called man a 'political animal'.
This certainly applied in their case. Nonetheless, one could argue that
when politicians speak too much about deception, disinformation and
double agents they sound more like amateur spymasters. Both men
served in the military during World War II. Nixon was a staff officer;
Kissinger a sergeant in the Counter-Intelligence Corps. Nixon was
commissioned in the United States Naval Reserve in June 1942. He
saw sea duty as the officer in charge of the cargo handling units of the
South Pacific Combat Air Transport Command at Guadalcanal in the
Solomon Islands and later at Green Island. In 1944, Kissinger was tasked
with intelligence duties in Belgium and during the occupation of
Germany he was put in charge of a team in Hannover, searching for
Gestapo officers and other Nazis who could turn to guerrilla warfare
against the Allied forces. Kissinger was awarded the Bronze Star for
'performing duty in charge of a Counter Intelligence team operating
under difficult and extremely hazardous conditions'. He 'successfully
established chains of informants reaching into every phase of civilian life,
resulting in the detection and arrest of numerous persons identified.as
enemy agents engaged in espionage and sabotage'. In 1946, Sergeant
Kissinger was an instructor at the European Command Intelligence
School at Camp King.[1]

Nixon was strongly interested in psychological warfare and disinformation. On 24 November 1969, he wrote to Kissinger: 'Are we doing everything we can with regard to trying to disrupt morale in North Vietnam and among the VC? On several of my visits to Vietnam, people told me that there could be programs which would be effective in reducing morale in those areas. I know that CIA, of course, is a miserable flop in this field, but will you give me a report as to whether our program, if any, is adequate.'[2] Kissinger sought to sound optimistic towards an overconfident president: 'Despite the formidable difficulty of measuring the effectiveness of covert operations in denied areas, there is tangible evidence that these efforts have had some impact on North Vietnamese and Viet Cong morale.'[3] The national security adviser admitted that the overt psychological warfare schemes focused on South Vietnam and the NLF employing broadcasts and distributing leaflets. The only operation against Hanoi was the broadcast of a radio station, Voice of Freedom, which was deemed unreliable. Nixon wanted leaflets to be dropped in the DRV. Kissinger passed him the CIA's proposals:

a. Re-examination of the total allied broadcasting effort reaching the enemy in South Vietnam to determine if it is adequate. It is possible that some transmitter assets now being directed at North Vietnam should be reoriented to the enemy in South Vietnam.

b. Reintroduction of leaflets into North Vietnam using wind drift insertion from aircraft flying over international waters or third countries adjacent to North Vietnam.

c. Utilization of Viet Cong and North Vietnam Army rallies within the South Vietnam psychological warfare organizations.

d. Intensification of efforts to improve thematic guidance and selective targeting through better utilization of intelligence.[4]

Eventually, Nixon authorised Kissinger to 'step up this activity [of CIA psychological warfare programmes] to the maximum extent possible.'[5]

Richard Helms, the CIA director, admitted during a conference that 'because of the structure, security and discipline of the regime in both countries (in China and the DRV), we have no high-level penetrations'. He remarked that a recently published novel, *The Defector* by Charles Collingwood, had 'a good description of the political environment in Hanoi'. He continued revealing 'certain audio surveillance operations, using the take from some of these as illustrations of our capacity to monitor North Vietnamese attitudes and intentions' claiming that US assessments of the enemy's intentions had been accurate.[6]

From February 1970 onwards, the CIA dispatched 22 teams of Laotian commandos in the DRV on sabotage missions. In March 1972, Helms wrote to Kissinger, telling him that the results were meagre; he suggested that the operations stop and be replaced by a deception campaign which would take advantage of the DRV's security paranoia.[7] Deception operations were implemented during the incursion in Cambodia and the 'Lamson 719' operation. (Between 8 February and 25 March 1971, ARVN forces had invaded Laos to destroy PAVN forces and logistics infrastructure; eventually, they withdrew having had limited success.) Helms proposed a set of deception scenarios, which, if implemented, could support US diplomacy in the talks with the DRV delegation in Paris. A 'rumour' entailed: the DRV leadership was to be 'informed' by a secret source under the control of the CIA that Washington and Beijing were negotiating a 'secret protocol'. Accordingly, China would agree to stop its military assistance to the DRV. In return, the United States would continue with the 'open door policy', would guarantee the territorial integrity of China and would withdraw the ships of 7th Fleet from the Taiwan Straits. (Helms argued that if the Hanoi leadership believed this, they 'should expedite serious negotiations since it would point to the beginning of the end of military assistance either from or through China'.)[8]

An alternative rumour to be leaked by a controlled secret source to Hanoi, would claim that President Nixon was seriously examining cutting a deal with Moscow, binding the Russians to stopping their military aid to the DRV. In return, Washington would agree to a conference in Europe which could lead to the withdrawal of US forces from the region. Helms was confident that this rumour 'could have [a] high impact on Hanoi, since the USSR currently provides 80 per cent of DRV's foreign assistance'.[9]

Paranoia and suspicion within the top leadership circles of Hanoi were factors to be exploited by the CIA. Helms offered Kissinger an alternative rumour: a secret source would tell the North Vietnamese that there was a faction of the DRV Politburo that had decided to stage a coup so as to stop the war and save the country's economy. According to this rumour, the coup leaders were supported by Beijing, which was acting as Washington's proxy. China would receive industrial aid packages from the United States. This rumour could be supported by the atmosphere of the Hoang Minh Chinh affair in 1967, which, Helms hoped, offered 'plausible evidence to support the idea that Hoang and his cohorts were, in fact, Chinese – or Soviet – agents of influence. The result could be increased suspicion and repression within the leadership structure with a concomitant diminution in drive and efficiency.' (Hoang Minh Chinh, a prominent member of the Politburo, and his followers were arrested, accused of pro-Soviet sentiment; he was charged, among other crimes, with passing to a foreign power a secret document of Sino-Vietnamese consultations.)[10]

Another rumour would involve an upper-middle-level Soviet official's fabricated report, leaked by the controlled secret source to DRV intelligence. The Soviet official had a discussion with high-ranking members of the Japanese Communist Party. The Japanese communists would argue that Soviet interests and influence would suffer if Hanoi turned victorious after a humiliating American defeat. The best outcome would be for the war to continue, and Saigon to resist. As a result, the DRV, preoccupied with the war, would not seek to dominate the communist movements in Cambodia, Thailand and Malaysia. In addition, the Japanese had informed the Soviet official that it was not economically feasible for Japanese companies to invest in the DRV. Helms was certain that 'the objective here would be to reinforce whatever views the Hanoi leadership may have that the USSR is prepared to play big-power politics and sell the DRV down the river when the Soviets' own national interests are at stake'.

The Sino-US talks during Nixon's visit to Beijing formed the basis for more false rumours. Helms proposed to Kissinger that a secret source would inform DRV intelligence that the United States had told the China that it was prepared to grant aid to both North and South Vietnam; to which China would reply that the offer to the DRV should be either hard goods or light industrial aid, avoiding making Hanoi follow a hegemonic stance towards Laos and Cambodia. As Helms put

it, this rumour 'would reinforce to Hanoi's leadership the prospect of
an emerging conflict of interest between China and North Vietnam in
Indochina, with consequent worry that future Chinese aid might be
less generous'.[11]

In their turn, the PAVN made a bid to create a fait accompli.
Abandoning the negotiations on 30 March, the DRV leaders ordered an
invasion of South Vietnam, which the Americans called the Easter
Offensive. There was an initial advance of the PAVN. Nixon retaliated
by ordering the mining of Haiphong and massive bombings, which,
together with the counterattacks of the ARVN, saved Saigon from
defeat. On 3 May 1972, the ARVN retook Quang Tri, which had earlier
been captured by the PAVN.

Seeking ways to make the DRV fear the United States, Nixon himself
paid too much attention to the leaflets campaign and to psychological
warfare in general. On his request in May 1972, Kissinger informed him
of overt and covert propaganda schemes. The main theme of the leaflets
dropped in the DRV was that there was dissent among Hanoi's leaders
and that the people suffered from low morale and did not want to
continue the war.[12]

The national security adviser wrote about future psychological
operations with radio broadcasts giving the targeted audience 'an
aggregate message of North Vietnamese defeat, and accurate information
about such matters as killed or captured North Vietnamese soldiers'.
Nixon was briefed about the CIA's disinformation operations. The
agency was tasked with convincing 'the top Hanoi leadership that the
US Government is in clandestine communication with a high-level
dissident faction within the North Vietnamese Party Apparatus'. The
president wrote 'good' in the margin of the page. Kissinger continued:
'The first phase of this program involves "leaking" through a trusted
agent in Vientiane the alleged word of an American official that "there
are some people in Hanoi who also want to end this stupid war" and
"thank God not everybody on the Central Committee is crazy". –
"Evidence" will then be provided from a variety of sources and agents to
develop the legend that the US Government is in secret contact with a
dissident faction in the North Vietnamese hierarchy. It might even be
said that it was this faction which recommended the mining of
Haiphong as the only tangible way to break the power of the hardliners
in Hanoi.' (Nixon highlighted this phrase and, again, wrote 'good' in the

margin.) Kissinger hoped that 'the effects of this disinformation program could be significant – tensions and suspicions within the already paranoiac Hanoi leadership might increase, and the unity of this leadership might be weakened'.[13]

Psychological warfare operations were underway; parachuting of radios and military equipment created the impression of continuing commando operations in the DRV.[14] Nixon, seeking to show the escalation of the war, approved (with his usual 'good' remark pencilled in the margin) a set of other operations, such as the parachuting of supplies and the abandoning of amphibious warfare equipment on the coast so as to make the ever-suspicious DRV security services assume that more commandos were operating in their territory. He agreed to dispatch US Navy ships close to the coast, so as to make Hanoi fear an imminent invasion.[15] Admiral Thomas M. Moorer, the chairman of the Joint Chiefs of Staff, sent a message to Admiral John Sidney 'Jack' McCain Jr, the Commander in Chief of the Pacific, to coordinate authorised psychological operations. The operations for immediate implementation were: the insertion of counterfeit money into the DRV by air, secret agents or mail (the CIA would provide the money); the distribution of false documents showing the weaknesses of the communist regime; and the parachuting in of radio equipment and propaganda booklets.[16]

The double agent disinformation operation turned out not to be an easy affair. Carver, the special assistant for Vietnamese affairs at the CIA, wrote to Richard T. Kennedy of the NSC staff:

1. Our project to convince the Hanoi leadership that the U.S. Government is in clandestine communication with a high-level dissident faction within North Vietnam hit a snag when our double agent asset [less than one line not declassified] muffed his lines in a 22 May [1972] session with the North Vietnamese intelligence officer with whom he has been in contact. Unfortunately, at the point in the conversation where the agent was to allude to information about American contact with dissidents allegedly provided by the agent's notional 'American friend' (the purported source of the earlier data on mining), the agent strayed from his prepared script and the North Vietnamese did not pick up the point or pursue it.

2. Although we are disappointed in this setback, we had a stroke of luck the following day [23 May] when the press carried remarks by General Haig to the effect that there is 'no solidarity of views among the northern leadership' over the current invasion of the south and that moderates (in North Vietnam) want to 'scale down the ambitions of the regime' and 'draw back from the blood-letting in the south.' We plan to use these published comments of General Haig to get our disinformation program back on the rails. In their 22 May session, the North Vietnamese intelligence officer did ask our asset to find out how far the Americans are likely to go in applying pressure on North Vietnam and whether the U.S. will invade North Vietnam with American troops. Within the next few days, our asset will re-contact the North Vietnamese intelligence officer, report some filler-type generalizations on the troop and invasion issue (suitably slanted) and then re-broach the thought that the Americans are being advised by the high-level North Vietnamese dissidents with whom the U.S. is in contact, alluding to General Haig's remarks to buttress the fictional specifics provided by our asset's notional 'American contact'.[17]

In parallel, one-way voice radio messages would be broadcast so that the DRV security would assume that a dissident faction was getting instructions from abroad. There would also be a second double agent operation of disinformation, so as to give credence to the disinformation of the first. In any case, 'structuring this kind of disinformation in a manner that whets the target's appetite and remains plausible is a tricky proposition which cannot be rushed and which is always subject to the vagaries of chance and human nature'.[18]

On 1 June, the double agent met with the DRV intelligence officer. Kissinger himself informed Nixon, who was a keen enthusiast for these kinds of games: 'CIA has "revealed" to a North Vietnamese intelligence officer that the US Government has "clandestine contacts" with high-level dissidents in North Vietnam.' (Nixon wrote 'good' in the margin.) 'The [DRV] officer did not react to this revelation but took careful notes which may stimulate a reaction when his reports reach Hanoi. The channel used for this disinformation was the CIA asset [less than one line not declassified] who had established his credibility with the intelligence officer by reporting in advance on US intentions to mine Haiphong harbor. The officer told CIA's asset that Hanoi had cabled its congratulations on the Haiphong report. Because of the accuracy of his earlier reporting, the asset's current account of US "contacts" with dissidents may trigger probing questions from Hanoi. The intelligence officer plans to vacation in North Vietnam in July and seemed despondent, admitting that recent US actions had hurt North Vietnam and that his family was suffering hardships by being split up. He said he recognized that the US could carry on the war for a long time, but the US problem was that it did not know when or where the North Vietnamese will continue the struggle. He asked the CIA asset if the South Vietnamese Army would invade North Vietnam.'[19]

A second meeting between the double agent and the DRV officer took place on 13 June. On 29 June, Kissinger was informed: 'On balance, the double agent has the impression from this, and other recent conversations with DRV officials, that Hanoi is extremely anxious to find a way out of its dilemma and is reviewing the options to see what realistic bargaining points it has for renewed negotiations.'[20]

Nixon had turned himself into a master spy obsessed with disinformation. He pushed the concept of deception with the aim of making Hanoi believe that a secret campaign was taking place. Nonetheless, Melvin Laird, the secretary of defense, made a bid to persuade Nixon that this kind of operation had no value:

On 18 July 1972, I was notified of your desire to proceed with the task of creating notional agents/resistance groups in North Vietnam without the insertion of pseudo agents. A notional agents program implemented without concurrently conducting agent or direct action team operations might achieve limited credibility; however, the effectiveness of notional programs is directly related to and dependent upon actual operations to foster credibility. Although black radio operations, insertion of bogus documents, and dummy supply drops might cause some concern within North Vietnam, it is unlikely that significant reaction will result unless there is physical evidence of actions carried out by such a group. This credibility problem is compounded by the fact that tangible support of notional operations ceased within North Vietnam after the 1968 bombing halt and would be difficult to reestablish at this time. . . . Therefore, unless you indicate otherwise, I propose not to proceed with a notional agents/resistance group program in North Vietnam due to the marginal return anticipated and the risks to US personnel. The Chairman, Joint Chiefs of Staff concurs.[21]

Laird referred to a number of psychological warfare operations and their results. Ninety-two fabricated letters by Vietnamese to their compatriots to stop the war were sent from overseas – but the results were not yet known. A total of 30,000 radios would be parachuted in September into the DRV; results would be reported. The secretary of defense was not in favour of small-scale raids against PAVN installations out of fear of US casualties.

The CIA and the Pentagon had trained 20 former PAVN troopers to infiltrate the DRV in short-term missions. Nonetheless, Laird informed Nixon that the 'review of this concept suggests limited intelligence or sabotage potential with significant risk to personnel and supporting aircrews'. He also feared that if prisoners were taken, Washington would be blamed of contravening the 1954 Geneva Accords. The 7th Fleet retained the capability to launch diversionary amphibious attacks against the DRV coast. Laird reassured Nixon: 'The strategy of applying maximum military and psychological pressure on the enemy is proceeding with all available resources. Psychological operations, particularly, have been expanded dramatically with both leafletting and extensive broadcasting campaigns.'[22]

The secretary of defense's scepticism about the lack of credibility of the notional resistance proposed by Nixon was well founded. But the president would not change his mind. On 18 August, Kissinger replied to Laird: 'The President requests that a plan for creating notional/agent resistance groups in North Vietnam should be pursued vigorously in coordination with the Director of Central Intelligence. This would not require the insertion of personnel, but only give the appearance that we have done so (by dropping parachutes, agent radios, beaching rafts, etc.). This program can be further exploited by radio traffic directed to the notional agents. Even though the DRV may suspect this operation is a ploy, it cannot be sure and must consequently divert assets to counter it.'[23]

Meanwhile, the CIA managed to get hold of the COSVN resolution and assessments for offensives during the August–September period and on 26 July 1972 distributed them to key agencies. The next day, at a meeting in the White House chaired by Kissinger, the participants touched on the COSVN resolution and the secret source who had supplied it:

Kissinger: The other side wants us to set a terminal withdrawal date. Then there will be no progress in the negotiations, and the date will be upon us. We will have made a unilateral withdrawal – with nothing to show for it.

Sullivan (representative of the State Department): Incidentally, the COSVN assessment of the offensive and instructions on VC missions for August and September is very much like my analysis. If it isn't authentic, it is a great GVN forgery. [To Mr. Carver:] Do you think it is authentic?

Carver (representative of the CIA): The fellow who coughed it up is authentic. If he isn't, the North Vietnamese are paying a lot to authenticate a double agent. He has already cost them five companies, with information he's given us about tactical situations.

Kissinger: Have I seen this document?

Rush (representative of the Department of Defense): It's the one about VC tactics.

Kissinger: [To Mr. Sullivan:] Wouldn't you expect the North Vietnamese to be taking a harder line in Paris?

Sullivan: Yes, I would. Their propaganda line will be hard for the next couple of months, especially if there is flooding again.

Kissinger: I have concluded that the North Vietnamese are not very bright. I used to think they were diabolically clever. Not now, though. From their point of view, they would be better off now if they had taken one of our previous proposals.

[...]

Sullivan: The COSVN document makes interesting reading. It says: 'The VC/NVA will hit the GVN hard to force US President Nixon to settle the war on VC terms. If he does not end the war, he may lose the Presidential election in November. It is the intention of the Central Party Committee to force Nixon to accept the seven-point proposal and then to lose the election. The Party has come to know much about Nixon in four years. If he remains President, the VC will meet great difficulty despite a cease-fire. In the negotiations, the VC may have to make some concessions to end the war and to stop US bombing and blockade of North Vietnam. However, the negotiations must be based upon the seven points, and the VC will offer no other proposal.' This has the ring of truth to it, stubborn as it may sound.[24]

In any case, the precise effect of Nixon's and Kissinger's double agent deception on the DRV leadership's evolving stance towards the negotiations with the United States cannot be assessed. The evidence in this chapter shows that both top decision makers authorised and followed the handling of the double agent closely. It may be argued that we will never have a reliable (and not doctored) DRV account of the double agent disinformation and its impact on Vietnamese thinking. No doubt, the disclosure that the double agent succeeded in scaring off Hanoi would be an embarrassment to the Vietnamese leaders and their legacy.

After the resumption of the US–DRV negotiations in Paris on 8 October, Pham Xuan An remained the best-informed mole and journalist due to his connections with the head of the CIO.[25] Kissinger needed more information about Hanoi's plans, which looked intransigent despite yet another bombing campaign (operation Linebacker I); it was only after Linebacker II that Hanoi changed its stance. The CIA executed an operation to wiretap a landline of Hanoi's general staff communications. Air America employed a Hughes 500P (Penetrator) helicopter called the 'Quiet One'. Intelligence had revealed a telephone line outside the industrial city of Vinh. At one point, the phone line was not guarded. In a single operation, Laotian commandos taken there by a Hughes 500P installed a tap on the line as well a solar-powered relay station.[26] The CIA provided Kissinger with the secret intelligence.

Kissinger informed Nixon of 10 notional covert operations of infiltration of commandos in the DRV 'to lead the North Vietnamese to believe resistance groups are active in their midst'. The national security adviser claimed: 'We continue to receive indications we are touching sensitive North Vietnamese nerves. The DRV Premier's office recently issued a directive warning of US spy war schemes. . . . This warning has been repeated in North Vietnamese newspapers and on radios. Radio Hanoi recently reacted angrily against Voice of America about the DRV support of Arab terrorists. Numerous North Vietnamese POW and rallier reports are being received attesting to the effectiveness of one phase or another of our efforts – a recent rallier indicated he turned himself in as a result of listening to our "Mother Vietnam" broadcasts and stated that these have prompted other members of his unit to desert and return home.'[27] At least this was something Nixon would have liked to read about – psychological warfare effects.

After the signing of the Paris Peace Accords on 27 January, Kissinger asked James R. Schlesinger, the new CIA director, to secretly warn Hanoi to abstain from 'massive violations'. Schlesinger informed Kissinger: 'This message was passed on 16 March to well-placed North Vietnamese officials in both Vientiane [in Laos] and Paris under circumstances which should assure that it will reach the proper quarters in Hanoi.' The CIA director remarked that 'our disinformation program was designed specifically to lead the North Vietnamese to conclude that we were deliberately leaking our plans to them in such a way as to enable them, in effect, to save face vis-à-vis the American officials with whom they are engaged in on-going negotiations. By passing an identical message simultaneously in two widely separated portions of the globe, we sought to underscore the seriousness which we ascribed to this warning.'[28]

Psychological warfare continued, mainly in the form of radio broadcasts. The CIA proposed a black propaganda radio programme. 'Other radio efforts', however, were 'dropped as they became outmoded, and the mailing of letters to DRV officials abroad was terminated due to lack of response'. Mother Vietnam was a grey propaganda radio scheme, which for a year had been 'especially effective'. The new black propaganda radio scheme, called The Voice of Nam Bo Liberation, would target the South Vietnamese NLF fighters trying to make them antagonise their North Vietnamese comrades in arms.[29]

On 2 November 1973, Kissinger asked the CIA for yet another covert disinformation operation to make the DRV assume that any of their new major offensives would lead to US bombings. William Colby, the new CIA director, replied on 23 November: 'This program [of disinformation] has now been launched, and we have already received indications that at least some aspects of it have hit their mark.' Meanwhile, the CIA was examining ways 'to cause the North Vietnamese leadership to doubt the reliability of China as an ally in time of war'.[30]

CHAPTER 12

DESPERATE SPIES OF THE FALLING DOMINO

Thomas Polgar, a Hungarian-born OSS veteran with a heavy accent, was appointed station chief in Saigon, succeeding Shackley. He was the son of Jewish Hungarian parents and fled to the United States to avoid persecution – and death – by the Nazis. During the war he had joined the OSS and was eventually parachuted behind enemy lines to gather intelligence; by the end of the war he was operating on the outskirts of Berlin. Post-war, he joined the CIA and found himself working for the Berlin station, where he developed his later much-admired managerial skills. In the late 1960s, he was appointed chief of station in Buenos Aires, and eventually dealt with the hijacking of Americans on an aeroplane. He was called to negotiate with the hijackers to free the hostages. He observed that they were exasperated, narrating to Snepp, a young CIA intelligence officer: 'It was really a rather simple affair. The hijackers were getting pretty hot in the cabin with no air conditioning. I offered to send some Cokes into them. I drugged the Cokes and then, when the fellows were feeling relaxed, I walked in and took their guns away.'[1] Langley considered the station chief a hero and rewarded him with the Saigon station.

Soviet, Hungarian and Polish intelligence were interested in the new station chief. The Hungarians dispatched experienced operatives commanded by Anton Tolgyes, a Hungarian Jew, who, after being imprisoned by the Red Army, was committed to the communist regime. Snepp writes that 'an old and trusted axiom of the intelligence business that East European émigrés are the most nostalgic people in the world, particularly vulnerable to the blandishments of heritage and homeland'.[2] A back channel was opened: Polgar, Tolgyes and other Hungarians were secret interlocutors in Saigon.

On 3 May 1972, the ARVN retook Quang Tri, which was captured by the PAVN in the 1972 Easter Offensive. On 5 May at a reception at the Japanese embassy, Polgar met the head of the Polish International Commission for Control (ICC) delegation, whom, he wrote, 'happened to be [a] very experienced intelligence operative and also a man of the world'. The chief of station asked for the delegation head's views on the Quang Tri, only to hear him gloating that it was irrelevant 'because South Vietnam will lose the war in Washington'.[3]

The Paris Peace Accords were signed on 27 January 1973, facilitating the US military disengagement. The International Commission for Control and Supervision (ICCS) had been established to monitor the truce; it comprised two communist state delegations, from Poland and Hungary, and two neutral ones, from Iran and Indonesia (each delegation numbered about 200 members, officers and other ranks). Richard Hale, a CIA operative, wrote that the ICCS 'seemed like an excellent opportunity to recruit some defectors in place, prepared to report back to the agency after they returned home to Hungary and Poland. We were not looking for outright defections, and in fact refused more than one ... those of us not previously exposed to the Poles discovered how lightly the mantle of communism rested on their shoulders. We had so many volunteers that we had to turn some away and could afford to be selective. The Hungarians were a different matter. We eventually did have some limited success, but I have to say those boys were for the most part dedicated Communists.'[4] One future CIA mole who served in Vietnam, Ryszard Jerzy Kukliński, was a Polish colonel who served with the ICC from November 1967 to May 1968. He made contact with a US officer of Polish descent, but at that time did not offer to spy for the United States. Kukliński witnessed the Tet Offensive in Saigon and on returning to Poland was assigned work as a liaison with the Soviets on the operational plans for the invasion of Czechoslovakia. In 1971, he started spying for the CIA. During a 10-year period, he passed almost 35,000 documents (strategy plans, weaponry and tactics) of Soviet and Warsaw Pact forces to the CIA.[5]

Meanwhile the CIA targeted Soviet spies; a report of the CIA on potentially embarrassing episodes read: 'CIA [not declassified] technicians conducted tests in Miami area in August 1971 of DF [direction finding] gear intended for use against a Soviet agent in South Vietnam'.[6]

***

After the resignation of President Nixon in 1974, Pham Xuan An concluded that the United States would not intervene to save the South Vietnamese regime. In his messages to Hanoi, he insisted on a final largescale attack against Saigon.[7] According to Ba Minh, An's handler during the final phase of the war, the mole 'managed to obtain all US documents of strategic importance every year'.[8] An had access to the ARVN strategic studies report by General Nguyen Xuan Trien, who was involved in the coup against Diem; the report detailed the insufficient war supplies, low morale and the growing pessimism that Washington would ever employ B-52s to help the regime survive an attack by the PAVN.[9]

A high-ranking Viet Cong defector told Snepp in 1973 that the DRV had been planning for a ceasefire since 1971; the logistics units were assigned the task of setting up enclaves, predominantly along the western border of the Republic of Vietnam, to support the 'political struggle'. In addition, there was a scheme to move three million 'voters' into the south, in case elections were organised after an agreement with Saigon.[10]

In the summer of 1974, Kissinger authorised Polgar, who in turned assigned Snepp to provide intelligence briefings to the Polish and Hungarian ICCS delegations (who were in effect Warsaw's and Budapest's spies). Polgar and his staff were directed to argue in favour of the DRV, accepting demarcation of borders with the Republic of Vietnam. Snepp's aim was 'to convince them, and through them Hanoi, that we were fully aware of North Vietnamese plans and that the military stalemate was here to stay'. The briefing was the first in a series of secret contacts by Polgar that gave intelligence to the Hungarians on the assumption that they would persuade Hanoi's leadership to moderate its position. The United States had re-approached China and détente was achieved with the Soviet Union; thus it was (wrongly) assumed by Washington that Hanoi would feel isolated and abstain from any offensive.[11]

According to Polgar, the DRV 'did not keep their intentions secret'. 'Starting in October 1974 when we got the plan for 1975 I remember

I drove up to Bien Hoa to talk with my base chief in whose area this particular document was acquired. And we came to the conclusion that the language in this document was terribly similar to the COSVN 90 directive which came out a couple of months before the 1972 offensive.'[12]

By mid-December 1974, the PAVN commenced the first phase of the winter–spring campaign, with the aim of suffocating Saigon. By the end of December, General Viktor Kulikov, the head of the Soviet general staff, paid a visit to Hanoi; Polgar warned Langley that the Soviets were implicated in the campaign but found no willing ears.[13] Meanwhile, the station feared that possibly four members from Thieu's inner circle were assisting the DRV; among them the chief of counterintelligence of the Military Security Service.[14] However, no action was taken because the evidence was not deemed sufficient.

On the eve of the new year, Polgar boastfully reassured the CIA officers: 'I want you to know that everything is going OK. We don't see any problems in 1975. Our reading is that the situation is under control.'[15] But this was no reassurance to the officers, who were already anxious after the loss of half of Binh Long and Phuoc Long.[16]

In early 1975, DRV Public Security intercepted and successfully deciphered a cable from an embassy of a United States ally. The cable revealed that the Americans would not intervene with ground troops to support the Saigon regime. The cable with the vital intelligence was distributed to the Politburo and the high command.[17] Thus, the PAVN push to the south intensified. The ARVN units could not pose significant resistance to the PAVN, who were moving against the provinces of Kontum, Pleiku and Darlac, towards the east and southeast. ARVN forces, not willing to fight, took their families with them in retreat. The refugee columns were immense and unpredictable. Public order was broken in cities and villages. Air America and other airlines flew people to the south. The CIA bases and outposts in the areas were hastily abandoned; it was a developing situation, and the Saigon station and embassy had not issued pre-orders for evacuation. Classified material, Vietnamese employees and spy networks were all abandoned.[18] The ambassador insisted that evacuation orders would cause more chaos and panic.

In late February 1975, the mole codenamed Reaper was clear: Tay Ninh was about to be attacked by the PAVN. However, he did not report enemy intentions for a general offensive. Thus, the 25th Division of the

ARVN would be cut off and unable to retreat to Saigon. The mole Grandpa said that nothing was planned along the 1st Highway. The mole Goldmother reported nothing on an offensive in the western areas; nonetheless, there was a perceived enemy movement along the Central Highlands and the coast.[19]

In early March 1975, a spy inside Thieu's cabinet told the CIA station about Thieu's decision to withdraw all forces from the North and the highlands – at that time the ARVN almost abandoned the latter. Thieu sought a defensive perimeter north of Saigon, from Tay Ninh to Nha Trang. Polgar wanted to believe that despite all the retreats 'there's nothing strategic about them'.[20] DeForest wrote about a spy close to Thieu: 'One of the CIA's recruited agents in the Vietnamese government was a senior staff officer very close to President Nguyen Van Thieu. His crypt was Lingus, though I thought it could more appropriately have been Cunnilingus, especially when I read the synopses of his reports in the Agency's monthly intelligence bulletin. The man never reported a single thing that we wouldn't have found out regardless.'[21]

On 10 March, the final drive to Saigon commenced with the attack against Ban Me Thout. Washington continued to wrongly believe that that Danang (the place of the fanfare landing of the marines in 1965) would be bypassed; even Colby, now director of Central Intelligence, believed this.[22]

On 1 April in a safe house, Snepp met with 'a high reliable informant, who had just come out of the field'. He brought information about Hanoi's plans. The informant was clear: Hanoi was interested in total victory only; even a negotiated surrender would not be accepted.[23] For his part, Polgar (wrongly) assumed that Hanoi would seek a negotiation rather than a full attack against Saigon. He calculated that the DRV would have to abide by the 'détente-minded' Moscow; thus fake elections similar to the ones in Eastern Europe post World War II were a better choice for Hanoi.[24] Polgar was wrong in applying a lesson of history from the late 1940s to the situation in Vietnam.

On 8 April, a South Vietnamese Air Force F-5E fighter-bomber dropped two 500lb bombs on the presidential palace. It was an attempt against Thieu, who took shelter and survived. Only after 25 years did it become known that the pilot, Lieutenant Nguyen Thanh Trung, was a North Vietnamese mole with a later mission to bomb the US embassy.

Subsequently, on 28 April Trung headed a raid against Tan Son Nhut, with five PAVN-captured A-37 Dragonfly jet aircraft.[25]

On 9 April, Goldmother met with her CIA handlers. She claimed that PAVN and COSVN sapper units had been deployed to the Tan Son Nhut airport. She revealed that, according to COSVN directives, the intent was for total victory; the enemy was not willing to negotiate with Saigon. Other secret agents with access to the COSVN reported the same.[26] A few days later, the moles Reaper and Grandpa warned the CIA that the action against Tay Ninh was a diversion.[27]

Meanwhile, Bill Johnson, the chief of CIA operations in Saigon, pressured Polgar to establish stay-behind networks after the ensuing US withdrawal. At this time, neither Shackley (now the head of the Near East division at Langley) nor Ambassador Martin and Polgar believed that a withdrawal would occur. Shackley viewed 'no one [in Washington and in particular in the hostile Congress] will want to spend the money on such frivolities' as the stay-behind networks. The concept of stay-behind agents, initiated in Indochina by Lansdale back in the 1950s, had lost its appeal. Snepp remarked that Johnson 'eventually was allowed to undertake a few limited initiatives ... [but] when South Vietnam did collapse, the CIA had no significant intelligence networks in place'.[28] This phrasing shows that spies were indeed left behind to operate. Moreover, under an authorised scheme Johnson had documents planted to be found in the embassy safes after withdrawal. The documents named top ranking communists in Hanoi as CIA sources. Snepp writes that eventually 'the end came so fast, none of the documents were ever distributed'.[29] But this does not mean that they had not been drafted or typed.

Johnson was gradually growing desperate, fearing that the ARVN defence around Saigon would collapse and that he and his wife, Pat, a CIA analyst, would be captured. Snepp wrote that both had made a death pact in case of imminent arrest: Johnson would shoot his wife and then commit suicide.[30] CIA officers, worrying about a general uprising, each gathered a personal arsenal of Smith and Wesson .38 revolvers, .45 Colts and M16s in a vain attempt to protect themselves from mobs.[31]

The station issued an order for destruction of classified materials (reports and archives) which amounted to 14 tonnes. Nonetheless, Ambassador Martin objected to incineration during daytime hours, to avoid an impression of panic.[32]

Snepp writes that on the evening of 8 April 'the Station's best agent', a North Vietnamese, claimed that the PAVN high command had issued a 'resolution'; all areas north of Saigon were to be 'liberated' in April, and forces would move into the capital without a settlement. Hanoi was not interested in giving the Americans time to withdraw.[33]

On 9 April, during the National Security Council meeting chaired by President Ford, Colby spoke of escalation and informed the president of the spy's report: 'Our best clandestine source on Communist plans in the South has recently reported on new COSVN instructions which call for achieving final victory *this* year rather than in 1976. According to the agent, Communist gains have far exceeded their expectations for 1975 and have created the "most opportune moment" for total victory this year. The COSVN instructions call for the Communists to press the attack and expand Communist territorial holdings during April by "liberating" Tay Ninh, Hau Nghia, and Binh Duong provinces. The agent also claims that when "the time comes" the North Vietnamese will attack Saigon. Another clandestine source reported yesterday that the Communists are planning a three-pronged assault from the south, west and north of the capital itself.'[34]

The PAVN/Viet Cong final attack was launched on 9 April 1975. One senior Hungarian official with the ICCS in Saigon contacted Polgar, who reconstructed their conversation in a blog entry in 2013:

Hungarian: Look, you must be a realist. You must know that this war is lost.

Polgar: Okay. I admit the war is lost.

Hungarian: Every lost war must have political consequences.

Polgar: I agree with you.

Hungarian: These political consequences are obviously going to be bitter. But there is no interest in the side which I represent ... to unduly humiliate the United States. Maybe something can be worked out not to change the outcome of the war, that's finished, but to permit an ending which would not be unduly humiliating to the United States.

Polgar: What have you got in mind?

Hungarian: Well, you know we are out at Tan Son Nhut talking to our North Vietnamese colleagues. We have people in Hanoi. I have the impression that perhaps something could be worked out along the following lines. Thieu must resign. The United States must pledge non-intervention in South Vietnamese affairs beyond the maintenance of a normal Embassy structure. And in South Vietnam the government must be created consisting of people that the North Vietnamese find acceptable. These are the essential problems.

Polgar: Well, thank you very much. I will naturally report our conversation. I will discuss it with the Ambassador so we can get it back to Washington. And I will be back to you. And while we are awaiting the answer from Washington, would you be kind enough to talk to your friends again and find out who might be some of the people that they would consider acceptable in the government?[35]

The spy codenamed Whisper was a major in the ARVN, recruited by the CIA. On 15 April 1975, he warned his handlers that President Thieu had ordered the evacuation despite his official denials. Polgar directed all CIA personnel to leave, saving them from capture by the advancing PAVN.[36] CIA officer Sullivan remarked on the mood at the Duc hotel (where all CIA personnel gathered in Saigon) the same night: '[T]he main topic of conversation was Thieu's order to pull out of Pleiku without letting the Americans know. I saw no one panicking, but it was mentioned that the only thing between us and the NVA [i.e. PAVN] was the ARVN rabble.'[37]

On 17 April, a secret agent returned with more intelligence and met again with Snepp: 'He arrived in full disguise, and though we had met several times before, I hardly recognised him behind the false glasses and other paraphernalia.' The agent insisted that Hanoi was interested in total victory regardless of the casualties; neither a coalition government, negotiations nor US aid to Thieu could save the South Vietnamese regime. An attack against Saigon was initially planned to commence on 19 April (but it would not materialise on this date). General Van Tien Dung, the commander in chief of the PAVN, wanted to celebrate Ho Chi

Minh's birthday in Saigon on 19 May. The secret agent estimated that this timetable compelled the PAVN to attack the capital by early May at the latest. On hearing the report, Polgar was not surprised. But Kissinger's staff highly valued the intelligence provided.[38] Secret agent Fireball was the one whom Snepp met; he was the top-secret source for the CIA. His handlers offered him and his family help to leave Vietnam, but he declined. 'I could not understand his refusal', wrote Sullivan, the polygraph expert, suspecting him of being under some form of hostile control.[39]

The same night 'corroborating information' coming from 'highly sensitive sources' showed that DRV pilots were training with captured fighters in Danang; an agent deemed reliable said that the attack against Saigon had been cancelled, not aborted.[40] The highly sensitive sources had to be NSA intercepts. At the 17 April Special Actions Group Meeting, the evacuation of US personnel was discussed. Colby criticised Ambassador Martin's procrastination:

Colby: The way we are going about it now, we're going to look pretty foolish when the crunch comes.

General Scowcroft: Yes, but the way Graham is going about it is designed to keep Saigon from disintegrating into chaos.

Kissinger: If Saigon disintegrates into chaos, nobody is going to get out. You have to balance off the risks. It's a tight rope that he is walking.

Colby: I think we should get at least a trickle moving.[41]

Kissinger persuaded Ford to authorise a letter to Brezhnev. Washington was concerned about the developing situation; therefore, 'controlled conditions' for the US evacuation had to be implemented and Moscow had to exert its influence over Hanoi. A ceasefire and 'political problems' would be discussed between the Vietnamese.[42] When on 19 April the PAVN did not attack Saigon, Polgar's hopes for a last-minute settlement were boosted. He continued talking with his Hungarian contacts. Polgar consulted with Thieu, prompting him to resign and Vice President Huong to assume power. He hoped that a change could avert the takeover and buy time.[43]

At the 20 April Special Actions Group meeting, Kissinger turned against Colby: 'Yesterday you said that Vietnam would collapse in two to ten days. Now you are saying two days. What do you mean?' Colby elaborated: 'The point is that Vietnam could collapse in one or two days – ten days at the outside. In the best case situation, it would take three weeks.'[44]

On 21 April, Thieu resigned. Vice President Tran Van Huong was left behind, but eventually he stepped down and General Minh assumed the presidency. Polgar arranged for the secret departure of Thieu and his close associates. The station chief contacted the Hungarian official:

Polgar: Look, I have delivered on your first point. We still don't have a definitive answer. Have you got any suggestion as to people's names?

Hungarian: Well, as a matter of fact, I do. But I am very poor on Vietnamese names, so I wrote them all down.

{The Hungarian started reading names out of a notebook.}

Polgar: That's very interesting. I will of course follow up on our previous conversation and I'll get back to you.

Hungarian: I have an additional word from my colleagues here and they tell me that when they said you must move fast, they meant within a matter of days, not weeks.[45]

That same day, DeForest met Goldmother and Grandpa at the safe house. They gave the latest details of the PAVN advance. The CIA officer offered to help them to escape Vietnam. Both declined, saying that they were considered heroes by Hanoi. DeForest remarked that they looked neither happy nor excited about the final victory of their army. Of Grandpa he wrote: 'Nothing ever shocked this man or put him off balance. He loved this game he was playing, the intrigue, the danger, the need to mask every emotion and keep all the conflicts in balance. Like Goldmother, Grandpa was an adrenaline junkie.'[46]

Four days later, while the panic had spread in South Vietnam following the unopposed PAVN advance, Radio Saigon broadcasted: 'Le Duan murders his chief political rival in Hanoi! Chinese troops pour across the border into North Vietnam to avenge the death.' American journalists rushed to the CIA station to get confirmation of this unexpected, dramatic news, which they assumed could turn the politico-military situation. But intelligence officers reassured them that this was a crude psychological operation of the South Vietnamese regime. Hanoi's leadership was safe and sound.[47]

Meanwhile, Kissinger did not want to have any negotiations with the DRV, despite Ambassador Martin being strongly in favour. Polgar met his Hungarian contact on 26 or 27 April. His reply was that it was now too late for any agreement. The PAVN and the Viet Cong were coming to Saigon, and no one could save the Americans from humiliation.[48]

Martin threatened Polish Ambassador Ryzard Fialkowski, warning that if the PAVN launched SA-2 missiles or other weapons against the evacuation aircraft, the United States would bomb Hanoi. The Pole had to transfer this message to the DRV. Martin had the reputation of an uncompromising hawk. General Murray, the defence attaché under Ambassador Bunker, once said that: 'If [USAF General] Curtis LeMay had invented an ambassador, he would have invented Martin. You know: "Bomb them back to the Stone Age".'[49]

On 26 April Ambassador Martin informed Kissinger:

I really think we have about come to the end of the road on any further pressure on us here about the American community. Since you have left the decision to me, I am not going to reduce any more on the American official community. We have notified other Americans that they are now staying at their own risk.

[...] As far as the military pressures on the President are concerned, you might care to inform him that the reports of the SA 2s [missiles], which so panicked one of your WSAG [Washington Special Action Group] meetings, and which resulted in the closing of the Saigon airport to American commercial airlines, turns out to be incorrect.[50]

On 28 April, before noon, the WSAG was summoned. Kissinger and his interlocutors were worried and confused about reports that anti-aircraft artillery had fired against evacuation planes. Martin had just talked to General Scowcroft on the phone, who said: 'Those planes that attacked

Tan Son Nhut today were probably South Vietnamese defectors or
VNAF pilots disgruntled with the new Minh Government. It is also
possible that the North Vietnamese held a gun to their head and told
them to go down and do some damage. It isn't clear as to who it was, but
they bombed only the VNAF side of Tan Son Nhut. They did not attack
the DAO [Defense Attaché Office] side of the field. Also, our C–130
pilots report that they were trailed by the A–37s. They were not fired
on, and there was no damage. The planes flew over the Presidential
Palace, but did not release any ordnance. They didn't hit the Palace.'[51]

On the evening of 28 April, during the meeting of the National
Security Council, Colby provided the latest intelligence; the Viet Cong
had rejected General Minh's proposal for a ceasefire and continued
advancing. CIA director said: 'It is a very dangerous situation. The
North Vietnamese are bringing artillery within range of Tan Son Nhut
airport. At 4:00 a.m. they had a salvo of rockets against Tan Son Nhut.
This is what killed the [two] Marines. This salvo was followed by 130
millimetre artillery fire. Some of this artillery fire hit the American side,
not the Vietnamese side like last night. Three aircraft have been shot
down. All are Vietnamese. They include a C–119, an A–1, and an A–37
helicopter. The latter was shot down by an SA–7 missile. The presence of
these missiles increases the risk factor greatly.'[52] The discussion turned
again to the threat of anti-aircraft missiles:

General Brown (chairman of the JCS): What worries me more than
the artillery fire is the report of an aircraft being shot down by an
SA–7. Choppers or aircraft are defenseless against the SA–7. The
only way to deflect the missiles is to use flares, but I am not sure
whether the aircraft we are using are equipped for that. Of course,
we have to do our mission, but if the risk becomes too great, we
may need to turn off the lift.

President: If the risk is too great, the man on the ground has to
judge. We cannot. That means we have to move to get the DAO
people out as well as the Embassy. That is one possibility. If they
can land, they should carry out the operation as before. But when
they find that it is getting too hazardous the last two C–130's have
to take the DAO out. I think we have to continue operations if the
people on the ground say that conditions are alright, but if it is a

question of two remaining aircraft they should be filled by the DAO personnel and not by Vietnamese.

Kissinger: I have talked to Graham Martin. I think the DAO should come out anyway. I also think the Embassy should be thinned down. If we have to go to suppressive fire, then we must remove the Americans. Otherwise, it is too risky.

Schlesinger: There is no authority now for suppressive fire, only for the chopper lift.

President: If we do not fire until they do, we are bound to lose some choppers to the SA–7's.

Schlesinger: It is a hard weapon to counter.

General Brown: We cannot do much about them.

[. . .] President: If we have air cover but do not use it, they would still have enough radar to pick up our presence.

General Brown: The artillery people do not. Nor do the SA–7 people. I think we should not commit the air cover until we are ready to use it. The risk is such that they should only be used for a job, rather than to be picked up on radar.

[. . .] President: Can the SA–7 not be jammed?

Brown: No. It is heat-seeking.

Scowcroft: We have just received a report that the airport is still taking fire. The two North Vietnamese platoons are still in the cemetery near Tan Son Nhut. The C–119 was shot down over the airport and the other aircraft elsewhere. We also understand the C–130's are still on the way but are not landing.

Schlesinger: The North Vietnamese have 4,000 sappers in Saigon. They will hit the Embassy if we attack by fire.

Kissinger: I think that, if we fire, we have to pull out the entire Embassy. Maybe we should consider leaving in a nucleus of volunteers, but I would pull everybody out. The North

Vietnamese have the intention of humiliating us, and it seems unwise to leave people there.

President: I agree. All should leave.[53]

At the early morning meeting of the Special Actions Group on 29 April, Kissinger was informed of more refugees besieging the embassy, trying to get in:

Kissinger: Where are all these extra people coming from?

General Brown: Over the wall and through the gates. I don't know where they are all coming from.

Kissinger: Can someone explain to me what the hell is going on! The orders are that only Americans are to be evacuated. Now, what the hell is going on?

Clements: There are still something like 350 to 400 Americans still to be evacuated.

Ambassador L. Dean Brown: There have been 4,500 people taken out so far. That's raw information.

Kissinger: And there are still Americans to be evacuated?

General Brown: Yes, there are 500 – close to 600 still to be evacuated.

Kissinger: And there is still no sign of opposition to the evacuation?

General Brown: There has been some sniper fire from the roofs of buildings near the Embassy. One problem is that the weather is bad.

[. . .] {Secretary Kissinger was handed a note at this point.}

Kissinger: This says that the helicopters are taking fire from small arms, tracers, and anti-aircraft. It's an NSA message. Who could they be, ARVN?

General Brown: It's hard to say.

Colby: Probably some ARVN and the local police. When they say small arms fire and tracers, it is probably police and ARVN.

Kissinger: Who's firing the anti-aircraft?

Colby: It's hard to say. Flying bullets sound like anti-aircraft to pilots under fire. It's just hard to tell.

Shackley: The only anti-aircraft guns in Saigon are those controlled by the South Vietnamese at the Presidential Palace grounds.

Kissinger: Do they [the US forces] have authority to fire back?

General Brown: Yes, but it's hard to do, particularly at night. There's no coordination with the ground, and they can't see anything. It's just damn tricky to fire back at night.[54]

As of the morning of 29 April, the available communication intercepts confirmed that Hanoi wanted to take over Saigon militarily.[55] Meanwhile, the same morning, the Polish and Hungarian delegations had panicked under the PAVN shelling around Saigon. Polish Colonel Toth came to the embassy and asked for Polgar's help so that the CIA could arrange to transfer its delegations to a downtown hotel. Polgar assigned this task to Johnson, who took the delegations to safety at the Majestic Hotel to await the approaching PAVN. Johnson is the only CIA officer to have received an official hero citation from a communist country for his aid.[56]

By noon on 29 April, Ambassador Martin, at that point seriously ill with pneumonia, realised that evacuation of all US personnel and South Vietnamese personnel and dependents was the only option. There was no possibility of an arrangement with Hanoi. The PAVN were deployed outside the city and bombed the airport. No fixed-wing aircraft could now serve for the evacuation. Only helicopters from the embassy and other designated areas could save the Americans and South Vietnamese from capture or death.

The embassy building was full of desperate, panic-stricken refugees. Foreign Service Officers and CIA personnel were trying to accommodate them, as well as to arrange for classified material to be destroyed. Snepp witnessed many episodes of panic: 'Others in the front office also were beginning to succumb to their nerves. One of Polgar's secretaries had grown so agitated, she was no longer functioning in her usual practical and efficient way. At one point I caught her hammering away at the frame of a wall picture in Polgar's office with the butt of a cocked pistol. "Just taking the pictures down for Mr.P," she murmured as I grabbed her hand and thumbed the safety catch.'[57]

At about 5 p.m. hysteria broke out. An embassy finance officer saw a Vietnamese-looking man with an automatic rifle climbing the stairwell to the fifth floor. He assumed that he was a guerrilla followed by his comrades. The officer shouted to the refugees that the Viet Cong were inside the embassy. Screams and a rush up the stairs and the corridors followed. DeForest narrated the episode: 'I yelled at everyone to get into the walk-in vault we had in the room – the former finance office. In a moment, everyone there had grabbed Uzis and pistols, crowded into the vault, and pulled the door to, leaving it open a crack. After a tense couple of minutes, we heard someone shout "False alarm," and we carefully moved back into the office.' The 'Viet Cong' with the rifle was an American Nisei State Department guard.[58]

On 29 April at about 9 p.m., Polgar and Martin were about to leave together with their staff. The station chief felt insulted when asked by a marine to hand over his pistol. 'Polgar pulled his own Browning automatic out of his hip holster and stared down at it for a moment', Snepp witnessed; 'at last he let out a forlorn sigh. "I've gotta stay." The Ambassador insists on holding on a bit longer.'[59] Snepp left having seen his helicopter fired at, possibly by PAVN units closing in.

Meanwhile, Pham Xuan An helped Tran Kim Tuyen, the old spymaster of SEPES, to escape. Tuyen boarded the last helicopter from the rooftop of 22 Gia Lon Street, half a mile from the US embassy. An, who had arranged for his own wife and four children also to leave, watched Tuyen, the man who brought him into the South Vietnamese secret services back in 1954. An said helping Tuyen to escape 'was an act of the heart . . . his wife was expecting a baby. He could have left anytime earlier, but he stayed to get his men out, and then it was too late. The CIA could not help him. [Journalist] Bob Shaplen could not help him. It was up to me.'[60]

The White House demanded that the evacuation be completed at 3.45 a.m. on 30 April. A CH-46 helicopter landed on the embassy rooftop at approximately 4.45 a.m., Saigon time. The pilot insisted that his presidential orders were to evacuate Ambassador Martin, who climbed in; the CH-46 flew away at 4.58 a.m. The pilot confirmed by the call-sign 'Tiger', meaning the departure of Martin. DRV signals intelligence intercepted this. General Dung was now preparing to take over Saigon.[61] Another CH-46 landed soon after for the remaining embassy and CIA staff. Polgar wrote of his last view of Saigon:

It was really quite dark when we left. Out toward Tan Son Nhut you could see a few fires, but basically the city had its normal night time picture. The street lights were on, the traffic lights were working. It was a very eerie thing and this was what so unusual about those last days. I'm not speaking only for the last night, but any of the last weeks in Saigon. They were so unreal because everything appeared to be so normal. It wasn't like the long siege of Warsaw, you know. A day before the collapse, you could still go to restaurants and get a very nice meal and a good wine. Nobody fired at us on the way out. And that's another thing. The North Vietnamese are a rational people.... Our reception on the [USS] Blue Ridge showed the American military at its worst. They started out by searching everybody. I think the Ambassador was the only one who was not searched. They searched us, and they searched our belongings. And in normal peace time I far outranked the admiral commanding the ship. Nobody objected, though. We were tired. We were pretty placid. And we were a defeated army.[62]

On 30 April at 7.51 a.m., a CH-46 Sea King helicopter, after the withdrawal of the Marines' detachment from the embassy compounds, sent the final message: 'All the Americans are out, repeat out.' (However, Tucker Gougelmann, a former CIA high-ranking paramilitary specialist who was trying to extract his Vietnamese family, did not leave South Vietnam. Eventually, he was discovered by the DRV security services; he was arrested and tortured, and died in captivity in 1976.)[63] More than 100,000 Vietnamese were evacuated by 30 April.[64]

The story of the American evacuation of Saigon shows that Hanoi did not want to humiliate them by seizing the US embassy. The PAVN increased the pressure with military deployments around the city so as to scare Washington and force the US government to issue an evacuation order immediately. In these days and hours the tactical intercepts of US communications as well as of PAVN signals turned into an indirect communication channel. These intercepts confirmed to the PAVN the rapidly increasing US pessimism concerning both the outcome of the war and the arrangements for a speedy evacuation. If the US personnel in Saigon had been slow in carrying out the White House's all-out evacuation order, we are convinced that the PAVN would have delayed its advance, giving the Americans more time to leave.

Pham Xuan An remained in Saigon, continuing to pose as a journalist and fearing for his life: 'It was a dangerous moment for me. . . . It would have been easy for someone to put a bullet through my skull. I was afraid they would kill me and barbecue my dogs alive. All I could do was wait for someone from the jungle to come out and recognize me.'[65]

Colonel Bui Tin was the highest ranking officer to first reach the presidential palace in Saigon at midday on 30 April. Tin met with General Minh, who asked for a former surrender ceremony only to be rebuffed: 'You cannot surrender what you do not have. You must surrender immediately.'[66] The next day, Colonel Tin sought out news correspondents, among them Pham Xuan An (Tin did not know that An was a Hanoi spy).[67] An worked as acting bureau chief of *Time* magazine until May 1976. He commented on the communist censorship: 'They cut off the teletype machine. . . . They crossed out this, crossed out that. The censorship was so tight it was like back in the days of Graham Greene. I didn't file many stories because I didn't know how to dodge the censors. All they wanted was propaganda for the new regime, so I spent my days going to cockfights and fish fights.'[68]

Back in United States on 1 May 1975, Neil Sheehan, a prominent war correspondent, called the now-retired General Lansdale on the phone. His wife, Pat, answered. Sheehan wanted a comment on the fall of Saigon. She replied that her husband, together with others, 'are trying to figure out how to save Vietnam'.[69] The once celebrated planner of black propaganda operations and secret missions had illusions that there could be a way to avert the DRV victory. By September 1976, Conein, the onetime Lansdale associate, confided to Sheehan that there were indications that Pham Xuan An was either a Viet Cong or a Hanoi sympathiser. Conein was puzzled that An's family were able to return to Vietnam without being blocked by the authorities.[70]

The spy codenamed Fireball was a district cadre for the Cao Dai sect in Tay Ninh. According to the available accounts, and to a July 1995 article in a PAVN newsletter, he was betrayed by a South Vietnamese security officer and committed suicide in April or May 1975 to avoid arrest. Sullivan remarked that the NLF 'might have used him [i.e. Fireball] not to pass us disinformation but as a conduit for [real] information they wanted us to have'.[71] This may have been the case on the eve of the fall of Saigon. This spy, however, had been operating from 1969 until early 1975; Hanoi could not be certain of the outcome of the war so as to launch a secret strategy of *informing* the CIA of actual NLF and PAVN military intentions.

AFTERMATH

US INTELLIGENCE AND THE SINO-VIETNAMESE WAR

For a spy the war never ends. A new, ensuing confrontation between China and Vietnam required the attention of US and British intelligence. Following the US–Chinese Shanghai Communiqué on 28 February 1972, the NSA was ordered to downgrade China as a priority intelligence target. Nonetheless the CIA operated radio intercept equipment on the roof of the US Liaison Office headquarters in Beijing. In addition the Canyon and Rhyolite signals intelligence satellites would ensure a steady stream of military intelligence in the coming conflict in Southeast Asia. In their turn, the DRV intelligence services recruited a mole. Ronald Humphrey was a United States Information Agency (USIA) officer who in 1969 had served in Vietnam, where he fell in love with a Vietnamese woman; she once warned him of mine attack, and he became convinced that she had saved his life. Eventually, the DRV security services arrested her. In 1975, Humphrey offered a Vietnamese classified documents relating to the US–DRV talks on the prisoners of war; the secret intelligence reached the DRV delegation in Paris. Humphrey wanted to negotiate the release of his lover and her children. The following year he began spying. The DRV intelligence freed her with her children in July 1977. Humphrey delivered classified material relating to US policy towards the DRV to David Truong (born Truong Dinh Hung), who in his turn handed it over to the DRV intelligence courier Yung Krall – her father was the DRV ambassador in Moscow. Krall was married to a US Navy officer. She had agreed to act as a double agent for the CIA to trap Humphrey. She was codenamed Agent Keyseat, and her trap led to the arrest of Humphrey and Truong by the FBI in January 1978.[1] At the time of his arrest, Truong was a postgraduate student of the American University and also worked as a lobbyist in Washington, promoting the normalisation of US–Vietnamese relations. He admitted giving the secret documents supplied by Humphrey to the Vietnamese in Paris; however, he claimed that he thought that they were correspondents of a Vietnamese newspaper in Paris – not diplomats or intelligence officers. The handling of the case drew criticism because no court warrants had been sought by the FBI to tap Truong's phone or to arrange for hidden cameras in Humphrey's office. Critics claimed that the FBI had violated the Fourth Amendment against illegal search and seizure. President Carter took an interest in the case, and personally authorised parts of the surveillance, citing grounds of national security.[2]

Meanwhile, Mao, seeking to control the expansion of the influence of the DRV (which was siding with Moscow), backed the Pol Pot regime, which seized Phnom Penh on 17 April 1975. In an act of desperation, the Soviet Ambassador in Phnom Penh hid the codebooks and other classified materials so that they would not be found by the Khmer Rouge; for this he was awarded the Order of Lenin. The CIA was informed of this episode by KGB defector Stan Levchenko.[3]

Indeed, by the early 1970s the Chinese troops in the DRV had left the country (Chinese presence had peaked in 1967, with 170,000 Chinese).[4] Most important, from 1973 onwards, border clashes between Chinese and DRV troops took place, and no settlement was reached. (The DRV claimed that by 1975, 179 'skirmishes' had taken place; China claimed 121.) China was no longer interested in granting aid to Hanoi. The disputes over the sovereignty of the Paracel and Spratley group of islands resurfaced.[5] Tensions peaked. Deng Xiaoping, who took a hard line towards Hanoi, told Le Duen in their 29 September 1975 meeting: 'We are not at ease when we get to read Vietnamese newspapers and know [Vietnamese] public opinion. In fact, you stress the threat from the North. The threat from the North for us is the existence of Soviet troops on our northern borders, but for you, it means China.'[6]

On 20 January 1975, Chinese forces occupied several of the ARVN-controlled Paracel islands. In April, on the eve of the fall of Saigon, the PAVN occupied six islands in the Spratley group. China sought a settlement during the DRV–US war, assuming the weak position of Hanoi; however, the North Vietnamese did not succumb.[7] In 1977, the Khmer Rouge under Pol Pot invaded DRV provinces; the DRV fought back, invading Cambodia in December 1978.

In the summer of 1978 the CIA believed that Hanoi-Beijing relations were about to lead to a confrontation. CIA analysts wrote that 'bitterness is so deep that the situation could deteriorate further, especially if the Vietnam-Cambodian fighting intensifies'.[8]

Armed incidents were reported on the Sino-Vietnamese borders. In September and October 1978, a secret source reported the build-up of defences on the Vietnamese side and its reinforcement with more troops, SA-3 surface to air missiles and more artillery batteries. In a mid-October interagency memorandum, the CIA's national intelligence officer for East Asia and the Pacific predicted a Chinese invasion/action against the DRV. Beijing would opt for war with the DRV, which was about to defeat the Pol Pot regime.[9] In the meantime, the PAVN used the cover of the Khmer National United Front for National Salvation (KNUFNS).[10] The Pol Pot regime, which was responsible for genocide, was also targeted by Moscow, which backed Hanoi. By late 1978, the Vietnamese forces deposed Pol Pot, occupying the capital.

Indications of a coming war between China and Vietnam were initially fragmented; on 3 November 1978, Moscow and Hanoi signed a mutual defence treaty; Beijing assumed that this was to 'contain' Chinese influence in Southeast Asia. China sought to intervene in the DRV, accusing Hanoi of mistreating ethnic Chinese and occupying the Spratly Islands (claimed by China). The Chinese, fearing that the Soviets would intervene to help Hanoi, deployed more forces along the Sino-Soviet border. In early January 1979, the CIA reported of an increased readiness of the PAVN's missiles, anti-aircraft and artillery units on the border. The likelihood of a confrontation was deemed very high. By mid-January, a secret source gave indications of the coming of war with the upgrade of Chinese forces along the other parts of the border.[11]

US Secretary of State Cyrus Vance informed President Carter on 26 January 1979, the eve of Chinese Vice Premier Deng Xiaoping's visit to Washington:

> China has suffered a public setback with the fall of Pol Pot, and they are looking for ways to recoup some of their losses.

A critical question, to which we do not know the answer, is whether or not the Chinese are likely to take any sort of military action against Vietnam.

[. . .] In regard to Vietnam, we wish to make clear to the Chinese that we strongly condemn the Vietnamese invasion of Cambodia, but could not support action by China in the region which could widen or escalate the fighting.

If the Chinese were to attack Vietnam shortly after Deng leaves the States, as is possible, we would be viewed as implicated in such action.[12]

Deng hoped to get Carter's support for his war plan against Vietnam. On the evening of 28 January, when Deng had just reached Washington DC, he asked for a special meeting with the president. The Americans did not anticipate this, but agreed. At the meeting with President Carter in the Oval Office, Deng disclosed the Chinese intention to wage war on Vietnam and sounded willing to be informed of the US policy with reference to the Soviets backing the DRV. Deng presented hypotheses of Moscow's responses to the coming war. He spoke of the 'the worst possibility'; China 'would hold out' a Soviet offensive, asking only for American 'moral support'. Carter asked Deng not to wage war. The next day he wrote to the Chinese leader trying to dissuade him from the war option. He claimed that a limited war would not have an impact on Vietnam's bid to control Cambodia, and there was a danger of a quagmire for China. An invasion would also make China be seen as an aggressor in front of world opinion. The next day, at another meeting with Carter, Deng repeated the willingness of Beijing to launch a war, which in any case would be a small operation with limited objectives; China had to 'punish' the DRV. Carter again tried to restrain the Chinese. Nonetheless, former CIA Director Robert Gates, then a staff officer at the National Security Council, wrote that the 'signals' to the Chinese leader were positive to the extent that Carter and his administration did not mention a disruption of normalisation of US–China relations and military and economic cooperation as a side-effect of the Chinese invasion of Vietnam. Gates remarked: 'Further [there was] no indication that the secret just shared [i.e. the planned Chinese invasion] would be violated to warn the intended victim or complicate Chinese plans. And, I suspect, but can't prove, that there were comments made by Brzezinski and others that the Chinese found even more encouraging, however subtly expressed.'[13] In any case, the president surprised Deng by discussing a proposal for a joint US–Sino signals intelligence base to target Soviet missile tests.[14]

According to a CIA article published in *Intelligence Studies* in 1986 and only declassified in 2014, despite the warning of the agency about the coming of the war with a Chinese action, some decision makers in Washington wrongly concluded that Deng's visit to the US capital proved that the Chinese were not willing to go to war, but were simply bluffing.[15]

The NSA intercepted the communications of the Vietnamese and Chinese forces on the eve of the war.[16] At the National Security Council Meeting on 16 February 1979, Admiral Turner, the director of the CIA, presented an outline of the Chinese military and air force deployments: 'On the ground, 14 divisions, with nine amassed at an attack point in the NE portion of the Sino-Vietnamese border and five amassed at a point in the NW. The two attack points are at the traditional entry points to Vietnam.' The total reached 170,000 troops. The president was interested Hanoi's intentions:

President Carter: Is it fair to say the Vietnamese thus far have not responded to the Chinese military build-up, and that their main posture is to defend Hanoi?

Turner: Yes.

President Carter: Have the Chinese been provoked to undertake this action?

Turner: We don't know.

President Carter: What will the Chinese do?

Turner: We believe the Chinese will confine themselves to the hilly areas and not enter the plain. But the Vietnamese may not come after them. The area of the border clashes and provocations which the Chinese claim require the attack is here. [One-and-a-half lines not declassified] The terrain is one through which armor can move. The hills are up to 3,000 feet, and the valleys can be used.

President Carter: Is there any [less than one line not declassified] on the level of activity on the North Vietnamese border?

Turner: No.[17]

The Chinese gave an embarrassing advance notice to Carter on their coming intervention. Carter (who had received the relevant intelligence from the CIA) admitted to his staff that China's warning 'places us in a difficult position'.[18]

On 17 February, the Chinese divisions invaded Vietnam, supported by 200 T59s, T62s and T63s. The Chinese concentrated on six border provinces: Quang Ninh, Lang Son, Cao Bang, Ha Tuyen, Hoang Lien Son and Lai Chau. The PAVN forces were initially surprised but their defence did not collapse. US spy satellites, and the KH-9 Big Bird photographic reconnaissance satellites, kept track of the deployments of the adversaries. The Chinese proceeded 15–20 km into Vietnam. Initially, the PAVN employed guerrilla tactics, concentrating on the defence of Hanoi, with about 300,000 troops. The Vietnamese received intelligence from Soviet satellites. In spite of the fierce battles in provincial capitals, by late February the PAVN had not yet mobilised its forces in full. Gates wrote that 'before too many days passed it became apparent through our overhead collection systems that the Vietnamese were giving a good account of themselves and that the Chinese were having problems maintaining command and control, that their equipment was outdated, and that Hanoi's troops were seasoned veterans compared to the Chinese'.[19] The CIA had noted the limited Soviet airlift of supplies to Hanoi, which commenced four days after the invasion. Moscow sought to support the DRV without provoking Beijing.[20]

According to some accounts, throughout the conflict Brzezinski met with the Chinese ambassador almost every night to discuss intelligence related to Soviet troop movements. Brzezinski admitted to meeting with Chinese officials for 'diplomatic consultations' throughout the war. He told the Chinese that US intelligence would keep all Soviet deployments near China under surveillance. Initially, Deng was afraid of a Russian bid to come to the support of Vietnam.[21] Gates was clear: 'We didn't know for sure how the Soviets would respond, however, and neither did the Chinese. So, as part of the new US–China relationship, each evening during the Sino-Vietnamese conflict Brzezinski would meet with the Chinese ambassador or his representatives and provide the latest American intelligence on what the Soviets were doing.'[22]

On 6 March, Beijing announced that though its forces could reach for Hanoi its 'punitive mission' was accomplished, and so commenced its withdrawal, destroying the infrastructure. On 16 March, all Chinese troops were within Chinese territory. Both states declared victory. In March, after the end of the war, Deng boasted at the CCP Central Committee that although the Americans 'spoke with an official tone' against China's invasion, 'in private had spoken differently' and had given China intelligence on the 54 Soviet divisions stationed on the Sino-Soviet borders.[23]

For the Bureau of Intelligence and Research of the State Department, 'the Chinese attack on Vietnam was a milestone in the development of the Sino-Soviet struggle. China, for the first time, challenged a Soviet treaty ally with force. Considering the high stakes, China, the Soviet Union, and Vietnam all acted with prudence.'[24] For the CIA, 'Kampuchea was a key catalytic factor in Chinese thinking. The Sino-Vietnamese border dispute escalated against the backdrop of Vietnam's occupation of Kampuchea and Beijing's inability to protect its client regime there. In short, two factors – Vietnamese action against Kampuchea and Hanoi's refusal to assume a less provocative posture along the Sino-Vietnamese border – seem to have been mutually reinforcing, impelling Beijing to try to "punish" Vietnam militarily by invading the north.'[25] For the CIA, 'the intelligence community's forecast of a break in relations between China and Vietnam and the subsequent tactical warning of war were accurate and timely. But the effect was dampened significantly by Washington's lack of interest in Indochina, and by a zealous pursuit of better political and economic relations with Beijing, at the expense of a new and decisive foreign policy toward Southeast Asia.'[26]

In 1980, after the end of the war, Hanoi signed treaties of cooperation with the KGB and the Stasi, as well as with the interior ministries of Cuba, Czechoslovakia and Hungary. The provisions of the agreement with Stasi included the exchange of intelligence and German aid in telecommunications and surveillance technology.[27] Hanoi agreed to allow Soviet ships to use the Cam Ranh Bay base, and to allow the construction of a signals intelligence base nearby.

The agreement covered a 25-year period. As the Cold War entered its final decade, the signals intelligence base, which covered the East and South China Sea and the Western Pacific, considerably enhanced Soviet military intelligence capabilities.[28] The base was considered the largest outside the Soviet Union and survived the end of the Cold War. After negotiations which led to no agreement, the Russians withdrew from Cam Ranh Bay in May 2002.

NOTES

Introduction   The Killing Maze

1. Sophie Quinn-Judge, *Ho Chi Minh: The Missing Years* (London: Hurst, 2003), pp. 11–13, 30.
2. Ibid., pp. 43, 71, 92.
3. Calder Walton, *Empire of Secrets: British Intelligence, the Cold War and the Twilight of Empire* (London: Harper Press, 2013), p. 168; Quinn-Judge, *Ho Chi Minh*, pp. 191–5.
4. Quinn-Judge, *Ho Chi Minh*, p. 247.
5. Geraint Hughes, 'A "Post-war" War: The British Occupation of French Indochina, September 1945–March 1946', *Small Wars and Insurgencies*, Vol. 17, No. 3 (September 2006), p. 266.
6. Dixee R. Bartholomew-Feis, *The OSS and Ho Chi Minh: Unexpected Allies in the War against Japan* (Lawrence: University Press of Kansas 2006), p. 235.
7. Christopher Goscha, 'Wiring Decolonization: Turning Technology against Coloniezer during the Indochina War, 1945–1954', *Comparative Studies in Society and History*, Vol. 54, Issue 4 (2012), p. 803.
8. Ibid., p. 814.
9. Bartholomew-Feis, *The OSS and Ho Chi Minh*, pp. 232–3.
10. Archimedes L.A. Patti, *Why Viet Nam?: Prelude to America's Albatross* (University of California Press, 1982), p. 162; Bartholomew-Feis, *The OSS and Ho Chi Minh*, p. 233.
11. Bartholomew-Feis, *The OSS and Ho Chi Minh*, p. 267.
12. Ibid., pp. 239–43.
13. Fredrik Logevall, *Ambers of War: The Fall of an Empire and the Making of America's Vietnam* (New York: Random House, 2012), p. 95.
14. Conein quoted in Bartholomew-Feis, *The OSS and Ho Chi Minh*, p. 251.
15. Ibid.

16. Peter Neville, *Britain in Vietnam: Prelude to Disaster, 1945–6* (London: Routledge, 2007), p. 117.
17. Hughes, 'A "Post-war" War', p. 267.
18. Quoted in Lawrence Mark Atwood and Fredrik Logevall, eds, *The First Vietnam War: Colonial Conflict and Cold War Crisis* (Cambridge MA: Harvard University Press, 2007), p. 109.
19. Hughes, 'A "Post-war" War', p. 267.
20. Bartholomew-Feis, *The OSS and Ho Chi Minh*, pp. 275, 385 note 46.
21. Patti, *Why Viet Nam?*, p. 341.
22. Bartholomew-Feis, *The OSS and Ho Chi Minh*, pp. 274, 277.
23. Hughes, 'A "Post-war" War', p. 268.
24. Bartholomew-Feis, *The OSS and Ho Chi Minh*, pp. 231, 247–8, 272.
25. Quoted in Christopher E. Goscha, 'Intelligence in a Time of Decolonization: The Case of the Democratic Republic of Vietnam at War (1945–50)', *Intelligence and National Security*, Vol. 22, No. 1 (February 2007), p. 105.
26. Bartholomew-Feis, *The OSS and Ho Chi Minh*, p 279.
27. Quoted in Logevall, *Embers of War*, p. 113.
28. Hughes, 'A "Post-war" War', p. 268.
29. Bartholomew-Feis, *The OSS and Ho Chi Minh*, pp. 260–1.
30. Logevall, *Embers of War*, pp. 126–8.
31. Ilya V. Gayduk, *Confronting Vietnam: Soviet Policy toward the Indochina Conflict, 1954–1963* (Stanford CA: Stanford University Press, 2003), p. 3.
32. Hughes, 'A "Post-war" War', p. 269; Neville, *Britain in Vietnam*, p. 81.
33. Hughes, 'A "Post-war" War', p. 269.
34. Bartholomew-Feis, *The OSS and Ho Chi Minh*, p. 287.
35. Nevile, *Britain in Vietnam*, p. 83.
36. Bartholomew-Feis, *The OSS and Ho Chi Minh*, pp. 269, 280, 284, 287.
37. Hughes, 'A "Post-war" War', p. 269.
38. Bartholomew-Feis, *The OSS and Ho Chi Minh*, p. 288.
39. Robert J. Hanyok, *Spartans in Darkness: American SIGINT and the Indochina War, 1945–1975*, Series VI, Vol. 7 (National Security Agency/Central Security Service, 2002), pp. 18–19.
40. Goscha, 'Wiring Decolonization', p. 804.
41. Bartholomew-Feis, *The OSS and Ho Chi Minh*, p. 289.
42. Hughes, 'A "Post-war" War', p. 269.
43. Ibid., p. 270; Bartholomew-Feis, *The OSS and Ho Chi Minh*, p. 291.
44. Bartholomew-Feis, *The OSS and Ho Chi Minh*, pp. 292–5, 298.
45. Thomas A. Bass, *The Spy Who Loved Us: The Vietnam War and Pham Xuan AN's Dangerous Game* (New York: Public Affairs, 2009), p. 133.
46. Bartholomew-Feis, *The OSS and Ho Chi Minh*, pp. 252, 263, 298
47. MacKenzie to Dening, 29 September 1945, WO 203/5568 The National Archives (TNA), UK.
48. Neville, *Britain in Vietnam*, p. 107.
49. Hughes, 'A "Post-war" War', p. 270.

50. T.O. Smith, *Britain and the Origins of the Vietnam War: UK Policy in Indo-China, 1943–50* (London: Palgrave Macmillan, 2007), p. 46.
51. Hughes, 'A "Post-war" War', p. 271.
52. Smith, *Britain and the Origins of the Vietnam War*, p. 43.
53. Myers to Mountbatten, 31 October 1945, WO 172/1786 TNA.
54. Hughes, 'A "Post-war" War', p. 272.
55. Neville, *Britain in Vietnam*, pp. 95, 99, 104.

Chapter 1   Our Man in Hanoi

1. Narrative by Lt Col. A.G. Trevor-Wilson, Papers of Trevor-Wilson, p. 1. Vietnam Virtual Archive, available at http://www.virtual.vietnam.ttu.edu/cgi-bin/starfetch.exe?vYSs7CuDelG1c@Wzc5a4Kxglv4iskwi5WJwzGgP6lo91 Ith018FTZsO3eopXylsZnU3AcQc@XJ3Z.KI2cZh9i1pQ19sFGeLIEy4mn PhaYn0/0800115010.pdf (accessed 19 June 2013).
2. Ibid.
3. Ibid., p. 2.
4. Mervyn Brown, *War in Shangri-La: A Memoir of Civil War in Laos* (London: Radcliffe Press, 2001), p. 33.
5. Narrative by Lt Col. A.G. Trevor-Wilson, Papers of Trevor-Wilson, p. 2.
6. Ibid., p. 3.
7. Ibid.
8. Douglas Porch, *The French Secret Services: A History of French Intelligence from the Dreyfus Affair to the Gulf War* (New York: Farrar, Straus and Giroux, 1995), pp. 575–6, note 18.
9. Narrative by Lt Col. A.G. Trevor-Wilson, Papers of Trevor-Wilson, p. 3.
10. Ibid., p. 4.
11. Richard Aldrich, 'Britain's Secret Intelligence Service in Asia during the Second World War', *Modern Asian Studies*, Vol. 32, No. 1 (February 1998), p. 214; Report by Trevor-Wilson, 28 December 1945, WO 203/5563 TNA; Neville, *Britain in Vietnam*, p. 118.
12. Narrative by Lt Col. A.G. Trevor-Wilson, Papers of Trevor-Wilson, p. 1.
13. Ibid., p. 4.
14. Ibid., pp. 4–5.
15. Hughes, 'A "Post-war" War', p. 275.
16. Ibid.
17. Ibid.
18. Quoted in Smith, *Britain and the Origins of the Vietnam War*, p. 48.
19. Logevall, *Embers of War*, pp. 129–32.
20. Ibid., p. 132.
21. Ibid.
22. Neville, *Britain in Vietnam*, p. 13; Narrative by Lt Col. A.G. Trevor-Wilson, Papers of Trevor-Wilson, p. 5.
23. Goscha, 'Intelligence in a Time of Decolonization', p. 114.

24. Logevall, *Embers of War*, pp. 133–4.
25. Personal narrative of Lt Col. A.G. Trevor-Wilson, Trevor-Wilson Papers, p. 6.
26. Orrin DeForest and David Chanoff, *Slow Burn: The Rise and Bitter Fall of American Intelligence in Vietnam* (New York: Simon & Schuster, 1990), p. 83.
27. The Consul at Saigon (Reed) to the Secretary of State, 1 April 1946, *FRUS* 1946, Vol. VIII: *The Far East*, p. 34.
28. The Consul at Saigon (Reed) to the Secretary of State, 4 May 1946, ibid., pp. 39–40.
29. David Marr, *Vietnam: State, War, and Revolution (1945–1946)* (Berkeley: California University Press, 2013), p. 227.
30. Logevall, *Embers of War*, pp. 137–43.
31. The Acting Secretary of State to the Concul at Saigon (Reed), *FRUS* 1946, Vol. VIII: *The Far East*, p. 57.
32. Logevall, *Embers of War*, p. 144.
33. Neville, *Britain in Vietnam*, p. 156.
34. Logevall, *Embers of War*, p. 737, note 1.
35. The Consul at Saigon (Reed) to the Secretary of State, 17 September 1946, *FRUS* 1946, Vol. VIII: *The Far East*, p. 59.
36. Logevall, *Embers of War*, p. 151.
37. Ibid., p. 154.
38. Quoted in Porch, *The French Secret Services*, p. 305.
39. Logevall, *Embers of War*, pp. 155–7.
40. The Secretary of State to Certain Missions, 17 December 1946, *FRUS* 1946, Vol. VIII: *The Far East*, p. 72.
41. Logevall, *Embers of War*, p. 159.
42. Foreign Office to British embassy (Washington), 14 April 1948, FO 371/69654TNA quoted in Atwood, 'Fording the "Great Combination"', p. 122.
43. Thompson to Foreign Office, 14 December 1948, FO 371/69684 TNA quoted in ibid.
44. Goscha, 'Wiring Decolonization', p. 815.
45. Neville, *Britain in Vietnam*, p. 168.
46. Ibid., p. 167.
47. Jean-Marc LePage, *Les Services Secrets en Indochine* (Paris: Nouveau Monde, 2012), p. 48.
48. Logevall, *Embers of War*, pp. 162–3.
49. Personal narrative of Lt Col. A.G. Trevor-Wilson, Trevor Wilson Papers, p. 6.
50. Logevall, *Embers of War*, pp. 161–7, 189, 192.
51. The Ambassador in France (Caffery) to the Secretary of State, 15 January 1947, *FRUS* 1947, Vol. VI: *The Far East*, pp. 62–3.
52. Quoted in Jeffery, *MI6*, p. 698.
53. Events of week ending 4 June 1947, FO 371/63455TNA.
54. Consulate General (Saigon) to Foreign Office, 25 June 1947, FO 371/63455 TNA.

55. Consulate General (Saigon) to Foreign Office, 27 June 1947, ibid.
56. Military intelligence report No. 2 of 6 February 1949 submitted by British Military Liaison Officer, Saigon, p. 3, FO 371/75960 TNA.
57. Monthly Report for September 1950, p. 1, FO 959/70 TNA.
58. Smith, *Britain and the Origins of the Vietnam War*, pp. 52, 76, 78.
59. Quoted in Rotter, 'Chronicle of a War Foretold' in Atwood-Lawrence and Logevall, eds, *The First Vietnam War*, p. 294.
60. Ibid., pp. 80–1.
61. All quoted in Smith, *Britain and the Origins of the Vietnam War*, pp. 77–81, 109.
62. The Vice Consul at Hanoi (O'Sullivan) to the Secretary of State, 1 November 1946, *FRUS* 1946, Vol. VIII: *The Far East*, pp. 62–3.
63. The Ambassador in France (Caffery) to the Secretary of State, 29 November 1946, ibid., p. 63.
64. The Vice Consul at Hanoi (O'Sullivan) to the Secretary of State, 3 December 1946, ibid., pp. 64–5.
65. The Vice Consul at Hanoi (O'Sullivan) to the Secretary of State, 23 December 1946, ibid., p. 77.
66. The Ambassador in France (Caffery) to the Secretary of State, 29 November 1946, ibid., p. 63.
67. Hanyok, *Spartans in Darkness*, p. 12.
68. Memorandum of Conversation by Mr Charlton Ogburn Jr of the Division of Southeast Asian Affairs, 31 December 1946, *FRUS* 1946, Vol. VIII: *The Far East*, p. 83.
69. Gibbs to Foreign Office, 21 October 1948, CO 537/3334 TNA.
70. Gibbs to Foreign Office, 13 December 1948, CO 537/3334 TNA.
71. Report by Major J.E.D. Street, 12 June 1947, FO 371/63455 TNA.
72. Ibid.
73. Consulate General (Saigon) to N. Brain (Office of HM Special Commissioner in Southeast Asia), 25 June 1947, p. 1, FO 371/63455 TNA.
74. Killearn to Bevin, 2 February 1948, FO 371/69694 TNA, Smith, *Britain and the Origins of the Vietnam War*, p. 84.
75. Street (minute), 12 June 1947, FO 371/63455 TNA in ibid., p. 99.
76. Ibid., p. 107.
77. Mackworth Young (minute) 2 February 1949; Scott (minute) 5 February 1949; Dening to Clarke, 8 February 1949, FO 371/75960 TNA.
78. Smith, *Britain and the Origins of the Vietnam war*, p. 108.
79. Hopson to Foreign Office, 29 November 1948, CO 537/3334 TNA in ibid., p. 105.
80. Quoted in ibid., p. 112.
81. Smith, *Britain and the Origins of the Vietnam War*, p. 120.
82. Jean-Marc LePage and Elie Tenenbaum, 'French and American Intelligence Relations during the First Indochina War, 1950–54', *Studies in Intelligence*, Vol. 55, No. 3 (September 2001), p. 26.
83. Porch, *The French Secret Services*, p. 316.

84. Blackham (minute) 9 March 1949, FO 371/75961 TNA in Smith, *Britain and the Origins of the Vietnam War*, p. 122.
85. Clarke to Foreign Office 30 March 1949 FO 371/75961; Palliser (minute) 7 April 1949 FO 371/75962 TNA Smith, *Britain and the Origins of the Vietnam War*, p. 123.
86. The Military Situation in Tonkin, March 1949, FO 371/75961 TNA.
87. British embassy (Paris) to Foreign Office, 30 March 1949, ibid.
88. Military Intelligence Report No. 5 dated 18 April 1949, p. 1, FO 371/75962 TNA.
89. Ibid., p. 2.
90. Smith, *Britain and the Origins of the Vietnam War*, p. 121.
91. Quoted in ibid., p. 125.
92. Gibbs to Scott, 15 March 1949, pp. 1–2, FO 371/75961 TNA.
93. Smith, *Britain and the Origins of the Vietnam War*, p. 117.
94. British Consulate-General (Saigon) to the Office of the Commissioner-General (Singapore), 6 April 1949, FO371/75962 TNA.
95. Military intelligence report No. 6. French Indochina, 3 May 1949, p. 2, FO371/75962 TNA.
96. GHQ Far East Land Forces to COS, 3 October 1949 AIR 8/1584 TNA; VCOS meeting, 10 October 1949, AIR 8/1584 TNA in Smith, *Britain and the Origins of the Vietnam War*, p. 125.
97. Smith, *Britain and the Origins of the Vietnam War*, pp. 128, 136.
98. Lunn-Rockliffe to Gibbs, 31 January 1950, FO 371/83656 TNA.
99. Gibbs to Scott, 4 February 1950, FO 371/83656 TNA.
100. Smith, *Britain and the Origins of the Vietnam war*, pp. 128–9.
101. Kelly to Foreign Office, 31 January 1950, FO 371/ 83604 TNA.
102. Lloyd to Hobson (Saigon), 29 November 1949, FO 959/33 TNA
103. Ministry of Defence to Attlee, 29 March 1950, PREM 8/1221 TNA.
104. Graves to Eden, 18 January 1952, p. 8, FO 474/6 TNA.
105. Graves to Eden 3 January 1952, p. 2, ibid.

Chapter 2   French Intelligence at War

1. Alexander Zervoudakis, 'Nihil mirare, nihil contemptare, omnia intelligere: Franco-Vietnamese Intelligence in Indochina, 1950–1954', *Intelligence and National Security*, Vol. 13, Issue 1 (1998), pp. 201–2.
2. LePage, *Les Services Secrets en Indochine*, pp. 58–9, 97.
3. Zervoudakis, 'Nihil mirare, nihil contemptare, omnia intelligere', pp. 202–4.
4. Porch, *The French Secret Services*, pp. 328, 575.
5. LePage, *Les Services Secrets en Indochine*, pp. 196–7.
6. Zervoudakis, 'Nihil mirare, nihil contemptare, omnia intelligere', pp. 204–5.
7. Hanyok, *Spartans in Darkness*, pp. 18, 20, 28.
8. Zervoudakis, 'Nihil mirare, nihil contemptare, omnia intelligere' pp. 206–7.
9. Goscha, 'Intelligence in a Time of Decolonization', pp. 116–17, 123.

10. LePage, *Les Services Secrets en Indochina*, p. 66.
11. Porch, *The French Secret Services*, pp. 309, 311–12.
12. Merle Pribbenow, 'The Soviet-Vietnamese Intelligence Relationship during the Vietnam War: Cooperation and Conflict', *CWIHP* Working Paper No. 73, December 2014, p. 1.
13. Zervoudakis, 'Nihil mirare, nihil contemptare, omnia intelligere', p. 209.
14. Gosha, 'Intelligence in a Time of Decolonization', pp. 107–20.
15. The Vice Consul at Hanoi (O'Sullivan) to the Secretary of State, 3 July 1947, *FRUS* 1947, Vol. VI: *The Far East*, p. 108.
16. Ibid.
17. The Consul at Saigon (Reed) to the Secretary of State, 11 July 1947, ibid., p. 113.
18. The Consul at Saigon (Reed) to the Secretary of State, 22 September 1947, ibid., p. 139.
19. Whitworth to Graves, 3 March 1952, p. 35, FO 474/6 TNA.
20. The Consul at Saigon (Reed) to the Secretary of State, 27 February 1947, *FRUS* 1947, Vol. VI: *The Far East*, pp. 75–6.
21. The Ambassador in France (Caffery) to the Secretary of State, 27 March 1947, ibid., p. 81.
22. The Vice Consul at Hanoi (O'Sullivan) to the Secretary of State, 11 April 1947, ibid., pp. 85–6.
23. *FRUS* 1947, Vol. VI: *The Far East*, p. 67 note 44.
24. Logevall, *Embers of War*, p. 237.
25. Monthly Report for October 1950, FO 959/70 TNA.
26. Quoted in Goscha, 'Intelligence in a Time of Decolonization', p. 130.
27. All quoted in ibid., pp. 126–31.
28. Porch, *The French Secret Services*, pp. 307, 572, note 37.
29. Zervoudakis, 'Nihil mirare, nihil contemptare, omnia intelligere', p. 205.
30. Porch, *The French Secret Services*, p. 321.
31. Ibid; LePage, *Les Services Secrets en Indochine*, pp. 121–2.
32. Porch, *The French Secret Services*, pp. 322–4.
33. LePage, *Les Services Secrets en Indochine*, p. 119.
34. Shawn McHale, 'Understanding the Fanatic Mind? The Viêt Minh and Race Hatred in the First Indochina War (1945–1954)', *Journal of Vietnamese Studies*, Vol. 4, Issue 3 (2009), p. 121.
35. Military Intelligence Report No. 2, French Indochina to MI2, 6 February 1949, FO 371/75960 TNA.
36. Enclosure to Saigon letter to R.H.Scott No. XIII/3/49 of 9 December 1940, FO 959/33 TNA.
37. On opium and child spies: LePage, *Les Services Secrets en Indochine*, pp. 96, 108–9, 124–6, 200–1, 207.
38. Trevor-Wilson to Gibbs, 5 May 1950; Monthly Report for the month of April 1950, 4 May 1950, FO 959/70 TNA.
39. Zervoudakis, 'Nihil mirare, nihil contemptare, omnia intelligere', pp. 202–3, 212–14, 218–23.

40. Porch, *The French Secret Services*, pp. 309, 313.
41. Goscha, 'Wiring Decolonization', p. 826.
42. Zervoudakis, 'Nihil mirare, nihil contemptare, omnia intelligere', pp. 203–5.
43. Porch, *The French Secret Services*, pp. 314–15.

Chapter 3   With Extreme Prejudice

1. McHale, 'Understanding the Fanatic Mind?', p. 114.
2. Ibid., p. 110.
3. Ibid., pp. 111–12.
4. Ibid., pp. 107–8.
5. Ibid., p. 112.
6. Ibid.
7. Ibid., p. 113.
8. Ibid., p. 114.
9. Goscha, 'Intelligence in a Time of Decolonization', p. 112.
10. Logevall, *Embers of War*, p. 209.
11. Porch, *The French Secret Services*, p. 302.
12. Goscha, 'Wiring Decolonization', p. 822.
13. Pirrie to Consulate-General (Saigon), 3 April 1950, FO 959/70 TNA.
14. Goscha, 'Intelligence in a Time of Decolonization', p. 122.
15. Quoted in Norman Sherry, *The Life of Graham Greene*, Vol. 2: *1939–1955* (New York: Penguin, 1994), p. 367.
16. McHale, 'Understanding the Fanatic Mind?', p. 110.
17. Goscha, 'Intelligence in a Time of Decolonization', p. 122.
18. Ibid., p. 123.
19. Ibid., p. 125.
20. Graves to Morrison, 11 August 1951, p. 1, FO 959/107 TNA.
21. Ibid., p. 2; Graves to South East Asia Department (Foreign Office), 15 August 1951, FO 959/107 TNA.
22. Graves to Morrison, 11 August 1951, p. 3, FO 959/107 TNA.
23. Graves to South East Asia Department (Foreign Office), 15 August 1951, FO 959/107 TNA.
24. Graves to Eden, 29 February 1952, pp. 29–30, FO 474/6 TNA.
25. Michael Thompson, 'Thoughts Provoked by The Very Best Men: The Need for Integrity'. Available at https://www.cia.gov/library/center-for-the-study-of-intelligence/csi-publications/csi-studies/studies/96unclass/bestmen.htm#ft7 (accessed 25 July 2013).
26. Ibid.
27. All quoted in Thomas A. Bass, *The Spy Who Loved Us: The Vietnam War and Pham Xuan An's Dangerous Game* (New York: Public Affairs, 2009), pp. 56–7.
28. Narrative of Lt Col. A.G. Trevor-Wilson, Trevor-Wilson Papers, p. 3.
29. Ibid., p. 7.
30. Ibid.
31. Quoted in Bass, *The Spy Who Loved Us*, p. 55.

32. Quoted in ibid.
33. Ibid., p. 57.
34. Narrative of Lt.Col.A.G.Trevor-Wilson, p. 7.
35. Norman Sherry, *The Life of Graham Greene*, pp. 417–19.
36. Quoted in ibid., p. 417.
37. A report dated 4 April 1952 by Lansdale held at the Lansdale Papers in the UCLA quoted in Jonathan Nashel, *Edward Lansdale's Cold War* (Amherst: Massachusetts Press, 2005), pp. 22, 253 note. 22.
38. Quoted in Tim Weiner, *Legacy of Ashes: The History of the CIA* (New York, 2007), pp. 246–7; DeForest and Chanoff, *Slow Burn*, p. 140.
39. Tim Weiner, *Legacy of Ashes*, p. 246.
40. Peer DeSilva, *Sub Rosa: The CIA and the Uses of Intelligence* (New York: New York Times Books, 1978), p. 250.
41. William Rosenau and Austin Long, *The Phoenix Program and Contemporary Counterinsurgency*, RAND Occasional Paper 2009, pp. 7–8; see also Kevin M. Boylan, '"Goodnight Saigon: American Provincial Advisors' Final Impressions of the Vietnam War', *The Journal of Military History*, Vol. 78, No. 1 (January 2014), pp. 233–70.
42. Quoted in Rosenau and Long, *The Phoenix Program and Contemporary Counterinsurgency*, p. 10.
43. John Prados, *Lost Crusader: The Secret Wars of CIA Director William Colby* (New York: Oxford University Press, 2003), p. 213.
44. Michael Howard Holzman, *James Jesus Angleton, the CIA, and the Craft of Counterintelligence* (Amherst: University of Massachusetts, 2008), p. 229.
45. 'The Pacification Effort in Vietnam', Special National Intelligence Estimate 14–69, 16 January 1969, p. 6, available at http.www.foia.cia.govsitesdefault filesdocument_conversions89801DOC_0000022669.pdf (accessed 22 November 2013).
46. Rosenau and Long, *The Phoenix Program and Contemporary Counterinsurgency*, pp. 10–13.
47. Prados, *Lost Crusader*, p. 216.
48. Gregory L. Vistica, 'One Awful Night in Thanh Phong', *New York Times Magazine*, 25 April 2001, available at http://www.nytimes.com/2001/04/25/magazine/25KERREY.html?pagewanted=1&ei=5070&en=3db9255f522f13f6&ex=1138251600? (accessed 22 November 2013).
49. Ted Shackley and Richard A. Finney, *Spymaster: My Life in the CIA* (Dulles VA: Potomac Books, 2005), pp. 233–4.
50. Woods, *Shadow Warrior*, p. 331.
51. Quoted in ibid., p. 316.
52. Quoted in ibid., p. 315.
53. Ibid., p. 314.
54. Dale Andrade, 'Three Lessons from Vietnam', *Washington Post*, 29 December 2005, p. A23; Mark Moyar, *Phoenix and the Birds of Prey: The CIA's Secret Campaign to Destroy the Viet Cong* (Annapolis: Naval Institute Press, 1997), p. 236.

55. Prados, *Lost Crusader*, p. 236.
56. Quoted in Woods, *Shadow Warrior*, p. 313; Prados, *Lost Crusader*, p. 219.
57. Richard A. Hunt, *Pacification: The American Struggle for Vietnam's Hearts and Minds* (Boulder: Westview Press, 1995), pp. 247–8; Prados, *Lost Crusader*, p. 230.
58. Kevin M. Boylan, 'Goodnight Saigon: American Provincial Advisors' Final Impressions of the Vietnam War', *Journal of Military History*, Vol. 78, No. 1, p. 249.
59. Merle Pribbenow (translation), *Victory in Vietnam: The Official History of the People's Army of Vietnam, 1954–1975* (Lawrence, KS: University Press of Kansas, 2002), pp. 246–7.
60. Boylan, 'Goodnight Saigon', p. 249.
61. Hunt, *Pacification*, pp. 247–8.
62. Quoted in Woods, *Shadow Warrior*, p. 288.
63. Boylan, 'Goodnight Saigon', pp. 244–5.
64. Quoted in ibid., p. 245.
65. Quoted in ibid.
66. Quoted in ibid., p. 246.
67. Ibid., p. 247.

Chapter 4   Spymasters' Fear

1. Pirrie to Consulate-General (Saigon), 8 February 1950, FO 959/70 TNA.
2. Monthly report for March 1950, ibid.
3. American Foreign Service Officer's Conference held in Bangkok in June 1948: Communism in South East Asia, 7 September 1948, p. 3, FO 371/69694 TNA.
4. Charles Kraus, 'A border region "exuded with militant friendship": Provincial narratives of China's participation in the First Indochina War, 1949–1954', *Cold War History*, Vol. 12, Issue 3 (August 2012), p. 4.
5. Kraus, 'A border region "exuded with militant friendship"', pp. 5–7.
6. Pirrie to Minister (British legation, Saigon), 2 June 1950, FO 959/70 TNA.
7. Pirrie to Consulate General (Hanoi), 6 July 1950, ibid.
8. Trevor-Wilson to Gibbs (Saigon), 20 July 1950, ibid.
9. Pirrie to the Minister (British legation, Saigon), 3 December 1950, ibid.
10. Qiang Zhai, *China and the Vietnam Wars, 1950–1975* (Chapel Hill: University of North Carolina Press, 2000), p. 37.
11. Quoted in ibid., p. 53.
12. Kraus, 'A border region "exuded with militant friendship"', p. 10.
13. Qiang, *China and the Vietnam Wars*, p. 20.
14. Goscha, 'Intelligence in a Time of Decolonization', p. 118.
15. Goscha, 'The Maritime Nature of the Wars for Vietnam'.
16. The Secretary of State to the Embassy in China, 2 July 1948, *FRUS 1948*, Vol. VI: *The Far East and Australasia*, p. 28.
17. Logewall, *Embers of War*, p. 211.

18. Ibid., pp. 212, 225.
19. Memorandum by the Director of the Office of Eastern European Affairs (Yost) to the Assistant Secretary of State for European Affairs (Perkings), 31 January 1950, *FRUS 1950*, Vol. VI: *East Asia and the Pacific*, p. 710.
20. Memorandum by the Assistant Secretary of State for Far Eastern Affairs (Butterworth) to the Deputy Under Secretary of State for Political Affairs (Rusk), 5 January 1950, ibid., pp. 690–1.
21. The Charge at Saigon (Gullion) to the Secretary of State, 6 May 1950, ibid., p. 808.
22. LePage and Tenenbaum, 'French and American Intelligence Relations during the First Indochina War', p. 26.
23. Graves to Scott, 21 December 1950, FO 959/107 TNA.
24. Murray to Gibbs, 10 January 1951, ibid.
25. Gibbs to Murray, 20 January 1951, ibid.
26. LePage and Tenenbaum, 'French and American Intelligence Relations during the First Indochina War', p. 28.
27. Ibid., pp. 27–9.
28. Quoted in Ted Morgan, *Valley of Death: The Tragedy at Dien Bien Phu that Led America into the Vietnam War* (New York: Random House, 2010), p. 140.
29. LePage and Tenenbaum, 'French and American Intelligence Relations during the First Indochina War', pp. 27–9.
30. Logevall, *Embers of War*, p. 225.
31. The Minister at Saigon (Heath) to the Secretary of State, 30 November 1951, *FRUS 1951*, Vol. VI: *Asia and the Pacific*, p. 547.
32. The Minister at Saigon (Heath) to the Secretary of State, 18 July 1951, ibid., p. 456.
33. The Ambassador at Saigon (Heath) to the Department of State, 18 October 1952, *FRUS 1953*, Vol. XIII: *Indochina*, p. 267.
34. *FRUS 1953*, Vol. XIII: *Indochina*, p. 563, note 1.
35. Jean-Marc LePage and Elie Tenenbaum, 'French and American Intelligence Relations during the First Indochina War, 1950–54', *Studies in Intelligence*, Vol. 55, No. 3 (September 2001), pp. 29–32.
36. Porch, *The French Secret Services*, p. 317.
37. Draft report by the National Security Council, 27 February 1950, *FRUS 1950*, Vol. VI: *East Asia and the Pacific*, pp. 745, 747.
38. Quoted in Andrew J. Rotter, 'A Chronicle of a War Foretold: The United States and Vietnam, 1945–1954' in Atwood-Lawrence and Logevall, eds, *The First Indochina War*, p. 290.
39. The Ambassador in France (Bruce) to the Secretary of State, 8 April 1950, *FRUS 1950*, Vol. VI: *East Asia and the Pacific*, pp. 772–3.
40. The Ambassador in France (Bruce) to the Secretary of State, 12 August 1950, ibid., pp. 851–2.
41. The Secretary of State to the Embassy in France, 15 August 1950, ibid., p. 854.

42. Memorandum by the Assistant Secretary of State for Far Eastern Affairs (Rusk) to the Secretary of State, 11 September 1950, ibid., p. 878.
43. The Minister at Saigon (Heath) to the Secretary of State, 15 October 1950, ibid., p. 894.
44. Ibid., p. 896.
45. National Intelligence Estimate, NIE-5, 29 December 1950, ibid., pp. 959–60.
46. Telegram from Hanoi (Consulate General), 1 January 1951, FO 959/107 TNA.
47. Military attaché (Saigon) to Minister (Saigon/War Office (MI2)/ 22 January 1951, p. 2, FO 959/107 TNA.
48. Assistant Military Attaché (Hanoi) to Military Attaché (Saigon), 8 June 1951, ibid.
49. 'Extract of a letter received from Hanoi dated 7th June 1951', ibid.
50. Gibbs to Foreign Office, 1 February 1051, ibid.
51. Minute by Frank S. Gibbs, 7 February 1951, ibid.
52. Handwritten note in ibid.
53. Brigadier L.F. Field to Troopers for MI2, 11 June 1951, ibid.
54. The Minister at Saigon (Heath) to the Secretary of State, 14 March 1951, FRUS 1951, Vol. VI: Asia and the Pacific, p. 396.
55. The Minister at Saigon (Heath) to the Secretary of State, 23 March 1951, ibid., p. 409.
56. NIE-35, National Intelligence Estimate, 7 August 1951, ibid., pp. 473, 475.
57. Memorandum by the Minister at Saigon (Heath), undated, ibid., pp. 485–6.
58. Memorandum of conversation by Mr William M. Gibson of the Office of Philippine and Southeast Asian Affairs, 14 September 1951, ibid., p. 503.
59. Memorandum by the Acting Assistant Secretary of State for Far Eastern Affairs (Allison) to the Secretary of State, 19 December 1951, ibid., p. 563.
60. The Secretary of State to the Embassy in France, 20 December 1951, ibid.
61. Substance of discussions of State Joint Chiefs of Staff meeting at the Pentagon building, December 21, 1951, 11:30 am. Ibid., p. 569.
62. The Ambassador in France (Bruce) to the Secretary of State, 22 December 1951, ibid., pp. 571–2.
63. The Ambassador in France (Bruce) to the Secretary of State, 29 December 1951, ibid., pp. 580–1.
64. Graves to Eden, 24 January 1952, p. 11, FO 474/6, TNA.
65. Graves to Eden, 4 February 1952, p. 21, ibid.
66. Peter Lowe, Contending with Nationalism and Communism: British Policy Towards Southeast Asia, 1945–65 (London: Palgrave Macmillan, 2009), p. 62.
67. H.A. Graves quoting the military attaché in Graves to Foreign Office, 23 December 1952, FO 371/101077 TNA quoted in Atwood, 'Forging the "Great Combination"', p. 127.
68. MacDonald to Eden, 26 July 1952, p. 55, FO 474/6 TNA.
69. National Intelligence Estimate NIE 35/1, 3 March 1952, FRUS 1952–1954, Vol. XIII: Indochina, Part 1, pp. 54–5.

70. Draft memorandum prepared in the Department of Defense, 3 April 1952, ibid., p. 119.
71. United States minute of tripartite Foreign Ministers meeting with France and the United Kingdom at the Quai d'Orsay, Paris, May 28, 1952, ibid., p. 164.
72. NIE 35/2 National Intelligence Estimate: 'Probable Developments in Indochina through mid-1953', 29 August 1952, ibid., p. 243.
73. Memorandum by the Assistant Secretary of State for Far Easter Affairs (Allison) to the Undersecretary of State (Bruce), 24 November 1952, ibid., p. 303.
74. NIE 91 'Probable Developments in Indochina through mid-1954', 4 June 1953, ibid., p. 593.
75. Ibid., p. 594.
76. Memorandum of Conversation by the Counselor (MacArthur), 9 October 1953, ibid., p. 823.
77. Kraus, 'A border region "exuded with militant friendship"', p. 6.
78. 'Anti-Soviet Communism', JIC (memorandum), 19 December 1953, JIC (53)119, CAB 158/16 TNA.
79. Morgan, Valley of Death, pp. 169–70.
80. Ibid., pp. 176–8.
81. Qiang, China and the Vietnam Wars, p. 45.
82. Memorandum by the Director of the office of Philippine and Southeast Asian affairs (Bonsal) to the Assistant Secretary of State For Far Eastern Affairs (Robertson), 27 November 1953, FRUS 1952–1954, Vol. XIII: Indochina, p. 886; Zervoudakis, 'Nihil mirare, nihil contemptare, omnia intelligere', p. 216.
83. Porch, The French Secret Services, p. 309.
84. Morgan, Valley of Death, p. 338.
85. Dwight D. Eisenhower, Mandate for Change: The White House Years, 1953–1956: A Personal Account (New York: Doubleday, 1963), p. 339.
86. Military attache (Saigon) to Minister (Saigon/War Office, MI2), 22 January 1951, p. 2, FO 959/107 TNA.
87. Qiang, China and the Vietnam Wars, ibid., p. 47.
88. Zervoudakis, 'Nihil mirare, nihil contemptare, omnia intelligere', p. 216.
89. John R. Nordell Jr, The Undetected Enemy: French and American Miscalculations at Dien Bien Phu, 1953 (College Station: Texas A&M University Press, 1995), pp. 141–4.
90. Morgan, Valley of Death, p. 251.
91. Memorandum of Discussion at the 189th Meeting of the National Security Council, Thursday, March 18, 1954, FRUS 1952–1954, Vol. XIII: Indochina, pp. 1132–3.
92. Ibid., p. 1133.
93. Quoted in Morgan, Valley of Death, p. 393.
94. John Prados, 'Assessing Dien Bien Phu' in Atwood and Logevall, eds, The First Vietnam War, pp. 230–6; Logevall, Embers of War, pp. 457–509; Morgan, Valley of Death, pp. 478–9.

95. Ibid., p. 482.
96. Quoted in ibid., p. 481.
97. See also Rotter, 'Chronicle of a War Foretold' in ibid., p. 301.
98. Panagiotis Dimitrakis, *Failed Alliances of the Cold War: Britain's Strategy and Ambitions in Asia and the Middle East* (London: I.B.Tauris, 2012).
99. Morgan, *Valley of Death*, p. 407.
100. Quoted in Rotter, 'Chronicle of a War Foretold', p. 305.
101. Quoted in ibid., p. 304.
102. Morgan, *Valley of Death*, p. 409.
103. Qiang, *China and the Vietnam Wars*, p. 48.
104. Ibid., p. 47.
105. Ibid., p. 49.
106. Morgan, *Valley of Death*, p. 490.
107. Ibid., p. 515.
108. Ibid., p. 516.
109. Hanyok, *Spartans in Darkness*, p. 45.

Chapter 5   The Colonel and the Mole

1. An quoted in Bass, *The Spy Who Loved US*, p. 66.
2. Ibid., p. 2.
3. An quoted in ibid., p. 64.
4. Ibid.
5. Quoted in Cecil B. Currey, *Edward Lansdale: The Unquiet American* (Boston: Houghton Mifflin, 1988), p. 8.
6. Thomas L. Ahern Jr, *CIA and the House of Ngo: Covert Action in South Vietnam, 1954–1963* (Washington, DC: Center for the Study of Intelligence), p. 15.
7. LePage and Tenenbaum, 'French and American Intelligence Relations during the First Indochina War', p. 26.
8. Ibid., pp. 16–17.
9. Lansdale Team's Report on Covert Saigon Mission in 1954 and 1955, *The Pentagon Papers* (Gravel Edition), Vol. 1, pp. 573–83, available at https://www.mtholyoke.edu/acad/intrel/pentagon/doc95.htm (accessed 14 October 2013).
10. Ahern, *CIA and the House of Ngo*, p. 33 note 37.
11. Lansdale Team's Report on Covert Saigon Mission.
12. 'Lieutenant Colonel Lucien E. Conein', available at http://www.arlington cemetery.net/conein.htm (accessed 16 October 2013).
13. Lansdale Team's Report on Covert Saigon Mission.
14. Ibid.
15. Edward Lansdale, 'Military Operations', Box 80, Lansdale Papers (Hoover Institution, Stanford) quoted in Alison Baier, 'Edward Lansdale: The Image of the United States in Vietnam', p. 25, available at history.rutgers.edu/.../269-edward-lansdale (accessed 26 October 2013).

16. Lansdale Team's Report on Covert Saigon Mission.
17. All quoted in McHale, 'Understanding the Fanatic Mind?', pp. 98–9, 122.
18. Lansdale Team's Report on Covert Saigon Mission.
19. Ibid.
20. Kenneth Conboy and Dale Andrade, *Spies and Commandos: How America Lost the Secret War in North Vietnam* (University Press of Kansas, 2001), p. 9.
21. Ahern, *CIA and the House of Ngo*, p. 45, note 24.
22. Lansdale Team's Report on Covert Saigon Mission.
23. Bass, *The Spy Who Loved Us*, p. 82.
24. Ibid., pp. 83–4.
25. Ellsberg quoted in ibid., pp. 89–90.
26. Ahern, *CIA and the House of Ngo*, p. 35.
27. Douglas Little, 'Mission Impossible: The CIA and the Cult of Covert Action in the Middle East', *Diplomatic History*, Vol. 28, No. 5 (November 2004), p. 678.
28. Lansdale Team's Report on Covert Saigon Mission.
29. Ibid.
30. Ibid.
31. Bass, *The Spy Who Loved Us*, p. 76.
32. Mark Moyar, *Triumph Forsaken: The Vietnam War, 1954–1965* (Cambridge: Cambridge University Press, 2006), pp. 428–9, note 22.
33. Quoted in Bass, *The Spy Who Loved Us*, p. 77.
34. Ibid., p. 65.
35. Ibid., p. 94.
36. Stuart A. Herrington, *Stalking the Vietcong - Inside Operation Phoenix: A Personal Account* (New York: Ballantine Books, 2004), p. 31.
37. Nashel, Jonathan, *Edward Lansdale's Cold War* (Amherst: University of Massachusetts Press, 2005), p. 92.
38. Quoted in Bass, *The Spy Who Loved Us*, pp. 65, 73, 94.
39. As quoted in ibid., pp. 66–7.
40. Ibid., p. 73.
41. As quoted in ibid., pp. 88–9.
42. Ibid., p. 95.
43. An quoted in ibid., pp. 95–6, 99.
44. An quoted in ibid.
45. Lansdale Team's Report on Covert Saigon Mission.
46. Ibid.
47. Ibid.
48. Ibid.
49. Ibid.
50. 'PAVN March into Haiphong', *The Canberra Times*, 14 May 1955.
51. Lansdale Team's Report on Covert Saigon Mission.
52. Moyar, *Triumph Forsaken*, p. 41.
53. Ahern, *CIA and the House of Ngo*, pp. 41–3.
54. Ahern, *CIA and the House of Ngo*, p. 44; Moyar, *Triumph Forsaken*, p. 45.

55. Larry Berman, *Perfect Spy: The Incredible Double Life of Pham Xuan An, Time Magazine Reporter & Vietnamese Communist Agent* (New York: Smithsonian Books, 2007), p. 78.

56. Ahern, *CIA and the House of Ngo*, p. 69.

57. Moyar, *Triumph Forsaken*, p. 47.

58. Ahern, *CIA and the House of Ngo*, p. 70.

59. Moyar, *Triumph Forsaken*, p. 48.

60. Ibid., p. 49.

61. Abern, *CIA and the House of Ngo*, p. 78.

62. Quoted in Ahern, *CIA and the House of Ngo*, p. 79.

63. Moyar, *Triumph Forsaken*, p. 50.

64. Ibid., p. 51.

65. Ibid., p. 429 note 48.

66. Ahern, *CIA and the House of Ngo*, p. 81.

67. Berman, *Perfect Spy*, p. 79.

68. Howard R. Simpson, *Tiger in the Barbed Wire: An American in Vietnam, 1952– 1991* (New York: Kodansha, 1992), p. 172.

69. Moyar, *Triumph Forsaken*, p. 54.

70. Ibid., p. 55.

71. Bass, *The Spy Who Loved Us*, pp. 103–5.

Chapter 6   Secret Sources and Double Cross

1. Ahern, *CIA and the House of Ngo*, pp. 90, 108, 169.

2. Quoted in ibid., p. 105.

3. Ibid., p. 106.

4. Ibid., p. 111.

5. Prados, *Lost Crusader*, p. 65.

6. Ahern, *CIA and the House of Ngo*, p. 113.

7. All quoted in ibid., pp. 116, 118–20.

8. Richard H. Shultz Jr, *The Secret War against Hanoi: The Untold Story of Spies, Saboteurs, and Covert Warriors in North Vietnam* (New York: Harper Perennial, 1999), p. 14.

9. Ahern, *CIA and the House of Ngo*, pp. 60, 121–5.

10. Quoted in Thomas L. Ahern Jr, *The Way We Do Things: Black Entry Operations Into North Vietnam* (CIA: Center for the Study of Intelligence, 2005), p. 8.

11. Quoted Ahern, *CIA and the House of Ngo*, p. 129.

12. Ibid., p. 130.

13. Woods, *Shadow Warrior*, p. 144.

14. Shultz, *The Secret War against Hanoi*, p. 14.

15. Circular 13 November 1955, p. 1, FO 959/152 TNA.

16. Ibid., p. 2.

17. Ibid., p. 3.

18. Vietnamese Workers Party Central Committee to Comrade Muoi, 23 March 1956, FO 959/152 TNA.

19. Conboy and Andrade, *Spies and Commandos*, p. 282.
20. Consulate General (Hanoi) to Foreign Office, 25 March 1958, FO 371/136167 TNA.
21. Consulate General (Hanoi) to Foreign Office, 7 April 1959; Consulate General (Hanoi) to Foreign Office, 7 July 1959, all in FO 371/144452 TNA.
22. British Embassy (Saigon) to Foreign Office, 25 July 1959, FO 371/144453 TNA.
23. Goscha, 'The Maritime Nature of the Wars for Vietnam'.
24. Hanyok, *Spartans in Darkness*, pp. 147–9.
25. Ahern, *CIA and the House of Ngo*, pp. 133–4.
26. Ibid., p. 135.
27. Woods, *Shadow Warrior*, p. 149.
28. Bruce Hoffman and Christian Ostermann, eds, *Moles, Defectors, and Deceptions: James Angleton and his Influence on US Counterintelligence* (Woodrow Wilson International Center for Scholars and Georgetown University Center for Peace & Security Studies Joint Conference, 2012), p. 37.
29. Ahern, *CIA and the House of Ngo*, pp. 140–3.
30. Ibid., p. 147; George W. Allen, 'Coups Covering in Saigon', *Studies in Intelligence*, Vol. 33 (Winter 1989), p. 59.
31. Ahern, *CIA and the House of Ngo*, p. 165.
32. Ibid., p. 165.
33. Woods, *Shadow Warrior*, pp. 156–7.
34. Ahern, *CIA and the House of Ngo*, p. 149.
35. Ibid., p. 151.
36. Ibid., p. 156.
37. Ibid., p. 164.
38. Woods, *Shadow Warrior*, p. 181.
39. Ahern, *CIA and the House of Ngo*, p. 166.
40. Ibid., p. 163.
41. Quoted in Berman, *Perfect Spy*, p. 183.
42. Quoted in ibid., p. 137.
43. Quoted in ibid., p. 144.
44. Quoted in Bass, *The Spy Who Loved Us*, pp. 137–8.
45. Quoted in Berman, *Perfect Spy*, p. 135.
46. Ibid.
47. Bass, *The Spy Who Loved Us*, p. 136.
48. Ahern, *The Way We Do Things*, p. 10.
49. Ibid., p. 21.
50. Woods, *Shadow Warrior*, p. 196.
51. See the three main books: Richard H. Shultz, *The Secret War Against Hanoi: The Untold Story of Spies, Saboteurs, and Covert Warriors in North Vietnam* (New York: Harper Perennial, 1999); Kenneth Conboy and Dale Andrade, *Spies and Commandos: How America Lost the Secret War in North Vietnam* (University Press of Kansas, 2000); Tourison Sedgwick, *Secret Army, Secret War: Washington's*

Tragic Spy Operations in North Vietnam (Annapolis, MD: Naval Institute Press, 1995).

52. Ahern, *The Way We Do Things*, p. 13.
53. Ibid.
54. Ibid., p. 14.
55. Ibid.
56. Ibid., p. 15.
57. Ibid., pp. 15–17.
58. Ibid.
59. Ibid., p. 18.
60. Ibid., p. 19.
61. Ibid., p. 21.
62. Ibid.
63. Ibid., p. 22.
64. Ibid., p. 23.
65. Ibid.
66. Ibid., p. 24.
67. Ibid.
68. Ibid., p. 25.
69. Ibid.
70. Ibid., p. 26.
71. Ibid., p. 27.
72. Ibid.
73. Ibid., p. 29.
74. Ibid., p. 30.
75. Ibid., p. 31.
76. Ibid., p. 33.
77. Ibid., p. 35.
78. Ibid., p. 37.
79. Ibid., p. 38.
80. Ibid., pp. 38–9.
81. Quoted in ibid., p. 41.
82. Ibid.
83. Ibid., pp. 42–3.
84. Ibid., pp. 47, 49.
85. Ibid., p. 49.
86. Ibid., p. 52.
87. Shultz, *The Secret War against Hanoi*, pp. 36–7.
88. Ahern, *The Way We Do Things*, p. 58.

Chapter 7   The Spy and the Coup

1. Tim Weiner, 'Lucien Conein, 79, Legendary Cold War Spy', *New York Times*, 7 June 1998.

2. Quoted in Thomas L. Ahern Jr, *CIA and the Generals: Covert Support to Military Government in South Vietnam* (CIA: Center for the Study of Intelligence, October 1998), p. 11.

3. Thomas L. Ahern Jr, *CIA and the House of Ngo: Covert Action in South Vietnam, 1954–1963* (CIA: Center for the Study of Intelligence, June 2000), p. 166.

4. Ibid., p. 167.

5. Ibid.

6. Quoted in Bass, *The Spy Who Loved Us*, p. 139.

7. Ahern, *CIA and the House of Ngo*, p. 167.

8. Quoted in William Prochnau, *Once Upon a Distant War* (New York: Vintage, 1995), p. 46.

9. Ahern, *CIA and the House of Ngo*, pp. 169–72.

10. Ibid., p. 174.

11. Ball to US Embassy-Operation Immediate, 24 August 1963, p. 2, available at www2.gwu.edu~ nsarchivNSAEBBNSAEBB101vn02.pdf (accessed 7 November 2013).

12. Quoted in Nashel, *Edward Landsdale's Cold War*, p. 67.

13. Ibid., p. 3.

14. Audio tape record available at: http://www2.gwu.edu/~ nsarchiv/NSAEBB/ NSAEBB444/docs/audio02.mp3 (accessed 11 November 2013).

15. Ahern, *CIA and the House of Ngo*, p. 174.

16. Ibid., p. 175.

17. Ibid.

18. Woods, *Shadow Warrior*, p. 191.

19. Ahern, *CIA and the House of Ngo*, p. 178.

20. Ibid., p. 179.

21. Bundy's notes on the paper 'Cast of Characters in South Vietnam' OCI no. 2703/63, August 28, 1963 28 August 1963, John F. Kennedy Library: Kennedy Papers: National Security File, Country File, box 201, folder: 'Vietnam: General, CIA Reports 11/3/63–11/5/63', available at http://www2.gwu.edu/~ nsarchiv/NSAEBB/NSAEBB444/docs/diem18.pdf (accessed 11 November 2013).

22. 'Memorandum of Conference with the President, August 28, 1963, Noon', John F. Kennedy Library: Kennedy Papers, National Security File, Meetings & Memoranda series, box 316, folder: 'Meetings on Vietnam 8/24/63–8/31/63', available at http://www2.gwu.edu/~ nsarchiv/NSAEBB/NSAEBB444/diem10.pdf (accessed 11 November 2013).

23. Memorandum of conference with the President, 28 August 1963, Noon, p. 4, available at http://www2.gwu.edu/~ nsarchiv/NSAEBB/NSAEBB444/diem10.pdf (accessed 13 November 2013).

24. Tape Recording of Presidential Meeting, 29 August 1963, Noon (56:03 minutes elapsed), John F. Kennedy Library, NARA, available at http://www2.gwu.edu/~ nsarchiv/NSAEBB/NSAEBB444/audio12.mp3 (accessed 13 November 2013).

25. Ahern, *CIA and the House of Ngo*, p. 180.
26. Ibid.
27. Ibid., p. 182.
28. Quoted in ibid., p. 183.
29. Quoted in ibid., p. 185.
30. Ibid., p. 185.
31. Ibid., p. 186.
32. Quoted in ibid., p. 187.
33. Ibid., p. 187.
34. Hanyok, *Spartans in Darkness*, p. 158.
35. Ahern, *CIA and the House of Ngo*, p. 189.
36. Nashel, *Edward Lansdale's Cold War*, p. 57.
37. Ahern, *CIA and the House of Ngo*, p. 188.
38. Quoted in Woods, *Shadow Warrior*, p. 177.
39. Ahern, *CIA and the House of Ngo*, p. 191.
40. Quoted in Hanyok, *Spartans in Darkness*, p. 160.
41. Ahern, *CIA and the House of Ngo*, p. 191.
42. Ibid., p. 192.
43. Howard Jones, *Death of a Generation: How the Assassinations of Diem and JFK Prolonged the Vietnam War* (Oxford: Oxford University Press, 2004), p. 384.
44. Conein testimony, June 20, 1975, pp. 23, 38–9, Record No. 157–10014-10094, SSCIA, Church Committee Hearings (NA) quoted in Jones, *Death of a Generation*, pp. 386–7.
46. Jones, *Death of a Generation*, p. 389.
47. Quoted in ibid., pp. 388–9.
48. Ibid., p. 389.
49. Quoted in ibid., p. 392.
50. Ahern, *CIA and the House of Ngo*, p. 196.
51. Lodge to Rusk, 8 October 1963, *FRUS 1961–1963*, Vol. IV: *Vietnam, August–December 1963*, pp. 394–5.
52. Ibid., p. 395 note 3.
53. Ahern, *CIA and the House of Ngo*, p. 197.
54. Ibid., p. 199.
55. Ibid., p. 198.
56. Ibid., pp. 198–9.
57. Ibid., p. 200.
58. Quoted in Jones, *Death of a Generation*, p. 395.
59. Quoted in Ahern, *CIA and the House of Ngo*, p. 200.
60. Ibid., p. 201.
61. Quoted in Jones, *Death of a Generation*, p. 396.
62. Quoted in ibid., pp. 396–7.
63. Quoted in Ahern, *The CIA and the House of Ngo*, p. 201.
64. Ibid., p. 201–2.
65. Ibid., p. 202.

66. Ibid.
67. Ibid; Jones, *Death of a Generation*, pp. 398–9.
68. Ahern, *CIA and the House of Ngo*, p. 204.
69. Ibid., p. 205.
70. All quoted in Freedman, *Kennedy's Wars*, p. 394.
71. Ahern, *CIA and the House of Ngo*, p. 205.
72. Ibid., p. 205.
73. Quoted in Jones, *Death of a Generation*, p. 403.
74. Ahern, *CIA and the House of Ngo*, p. 205.
75. Ibid., p. 206.
76. Ibid.
77. Ibid., pp. 206–7.
78. Quoted in ibid., p. 207.
79. Ibid.
80. Ibid., p. 208.
81. A US News of World Report dated 10 October 1983 quoted in Moyar, *Triumph Forsaken*, p. 265.
82. Ibid.
83. Quoted in Jones, *Death of a Generation*, p. 410–11, 524 note 10.
84. Stuart E. Methven, *Laughter in the Shadows: A CIA Memoir* (Annapolis: Naval Institute Press, 2008), p. 103.
85. Quoted in Jones, *Death of a Generation*, p. 411.
86. Ahern, *CIA and the House of Ngo*, p. 209.
87. Jones, *Death of a Generation*, p. 414.
88. Ibid., p. 410.
89. Quoted in Ahern, *CIA and the House of Ngo*, p. 210.
90. Memorandum for the record by John M.Dunn Personal Assistant to the Ambassador, available at www2.gwu.edu~nsarchivNSAEBBNSAEBB 101vn23.pdf (accessed 6 November 2013).
91. Moyar, *Triumph Forsaken*, p. 269.
92. Quoted in Jones, *Death of a Generation*, p. 413.
93. Quoted in Moyar, *Triumph Forsaken*, p. 270.
94. Quoted in ibid.
95. Ibid.
96. Ibid.
97. Ahern, *CIA and the House of Ngo*, p. 211.
98. Ibid., p. 212.
99. Jones, *Death of a Generation*, pp. 428–9.
100. Francis X. Winters, *The Year of the Hare: America in Vietnam, January 25, 1963–February 15, 1964* (Athens: University of Georgia Press, 1999), p. 104.
101. Ibid.
102. Ibid.
103. Ibid.
104. Quoted in Jones, *Death of a Generation*, p. 430.

105. Maxwell D. Taylor, *Swords and Plowshares* (New York: Da Capo Press, 1990), p. 301.
106. Ahern, *CIA and the House of Ngo*, p. 214.
107. Ellen J. Hammer, *A Death in November: America in Vietnam, 1963* (New York: Oxford University Press, 1987), pp. 306–7.
108. Quoted in Jones, p. 426.
109. Ken Hughes, 'JFK and the Fall of Diem', available at http://cache.boston.com/globe/magazine/1999/10–24/featurestory1.shtml (accessed 16 November 2013); Jones, *Death of a Generation*, pp. 427.
110. Telegram From the Central Intelligence Agency Station in Saigon to the Director of the National Security Agency (Blake) 3 November 1963, available at http://history.state.gov/historicaldocuments/frus1961–63v04/d283 (accessed 11 November 2013).
111. Current Intelligence Memorandum; Press version of how Diem and Nhu died, 12 November 1963, available at www2.gwu.edu~ nsarchivNSAEBBNSAE BB101vn28.pdf (accessed 6 November 2013).
112. Ken Hughes, 'JFK and the Fall of Diem', available at http://cache.boston.com/globe/magazine/1999/10–24/featurestory1.shtml (accessed 15 November 2013).
113. Ahern, *CIA and the House of Ngo*, p. 214; Stanley Karnow, *Vietnam: A History* (New York: Penguin 1997), p. 325.
114. George W. Allen, 'Coups Covering in Saigon', *Studies in Intelligence*, Vol. 33 (Winter 1989), p. 59.
115. Berman, *Perfect Spy*, p. 151.
116. Ibid., p. 152.
117. George W. Allen, 'Coups Covering in Saigon', *Studies in Intelligence*, Vol. 33 (Winter 1989), p. 60.

Chapter 8   Distortions and Escalation

1. Pierre Asselin, *Hanoi's Road to the Vietnam War, 1954–1965* (Berkeley: University of California Press, 2013), pp. 164–5.
2. Quoted in ibid., p. 166.
3. Ibid., p. 167.
4. Quoted in ibid., pp. 177–8.
5. Memorandum From Michael V. Forrestal of the National Security Council Staff to the President's Special Assistant for National Security Affairs (Bundy), 5 May 1964, *FRUS 1964–1968*, Vol. I: *Vietnam, 1964*, available at http://history.state.gov/historicaldocuments/frus1964–68v01/d138 (accessed 3 January 2014).
6. Roger Thompson, *Lessons Not Learned: The U.S. Navy's Status Quo Culture* (Annapolis: Naval Institute Press, 2007), pp. 64–5.
7. Hanyok, *Spartans in Darkness*, pp. 187–8 (declassified in 2007).
8. Ibid., p. 222.
9. Ibid.

10. Ibid., pp. 195–6.
11. Ibid., p. 197.
12. Ibid., p. 198.
13. Ibid.
14. Ibid., p. 212.
15. Ibid., p. 213.
16. Ibid., pp. 198–9.
17. Quoted in ibid., p. 221.
18. Quoted in ibid., p. 220; Johnson and McNamara discuss the crisis in Michael R. Beschloss, ed., *Taking Charge: The Johnson White House Tapes, 1963–1964* (New York: Simon & Schuster, 1997), pp. 498–501, 506–8.
19. Quoted in Qiang Zhai, *China & The Vietnam Wars, 1950–1975* (Chapel Hill: The University of North Carolina Press, 2000), p. 132; Yang Kuisong (translated by Qiang Zhai), *Changes in Mao Zedong's Attitude toward the Indochina War, 1949–1973*, Working Paper No. 34, Woodrow Wilson International Center for Scholars, p. 29.
20. Hanyok, *Spartans in Darkness*, pp. 219–20.
21. Quoted in Asselin, *Hanoi's Road to War*, p. 198.
22. Ibid., p. 201.
23. Ibid., p. 200.
24. Qiang Zhai, 'Beijing and the Vietnam Conflict, 1964–1965: New Chinese Evidence', available at http://the-puzzle-palace.com/files/china.html (accessed 10 December 2013).
25. Bass, *The Spy Who Loved Us*, p. 238.
26. Hanyok, *Spartans in Darkness*, p. 98.
27. Quoted in Shultz, *The Secret War against Hanoi*, p. 250.
28. Quoted in ibid.
29. Memorandum From the Ambassador's Special Assistant (Lansdale) to the Ambassador to Vietnam (Bunker), 2 September 1967, *FRUS 1964–1968*, Vol. V: *Vietnam, 1967*, available at http://history.state.gov/historicaldocuments/frus1964–68v05/d302 (accessed 28 November 2013).
30. Bass, *The Spy Who Loved Us*, p. 141.
31. Ibid., p. 143.
32. Ibid., p. 141.
33. Ibid., p. 149.
34. Ibid., pp. 172–5.
35. Merle L. Pribbenow, II, 'Vo Nguyen Giap and the Mysterious Evolution of the Plan for the 1968 Tet Offensive', *Journal of Vietnamese Studies*, Vol. 3, No. 2 (Summer 2008), pp. 1–33.
36. Sophie Quinn-Judge, 'The Urban Movement and the Planning and Execution of the Tet Offensive', Cold War International History Project, October 2014, available at http://www.wilsoncenter.org/publication/the-urban-movement-and-the-planning-and-execution-the-tet-offensive (accessed 24 October 2014).

37. Hanyok, *Spartans in Darkness*, p. 317 (declassified in 2007).
38. Quoted in ibid., p. 320.
39. Ibid., p. 318 (declassified in 2008).
40. Ibid., p. 320.
41. Ibid., p. 321 (declassified in 2007).
42. Ibid., p. 322.
43. Ibid., p. 324–5.
44. Quoted in Karnow, *Vietnam*, p. 554.
45. Hanyok, *Spartans in Darkness*, p. 326 (declassified in 2007).
46. Ibid., p. 337.
47. Ibid., pp. 329–31.
48. Quoted in ibid., p. 332.
49. Quoted in ibid., p. 335.
50. Quoted in ibid., p. 345.
51. Ibid.
52. Ibid.
53. Ibid., p. 333.
54. Ibid., pp. 343, 311 (declassified in 2008).
55. Ibid., p. 344 (declassified in 2007).
56. Ibid.
57. Quoted in ibid., pp. 334–5.
58. Quinn-Judge, 'The Urban Movement and the Planning and Execution of the Tet Offensive'.
59. Hanyok, *Spartans in Darkness* (declassified in 2007), p. 337.
60. The author refers to January 29 (January 30 in Saigon), Matthew M. Aid, *The Secret Sentry: The Untold History of the National Security Agency* (New York: Bloomsbury Press, 2009), p. 119.
61. Hanyok, *Spartans in Darkness*, p. 338 (declassified in 2007).
62. Ibid., p. 339.
63. Ibid., p. 342.
64. Christopher Andrew, *For the President's Eyes Only: Secret Intelligence and the American Presidency from Washington to Bush* (New York: Harper Collins, 1995), p. 341.
65. Hayonk, *Spartans in Darkness*, p. 339 (declassified in 2007).
66. Ibid., p. 340.
67. Ibid., p. 343.
68. Ibid., p. 344.
69. Alexander Ovodenko, 'Visions of the Enemy from the Field and from Abroad: Revisiting CIA and Military Expectations of the Tet Offensive', *Journal of Strategic Studies*, Vol. 34, No. 1 (February 2011), pp. 138–9.
70. Ibid., p. 142.
71. Bass, *The Spy Who Loved Us*, p. 196.
72. Berman, *Perfect Spy*, p. 174; Bass, *The Spy Who Loved Us*, p. 196.
73. Bass, *The Spy Who Loved Us*, p. 196.

74. Quoted in Lewis Sorley, *Westmoreland: The General Who Lost Vietnam* (New York: Houghton Mifflin Harcourt, 2011), p. 177.
75. Ibid.
76. Quoted in ibid., p. 178.
77. Quoted in ibid., p. 179.
78. Quoted in ibid., p. 182.
79. Quoted in Bass, *The Spy Who Loved Us*, p. 198.
80. Sorley, *Westmoreland*, p. 171.
81. Nicholas Khoo, *Collateral Damage: Sino-Soviet Rivalry and the Termination of the Sino-Vietnamese Alliance* (New York: Columbia University Press, 2011), p. 51.
82. Quoted in Bass, *The Spy Who Loved Us*, p. 198.
83. Quoted in ibid., p. 203.
84. Ibid., pp. 203–4.
85. Ibid., p. 205.
86. Quoted in ibid., p. 208.
87. Berman, *Perfect Spy*, p. 177.
88. Ibid., pp. 181–3.

Chapter 9   Molehunt and Spies in the Viet Cong

1. Charles R. Myer, *Division-Level Communications, 1962–1973* (Washington DC: Department of the Army, 1982), pp. 65–6.
2. Ibid., p. 67.
3. Douglass H. Hubbard Jr, *Special Agent, Vietnam: A Naval Intelligence Memoir* (Washington DC: Potomac Books, 2006), p. 56.
4. Berman, *Perfect Spy*, p. 237.
5. David Stout, 'Vu Ngoc Nha, 74, a Top Communist Spy in Vietnam, Dies', *New York Times*, 11 August 2002, available at http://www.nytimes.com/2002/08/11/world/vu-ngoc-nha-74-a-top-communist-spy-in-vietnam-dies.html?pagewanted=print&src=pm (accessed 27 November 2013); Shackley and Finney, *Spymaster*, pp. 234–5.
6. Quoted in Antonio J. Mendez and Malcolm McConnell, *The Master of Disguise: My Secret Life in the CIA* (New York: Harper Collins, 1999), p. 110.
7. Ibid., p. 111.
8. Shackley and Finney, *Spymaster*, p. 238.
9. Ibid.
10. Quoted in ibid., p. 239.
11. Quoted in ibid., p. 240.
12. Quoted in ibid., p. 241.
13. Ibid.
14. John F. Sullivan, *Of Spies and Lies: A CIA Lie Detector Remembers Vietnam* (Lawrence KS: University Press of Kansas, 2002), pp. 82–4.
15. Ibid., pp. 149–52.

16. Ibid., p. 153.
17. Ibid., p. 84.
18. Ibid., pp. 78–82.
19. Ibid., p. 154.
20. Ibid., p. 156.
21. Ibid.
22. Ibid., pp. 156–7.
23. Ibid., pp. 161–2.
24. Shackley and Finney, *Spymaster*, p. 243.
25. Ibid., p. 244.
26. Memorandum for the record, 'Covert Actions in Support of U.S. Objective in South Vietnam's 1971 Elections', 3 February 1971, *FRUS 1969–1976*, Vol. VII: *Vietnam, July 1970–January 1972*, pp. 351–5.
27. Snepp, *Decent Interval*, p. 40.
28. Merle L. Pribbenow, 'The Man in the Snow White Cell: Limits to Interrogation', available at https://www.cia.gov/library/center-for-the-study-of-intelligence/csi-publications/csi-studies/studies/vol48no1/article06.html (accessed 25 November 2013); Frank Snepp, *Decent Interval: An Insider's Account of Saigon's Indecent End told by the CIA's Chief Strategy Analyst in Vietnam* (Lawrence KS: University Press of Kansas, 2002), pp. 31–7.
29. Pribbenow,'The Man in the Snow White Cell'.
30. Snepp, *Decent Interval*, p. 38.
31. Pribbenow, 'The Man in the Snow White Cell'.
32. All quoted in Snepp, *Decent Interval*, pp. 35–6.
33. Ibid., p. 37.
34. Pribbenow, 'The Man in the Snow White Cell'.
35. Snepp, *Decent Interval*, p. 38.
36. Conboy and Dale, *Spies and Commandos*, p. 211.
37. Schultz, *The Secret War Against Hanoi*, pp. 148, 156.
38. Merle L. Pribbenow, 'Jane Fonda and Her Friendly North Vietnamese Intelligence Officer', 10 August 2011, available at http://www.washington decoded.com/site/2011/08/fonda.html (accessed 20 May 2014).
39. DeForest and Chanoff, *Slow Burn*, p. 70; see also Stuart A. Herrington, *Stalking the Vietcong – Inside Operation Phoenix: a Personal Account* (New York: Ballantine Books, 1982), pp. 136–40.
40. DeForest and Chanoff, *Slow Burn*, pp. 123–4, 129.
41. Ibid., pp. 141–5.
42. Ibid., pp. 51–2.
43. Ibid., p. 69.
44. Ibid., pp. 115–16.
45. Ibid., pp. 116–17.
46. Ibid., pp. 169–72.
47. Ibid., p. 173.
48. Ibid.

49. Ibid., p. 174.
50. Ibid., p. 197.
51. Ibid., pp. 199-200.
52. Ibid., pp. 185-6.
53. Ibid., p. 203.
54. Ibid., p. 205.
55. Ibid., pp. 221-4.
56. Ibid., p. 225.
57. Ibid., p. 231.
58. Ibid., pp. 228-9.

Chapter 10   Ms Daphne Park, MI6 and Soviet Espionage

1. Hirst to FCO, 14 February 1969 FCO 15/1000 TNA.
2. Philo to FCO, 13 March 1969, p. 2, ibid.
3. Philo to FCO, 27 March 1969, p. 2, ibid.
4. Philo to FCO, 16 May 1969, p. 2, ibid.
5. Townend to FCO, 29 May 1969, p. 2, ibid.
6. Philo to FCO, 5 June 1969, p. 1, ibid.
7. Philo to FCO, 17 July 1969, p. 2, ibid.
8. Philo to FCO, 8 May 1969, p. 1, ibid.
9. Townend to FCO, 5 June 1969, p. 1, ibid.
10. Philo to FCO, 3 June 1969, p. 3, ibid.
11. Gordon Corera, The Art of Betrayal: Life and Death in the British Secret Service (London: Weidenfeld and Nicolson, 2011), pp. 36-7, 94-5.
12. Ibid., p. 97.
13. Park quoted in ibid., p. 100.
14. Ibid., p. 101.
15. Ibid., p. 133.
16. Ibid., p. 119.
17. Ibid., pp. 118-31.
18. The British Consul General in North Viet-Nam to the Secretary of State for Foreign and Commonwealth Affairs, 25 October 1970, p. 6. FCO 15/1335 TNA.
19. Philo to FCO, 25 September 1969, p. 2, FCO 15/1000 TNA.
20. Park to FCO, 23 October 1969, p. 2, ibid.
21. Park to FCO, 29 December 1969, p. 3, ibid.
22. The British Consul General in North Viet-Nam to the Secretary of State for Foreign and Commonwealth Affairs: Her Majesty's Representative in Limbo: A Valedictory, 25 October 1970, pp. 1-2, FCO 15/1335 TNA.
23. Ibid., p. 2.
24. Ibid.
25. Ibid.
26. Ibid., p. 3.

27. Ibid., p. 4.
28. Ibid., p. 5.
29. The British Consul-General in North Viet-Nam to the Secretary of State for Foreign and Commonwealth Affairs, 25 October 1970, p. 6. FCO 15/1335 TNA.
30. Park to Gordon, 26 June 1970, FCO 15/1355 TNA.
31. Richard Aldrich, *GCHQ: The Uncensored Story of Britain's Most Secret Intelligence Agency* (London: Harper Press, 2011), p. 278.
32. Quoted in ibid., p. 279.
33. Ibid., p. 280.
34. Quoted in ibid., p. 243.
35. Pribbenow, 'The Soviet–Vietnamese Intelligence Relationship during the Vietnam War', p. 6.
36. Ibid., pp. 7–8.
37. Ibid., pp. 4–5.
38. Martin Grossheim, 'The East German "Stasi" and the Modernization of the Vietnamese Security Apparatus, 1965–1989', CWIHP e-Dossier No. 51, available at http://www.wilsoncenter.org/publication/stasi-aid-and-the-modernization-the-vietnamese-secret-police (accessed 28 August 2014).
39. Pribbenow, 'The Soviet-Vietnamese Intelligence Relationship during the Vietnam War', p. 11.
40. Ibid.
41. Ibid., pp. 11–12.
42. Ibid., pp. 9, 13.
43. Nicholas Khoo, *Collateral Damage: Sino-Soviet Rivalry and the Termination of the Sino-Vietnamese Alliance* (New York: Columbia University Press, 2011), p. 33.
44. Christopher Andrew and Vasili Mitrokhin, *The KGB and the World: The Mitrokhin Archive II* (London: Penguin, 2006), p. 265.
45. Pribbenow, 'The Soviet-Vietnamese Intelligence Relationship during the Vietnam War', pp. 13–14.
46. Ibid., pp. 14–15.
47. Andrew and Mitrokhin, *The KGB and the World*, p. 266.
48. Ibid., p. 318.
49. Oleg Kalugin, *Spymaster: My Thirty-two Years in Intelligence and Espionage Against the West* (New York: Basic Books, 2009), pp. 220–1.
50. Barbara Crossette, 'Vietnam Admits KGB Interrogated American' *New York Times*, 22 January 1992, available at http://www.nytimes.com/1992/01/22/world/vietnam-admits-kgb-interrogated-american.html (accessed 2 July 2014); Anonymous, 'Eugene A. Weaver', available at http://projects.militarytimes.com/citations-medals-awards/recipient.php?recipientid=28107 (accessed 7 July 2014); Anonymous, 'Eugene A. Weaver', available at http://www.pownetwork.org/bios/w/w600.htm (accessed 7 July 2014); Anonymous, 'Eugene A. Weaver', available at http://taskforceomegainc.org/w600.html (accessed 7 July 2014).

Chapter 11   The Double Agent Games of the White House

1. Walter Isaacson, *Kissinger: A Biography* (New York: Simon & Schuster, 2005), pp. 48–9.
2. Memorandum From the President's Assistant for National Security Affairs (Kissinger) to President Nixon, 9 December 1969, *FRUS* 1969–1976, Vol. VI: *Vietnam, January 1969–July 1970*, p. 509.
3. Ibid.
4. Ibid., p. 510.
5. Ibid.
6. Memorandum for the Record, Washington, 6 August 1970, *FRUS* 1969–1976, Vol. VII: *Vietnam, July 1970–January 1972*, pp. 17–18.
7. Memorandum From Director of Central Intelligence Helms to the President's Assistant for National Security Affairs (Kissinger), 10 March 1972, *FRUS* 1969–1976, Vol. VIII: *Vietnam, January–October 1972*, p. 126.
8. Ibid., p. 128.
9. Ibid.
10. See Sophie Quinn-Judge, 'The Ideological Debate in the DRV and the Significance of the Anti-Party Affair, 1967–1968', *Cold War History*, Vol. 5, Issue 4 (November 2005).
11. All quoted in the Memorandum From Director of Central Intelligence Helms to the President's Assistant for National Security Affairs (Kissinger) 10 March 1972, *FRUS* 1969–1976, Vol. VIII: *Vietnam, January–October 1972*, p. 129.
12. Memorandum From the President's Assistant for National Security Affairs (Kissinger) to President Nixon, 18 May 1972, ibid., p. 588.
13. Ibid., pp. 590–1.
14. Ibid., p. 592.
15. Ibid.
16. Message From the Chairman of the Joint Chiefs of Staff (Moorer) to the Commander in Chief, Pacific (McCain), 21 May 1972, ibid., pp. 625–6.
17. Memorandum From the Special Assistant for Vietnamese Affairs, Central Intelligence Agency (Carver) to Richard T. Kennedy of the National Security Council Staff, 31 May 1972, ibid., p. 645.
18. Ibid., p. 646.
19. Memorandum From the President's Assistant for National Security Affairs (Kissinger) to President Nixon, 8 June 1972, ibid., pp. 657–8.
20. Ibid., p. 658.
21. Memorandum From Secretary of Defense Laird to President Nixon, 10 August 1972, ibid., p. 818.
22. Ibid., p. 819.
23. Ibid., p. 819, note 2.
24. Minutes of a Washington Special Actions Group Meeting, 27 July 1972, ibid., pp. 775–6.
25. Bass, *The Spy Who Loved Us*, p. 218.

26. James R. Chiles, 'Air America's Black Helicopter: The secret aircraft that helped the CIA tap phones in North Vietnam', *Air & Space* magazine, March 2008, available at http://www.airspacemag.com/military-aviation/the_quiet_one.html (accessed 13 December 2013).
27. Memorandum From the President's Assistant for National Security Affairs (Kissinger) to President Nixon, 24 October 1972, *FRUS* 1969–1976, Vol. IX: *Vietnam, October 1972–January 1973*, p. 291.
28. Memorandum From the Director of Central Intelligence (Schlesinger) to the President's Assistant for National Security Affairs (Kissinger), 21 March 1973. *FRUS* 1969–1976, Vol. X: *Vietnam, January 1973–July 1975*, p. 162.
29. Memorandum From Rob Roy Ratliff of the National Security Council Staff to the President's Assistant for National Security Affairs (Kissinger) 11 July 1973, ibid., pp. 383–4.
30. Memorandum From the Director of Central Intelligence (Colby) to the President's Assistant for National Security Affairs (Kissinger), 23 November 1973, ibid., p. 458.

Chapter 12   Desperate Spies of the Falling Domino

1. As quoted in Snepp, *Decent Interval*, p. 86; see also Thomas Polgar, 'Assignment: Skyjacker', *Studies in Intelligence*, Vol. 16, No. 3 (Fall 1972), pp. 53–63.
2. Snepp, *Decent Interval*, p. 89.
3. Thomas Polgar, 'We Were a Defeated Army', 27 January 2013, available at http://lde421.blogspot.gr/2013/01/tom-polgar-remembers.html (accessed 5 December 2013).
4. Richard Hale, 'Firsthand Account of a CIA Officer in Saigon', available at http://www.historynet.com/richard-hale-firsthand-account-of-a-cia-officer-in-saigon.htm (accessed 13 December 2013).
5. Benjamin Weiser, *A Secret Life: The Polish Officer, His Covert Mission, and the Price He Paid to Save His Country* (New York: Public Affairs, 2005).
6. 'Potential Embarrassing Agency Activities', 8 May 1973, available at http://nsarchive.chadwyck.com/marketing/fj/displayItemPdf.do?id=FJ00058 (accessed 20 April 2014).
7. Bass, *The Spy Who Loved Us*, p. 218.
8. Quoted in Berman, *Perfect Spy*, p. 193.
9. Ibid., p. 203–4.
10. Snepp, *Decent Interval*, p. 53.
11. Ibid., p. 111.
12. Polgar, 'We Were a Defeated Army'.
13. Snepp, *Decent Interval*, p. 137.
14. Ibid., p. 135.
15. Quoted in DeForest and Chanoff, *Slow Burn*, p. 249.
16. Ibid.
17. Pribbenow, 'The Soviet-Vietnamese Intelligence Relationship during the Vietnam War', p. 6.

18. Snepp, *Decent Interval*, p. 200.
19. DeForest and Chanoff, *Slow Burn*, pp. 251-2.
20. Snepp, *Decent Interval*, p. 208.
21. DeForest and Chanoff, *Slow Burn*, p. 154.
22. Snepp, *Decent Interval*, p. 226.
23. Ibid., p. 288.
24. Ibid., p. 290.
25. Hale, 'Firsthand Account of a CIA Officer in Saigon'.
26. DeForest and Chanoff, *Slow Burn*, p. 253.
27. Ibid., p. 255.
28. Snepp, *Decent Interval*, p. 300.
29. Ibid., p. 456.
30. Ibid., p. 310.
31. Hale, 'Firsthand Account of a CIA Officer in Saigon'.
32. Snepp, *Decent Interval*, pp. 405-6.
33. Ibid., p. 326.
34. Minutes of National Security Council Meeting, Washington, 9 April 1975, *FRUS* 1969–1976, Vol. X: *Vietnam, January 1973–July 1975*, available at http://history.state.gov/historicaldocuments/frus1969–76v10/d212 (accessed 12 December 2013).
35. Polgar, 'We Were a Defeated Army'.
36. Ibid., pp. 200-1.
37. Ibid., p. 201.
38. Snepp, *Decent Interval*, p. 367.
39. Sullivan, p. 154.
40. Ibid., p. 368.
41. Minutes of Washington Special Actions Group Meeting, 17 April 1975, *FRUS* 1969–1976, Vol. X: *Vietnam, January 1973–July 1975*, available at http://history.state.gov/historicaldocuments/frus1969–76v10/d236 (accessed 20 December 2013).
42. Snepp, *Decent Interval*, p. 371.
43. Ibid., p. 382.
44. Minutes of Washington Special Actions Group Meeting, 20 April 1975, *FRUS* 1969–1976, Vol. X: *Vietnam, January 1973–July 1975*, available at http://history.state.gov/historicaldocuments/frus1969–76v10/d245 (accessed 20 December 2013).
45. Ibid.
46. DeForest and Chanoff, *Slow Burn*, p. 261.
47. Snepp, *Decent Interval*, p. 427.
48. Polgar, 'We Were a Defeated Army'.
49. Snepp, *Decent Interval*, pp. 74, 391.
50. Backchannel Message From the Ambassador to Vietnam (Martin) to the President's Assistant for National Security Affairs (Kissinger), 26 April 1975, *FRUS* 1969–1976, Vol. X: *Vietnam, January 1973–July 1975*, available at

http://history.state.gov/historicaldocuments/frus1969–76v10/d262 (accessed 10 December 2013).

51. Minutes of Washington Special Actions Group Meeting, 28 April 1975. *FRUS 1969–1976*, Vol. X: *Vietnam, January 1973–July 1975*, available at http://history.state.gov/historicaldocuments/frus1969–76v10/d266 (accessed 12 December 2013).

52. Minutes of National Security Council Meeting, 28 April 1975, *FRUS 1969–1976*, Vol. X: *Vietnam, January 1973–July 1975*, available at http://history.state.gov/historicaldocuments/frus1969–76v10/d268 (accessed 10 December 2013).

53. Ibid.

54. Minutes of Washington Special Actions Group Meeting, 29 April 1975, *FRUS 1969–1976*, Vol. X: *Vietnam, January 1973–July 1975*, available at http://history.state.gov/historicaldocuments/frus1969–76v10/d273 (accessed 12 December 2013).

55. Snepp, *Decent Interval*, p. 480.

56. Ibid., pp. 497–8.

57. Ibid., p. 524.

58. DeForest and Chanoff, *Slow Burn*, pp. 275–6.

59. Snepp, *Decent Interval*, p. 547.

60. Quoted in Berman, *Perfect Spy*, p. 226.

61. Hanyok, *Spartans in Darkness*, p. 445.

62. Polgar, 'We Were a Defeated Army'. There was a body search for drugs for all US personnel (except the ambassador) and the Vietnamese refugees. DeForest and Chanoff, *Slow Burn*, pp. 276–7.

63. DeForest and Chanoff, *Slow Burn*, pp. 263–4.

64. Jana K. Lipman, '"A Precedent Worth Setting." Military Humanitarianism: The U.S. Military and the 1975 Vietnamese Evacuation', *The Journal of Military History*, Vol. 79, Issue 1 (January 2015), pp. 151–79.

65. Quoted Bass, *The Spy Who Loved Us*, pp. 221–2.

66. Quoted in Berman, *Perfect Spy*, p. 224.

67. Bass, *The Spy Who Loved Us*, pp. 222–3.

68. Quoted in ibid., p. 223.

69. Quoted in Nashel, *Edward Lansdale's Cold War*, p. 211.

70. Berman, *Perfect Spy*, p. 240.

71. Sullivan, *Of Spies and Lies*, pp. 229–30; David Corn, *Blond Ghost: Ted Shackley and the CIA's Crusades* (New York: Simon & Schuster, 1994), p. 291.

Aftermath: US Intelligence and the Sino-Vietnamese War

1. Michael J. Sulik, *American Spies: Espionage against the United States from the Cold War to the Present* (Washington DC: Georgetown University Press, 2013), pp. 40–2.

2. Paul Vitellojuly, 'David Truong, Figure in U.S. Wiretap Case, Dies at 68', *New York Times*, 6 July 2014, available at http://www.nytimes.com/2014/07/

07/us/david-truong-figure-in-us-wiretap-case-dies-at-68.html?src=recg&
_r=0 (accessed 7 July 2014).

3. Sullivan, *Of Spies and Lies*, p. 147.

4. Zhai, *China and the Vietnam Wars*, p. 135; see also Nicholas Khoo, *Collateral Damage: Sino-Soviet Rivalry and the Termination of the Sino-Vietnamese Alliance* (New York: Columbia University Press, 2011).

5. Zhai, *China and the Vietnam Wars*, pp. 210–3.

6. Quoted in Kosal Path, 'The economic factor in the Sino-Vietnamese split, 1972–75: An analysis of Vietnamese archival sources', *Cold War History*, Vol. 11, No. 4 (November 2011), p. 542.

7. Zhai, *China and the Vietnam Wars*, pp. 210–13.

8. 'Forecasting the Sino-Vietnamese Split', *Studies in Intelligence*, Vol 30 (Winter 1986), p. 69.

9. Ibid., p. 70.

10. Sophie Quinn-Judge, 'Victory on the battlefield; isolation in Asia: Vietnam's Cambodia decade, 1979–1989' in Odd Arne Westad, and Sophie Quinn-Judge, eds, *The Third Indochina War: Conflict between China, Vietnam and Cambodia, 1972–79* (London: Routledge, 2006), pp. 207–27.

11. 'Forecasting the Sino-Vietnamese Split', p. 71.

12. Memorandum from Secretary of State Vance to President Carter, 26 January 1979, *FRUS* 1977–1980, Vol. XIII: *China*, available at http://history.state.gov/historicaldocuments/frus1977–80v13/d199 (accessed 22 December 2013).

13. Robert M. Gates, *From the Shadows: The Ultimate Insider's Story of Five Presidents and How They Won the Cold War* (New York: Simon & Schuster Paperbacks, 2006), p. 121.

14. Zbigniew Brzezinski, *Power and Principle: Memoirs of the National Security Adviser, 1977–1981* (New York: Farrar, Straus and Giroux, 1983), pp. 409–10; Xiaoming Zhang, 'Deng Xiaoping and China's Decision to go to War with Vietnam', *Journal of Cold War Studies*, Vol. 12, No. 3 (Summer 2010), p. 24.

15. 'Forecasting the Sino-Vietnamese Split', p. 71.

16. Aid and Richelson, *U.S. Intelligence and China: Collection, Analysis and Covert Action*, p. 10.

17. Record of a National Security Council Meeting, 16 February 1979, *FRUS* 1977–1980, Vol. XIII: *China*, available at http://history.state.gov/historical documents/frus1977–80v13/d214 (accessed 20 December 2013).

18. Ibid.

19. Gates, *From the Shadows*, p. 121.

20. Ibid., p. 122.

21. James Mann, *About Face: A History of America's Curious Relationship with China, From Nixon to Clinton* (New York: Alfred A. Knopf, 1999), p. 100; Interview of Brzezinski in Sam Brothers, *The Enemy of My Enemy: The Sino-Vietnamese War of 1979 and the Evolution of the Sino-American Covert Relationship*, Thesis, Georgetown University, 2014, pp. 56, 58.

22. Gates, *From the Shadows*, p. 122.

23. Xiaoming Zhang, 'Deng Xiaoping and China's Decision to go to War with Vietnam', p. 25.

24. Report Prepared in the Bureau of Intelligence and Research' 20 March 1979, No. 1148 'The Consequences of the Chinese Attack on Vietnam', *FRUS*, 1977–1980, Vol. XIII: *China*, available at http://history.state.gov/historical documents/frus1977–80v13/d231 (accessed 20 December 2013).

25. Research Paper Prepared in the National Foreign Assessment Center, Central Intelligence Agency 'The Sino-Vietnamese Border Dispute', Washington, March 1979, *FRUS*, Vol. 13, 1977–1980, Vol. XIII: *China*, available at http://history.state.gov/historicaldocuments/frus1977–80v13/d226 (accessed 20 December 2013).

26. 'Forecasting the Sino-Vietnamese Split', p. 71.

27. Martin Grossheim, 'The East German "Stasi" and the Modernization of the Vietnamese Security Apparatus, 1965–1989' CWIHP e-Dossier No. 51, available at http://www.wilsoncenter.org/publication/stasi-aid-and-the-modernization-the-vietnamese-secret-police (accessed 28 August 2014).

28. Gates, *From the Shadows*, p. 122.

BIBLIOGRAPHY

Archives

Central Intelligence Agency declassified archives and stories
Foreign Relations of the United States (FRUS) series
The National Archives (UK)
National Archives and Records Administration (NARA)
National Security Archive (US)
Vietnam Centre Archive, Texas Tech University

Select Published Works

Ahern Jr, Thomas L., *The Way We Do Things: Black Entry Operations Into North Vietnam* (CIA: Center for the Study of Intelligence, 2005).

——— *Good Questions, Wrong Answers: CIA Estimates of Arms Traffic Through Sihanoukville, Cambodia During the Vietnam War* (CIA: Centre for the Study of Intelligence, 2004).

——— *CIA and the House of Ngo: Covert Action in South Vietnam, 1954–1963* (CIA: Center for the Study of Intelligence, June 2000).

——— *CIA and the Generals: Covert Support to Military Government in South Vietnam* (CIA: Center for the Study of Intelligence, October 1998).

Aid, Matthew M., *Secret Sentry: The Untold History of the National Security Agency* (New York: Bloomsbury, 2009).

Aid, Matthew and Richelson, Jeffrey T., *U.S. Intelligence and China: Collection, Analysis and Covert Action*, available at http://nsarchive.chadwyck.com/collections/content/CI/intell_and_china_essay.pdf (accessed 4 January 2014).

Aldrich, Richard, *GCHQ: The Uncensored Story of Britain's Most Secret Intelligence Agency* (London: Harper Press, 2011).

——— 'Britain's Secret Intelligence Service in Asia during the Second World War', *Modern Asian Studies*, Vol. 32, No. 1 (February 1998).

Allen, George W., 'Coups Covering in Saigon', *Studies in Intelligence*, Vol. 33 (Winter 1989).

Andrew, Christopher and Mitrokhin, Vasili, *The KGB and the World: The Mitrokhin Archive II* (London: Penguin, 2006).

Anonymous, 'Lieutenant Colonel Lucien E. Conein', available at http://www.arlingtoncemetery.net/conein.htm (accessed 16 October 2013).

Anonymous, 'Forecasting the Sino-Vietnamese Split', *Studies in Intelligence*, Vol.30 (Winter 1986).

Anonymous, 'PAVN March into Haiphong', *The Canberra Times*, 14 May 1955.

Asselin, Pierre, *Hanoi's Road to the Vietnam War, 1954–1965* (Berkeley: University of California Press, 2013).

Atwood, Mark Lawrence and Logevall, Fredrik, eds, *The First Vietnam War: Colonial Conflict and Cold War Crisis* (Cambridge MA: Harvard University Press, 2007).

Baier, Alison, 'Edward Lansdale: The Image of the United States in Vietnam', available at history.rutgers.edu/.../269-edward-lansdale (accessed 26 October 2013).

Bartholomew-Feis, Dixee R., *The OSS and Ho Chi Minh: Unexpected Allies in the War against Japan* (Lawrence KS: University Press of Kansas, 2006).

Bass, Thomas A., *The Spy Who Loved Us: The Vietnam War and Pham Xuan An's Dangerous Game* (New York: Public Affairs, 2009).

Berman, Larry, *Perfect Spy: The Incredible Double Life of Pham Xuan An, Time Magazine Reporter & Vietnamese Communist Agent* (New York: Smithsonian Books, 2007).

Beschloss, Michael R., ed., *Taking Charge: The Johnson White House Tapes, 1963–1964* (New York: Simon & Schuster, 1997).

Blood, Jake, *The Tet Effect: Intelligence and the Public Perception of War* (London: Routledge, 2004).

Boylan, Kevin M., 'Goodnight Saigon: American Provincial Advisors' Final Impressions of the Vietnam War', *The Journal of Military History*, Vol. 78, No. 1 (January 2014).

Bradley, Mark Philip and Young, Marylin B., eds, *Making Sense of the Vietnam War: Local, National, and Transnational Perspectives* (New York: Oxford University Press, 2008).

Brothers, Sam, 'The Enemy of My Enemy: The Sino-Vietnamese War of 1979 and the Evolution of the Sino-American Covert Relationship', Thesis, Georgetown University, 2014.

Brown, Mervyn, *War in Shangri-La: A Memoir of Civil War in Laos* (London: The Radcliffe Press, 2001).

Brzezinski, Zbigniew, *Power and Principle: Memoirs of the National Security Adviser, 1977–1981* (New York: Farrar, Straus and Giroux, 1983).

Calkins, Laura M., *China and the First Vietnam War, 1947–54* (New York: Routledge, 2013).

Chapman, Jessica, *Cauldron of Resistance: Ngo Dinh Diem, the United States, and 1950s Southern Vietnam* (Ithaca: Cornell University Press, 2013).

Chen, Jian, *Mao's China and the Cold War* (Chapel Hill: University of North Carolina Press, 2001).

Chiles, James R., 'Air America's Black Helicopter: The Secret Aircraft that Helped the CIA Tap Phones in North Vietnam', *Air & Space*, February–March 1998, available at http://www.airspacemag.com/military-aviation/the_quiet_one.html (accessed 13 December 2013).

Conboy, Kenneth and Andrade, Dale, *Spies and Commandos: How America Lost the Secret War in North Vietnam* (Lawrence KS: University Press of Kansas, 2001).

Corera, Gordon, *The Art of Betrayal: Life and Death in the British Secret Service* (London: Weidenfeld and Nicolson, 2011).

Croizat, V.J. (translation), *Lessons of the War in Indochina* (RAND Memorandum RM-5271 PR, May 1967).

Currey, Cecil B., *Edward Lansdale: The Unquiet American* (Boston: Houghton Mifflin, 1988).

Daddis, Gregory A., 'Out of Balance: Evaluating American Strategy in Vietnam, 1968–72', *War & Society*, Vol. 32, No. 3 (October 2013).

Dale, Andrade, 'Three Lessons from Vietnam', *Washington Post*, 29 December 2005.

DeForest, Orrin and Chanoff, David, *Slow Burn: The Rise and Bitter Fall of American Intelligence in Vietnam* (New York: Simon & Schuster, 1990).

DeSilva, Peer, *Sub Rosa: The CIA and the Uses of Intelligence* (New York: New York Times Books, 1978).

Dimitrakis, Panagiotis, *Failed Alliances of the Cold War: Britain's Strategy and Ambitions in Asia and the Middle East* (London: I.B.Tauris, 2012).

Eisenhower, Dwight D., *Mandate for Change: The White House Years, 1953–1956: A Personal Account* (New York: Doubleday, 1963).

Elkind, Jessica, '"The Virgin Mary is Going South": Refugee Resettlement in South Vietnam, 1954–1956', *Diplomatic History*, Vol. 38, Issue 5 (2014).

Field Service Regulations, Operations FM 100-5 (Department of the Army, 1962).

Ford, Harold P., *CIA and the Vietnam Policymakers: Three Episodes 1962–1968* (CIA: Centre for the Study of Intelligence, 1998).

Freedman, Lawrence, *Kennedy's Wars: Berlin, Cuba, Laos, and Vietnam* (Oxford: Oxford University Press, 2000).

Gaiduk, Ilya V., *Confronting Vietnam: Soviet Policy toward the Indochina Conflict, 1954–1963* (Stanford: Stanford University Press, 2003).

Gates, Robert M., *From the Shadows: The Ultimate Insider's Story of Five Presidents and How They Won the Cold War* (New York: Simon & Schuster, 2006).

Goscha, Christopher E., 'Wiring Decolonization: Turning Technology against the Colonizer during the Indochina War, 1945–1954', *Comparative Studies in Society and History*, Vol. 54, Issue 4 (2012).

——— *Vietnam: Un État né de la Guerre, 1945–1954* (Paris: Armand Colin, 2011).

——— 'The Maritime Nature of the Wars for Vietnam (1945–75)', paper presented at the Texas Tech, Vietnam Center 4th Triennial Vietnam Symposium, 11–13 April 2003.

Goscha, Christopher E. and Ostermann, Christian F., eds, *Connecting Histories: Decolonization and the Cold War in Southeast Asia, 1945–1962* (Stanford: Stanford University Press, 2009).

Grossheim, Martin, 'The East German "Stasi" and the Modernization of the Vietnamese Security Apparatus, 1965–1989', *CWIHP e-Dossier*, No. 51, available at http://www.wilsoncenter.org/publication/stasi-aid-and-the-modernization-the-vietnamese-secret-police (accessed 28 August 2014).

Halberstam, David, *The Best and the Brightest* (New York: Ballantine Books, 1992).

Hale, Richard W., 'A CIA Officer in Saigon', available at http://www.historynet.com/richard-hale-firsthand-account-of-a-cia-officer-in-saigon.htm (accessed 11 February 2015).

Hammer, Ellen, *A Death in November: America in Vietnam, 1963* (New York: E.P. Dutton, 1987).

Herrington, Stuart A., *Stalking the Vietcong – Inside Operation Phoenix: a Personal Account* (New York: Ballantine Books, 1982).

Hershberg, James G., *Marigold: The Lost Chance for Peace in Vietnam* (Washington DC: Stanford University Press/Wilson Center Press, 2012).

Hilsman, Roger, *To Move a Nation: The Politics of Foreign Policy in the Administration of John F. Kennedy* (New York: Doubleday, 1967).

Hoffman, Bruce and Ostermann, Christian, eds, *Moles, Defectors, and Deceptions: James Angleton and his Influence on US Counterintelligence* (Woodrow Wilson International Center for Scholars and Georgetown University Center for Peace & Security Studies Joint Conference, 2012).

Holzman, Michael Howard, *James Jesus Angleton, the CIA, and the Craft of Counterintelligence* (Amherst: University of Massachusetts, 2008).

Hood, Steven J., *Dragons Entangled: Indochina and the China-Vietnam War* (New York: ME Sharp, 1993).

Hubbard, Douglass H., *Special Agent, Vietnam: A Naval Intelligence Memoir* (Washington DC: Potomac Books, 2006).

Hughes, Geraint, 'A "Post-war" War: The British Occupation of French Indochina, September 1945–March 1946', *Small Wars and Insurgencies*, Vol. 17, No. 3 (September 2006).

———— 'A "missed opportunity" for peace? Harold Wilson, British diplomacy, and the sun flower initiative to end the Vietnam war, February 1967', *Diplomacy & Statecraft*, Vol. 14, Issue 3 (2003).

Hughes, Ken, 'JFK and the Fall of Diem', available at http://cache.boston.com/globe/magazine/1999/10-24/featurestory1.shtml (accessed 16 November 2013).

Hunt, Richard A., *Pacification: The American Struggle for Vietnam's Hearts and Minds* (Boulder: Westview Press, 1995).

Jeffery, Keith, *MI6: The History of the Secret Intelligence Service, 1909–1949* (London: Bloomsbury, 2010).

Johnson, Lyndon B., *The Vantage Point: Perspectives on the Presidency, 1963–1969* (New York: Holt, Rinehart & Winston, 1971).

Jones, Howard, *Death of a Generation: How the Assassinations of Diem and JFK Prolonged the Vietnam War* (Oxford: Oxford University Press, 2004).

Kalugin, Oleg, *Spymaster: My Thirty-two Years in Intelligence and Espionage Against the West* (New York: Basic Books, 2009).

Karnow, Stanley, *Vietnam: A History* (New York: Penguin, 1997).

Kear, Simon, 'The British consulate-general in Hanoi, 1954–73', *Diplomacy & Statecraft*, Vol. 10, Issue 1 (March 1999).

King, Chen C., *China's War with Vietnam: Issues, Decisions, and Implications* (Stanford: Hoover Institution Press, 1987).

Kraus, Charles, 'A border region "exuded with militant friendship": Provincial narratives of China's participation in the First Indochina War, 1949–1954', *Cold War History*, Vol. 12, Issue 3 (August 2012).

'Lansdale Team's Report on Covert Saigon Mission in 1954 and 1955', *The Pentagon Papers (Gravel Edition)*, Vol. 1, available at https://www.mtholyoke.edu/acad/intrel/pentagon/doc95.htm (accessed 14 October 2013).

LePage, Jean-Marc, *Les Services Secrets en Indochine* (Paris: Nouveau Monde, 2012).

LePage, Jean-Marc and Tenenbaum, Elie, 'French and American Intelligence Relations during the First Indochina War, 1950–54', *Studies in Intelligence*, Vol. 55, No. 3 (September 2001).

Lipman, Jana K., "'A Precedent Worth Setting . . .'" Military Humanitarianism: The U.S. Military and the 1975 Vietnamese Evacuation', *The Journal of Military History*, Vol. 79, Issue 1 (January 2015).

Little, Douglas, 'Mission Impossible: The CIA and the Cult of Covert Action in the Middle East', *Diplomatic History*, Vol. 28, No. 5 (November 2004).

Logevall, Fredrik, *Ambers of War: The Fall of an Empire and the Making of America's Vietnam* (New York: Random House, 2012).

Lowe, Peter, *Contending with Nationalism and Communism: British Policy Towards Southeast Asia, 1945–65* (London: Palgrave Macmillan, 2009).

Mann, James, *About Face: A History of America's Curious Relationship with China, From Nixon to Clinton* (New York: Alfred A. Knopf, 1999).

Marr, David G., *Vietnam: State, War, and Revolution (1945–1946)* (Berkeley: University of California Press, 2013).

———— *Vietnam 1945: The Quest for Power* (Berkeley: University of California Press, 1995).

McHale, Shawn, 'Understanding the Fanatic Mind? The Việt Minh and Race Hatred in the First Indochina War (1945–1954)', *Journal of Vietnamese Studies*, Vol. 4, Issue 3 (2009).

McNamara, Robert S. and VanDeMark, Brian, *In Retrospect: The Tragedy and Lessons of Vietnam* (New York: Vintage Books, 1997).

Mendez, Antonio J. and McConnell, Malcolm, *The Master of Disguise: My Secret Life in the CIA* (New York: Harper Collins, 1999).

Methven, Stuart E., *Laughter in the Shadows: A CIA Memoir* (Annapolis MD: Naval Institute Press, 2008).

Miller, Edward, *Misalliance: Ngo Dinh Diem, the United States, and the Fate of South Vietnam* (Cambridge MA: Harvard University Press, 2013).

Morgan, Ted, *Valley of Death: The Tragedy at Dien Bien Phu that Led America into the Vietnam War* (New York: Random House, 2010).

Moyar, Mark, *Triumph Forsaken: The Vietnam War, 1954–1965* (Cambridge: Cambridge University Press, 2006).

Myer, Charles R., *Division-Level Communications, 1962–1973* (Washington DC: Department of the Army, 1982).

Nashel, Jonathan, *Edward Lansdale's Cold War* (Armherst: University of Massachusetts Press, 2005).

Neville, Peter, *Britain in Vietnam: Prelude to Disaster, 1945–6* (London: Routledge, 2007).

Nolting, Frederick C., *From Trust to Tragedy: The Political Memoirs of Frederick Nolting, Kennedy's Ambassador to Diem's Vietnam* (New York: Praeger, 1988).

Nordell Jr, John R., *The Undetected Enemy: French and American Miscalculations at Dien Bien Phu, 1953* (College Station: Texas A&M University Press, 1995).

Olsen, Mari, *Soviet–Vietnam Relations and the Role of China, 1949–64* (New York: Routledge, 2006).

Ovodenko, Alexander, 'Visions of the Enemy from the Field and from Abroad: Revisiting CIA and Military Expectations of the Tet Offensive', *Journal of Strategic Studies*, Vol. 34, No. 1 (February 2011).

Path, Kosal, 'The economic factor in the Sino-Vietnamese split, 1972–75: An analysis of Vietnamese archival sources', *Cold War History*, Vol. 11, No. 4 (November 2011).

Phillips, Rufus, *Why Vietnam Matters: An Eyewitness Account of Lessons Not Learned* (Annapolis MD: Naval Institute Press, 2009).

Polgar, Thomas, 'Assignment: Skyjacker', *Studies in Intelligence*, Vol. 16, No. 3 (Fall 1972).

Porch, Douglas, *The French Secret Services: A History of French Intelligence from the Dreyfus Affair to the Gulf War* (New York: Farrar, Straus and Giroux, 1995).

Powers, Thomas, *The Man Who Kept the Secrets: Richard Helms and the CIA* (New York: Knopf, 1979).

Prados, John, *Vietnam: The History of an Unwinnable War, 1945–1975* (Lawrence KS: University Press of Kansas, 2009).

――― *William Colby and the CIA: The Secret Wars of a Controversial Spymaster* (Lawrence KS: University Press of Kansas, 2009).

Pribbenow, Merle L. II, 'The Soviet-Vietnamese Intelligence Relationship during the Vietnam War: Cooperation and Conflict', *CWIHP Working Paper*, No. 73 (December 2014).

――― 'The Man in the Snow White Cell: Limits to Interrogation', available at https://www.cia.gov/library/center-for-the-study-of-intelligence/csi-publications/csi-studies/studies/vol48no1/article06.html (accessed 25 November 2013).

――― 'Jane Fonda and Her Friendly North Vietnamese Intelligence Officer', 2011, available at http://www.washingtondecoded.com/site/2011/08/fonda.html (accessed 20 May 2014).

――― 'Vo Nguyen Giap and the Mysterious Evolution of the Plan for the 1968 Tet Offensive', *Journal of Vietnamese Studies*, Vol. 3, No. 2 (Summer 2008).

――― 'North Vietnam's Final Offensive: Strategic Endgame Nonpareil', *Parameters* (Winter 1999–2000).

Prochnau, William, *Once Upon a Distant War* (New York: New York Times Books, 1995).

Qiang Zhai, *China and the Vietnam Wars, 1950–1975* (Chapel Hill: The University of North Carolina Press, 2000).

Quinn-Judge, Sophie, 'The Urban Movement and the Planning and Execution of the Tet Offensive', *Cold War International History Project* (October 2014). Available at http://www.wilsoncenter.org/publication/the-urban-movement-and-the-planning-and-execution-the-tet-offensive (accessed 24 October 2014).

――― *Ho Chi Minh: The Missing Years* (London: Hurst, 2003).

Robbins, James S., *This Time We Win: Revisiting the Tet Offensive* (New York: Encounter Books, 2012).

Roberts, Priscilla, ed., *Behind the Bamboo Curtain: China, Vietnam, and the World beyond Asia* (Stanford: Stanford University Press, 2006).

Rosenau, William and Long, Austin, *The Phoenix Program and Contemporary Counterinsurgency*, RAND Occasional Paper (2009).

Sedgwick, Tourison, *Secret Army, Secret War: Washington's Tragic Spy Operations in North Vietnam* (Annapolis MD: Naval Institute Press, 1995).

Shackley, Ted and Finney, Richard A., *Spymaster: My Life in the CIA* (Dulles VA: Potomac Books, 2005).

Sheehan, Neil, *A Bright Shining Lie: John Paul Vann and America in Vietnam* (New York: Pimlico, 1998).

Sherry, Norman, *The Life of Graham Greene*, Vol. 2: *1939–1955* (New York: Viking, 1994).

Shultz, Richard H., *The Secret War Against Hanoi: The Untold Story of Spies, Saboteurs, and Covert Warriors in North Vietnam* (New York: Harper Perennial, 1999).

Simpson, Howard R., *Tiger in the Barbed Wire: An American in Vietnam, 1952–1991* (New York: Brasseys, 1992).

Smith, T.O., 'Major-General Sir Douglas Gracey: Peacekeeper or Peace Enforcer?' *Diplomacy & Statecraft*, Vol. 21, Issue 2 (2010).

Snepp, Frank, *Decent Interval: An Insider's Account of Saigon's Indecent End* told by the CIA's Chief Strategy Analyst in Vietnam (Lawrence KS: University Press of Kansas, 2002).

Staininger, Rolf, "The Americans are in a hopeless position": Great Britain and the war in Vietnam, 1964–65', *Diplomacy & Statecraft*, Vol. 8, Issue 3 (1997).

Sulick, Michael J., *American Spies: Espionage against the United States from the Cold War to the Present* (Washington DC: Georgetown University Press, 2013).

Sullivan, John F., *Of Spies and Lies: A CIA Lie Detector Remembers Vietnam* (Lawrence KS: University Press of Kansas, 2002).

Taylor, Maxwell D., *Swords and Plowshares* (New York: Da Capo Press, 1990).

Thompson, Michael, 'Thoughts Provoked by The Very Best Men: The Need for Integrity'. Available at https://www.cia.gov/library/center-for-the-study-of-intelligence/csi-publications/csi-studies/studies/96unclass/bestmen.htm#ft7 (accessed 1 June 2015).

Thompson, Roger, *Lessons Not Learned: The U.S. Navy's Status Quo Culture* (Annapolis: Naval Institute Press, 2007).

Vistica, Gregory L., 'One Awful Night in Thanh Phong', *New York Times Magazine*, 2001, available at http://www.nytimes.com/2001/04/25/magazine/25KERREY.html?pagewanted=1&ei=5070&en=3db9255f522f13f6&ex=1138251600? (accessed 22 November 2013).

Walton, Calder, *Empire of Secrets: British Intelligence, the Cold War and the Twilight of Empire* (London: Harper Press, 2013).

Warren, James A., *GIAP: The General Who Defeated America in Vietnam* (New York: Palgrave Macmillan, 2013).

Weiner, Tim, *Legacy of Ashes: The History of the CIA* (New York: Doubleday, 2007).

——— 'Lucien Conein, 79, Legendary Cold War Spy', *New York Times* (7 June 1998).

Westad, Odd Arne and Quinn-Judge, Sophie, eds, *The Third Indochina War: Conflict between China, Vietnam and Cambodia, 1972–79* (London: Routledge, 2006).

Winters, Francis X., *The Year of the Hare: America in Vietnam, January 25, 1963–February 15, 1964* (Athens GA: University of Georgia Press, 1999).

Xiaoming, Zhang, 'Deng Xiaoping and China's Decision to go to War with Vietnam', *Journal of Cold War Studies*, Vol. 12, No. 3 (Summer 2010).

Yang, Kuisong and Zhai, Qiang (translation), *Changes in Mao Zedong's Attitude toward the Indochina War, 1949–1973*, Working Paper No. 34, Woodrow Wilson International Center for Scholars (February 2002).

Zervoudakis, Alexander, 'Nihil mirare, nihil contemptare, omnia intelligere: Franco-Vietnamese Intelligence in Indochina, 1950–1954', *Intelligence and National Security*, Vol. 13, Issue 1 (1998).

INDEX

Lightning Source UK Ltd.
Milton Keynes UK
UKHW021627040123
414801UK00009B/255